THE NEW WORKPLACE AND TRADE UNIONISM

E. Kevin Kelloway, Ph.D
Professor
Department of Management
Saint Mary's University
Halifax, NS B3H 3C3

Trade unions in Britain have experienced a major decline in membership over the past decade. From being important agents in British society, they are increasingly marginal to political action and work. Major legal and political constraints on their activity, changes in the nature of work and workers, and declining effectiveness have meant that they no longer occupy centre stage as they once did.

This book brings together authoritative accounts of the nature and meaning of trade unionism in the workplace today. It examines the beliefs and practices of union members in differing forms of employment, as well as analysing the non-union firm and the issues of collectivism and individualism in these settings. It critically engages with new management philosophies such as HRM, and new union ideas, such as partnership unionism.

Based on primary research into the new workplace in today's Britain, this book will be required reading for those wishing to obtain a critical understanding of collectivism in the workplace today. The future strategies of British trade unionism are also examined amid contradictory forces of exclusion, incorporation and renewal. The editors have gathered together contributions from leading academics who have systematically explored the nature of new industrial relations and new management philosophies and trade union responses.

Peter Ackers is Lecturer in Industrial Relations at Loughborough University. **Chris Smith** is Lecturer in Industrial Relations and Organisation Studies at Aston University. **Paul Smith** is Lecturer in Industrial Relations at Keele University.

CRITICAL PERSPECTIVES ON WORK AND ORGANIZATION

General Editors: David Knights, Chris Smith, Paul Thompson and Hugh Willmott

Since the appearance of Braverman's *Labor and Monopoly Capital*, the impact of labour process analysis has been debated in the fields of industrial sociology, organization theory, industrial relations, labour economics, politics and business studies. This series examines diverse aspects of the employment relationship across the range of productive and service industries. Some volumes explore further the established terrain of management control, the intensification of work, the deskilling of labour. Others are attentive to associated topics such as gender relations at work, new technology, workplace democracy and the international dimensions of the labour process.

LABOUR IN TRANSITION
The Labour Process in East Europe and China
Edited by Chris Smith and Paul Thompson

SKILL AND CONSENT
Contemporary Studies in the Labour Process
Edited by Andrew Sturdy, David Knights and Hugh Willmott

GLOBAL JAPANIZATION?
Transnational Transformation of the Labour Process
Edited by Tony Elger and Chris Smith

RESISTANCE AND POWER IN ORGANIZATIONS
Edited by John Jermier, David Knights and Walter Nord

MAKING QUALITY CRITICAL
Critical Perspectives on Work and Organization
Edited by Adrian Wilkinson and Hugh Willmott

THE NEW WORKPLACE AND TRADE UNIONISM

Edited by Peter Ackers,
Chris Smith and Paul Smith

London and New York

First published 1996
by Routledge
11 New Fetter Lane, London EC4P 4EE

Simultaneously published in the USA and Canada
by Routledge
29 West 35th Street, New York, NY 10001

Typeset in Garamond by LaserScript, Mitcham, Surrey
Printed and bound in Great Britain by
Clays Ltd, St Ives plc

British Library Cataloguing in Publication Data
A catalogue record for this book is available from the British Library

Library of Congress Cataloguing in Publication Data
A catalogue record for this book has been requested

ISBN 0–415–11676–7 (hbk)
ISBN 0–415–11677–5 (pbk)

CONTENTS

v

FIGURES

TABLES

CONTRIBUTORS

Peter Ackers is Lecturer in Industrial Relations at the Business School, Loughborough University. He has published articles on employer paternalism, employee involvement, workplace industrial relations and labour history. He is currently engaged in further research on the history of NACODS, the pit deputies' union.

Nick Bacon is Teaching Fellow at the Business School, Loughborough University and a member of the Human Resource and Corporate Management Research Unit. His previous research has been conducted on the steel industry in the UK and Germany. Currently he is researching into employee attitudes towards companies and trade unions.

Peter Fairbrother is Senior Lecturer in Sociology, Warwick University, and has published a number of papers and books on trade unionism in the state sector, workplace unionism, and union democracy, including *Politics and the State as Employer* (1994) and *Unions at the Crossroads* (1995). He is also engaged in research on industrial relations in Russia and is joint author of *The Workers' Movement in Russia* (1995).

John Kelly is Senior Lecturer in Industrial Relations at the London School of Economics. His publications include an assessment of Marxist analyses of trade unionism, *Trade Unions and Socialist Politics* (1988), and he is joint author of a study of the role of contemporary union officers, *Working for the Union* (1994).

Alan McKinlay is Professor of Management and Organization Behaviour at Stirling University. He is currently researching the social history of industrial relations in the post-1945 engineering industry, and he is joint author of a study of the Ford Motor Company entitled *Strategy and the Human Resource* (1993).

Ian McLoughlin is Senior Lecturer in the Department of Management Studies at Brunel University. He has researched and written widely on the human and organisational aspects of technological change and on industrial relations issues. He is co-author of *The Process of Technological Change* (Cambridge University Press, 1988) and *Technological Change at Work* (Open University Press, 1988; second edition, 1994). His most recent book is a study of industrial relations in non-union firms, *Enterprise Without Unions* (Open University Press, 1994).

Anna Pollert is Principal Research Fellow in the Industrial Relations Research Unit, University of Warwick. She is author of *Girls, Wives, Factory Lives* and editor of *Farewell to Flexibility?* and has published widely in the areas of gender relations, workplace relations and employment change. Her current interests are internationalisation and workplace change, and management, industrial relations and social transformation in Eastern Europe.

Chris Smith is Lecturer in Industrial Relations and Organisation Studies, Aston Business School, Aston University. His research interests are in work reorganisation, the impact of Japanese investment on work, engineering labour and comparative work organisation. He is currently researching Japanese-invested firms in Britain. He is author of *Technical Workers* (Macmillan, 1987); co-author of *White-Collar Workers* (Croom Helm, 1986) and *Reshaping Work: The Cadbury Experience* (Cambridge University Press, 1990); and co-editor of *White-Collar Work* (Macmillan, 1991), *Labour in Transition* (Routledge, 1992), *Engineers and Management* (Routledge, 1992), and *Global Japanization?* (Routledge, 1994).

Paul Smith is Lecturer in Industrial Relations, Department of Industrial Relations, Keele University. He has published papers on the unionisation of the road haulage industry, union government, and union exclusion. He is joint author of *Managing the Unions* (1996).

Carol Stephenson is Lecturer in Sociology, Department of Social and International Studies, Sunderland University. Her research interests are in work organisation in Japanese-invested firms, change at work, gender and the labour process and trade unions in the workplace. She is an active trade unionist.

John Storey is Professor of Strategic Human Resource Management at the Business School, Loughborough University, Director of the Human Resource and Corporate Management Research Unit, also at Loughborough University, and editor of the *Human Resource Management Journal*. He has authored several books including *Developments in the Management of Human Resources* and (with Keith Sisson) *Managing Human Resources and Industrial Relations*. He has recently edited a collected work, *Human Resource Management: A Critical Text*.

Satnam Virdee is Research Fellow at the Policy Studies Institute. His research at PSI has included a study of the careers of nursing staff in a multi-racial society, and work on PSI's fourth national survey on minority ethnic groups, scheduled for publication in 1995. Recent publications include *Part of the Union: Trade Union Participation by Ethnic Minority Workers*, (London, CRE).

Jeremy Waddington is Senior Research Fellow, Industrial Relations Research Unit, University of Warwick. He has written widely on trade unions, and is currently researching the impact of recent workplace restructuring on trade union organisation and practice. His publications include *The Politics of Bargaining*.

Colin Whitston is Lecturer in the Department of Industrial Relations, Keele University. His research interests are in work restructuring, trade unions and absence at work. He is currently involved in a large-scale survey on the effects of new work practices on trade union representatives and members. Recent publications include *Attending to Work* (with Paul Edwards).

John Wrench is Senior Research Fellow at the Centre for Research in Ethnic Relations, University of Warwick. Before that he was a lecturer for seven years in the Sociology Group at the Management Centre at Aston University. He has researched and published in the area of industrial health and safety, and equal opportunities, racism and discrimination in the labour market. Recent publications include *Invisible Minorities: Racism in New Towns and New Contexts*, Monographs in Ethnic Relations No. 6 (University of Warwick, 1993) (with H. Brar and P. Martin) and *Racism and Migration in Western Europe* (Oxford: Berg, 1993) (edited with John Solomos).

ABBREVIATIONS

ACAS	Advisory, Conciliation and Arbitration Service
AEC	Advanced Engineering Craftsman
AEEU	Amalgamated Engineering and Electrical Union
AEU	Amalgamated Engineering Union
BIFU	Banking, Insurance and Finance Union
CBI	Confederation of British Industry
COHSE	Confederation of Health Service Employees
CPSA	Civil and Public Services Association
CRE	Commission for Racial Equality
DMU	District Management Units
DSS	Department of Social Security
EETPU	Electrical, Electronic, Telecommunications and Plumbing Union
EI	Employee Involvement
EO	Equal Opportunity
EU	European Union
GMB	General, Municipal and Boilermakers' and Allied Trades Union
HRM	Human Resource Management
IOD	Institute of Directors
IPA	Involvement and Participation Association
IT	Information Technology
IWA	Indian Workers Association
JIT	Just-in-Time
MSF	Manufacturing, Science and Finance
NALGO	National and Local Government Officers' Association
NHS	National Health Service
NUCPS	National Union of Civil and Public Servants
NUM	National Union of Mineworkers

NUPE	National Union of Public Employees
PBR	Payment by Results
PSI	Policy Studies Institute
TGWU	Transport and General Workers' Union
TQM	Total Quality Management
TUC	Trades Union Congress
TUPE	Transfer of Undertaking (Protection of Employment Regulations)
TURERA	Trade Union Reform and Employee Rights Act
UCW	Union of Communication Workers
UDM	Union of Democratic Mineworkers
USDAW	Union of Shop, Distributive and Allied Workers
VDU	Visual Display Unit
WIRS	Workplace Industrial Relations Survey

1

AGAINST ALL ODDS? BRITISH TRADE UNIONS IN THE NEW WORKPLACE

Peter Ackers, Chris Smith and Paul Smith

INTRODUCTION

A TRADE UNION . . . is a continuous association of wage-earners for the purpose of maintaining or improving the conditions of their working lives.

(Webb and Webb 1921b: 1)

Collective, self-help organisations of workers, as broadly defined by the Webbs, have been part of the landscape of virtually all capitalist societies since the industrial revolution. Trade unions emerged out of the need for workers to counter their subordinate role, exploitation and precarious existence as waged labour in the employment relationship. They mobilise the collective interests of sellers of labour power, and negotiate or impose conditions on the sale of labour power and terms of work within the labour process. To do so, they may adopt a variety of strategies, all of which revolve around the power of collective organisation. The most obvious is collective bargaining with employers, underwritten by the reality or threat of industrial action by striking, banning over-time or working to unilateral rules. However, unions may also regulate employer freedom of choice, and thus power, in the labour market, by exercising control over the type of labour they recruit, through apprenticeship systems or by insisting on certain professional qualifications. Moreover, within the workplace they may police job controls over both the general pace of work and the specific job descriptions of different categories of employees. Together with employment law, unions are the principal mechanisms for regulating the unfettered exercise of employer power in both market and authority relations.

1

While unions are found throughout the global economy, their position in the employment relationship, relative to the strength of employers, varies historically, sectorally and between capitalist societies, as do their complexion and role. Periods of union ascendancy, such as the 1890s and 1970s, and decline, as in the 1930s and 1980s, occur across countries, but significant differences nevertheless persist, as the employment relationship is constructed within very different historical contexts. National differences have created unions with distinctive religious, political and occupational forms and divisions. This is apparent even within Western Europe, where there is a Southern European model, found in France, Italy and Spain, and characterised by competing Catholic, Socialist and Communist national confederations; and a Northern European model, evident in Britain, Germany, the Netherlands and Scandinavia, of single centres under Social Democratic or Labour hegemony. Any such broad categorisation, however, conceals a myriad of local factors, such as linguistic divisions in Belgium or the relative strength of Catholic unionism in Italy. National differences produce variations in union membership, such as the high density in Sweden and low density in France. But equally, the meaning of unionism varies, from the more politicised agencies of community mobilisation of Southern Europe to the more institutionalised and workplace-orientated organisations of Northern Europe. Just as, in Britain, the Royal College of Nurses (RCN) and the National Union of Mineworkers are both unions, in their own ways, so are the French CGT and the German IG Metal. For this complex web of reasons, relative union strength cannot simply be inferred from membership figures.

There are strong links between the level and character of union membership and particular categories of worker, employment conditions, sectors and other factors. Thus coal mining has produced strong and combative unions virtually everywhere, whereas the retail sector is usually an area of union weakness. Yet such generalisations are only rules of thumb, as cross-national variations and contra-cases can always be found to undermine any safe correlations. Those who would rationalise unions out of the contemporary capitalist employment relation – and they have been in the ascendancy across many countries over the past decade (Hyman 1994) – are as quixotic as those who complacently assert that unions will always be reproduced in the same form by the abstract operation of those social relations. Unions make and remake themselves in different historical settings in response to detailed changes in the character of the employment relationship. Therefore, it is rarely, if ever, possible to draw a precise and predictable parity between patterns of work and forms of union organisation.

Orthodox labour process theory regards trade unions as playing an ambivalent role within capitalism. On the one hand, they defend the interests of workers within the wage labour system, and force changes in the nature of control within the firm. Yet, on the other, they do not challenge the fundamentals of the capitalist employment relationship. Marx (1976) acknowledged the role of unions in mobilising to shorten the working day in mid-nineteenth-century British capitalism. This had the effect of moving work organisation into a new phase as reduced time at work required labour power to be more intensively utilised with more machinery and systematic organisation. Braverman (1974) saw in Taylorism further evidence of that process of intensifying work, and regarded unions as a shield against managerial power which, nevertheless, failed to challenge the underlying forces which create wage labour. Other writers within a labour process tradition, Friedman (1977), Edwards (1979) and Littler (1982), for example, have continued to emphasise the way in which labour unions influence managerial control within the firm, by promoting internal labour markets and greater employment security, and by modifying areas of managerial discretion. Recent writing, including the previous volumes in this series, has paid more attention to management and its agencies than to trade unions. This book explores the nature of British unions in the new workplace, an arena which is being increasingly shaped without their direct intervention and influence.

This collection limits itself to the contemporary predicament of trade unions in Great Britain. The reason for this is not undue parochialism, but a recognition of the changes particular to British society in the 1980s, and the need to analyse these specificities in their own terms without recourse to what would only be arbitrary comparative cases. British trade unionism preceded the advent of socialist ideas, and emerged at the height of the nation's economic and imperial power, and this left a lasting imprint of occupational sectionalism and industrial pragmatism and reformism (Saville 1988). This contrasts most obviously with the Southern European model of highly politicised unions. The early strength and practicality of British unions also encouraged a form of 'voluntarist collectivism'. As late as the 1970s the principal battle cry of British union radicals was 'free collective bargaining'. Elsewhere, even in countries with a common cultural heritage, such as Australia, a much more proactive state has created quite different industrial relations institutions and modes of union action (Gardner and Palmer 1992). The post-war fragmentation of private-sector bargaining to company and workplace levels has further marked the difference between the localised modus operandi of British unionism and the highly centralised bargaining and national scope of their German and Scandinavian equivalents. After signs during the 1970s that Britain might be moving towards the Northern European model, with greater state regulation and more positive legal employment rights, the Thatcherite free market reform post-1979 differentiated the British experience still further from that on the continent. For all these reasons, the British trade union experience calls for a special treatment. That does not mean, however, that it is without wider relevance. On a negative note, recent years have proved a major test of the British voluntarist tradition, which in an unfavourable economic climate appears to many as less resilient than the more centralised, legalistic and bureaucratic approaches on mainland Europe and elsewhere (Terry 1994). More positive lessons arise from the likelihood that British unions, along with their US counterparts, have already encountered *laissez-faire* economic policies and new management strategies which have yet to find their way to the heart of the continental European union movement. In this respect, the argument between the 'collectivism' of the European Social Chapter and the free market, American 'individualist' alternative may be crucial to the future of trade unionism in Britain and Europe.

THE NEW AGENDA

In 1978, the historian Eric Hobsbawm (1981) pronounced, 'The Forward March of Labour Halted', and depicted a historic crisis in the British labour movement. The visible symptom of this malaise (dramatically confirmed the following year) was the declining vote of the British Labour Party. However, the heart of the matter was a controversial judgement about the state of the unions, which had just reached their highest ever membership (Marsh and Cox 1992). According to Hobsbawm, deep social changes had taken place over the post-war decades, including the declining weight of the manual working class, and the feminisation and growing ethnic diversity of the labour force. Moreover, union industrial action had become increasingly sectionalised and socially disruptive over this same period. The upshot was that the relatively homogeneous white, male, manual union movement which had emerged from the last war was in a process of decomposition. Many of the social trends to which Hobsbawm drew attention fifteen years ago remain familiar and some have accelerated in the interim. However, the passage of time has redefined the context of these changes, and several new factors have added to or modified his diagnosis. Viewed from 1979, the election of the first Thatcher Conservative government was merely symptomatic of the underlying crisis in the labour movement (Hall and Jacques 1983). Soon, however, the New Right political agenda became an active agent of social and industrial change in its own right, with grave consequences for the legal position of unions (Wedderburn 1989). Force of economic and legal circumstance obliterated the unions' (rather exaggerated) reputation for wages militancy for an entire generation (Bassett 1987). Subsequently, the 'special case' of the British free market experiment gained a wider world currency, and connected with more fundamental trends in global capitalism. Union movements almost everywhere, even in politically protected enclaves such as Australia and Scandinavia, began to experience difficulties similar to those in Britain, albeit on a lesser scale (Gardner and Palmer 1992). Moreover, Thatcherite 'Enterprise Culture' opened the floodgates to a plethora of new American popular management concepts, such as the Business School, Human Resource Management (HRM), Total Quality Management (TQM), Employee Involvement (EI), and Empowerment. Under these influences, a management language has emerged which redefines workers as employees, individuals and teams, but not as organised collectivities with some interests separate from management. At best, the new management thinking simply ignores the role of unions in its search for other ways of winning employee consent; at worst it sets out to destroy or weaken them (Guest 1987). In a belated response to these new conditions, the mainstream union movement has promoted a 'new realist' agenda of presenting a softer, more friendly image to employers and workers alike. Arguably, the precise form of this 'new unionism' has been most apparent in its public overtures to prospective members and business collaborators, and most obscure in relation to practical workplace unionism.

Today, most unions have behind them a decade or more of severe membership loss and declining influence (Marsh 1992). This book attempts to unravel the complex range of factors, described in shorthand as the 'new workplace', which have brought them to this pass, and to provide a critical assessment of the ways in which they are responding to these changed circumstances. Most of the chapters first appeared in a specially commissioned stream on 'The New Workplace and Trade Unionism' at the 1994 International Labour Process Conference at Aston University. The remainder were deliberately sought out by the editors to ensure a rounded representation of the main issues. This introductory chapter situates these themes within a broader world and national context. The chosen approach is to begin with the widest possible angle on trends in the global capitalist workplace; then to focus on the British political and legal scene; and, next, workplace unionism itself. Lastly, we outline the contribution that each individual chapter makes to the book's major themes.

THE CHANGING WORLD OF WORK

There is a well-established debate between industrial relations and sociological approaches over the fit between class, workplace, occupations and trade unionism (Lockwood 1958; Blackburn 1967; Roberts *et al.* 1972; Bain 1970; Carter 1979). Factors which normally encourage unionisation include: large-scale and highly bureaucratic employment situations; limited scope for occupational mobility; the need to defend skill structures; and specific sectoral conditions, such as close-knit occupational and/or geographical communities. Moreover, strong unions have both helped to create and thrived upon employment security, with higher membership levels among full-time than part-time workers. There is also a well-charted literature on the types of socio-political environments which favour and impede trade unionism. In broad terms, unions flourish where management perceive benefits in their presence and are not hostile adversaries, as was the case in the public sector before 1979 (Bain and Price 1983; Clegg 1976). Finally there is an extensive literature on the relationship between particular economic conditions and unionisation, especially the way in which the business cycle and employment rates influence union membership. (See Snape 1994 for a recent evaluation of the dominance of economic and political constraints on one union's internal growth strategies.)

Using these general criteria, we can readily identify a series of structural changes which have undermined UK union membership since 1979. These include: the contraction of manufacturing employment to just over 4 million employees; the privatisation of public industries; the growth of non-manual workers; the shift towards services; the expansion of self-employment – doubling between 1979 and 1990 – and part-time work (to over 7 million); reduction in the size of enterprises and growth of small, less bureaucratised firms; and the high structural and cyclical levels of unemployment throughout the 1980s and 1990s. Altogether, these forces have made for an unfavourable union environment. However, structural arguments about the decline of trade unions and the nature of the contemporary workplace are problematic. Do they indicate a causal or historical correlation between types of worker, workplaces and trade unionism? After all, similar incremental and radical change has always characterised work within capitalism, and produced the many varied forms of unionism that exist in the global economy. Furthermore, the disparate rates of unionisation between capitalist societies which share many similar structural features highlight the contingent and historical nature of these connections. Therefore strong statements about the causes of union growth and decline which ignore national context and history should be avoided (Turner 1991).

Despite these problems many writers have chosen to characterise current changes in the labour process through a single paradigm shift, as from Fordism to post-Fordism, or from mass production to flexible specialisation. Alternatively, they have stressed the alternating fortunes of national models, such as towards American or Japanese production methodologies and employment practices. These step changes are said to require a new union agenda. Kenney and Florida (1993: 300) use Fordist and post-Fordist production neologisms to suggest that unions which are locked within a Fordist paradigm remain reactionary in the face of the new demands of work in what they call 'innovation mediated production'. At the comparative international level, Katz and Sabel (1985: 300) suggest that German and Japanese 'corporate trade union practices' accord better with new trends in flexible manufacture, which must be more responsive to product market changes, than 'job control unionism', more characteristic of British and US union environments. Katz (1988: 220) describes the agenda for trade unions in the new workplace as having two basic policy

7

approaches: a 'cooperatist' and a 'militant' strategy (a dichotomy explored by Bacon and Storey, and Kelly in this book). Wickens (1993: 76) argues that just as 'fordism created a type of adversarial trade unionism, the new manufacturing system of lean production will favour a more co-operative partnership'. Again at the cross-national level, Lane (1989) is one of many writers who suggest that trends towards more flexibility in the workplace and 'flexible specialisation' fit better with German industrial relations than French or British practice. Within this literature, trade unions are said to require a new *raison d'être*, which typically represents a broader responsibility for company survival, partnership with capital and less in the way of an adversarial, 'them and us' social distance and class conflict. Chapters by Storey and Bacon and Kelly in this book engage in this debate. Arguments of this kind suggest that the best-known instances of 'high performance production systems' occur in unionised workplaces where the unions have allegedly moved away from adversarialism towards partnership – Corning, Saturn, Xerox, Levi Strauss, NUMMI and AT & T (Applebaum and Batt 1994: 152; Black and Ackers 1994). Often evidence is marshalled to meet a prescriptive agenda. American exponents of partnership unionism highlight best cases rather than worst or perhaps typical cases, in which American management continue to exclude unions from the workplace, or marginalise their role through restructuring measures which fragment or by-pass them (Harrison and Bluestone 1988; Guest 1990; Milkman 1991). Kochan and Weinstein (1994), in a recent overview of industrial relations in the USA, reveal that the historical hostility towards unions displayed by American employers has been actively reinforced by new trends in work reorganisation, which have seen a continued decline in union density, lowering of wages and non-wage compensation, and considerable investment in coercion against trade unionists, especially in the private sector.

For whatever political or policy reasons the agenda of matching types of production regime to types of union (or non-union) regime has become a popular project. The problems with all these 'best fit' theories and scenarios is that once we insert cross-national and historical comparison we find contra-cases, diversity and weak associations between unionism or non-unionism and particular working practices, management philosophies or production regimes. This suggests that we need to be precise about evidence, and cautious about generalisations, especially cross-national assertions involving radically different industrial relations arrangements and traditions. It also suggests that we need more evidence, of the sort this book provides, on workers' experience of these new practices. For these reasons, we want to focus now on aspects of changes in the new workplace and how they have been empirically investigated in Britain. Three elements can be highlighted. First, there is the arrival of new overseas employers in the UK, who bring with them their own distinctive trade union and industrial relations agendas. Second, there is the impact of new technologies, especially computer-based information systems. Third, there is the wide-ranging discussion around flexible work and the flexible workplace.

The impact of overseas entrants

Manufacturing employment halved between 1979 and 1994, and its ownership composition also changed, with foreign multinationals increasing their share of investment, jobs and exports. Significant entrants have been US, Japanese and continental European, especially German, firms. There has been limited academic discussion of European entrants and virtually nothing on whether or not they are transferring aspects of their national industrial relations practices to the UK. (On German and other continental firms see Guest and Hoque 1994; on Swedish firms see Thompson *et al.* 1995). Questions of whether foreign companies act as transmitters of new practices have almost exclusively focused on US and Japanese firms. Most research has been conducted on US firms, and even surveys of UK emulators of Japanese practices have identified significant numbers of US firms (see Oliver and Wilkinson 1992: 133). US firms have figured extensively in discussions around the diffusion of Taylorism (Littler 1982), employee involvement, multi-divisional forms, measured day work, corporate culture and more recently Human Resource Management (HRM) (Stopford and Turner 1985: 142–7; Purcell and Sisson 1983; Chandler 1990; Guest 1989; Storey 1992). Non-union US firms, such as IBM, Hewlett Packard, Mars and Motorola, have featured in descriptions and research of HRM practices in the UK and have been celebrated as 'sophisticated paternalists' (Purcell and Sisson 1983) or 'sophisticated unitarists' (Scott 1994), which has tended to legitimate their non-unionism as not necessarily inimical to workers' wages or conditions.

9

However, the greatest attention has been lavished upon the impact of Japanese MNCs, and those firms which have consciously set out to 'emulate' the lessons of these for work organisation, personnel, manufacturing and industrial relations. Assessing the impact of Japanese firms on trade unionism is simultaneously straightforward and difficult. Of foreign employers, the Japanese, in sharp contrast to US firms, have been more pro-union and collectivist, though strongly prescriptive about the type of unionism they want. The pattern of manufacturing entry into the UK has been overwhelmingly through greenfield investment, and of those new factories about half are unionised (Milsome 1993: 93). Unionisation reflects regional labour traditions, with higher recognition in South Wales and the North-East, regions with strong trade union roots, and less recognition in new towns, such as Milton Keynes, Telford and Livingstone (Scotland) (Turnbull and Delbridge 1994: 354). However, unionisation also reflects the choice of location, and therefore management strategy, and not simply the established traditions of specific regions. Of unionised Japanese workplaces, 85 per cent are single union, with the AEEU being the most favoured organisation, regardless of sector. Japanese firms employ management consultants to profile union political character for selection through union 'beauty contests' at national, regional and local levels (Bassett 1987), and have therefore reinforced inherent competitive trends within the British union movement. In the single union deals, density rates vary considerably, with some of the celebrated cases, such as Nissan's Sunderland plant, having membership coverage variously put at 33 and 45 per cent of employees (see Stephenson in this volume). On brownfield sites, the multi-union patterns have continued, but with some movement towards single centres of bargaining. Single union deals are not distinctively Japanese. Cadbury's factory in Chirk, North Wales, can be seen as a revolutionary British plant heralding, in the late 1960s, many of the aspects currently identified with the Japanese – single status, single union, flexible working, etc. (Milsome 1993: 1; Whitaker 1986; Smith *et al.* 1990). The same might be argued of the relationship between the GMWU and Pilkingtons in the 1960s (Lane and Roberts 1971), and there are more general similarities to be made between Japanese and UK paternalist employers (Ackers and Black 1991; Black and Ackers 1988). Since the early 1980s, however, Japanese firms have been the real and symbolic movers behind a more widespread adoption of single unionism, no-strike deals, new arbitration agreements, company councils and other forms of management-directed reforms of British industrial relations which have capitalised on union weakness and inter-union competition for declining members (Oliver and Wilkinson 1992). They have also broken with custom and practice in certain areas, such as the use of temporary labour by Nissan, the first time it had been used in the British motor industry since the 1940s (Milsome 1993: 61).

The more complex aspect of the influence of Japanese transplants on labour relations relates to its meaning and significance inside the labour process. Oliver and Wilkinson's (1992: 292) discussion of what they see as 'the emergence of non-adversarial trade union[ism]' in Japanese firms and emulators of Japanese-style practice focuses exclusively on formal agreements, and not their implementation or execution. They highlight the need for 'flexible working arrangements . . . to operate JIT systems of production' (p. 296), but conflate agreements for flexibility with their actual operation. JIT systems also fit within environments where trade unionism is absent, and management have exclusive control over the timing of labour deployment according to production dictates. Garrahan and Stewart (1992) show how unions have been marginalised from traditional labour process controls, and this may be typical – certainly it conforms to the situation in Japan. But as Stephenson (in this volume) makes clear, even under 'Japanese' systems marked variations arise in the meaning of trade unionism, which is conditioned not by ownership alone, but also by other influences, such as labour selection, the nature of the labour force, leadership and other factors more generally associated with union strength. More longitudinal research is needed into UK Japanese transplants before we can make definitive statements about the role unions play inside their factories. In North America, qualitative work on workers' control in Japanese car transplants suggests continued union influence in job regulation in unionised settings (Rinehart et al. 1994), and informal individual and collective resistance in non-union plants (Graham 1994). This research from the shop floor indicates the persistence of established work rules and customs and is in marked contrast to the managerialist or top-down literature which suggests a transformation in US labour relations (Florida and Kenney 1991). Similar research is yet to be conducted within the UK, and therefore case studies are needed to uncover the meaning of Quality Circles, Just-in-Time, or single status for workers and the impact these practices have on trade unions over an extended period of time (Peck and Stone 1992; Elger and Smith 1994).

Information technology

Information technology (IT) is no longer new. Already it has had a wide impact on all sectors, facilitating the dramatic break-up of unionised strongholds such as Fleet Street printing, destroying occupational identities, such as boilermakers and draughtsmen, and causing redundancies in many other occupations and industries. Information technology has been investigated for its effects on labour–capital relations in three respects: first, for its potential to increase direct forms of communication, and therefore side-step union channels and networks; second, for its use in increasing monitoring and surveillance of employees; and, third, for its capability for integrating employees into the company ethos and interests through the use of video and visual communications. Moreover, IT provides opportunities for fragmenting and geographically dispersing work. For example, there are over two million 'tele' (i.e. remote) workers in Britain, and the concept of the 'virtual office' suggests further fragmentation. Homeworkers have always been difficult for unions to organise and easy for employers to dominate, though many of these remote workers are management and related staff who might not unionise anyway. Bratton (1992: 59–70), reviewing the widespread literature on new technology and unions, says that despite TUC support for comprehensive 'technology agreements', these were limited to non-manual workers, and in most workplaces new technology has been introduced using conventional procedural agreements, or introduced unilaterally by management without negotiation or consultation. Most surveys of managers' assessment of union influence over technology introduction suggest unions have not been impediments to investment. Implementation procedures dominated research on new technology in the 1980s. The effects of new technology on skills and jobs are also important and recent research suggests that union influence has tended to be non-strategic. Case studies and surveys reveal positive attitudes towards new technology, though where it impacts on job boundaries, inter-union conflicts have not been uncommon, especially in areas where there is a split between office and shop-floor staff, as with the introduction of numerically controlled machine tools. The impact of new technology in the office, amongst clerical labour, has seen changes in the division of labour, the de-skilling and routinisation of labour, intensification of work and increasingly technical control. Unionisation has been associated with these trends (Crompton and Jones 1984), and resistance to technology which intensifies and de-skills labour is documented (O'Connell Davidson 1994). But overall, such resistance has been directed not at stopping new technology, but with alleviating some of its effects. We should note that IT is available to unions and union activists in the workplace, and may be used to further their interests. Fairbrother (1994: 347) has shown that union officers at BT used computers, VDUs and mobile telephones, 'making themselves more accessible to their members . . . often countering corporation newsletters within hours of their first appearance'. Arguably, IT changes the nature of the workplace, but not the nature of the capitalist employment relation, and may mean a different type of trade unionism, rather than no unionism or less unionism.

Flexibility

Flexibility has been a central watchword of the reform of company structure and work organisation in the 1980s and 1990s, signifying deregulation of labour markets; contracting out and in of services; amalgamation of skills and tasks between occupations and functions; and the segmentation and polarisation of employment between different categories of employees. Atkinson's (1985) model of the flexible firm projected a co-operative, unionised 'core' of employees, and a non-unionised 'periphery', which has parallels with labour organisation in the large Japanese firm and the Victorian split between a craft-unionised elite and a general union or non-unionised mass of unskilled workers. These and many other issues have been debated under the umbrella of flexibility (Pollert 1988; 1991). The debate around the regulation of employment contracts, occupational content and task activities is too big to review here. Instead, we consider briefly two aspects of flexibility with potential implications for unions in the workplace: the emergence of a new peripheral workforce; and the development of teamworking within the core workforce.

Evidence of the creation of a new 'periphery', through the growth of non-union, non-standard employment, and employers' strategic use of this group to change the employment opportunities of workers and weaken or exclude trade unions is thin (see Millward *et al.* 1992; Hunter *et al.* 1993; Penn 1993; IRRR 1994). While case evidence (Smith *et al.* 1990; O'Connell Davidson 1994: 97) suggests substitution of full-timers by part-timers, and a dilution of union influence, employers overwhelmingly use atypical or non-standard employees – temporary workers, part-timers, contract workers, freelancers, etc. – not to strategically segment and weaken the bargaining position of workers and trade unions, but for conventional reasons of covering for sickness absence and short-term peaks in demand or to supply specialist skills (*Employment Gazette* 1994). The gender composition of the non-standard workforce reveals typical patterns of female employment participation and not widespread adoption of a flexible workforce (Pollert 1991). Some of the most extreme forms of flexibility occur in the retail industry, which along with construction, comes closest to the flexible firm model. In some instances (Asda, for example), full-time and part-time posts have been abolished, to be replaced by 'key-timers', workers available to cover peak times or absences and called in at two hours' notice (IRRR 1994). But such workers receive the same wages, terms and conditions as full-time/part-time staff, and only a few retail stores are experimenting in this way. Moreover, unionism within the retail sector has rarely sought to regulate the labour process, but has been limited to bargaining at national level between employers and national union offices. Felstead (1993: 198–9) discusses the vertical disintegration of the corporation and the creation of franchisees, who, while similar to employees, appear to unionise only in countries with very regulated industrial relations institutions. Moves towards further temporal segmentation may weaken attachment to work, relevant for trade unionism, but again, these new practices reprise older forms of casualisation (notably in construction) and reinforce rather than radically recast particular employment patterns. As Wrench and Virdee (Chapter 8) make clear, union organisation in these areas has historically been difficult. Clearly, the recent abolition of the Wages Councils may well increase casualisation and weaken still further the foothold unions had in these service sectors.

The contracting-out of services in the public sector has been more directly detrimental to workplace trade unionism. In contrast to private services, the public sector entered the 1980s with high union membership and a centralised, pluralist industrial relations system. Since then the Conservative government has promoted decentralisation, stringent financial controls, compulsory competitive tendering and various forms of 'privatisation'. Ironically, for advocates of partnership unionism, the privatisation of public utilities has witnessed significant deterioration in union influence, as service ideology and genuine partnership ethos are undermined in favour of commercialism and a frequently aggressive, macho management keen to assert managerial prerogatives over union provision and interests (Ferner and Colling 1991; O'Connell Davidson 1993; Fairbrother 1994; Walsh 1995). Many of the 'efficiency' gains of privatisation and commercialisation appear to be predicated upon the weakening of union organisation, clearing the path for the adoption of non-union, private service-sector employment norms. To this end, the privatised electricity and gas companies have imposed large wage reductions to the 'market rate'. Waddington and Whitson (Chapter 5) trace these developments in the 'exposed sector'. Overall the consistency of the survey and case study evidence implies that attacks on trade unionism through aspects of 'flexibility' will be more significant in the public and former public sectors.

By far the greatest use of flexibility has been in employers' attempts to change the permanent workforce through measures such as multi-skilling and more flexible working patterns including annualised hours, team working, new shift patterns, and various attempts to stop up the pores of the working day (IRRR 1994). These changes have been as common in unionised as non-unionised workplaces, and as Waddington and Whitson reveal, union members do not see this type of flexibility as a major grievance issue, suggesting that it has not had the dramatic impact on workplace unionism predicted in certain futurological models or those committed to a 'flexible future' for the workforce. One change in the 'new workplace', especially in manufacturing, has been the growth of teamwork, teamleaders and shifts in the pattern of authority on the shop floor. Teamworking follows a long-standing effort by employers to weaken occupational consciousness and symbolises a move away from strict control hierarchies, where workers are tied to individual tasks, and paced either by foremen or technology along traditional control lines. Teamworking is supposed to delegate responsibility for task allocation and scheduling to groups of workers, and to transform the role of the supervisor from 'policeman' to 'coach' (Buchanan and Preston

1992: 71). Multi-skilled, self-regulating groups are assumed to perform tasks with more autonomy, and to be better able to respond to changes in demand without direction from above or other tight control structures which mitigate against worker responsibility and reinforce patterns of conflict which reduce performance. Such controls may or may not enhance or reduce union influence in the labour process. There is evidence that integrating workers into teams may weaken union communication networks, but as Pollert (in this volume) shows, shop steward involvement can be vital to sustain teamworking.

Comparative research between European countries and the USA reveal wide national differences in the definition of teamwork (Turner 1991; Turner and Auer 1994; Berggren 1992). Mueller (1994) has shown cross-national, cross-company and cross-plant variations in exactly how teams are put together and the different role organised worker interest plays within these structures. Applebaum and Batt (1994: 152) have shown that in the USA, teamworking is more prevalent in unionised workplaces, although the role teamwork plays in marginalising trade unions (Turner 1991) is not sufficiently highlighted by their work. Its use in Britain appears less widespread than in the USA, Japan or other European countries, such as Germany and Sweden. As Waddington and Whitston show, teamworking hardly featured as an issue in their extensive survey of trade union workplaces. A consistent finding in comparative research is the way in which national industrial relations systems and traditions continue to shape the character of teamworking experience, thus reinforcing our general point that such practices do not offer a single 'best way' of organising the new workplace, but absorb local traditions, customs and styles which are remade within the apparently common discourse on teamworking. All research indicates that the concept of teamworking remains both ambiguous and deeply controversial, referring to different units, sizes and compositions of employees, some of which are so big as to make any meaningful operation of a 'team' impossible (see Pollert, this volume). Dawson and Webb (1989), Dawson (1991), Elger and Fairbrother (1992) and Buchanan and Preston (1992) have all investigated teamworking practices within British manufacturing and found that, like HRM, these new techniques are grafted onto existing authority relations, and that deep-seated traditions of conflict between foremen (team-leaders) and rank and file (team) workers persist (see McKinlay and Taylor, this volume). Buchanan and Preston (1992) examined teamwork in advanced manufacturing systems engineering, and discovered that foremen persisted with policing rules, intervening in work scheduling and task allocation despite formal rules and best-practice rhetoric against such interventions. In other words, managerial authority through the teamleaders or foremen continues to run along traditional British lines, despite ideological or rhetorical claims for teamworking as a break with these practices. Promises of workers having greater discretion have not materialised; rather, as Dawson and Webb (1989) suggest, skills have become more company-specific within teams and therefore labour mobility between companies using general skills has declined, creating not multi-skilled 'teams' but a 'flexible cage'.

A NEW POLITICAL AND LEGAL FRAMEWORK

The restructuring of employment relations and work organisation in contemporary Britain has occurred in the context of an ongoing project to reform employment law, initiated by Conservative governments since 1979. This programme has constrained the power of trade unions and removed a number of important statutory rules governing the contract of employment. The result has been to increase employers' discretion to determine the terms of the employment relationship and the structure of work organisation.

When first elected the new Conservative government was determined in the aftermath of the strike movement of 1978–9, dubbed 'The Winter of Discontent', to impose 'order' in industrial relations. An immediate objective was to restrict workers' and unions' freedom to take industrial action and picket, thereby restoring power to employing organisations which, it was alleged, had been disadvantaged by the Trade Union and Labour Relations Acts 1974 and 1976, which had re-established unions' tort immunity in industrial disputes – their protection from claims for damages for inducement of breach of contract and other civil wrongs incurred in industrial action.[1] Thus the Employment Act 1980 withdrew tort immunity for inducing 'secondary' or supportive industrial action (apart from first suppliers and customers)[2] and for picketing except at workers' place of work, and restricted the ability to establish and enforce a union closed shop. Organisers of action outside these limits therefore became liable for damages. In addition, the scope of the unfair dismissal provisions of the Employment Protection Act

1975 was narrowed in 1979 by extending the qualifying period of employment from six months to a year, while the 1980 Act shifted the burden of proof in tribunal hearings to the employee.

Matters did not rest there, however, for in the early 1980s the Conservative government became explicitly committed to 'free market' solutions to the restructuring of the labour market and employment law (Wedderburn 1989).[3] In this schema, market and contractual relations between individuals are regarded as the most efficient mechanism for the allocation of the rational preferences of utility-seeking individuals. Therefore any intervention in the pricing mechanism or reallocation of factors or products cannot increase the sum total of utility but, on the contrary, may cause its reduction. Unions are conceived as monopolistic organisations which, through their power to impose a 'rent' upon the hire of labour (that is, an additional charge above the market rate), coerce individuals who wish to dispose of labour and capital at the market evaluation. As a result, the market is distorted: either labour costs are raised and profits reduced, causing unemployment, or the wages of non-union labour are lowered (Turnbull 1991). The proper object of public policy in this free market framework is the protection and enhancement of market imperatives. This requires measures to restrict unions' liberty to take industrial action and impose their authority over members, to improve the operation of the market in labour and capital, and to reform the structure and management of the machinery of government and state services. The latter also provides an exemplar to the private sector of the viability of new structures and policies for the management of labour. A policy of union exclusion is an integral element (Smith and Morton 1993; 1994).

This perspective came increasingly to dominate the agenda of the Conservative government during the 1980s, underpinning the radicalisation of its programme of employment law reform (hence the later measures have often required amendments to earlier Acts which were once considered innovative). To date, there have been nine major statutes plus other subordinate instruments (for details, see Kessler and Bayliss 1995, Chapter 5; Dickens and Hall 1995).[4] The cumulative effect of this incremental process has been to remove statutory and administrative supports for collective bargaining, partially deregulate the contract of employment, create statutory rights against unions for members and non-members alike (including model rules for union government), reduce unions' freedom to take industrial action (through narrowing the definition of a trade dispute and its restriction within organisational and geographical boundaries), introduce procedural rules for the initiation of industrial action (enforceable by employers, and other companies, members and other individuals), and make union funds liable for damages actionable by employers and other companies. The Trade Union Reform and Employee Rights Act 1993 (TURERA) marked another important step in the evolution of this policy, imposing new restrictions upon unions' freedom to take industrial action and determine membership eligibility and discipline, financial autonomy and administration. Government policy now positively incites employers to abandon collective bargaining (Department of Employment 1991: 9). In the wider sphere, unions' legitimacy has been eroded by the diminution of their role as representative institutions (through the abolition of tripartite institutions, such as the National Economic Development Council) and sustained criticism of their economic impact,[5] and by the imposition of extensive statutory rules on union government which presume the prevalence of undemocratic tendencies and practices within unions and the necessity for state intervention to eliminate them.

The Conservative project of deregulation of the labour market and employment law has co-existed uneasily with the requirements of European Union (EU) legislation (Ewing 1993). The government's policy here has been a mixed one, combining elements of obstruction, minimum compliance and acceptance. Thus the Maastricht 'opt-out' from the Social Chapter has allowed the UK government to refuse to implement a number of important EU Directives; as an alternative, it has championed deregulation along with voluntary and individualist, employer-sponsored forms of Employee Involvement (EI) (Department of Employment 1989). In other cases it has only complied with the strict letter of the Directives (and not even that in some cases), refusing to accept the incompatibility of UK law until forced to do so by court proceedings. For example, the Transfer of Undertakings (Protection of Employment) Regulations 1981 were only amended by the TURERA 1993 after they were declared in court[6] not to be in compliance with the EU Directive 77/187 as they improperly excluded non-commercial undertakings and operations (*ibid.*: 173–6). In other cases, legislation drafted in response to the requirements of EU Directives has created a body of rules so complex that they are of little effect – minimum regulation by over-regulation – for example, the Equal Pay for Work of Equal Value Regulations 1983 (Gregory 1992) and the maternity leave provisions of the TURERA 1993. Nonetheless, important changes have been introduced into UK law, for example the TURERA's provision of a statutory right to stop work and not to be dismissed or suffer detriment as a result of action taken to pursue a health and safety issue, and the same Act's amendment of the TUPE Regulations to embrace non-commercial undertakings.

British unions engaging in industrial action today must surmount both substantive and procedural statutory obstacles in order to retain their tort immunity. Industrial action no longer requires a breach of a contract of employment but comprises any collective dispute between a UK employer and employees, or self-employees or self-employed workers, concerned with pay, terms or working conditions. Such action must be authorised by the appropriate union body after a majority of the workers have voted in favour by postal ballot under a statutory-defined procedure, supervised by an external agency. Unions must give seven days' notice of a ballot paper, details of the result, an additional seven days' notice of the commencement of any action, and information as to its nature, including details as to which workers will be involved (in some cases giving names). Unions remain liable in law for all industrial action (including unofficial and unconstitutional action) in which any official or lay officer participates, unless this is expressly repudiated under a statutory procedure. Only then can a ballot be organised. The complexity of this procedure illustrates the extraordinary, and one-sided, legal regulation of unions that has taken place in an era when Conservative governments have devoted themselves to freeing employers from legal 'red tape'. Any failure on the part of a union to remain within the law entitles a range of parties – the employer, another affected company, a member, or a citizen – to apply to court for an injunction requiring the action to cease immediately pending the largely fictional trial of the case (Wedderburn 1989: 684–704). Non-compliance may threaten the viability of the union itself through fines for contempt and sequestration (Wedderburn 1989: 705–17), as the experience of the 1984 miners' strike testifies. Other forms of action, such as limited sanctions or working to contract, have been declared by the courts to constitute contractual non-performance, and employers are entitled to respond with the complete cessation of pay.[7]

The power of employers to restructure and determine work organisation and employment relations has been directly enhanced by both statutes and case law. The policy of 'enterprise confinement' – the restriction of union tort immunity to industrial action within discrete employing organisations located in the UK, and picketing to employees' specific place of work – seeks to contain workers' collective power and action within boundaries determined almost entirely by the decisions and requirements of external agencies.[8] The statutory rules impose a delay upon industrial action and renders union members' support more transparent, thereby facilitating the mobilisation of counter-strategies by employers. In the hands of a determined management, such as News International (Ewing and Napier 1986), P & O (Auberach (1988) and the National Association of Port Employers (Turnbull *et al.* 1992), the legislation is a practical tool which can decisively weaken industrial action and unions. Enterprise confinement is also important in reinforcing the attempt to confine employees' perspectives and action within subordinate business units (Purcell 1989: 77) – the so-called 'decentralisation' of bargaining within multi-divisional corporations. New greenfield sites are protected against unions already established within the sector or company which wish to win recognition or comparable levels of wages and conditions. The cancellation of Ford's component factory provisionally planned for Dundee, with its single-union recognition agreement negotiated by the AEU, and pay and conditions outside the existing Ford UK agreement, when threatened by a union boycott, was expressly cited by the Conservative government in justification of the 1990 Act (Department of Employment 1989: 11). Employers' power has also been indirectly strengthened by the statutory regulation of unions' government and administration, which reduces their autonomy, flexibility and resources, lessening their ability to react effectively to employers' policies. Moreover, the sustained legal assault on their legitimacy has created a climate in which unions are not perceived to 'add value' to a business or the economy and therefore may be excluded by employers.

Finally, employers' discretion over work organisation and employment relations has increased as a result of the repeal of legislation controlling payment methods, the employment of women and young persons, and minimum pay rates. Furthermore, the TURERA 1993 empowered employers to discriminate in terms of pay and conditions between employees who wish to adhere to collective agreements and those prepared to accept 'personal' and 'individual' contracts of employment, preventing in all but exceptional cases any appeal to a tribunal on the grounds of discrimination against union members.[9]

The law of unfair dismissal has been further liberalised in employers' favour: in 1985 the qualifying period was extended to two years, while in 1990 employers became entitled to dismiss unofficial strikers on a selective basis and industrial action taken in their defence is outside the statutory definition of a trade dispute and union tort immunity. The case law has widened the criteria of 'Some Substantial Reason' to permit 'essential' business reorganisation by employers, including offers of new contracts to workers at inferior pay and terms, as a legitimate defence against unfair dismissal (Wedderburn 1986: 241–3). Unions, of course, have no legal protection against derecognition and may as a consequence lose a number of statutory rights, for example, health and safety representation, time off for union representatives, and information for collective bargaining purposes.

Overall, more than a decade of Conservative policy and employment legislation has transformed the political and legal context of British trade unionism. Until 1979, a bi-partisan and pluralist (Fox 1966) public policy had encouraged the growth of trade unionism, particularly in the public sector. However, as we have seen, Conservative governments broke decisively with collectivism by promoting an 'individualist *laissez-faire*' political economy in which unions are regarded as an unwarranted distortion of the labour market and interference in the master and servant relationship. As a result, British unions not only have faced a difficult economic environment and great changes in the character of work, but have done so stripped of legal and institutional supports.

MANAGEMENT AND UNIONS

In the past, unions have proved highly adaptable in the face of huge changes in technology or work organisation, or major shifts in the economic, legal and political environment. Thus nineteenth-century craft societies reared in the domestic, hand- or water-powered industry, such as engineers or textile workers, were often adept at redefining and re-establishing their role for an age of huge steam-driven factories (Turner 1962). Moreover, entire new industries and occupations, such as the motor industry or clerical workers (Bain 1970), were eventually brought into the union movement. Equally, unions in industries like cotton or coal used to lose members during the downswing of the trade cycle, but recouped their losses with the upturn. And, in the recent past, governments operating within a framework of liberal capitalist democracy have found it difficult to enact legal controls on unions. Most famously, the Industrial Relations Act 1971 was ignored by employers, flouted by unions, and appeared to confirm the 'limits of the law' (Weekes *et al.* 1975). Therefore it would be mistaken to assume that any change in the environment of unions, however severe, would translate straightforwardly into a loss of influence (or vice versa). As we have seen, over the past decade or more, the shape of work and its economic, political and legal climate have changed in ways which are largely detrimental to trade unionism. In this case, the sheer combined weight of negative factors may cause us to anticipate dramatic change. After all, it is one thing to face a legal offensive during a period of full employment, or to confront major changes in the character of work with the aid of a friendly political and legal regime. It is quite another to cope with the 'slings and arrows of outrageous fortune' when the state is also providing the ammunition. This said, all these external industrial relations influences are also mediated through institutions, namely the unions and the members they represent, and the companies and managers with which they deal. It is at the level of workplace strategy on both sides that the contours of contemporary unionism has been shaped. This section will consider three dimensions to this problem of agency. First, there is the espoused policy of modern management, notably that cluster of initiatives around the concept of HRM. Second, there is the survey and case study evidence on the extent of real change in the workplace. Finally, there are the strategies adopted by unions in workplace, but also in the broader labour market, to accommodate or counter these new pressures, and the problems of translating them into work-place union practice. In short, the main questions are: what is management seeking, what has it obtained, and what can the unions do about it?

The new management agenda

In the early 1980s, the new management approach was widely characterised as a crude 'Macho Management' (Edwardes 1983,

Edwards 1985). Throughout that decade, a series of tough super-bosses, Michael Edwardes at BL, Ian MacGregor at steel and coal, Eddie Shah and Rupert Murdoch in the print industry, fought bitter public battles to break or weaken unions in their previous industrial heartlands. The government provided appropriate legal instruments and police support against striking workers, and generally cheered on their efforts. Important as these strategic battles were as examples to the rest of the union movement, they were clearly not typical of what management was attempting in the bulk of British industry. Elsewhere, businesses were talking the novel, emollient language of HRM, and initiating a raft of new EI schemes such as Quality Circles, team briefing and profit sharing (Storey 1989). In common with the 'macho managers', they began to address and involve individual workers directly through these new parallel channels; not confronting the unions directly, but merely diverting the energies of people management away from union-centred conflict resolution. The true import of HRM was ambiguous and unclear. Some suspected that it was merely trivial: a relabelling of age-old personnel practices in the attractive language of American popular management. To others it was potentially benign: a long-awaited conversion of authoritarian British management to the virtue of shopfloor creativity, within the Harvard framework of pluralist union–management 'jointism' (Beer *et al.* 1984). Finally, yet other commentators perceived a more sinister trend: the insinuation of 'welfare capitalist' methods from American non-union firms, such as Hewlett-Packard and IBM, into the unionised 'mainstream' with drastic long-term implications for the future role of unions there (Guest 1987). In the USA, HRM has a strongly anti-union intent. Evidence on the impact of HRM in the UK is mixed, with surveys suggesting application rates higher in unionised firms, but with case studies indicating peaceful, and not so peaceful, co-existence between new HRM techniques and collective bargaining machinery (Millward *et al.* 1992; Sisson 1993; Storey 1992). For example, Cadbury, a company with a history of pro-unionism (Smith *et al.* 1990), has recently been reported as using HRM techniques deliberately to marginalise trade unions, which its management see as facing long-term decline within the workplace (*Labour Research* 1994: 24).

The new industrial relations

The research record proffers some support for all three prognoses, and plenty of instances of unreconstructed 'macho management'. Our problem is how to discern some overall pattern from this variety; how to attach some appropriate weighting to the various developments. Storey (1992) has shown that 'mainstream' British business has embarked on serious HRM programmes which belie talk of mere relabelling. However, while he has identified the desirability of a benign 'jointist' approach in order to gain effective workforce consent (Storey and Sisson 1993), there is limited British evidence of management seeking to breathe new life into the union relationship. The suspicion remains that the active component of HRM dualism is the non-union EI channel, and that, far from there being a symbiotic relationship, the new individualist ivy is growing by draining the lifeblood from the old collective tree. Taking a more diverse business sample, Marchington et al. (1992) have also vouched for the currency of EI concepts, while questioning their impact and identifying both considerable triviality and a variety of contrasting consequences for unions. The major WIRS surveys (Daniel and Millward 1983; Millward and Stevens 1986; Millward et al. 1992) provide an intriguing longitudinal series of aerial photographs of trends in workplace industrial relations, stretching over a decade. The first two surveys confounded simplistic talk of 'macho management' sweeping British industry, by stressing the institutional stability of continuing workplaces, in terms of union recognition and shop steward representation (Kelly 1987). On the other hand, the latest survey, which charts a significant trend towards union derecognition, suggests that sophisticated HRM has been confined to large-unionised workplaces, while the reality across a large and growing part of the economy is a 'Bleak House' combination of no unions and no new HRM techniques (Sisson 1993; Guest and Hoque 1994).

These latest WIRS results suggest that, outside established union bastions, 'generous, warm-hearted' management is not the principal obstacle to union advance, as some HRM advocates have contended (a point developed by McLoughlin in this volume). Within the existing unionised sectors, these findings would be quite consistent with the benign 'dualism' scenario, if there were any substantial evidence of management drawing the union into the centre of its HRM policies, as GM did in the US car industry in the late 1980s (Black and Ackers 1994). More often, particularly in the public and recently privatised sectors, the current actions of management give more credence to the union by-passing scenario. Perhaps, this presents a false polarisation between coercion and consent. For companies, such as Ford UK, which initially were quite content to force through change, irrespective of union wishes, may wish to return later to a collaborative relationship with the weakened union body that remains.

Union responses

Union responses have also gone through a series of phases, each of which has occasioned major internal conflicts. The first phase, in the early 1980s, was one of disbelief, especially on the left of the union movement, bolstered by the conviction that the Thatcher government would soon be defeated, as its Heath predecessor had, and that industrial relations could return to the status quo ante (Gill 1981). Macho management was conceived in such terms as an unpleasant but short-lived shift in the 'frontier of control'. The TUC's 1980 'Day of Action' dramatised this conviction. By the mid-decade, the consolidation of Conservative rule, the reduced importance of union strongholds in traditional heavy, manual industry, and ever-tightening legal controls provoked a much more fundamental reassessment (TUC 1988). This movement towards the 'new realism' was sealed by the defeat of the militant miners' union in 1985. However, at least three different political strands remained within the British union movement, and these may be loosely attached to some major union bodies (Martinez Lucio and Weston 1992a). First, on the left, TASS (later to merge into MSF and change its political complexion) emphasised the traditional union bargaining agenda, and saw progress mainly via deepening its existing organisation and through merger with other unions. By contrast, on the right, the 'business unionism' of the EETPU (now part of AEEU) went furthest towards embracing the new 'Enterprise Culture', by openly courting employers into 'single-union, no-strike' deals, and trying to enlarge its 'market-share' of union membership, at the expense of other less conciliatory unions (Bassett 1987). In the broad centre, the TUC and the two great general unions, the TGWU and the GMB, emphasised more modest overtures to management, in the form of reform proposals for 'single-table bargaining', and by stressing 'link' campaigns to win the growing peripheral workforce of part-time women and ethnic minorities – with limited success (Snape 1994). For all the furious public debate, by the late 1980s a common practical agenda emerged of opportunist mergers, overtures to employers, recruitment campaigns, and improved public images and individual services for workers (TUC 1988).

The union campaigns to win both employers and members have yielded meagre returns, and perhaps the greatest gap in all the various strategies has been their practical response to management HRM strategies in the workplace. The post-war decentralisation of collective bargaining to the workplace (Brown 1981), and the multi-union reality of union representation at that level, created a chasm between national rhetoric and workplace practice, which more than matches the same management predicament. This problematic British relationship between workplace and union stands in stark contrast to the integrated and proactive policy pursued by a continental union like IG Metal. In one view, under adverse economic and legal conditions, the militant, autonomous shop stewards' organisations of old have partially metamorphosed into the compliant 'company unions' of today (Brown 1986). More likely, the decline in the TUC's already weak authority, and the absence of mechanisms for co-ordinating or translating national union policies into workplace union strategies, has created a remarkable local pragmatism which belies official union labels. Thus regional officers of the left-wing TGWU participate in employer 'beauty contests' for single-union deals, and TGWU activists in one workplace boycott the Quality Circle programme, while their colleagues elsewhere welcome it. By contrast, some former public-sector unions, such as the UCW, have retained a closer link between union and workplace which may make them more capable of translating union policy into shopfloor practice.

For these reasons, any proper understanding of either management or union strategy cannot confine its attention to the corporate boardroom and the union head office, the company report or mission statement and the union policy document. While it is important to grasp corporate policy 'Beyond the Workplace' (Marchington *et al.* 1992), the workplace remains the crucible for the implementation of management and union policy, as the chapters in this volume testify.

THE OTHER CHAPTERS

Chapter 2 by Bacon and Storey and Chapter 3 by Kelly rehearse a long-standing debate within the trade union movement, between moderate (pluralist) and militant (radical) strategies, in the context of current management rhetoric about HRM and the unions' search for 'new realist' policies which will attract employers as well as workers. Bacon and Storey articulate the prevailing TUC view that unions may turn the claims of HRM to their own benefits and suggest a co-operative style consistent with the consultative ideas emerging from the EU. Their chapter draws on the findings of a large-scale research project on individualist and collectivist approaches to the employment relationship. This has involved case studies of nine 'mainstream' organisations, interviews with union officials and representatives, and attitude surveys of employees. They conclude that unions need to develop a vocabulary of the individual to meet the challenge of HRM strategies, while at the same time pressing for a collective social partnership with employers. Against this, Kelly evaluates the arguments for labour–management co-operation and finds them wanting. The more radical forms of moderation can seriously weaken unions' autonomy and power, eroding members' capacity to challenge or resist employers' priorities. Advocates of moderate unionism have seriously underestimated the antagonism displayed by employers to workplace union organisation and collective bargaining. He argues that militant unionism better serves union members' interests because it is predicated upon a recognition of the different interests of employers and workers. Militant unionism does not preclude collective bargaining relations with employers; it embodies an element of contingency, taking different forms in different circumstances. Nevertheless, this antinomy between moderate and militant informs many of the chapters that follow.

Chapter 4 by Fairbrother and Chapter 5 by Waddington and Whitston consider the situation from the perspective of trade union activists. Fairbrother's chapter discusses the potential of union renewal – the creation of new participative values and social relations which constitute trade union organisation – within the context of restructuring of the state sector (separation of purchaser and provider, decentralisation, financial measures and controls) initiated by Conservative governments during the 1980s. Hitherto standard terms and conditions of employment – negotiated nationally – have been qualified within new specific organisations and discrete sections, providing opportunities for bargaining initiative by members and representatives. A particular danger is that the centrifugal forces thus unleashed may subvert unions' national cohesion to establish a form of enterprise unionism. However, union renewal remains only a possibility, dependent upon members' action, since existing centralised and hierarchical forms of union organisation may be reasserted. Waddington and Whitston present the findings of a major survey of union activists, which offers an important corrective to the customary managerial sample. They cover a wide range of new management practices, including new HRM and EI initiatives, and new forms of work organisation, and question whether management is empowering employees or merely intensifying the pressure of work. In the first instance, they report a substantial take-up of new EI techniques, but note that the most popular of these are 'soft on power', like team briefing. In addition, they identify an upsurge in grievances related to new forms of work flexibility, especially in the 'exposed sector' considered by Fairbrother. Crucially, they find that concerns about work intensification have eclipsed any sense of enhanced commitment and empowerment. This is because the EI techniques chosen are too 'weak on power' to make a difference, and because any positive impact they might have on employee attitudes has been swamped by the perception that managers are forcing through unfavourable changes in the quality of work. To revive an old labour process metaphor, the realities of the economic 'base' of workplace realities, as experienced by these union activists, has overwhelmed the EI 'superstructure'.

The relationship between new production practices, shopfloor workers and union is the subject of Chapter 6 by Anna Pollert, which explores the development and operation of 'teamworking' within a mature mass production food company. While the literature of new production concepts does, as discussed previously, support the idea of their prevalence in unionised workplaces, we know relatively little about the actual relationship between unions and these techniques in practice. This chapter uses as its method a 'vertical slice' through the company, interviewing senior management, teamleaders, workers and trade unionists about the operation of teamworking and what it takes to make it work within a mature unionised environment. The case records, in considerable ethnographic and representative detail, the reorganisation of authority within a well-unionised factory, and shows that in certain ways shop steward co-operation was required to facilitate the operation of teamworking. Far from creating an alternative path of communication which undermined union channels, teamworking unintentionally created a new niche for trade union activity and influence. This outcome arose from the contradictory delivery of the system and the lack of training and inexperience of team-leaders who were frequently thrown on to shop stewards for guidance and help. While this reinforces a well-trodden literature on unions as the lubricant and not irritant of production, Pollert is careful to avoid a complacent reading of this experience, stressing the perhaps transitional nature of team organisation, and the quite different experience of their performance in different areas of the factory. Indeed, she concludes by highlighting the longer-term threat to shopfloor unionism as teamworking becomes more embedded and management more sophisticated at reaping its potential for reducing the influence of union-controlled channels of communication on the shop floor.

In Chapter 7 Stephenson examines two case studies of workplace trade unionism on greenfield sites from inward investors in the North-East of England. Nissan is possibly the most celebrated of Japanese companies in the UK, being the first major Japanese car assembler, applauded by the Conservative government as introducing a new industrial relations into Britain, and given a high profile by its ex-Personnel Director, Peter Wickens, who through various publica-tions and media appearances has presented the 'Nissan Way' as a new phase of 'partnership' industrial relations for British industry. The second case, Ikeda Hoover, is a Japanese–US joint venture car seat supplier to Nissan, located on the industrial estate bought by Nissan to house its Just-in-Time (JIT) supplier firms. The US parent, Johnson Controls, has thirty-one automotive seat plants world-wide supplying customers on a JIT basis; nine of these are in Europe. The case therefore offers an interesting perspective on Japanese and North American attitudes towards unions.

The chapter contrasts the quality of unionism in the two plants through interviews with workers, conducted away from the work-place over several years. In contrast to the work of Garrahan and Stewart (1992), which predicted that Nissan would form the model of shopfloor unionism for all its suppliers in the industrial site, Stephenson highlights the major differences between the two plants. At Nissan, despite gaining the right to have one shop steward in the plant, the union exercises no control over the labour process, and conditions of a passive, enterprise union prevail. At Ikeda-Hoover, by contrast, trade unionism, inherited though recruiting union-experienced workers conscious of their skilled and relatively secure place at work, operates at shopfloor level as an outlet for worker discontent. Stephenson explores the nature of unionism in the two plants, and how workers are able, despite the restrictive nature of the imposed union deal set up behind their backs, to create their own voice on the shop floor. While the contrasts between the two plants are considerable, redundancies and increased employment uncertainty at Nissan may be a spur to changes in the direction of worker organisation in the Ikeda-Hoover factory, thereby potentially reversing the logic of Garrahan and Stewart's thesis. But what is clear from the chapter is that Japanese ownership and working methods in themselves are no guarantee of a standard form of workplace unionism, as other factors such as employee selection, skill levels and union experiences are critical intervening variables influencing workers' desire and opportunities for building unionism on the shop floor.

The process of bringing marginal groups of Asian workers into trade unionism forms the substance of Chapter 8 by Wrench and Virdee. They chart the relationship between ethnic minority workers and unionism, changing through the generations from a high propensity to unionise amongst early migrants to a reduced propensity and under-unionisation by Asian minorities in many areas today. The problematical association between British unions and ethnic minorities is analysed by way of background for two case studies which examine two typical employment situations of ethnic minority women workers in contemporary capitalism: a large service-sector employer and a small sweatshop manufacturer. The first explores a TGWU campaign to organise mainly Asian female cleaners at Heathrow Airport, and the difficulties encountered from management non-recognition, wider environmental obstacles and problems of the union's strategy itself in this process. While charting the failure of one particular union drive, the authors stress the lessons of this and the importance of unions linking with ethnic minority organisations, to pursue more innovative and community-specific unionisation strategies. The second case deals with the experience of mainly Asian women sweatshop workers in the West Midlands, who struck with the GMB over a series of grievances including low and unequal pay, health and safety, management-imposed overtime and union recognition. The lengthy strike by the twenty-six mostly Punjabi women strikers eventually ended without reinstatement, and bitter acrimony between the strikers, union officials and Asian community groups. Wrench and Virdee analyse the social and political dynamics of this dispute and place this within a wider context and the prevailing perspectives towards recruiting marginal and ethnic-minority workers in the sweated trades and beyond. Their conclusions speak of the need for unions to take far more seriously union-isation of small firms, which are becoming the employment experience for an increasing number of workers, but particularly ethnic-minority women.

Chapter 9 by McKinlay and Taylor is a case study of team-working in a large North American non-union firm. Their study of PhoneCo illustrates how workers challenged management-imposed boundaries and perceptions as to how teams should operate. They are critical of Foucauldian concepts of surveillance and discipline which overstate the panoptic reach of management organisation. They indicate that the nature of teamworking itself became a contested issue as workers probed managerial commit-ment to devolved decision-making. This suggests that the power of HRM techniques to diffuse employee resistance and channel their individual and collective aspirations through corporate agendas has been exaggerated. Management responded by an open as-sertion of power within the employment relation, restoring hier-archical structures and norms.

Chapter 10 by McLoughlin draws together some of the impli-cations of non-unionism, particularly in the high-technology sector, by characterising the various types of non-union business and hypothesising what sort of trade union strategy might succeed. In line with WIRS (Millward *et al.* 1992), he argues that, in general, non-unionism cannot be regarded as a product of seductive HRM policies promoted by 'sophisticated unitarists' since none of his cases fit this bill. This tallies with Waddington and Whitston's view, that even in those unionised workplaces where HRM techniques are most evident, the seduction factor is low. Rather, McLoughlin argues, these employees do not unionise, notwithstanding con-siderable grievances with their existing non-union employers, because they doubt the efficacy of union membership – whether it is feasible for them to gain union recognition against employer opposition, and whether it will make a difference. This returns us to the issues raised by Bacon and Storey, and by Kelly, though it offers no easy solution for union strategy. On the one hand, it might support a conciliatory and consultative overture to employers to nudge them in the direction of union recognition. On the other, it might support the view that unless unions are forceful and combative bargaining agents, employees are unlikely to regard the sacrifices of membership as worthwhile. Alternatively, the efficacy of trade unionism may depend, as it partly did in the period before 1970, on a supportive political and legal framework. In this third view, a change of British government, an alternative political economy, and a new rapport with the EU are prerequisites for any resumption of the 'forward march' of labour.

NOTES

1 The Trade Union and Labour Relations Acts 1974 and 1976 – the first passed by the minority Labour government, 1974–6, the second by the majority government, 1976–9 – had restored the legal position of trade unions to take industrial action to the position prior to the Industrial Relations Act 1971, as governed by the Trades Disputes Act 1906. But the language used was wider than the 1906 Act in order to give immunity to the various torts which had been developed by the courts during the 1960s (Wedderburn 1989: 565–8, 589–96, 619–23). The response of some judges, led by Lord Denning, Master of the Rolls (the senior civil judge), was hostile, and they interpreted union immunity narrowly. This was an important factor creating the favourable political climate for the subsequent imposition of statutory restrictions upon industrial action (*ibid.*, 596–7).

2 See Wedderburn (1989: 598–606) for the ineffectiveness of the 'gateways to legality', now abolished by the Employment Act 1990.

3 The Conservatives' free market programme is a pragmatic amalgam of maxims drawn from both neo-classical and Austrian economic schools; see Fine and Harris (1987). For other sources see Fosh *et al.* (1993).

4 Employment Act 1980, Employment Act 1982, Trade Union Act 1984, Wages Act 1986, Sex Discrimination Act 1986, Employment Act 1988, Employment Act 1989, Employment Act 1990, Trade Union Reform and Employee Rights Act 1993.

5 The detrimental effect of unions upon productivity has now attained the status of a self-evident truth in government pronouncements (Department of Employment 1988: 15; 1989: 5–6, on the pre-entry closed shop).

6 *Kenny* v. *South Manchester College* [1993] IRLR 265.

7 *Solihull MBC* v. *NUT* [1985] IRLR 211 (see Wedderburn 1989: 588); *Ticehurst and Thompson* v. *British Telecommunications* [1992] IRLR 219.

8 The only exception which still remains is the freedom of pickets (achieved through tort immunity) to seek to dissuade workers

employed by other organisations (or under contract to them) from the provision or collection of goods or services to the employer in dispute.
9 Claims, under s. 146(1) of the Trade Union and Labour Relations (Consolidation) Act 1992 (formerly s. 23 of the Employment Protection Act 1975), on the grounds of discrimination against union membership as a result of the introduction of personal contracts were successful at industrial tribunals, reversed by the EAT, but supported again by the Court of Appeal. *Associated Newspapers* v. *Wilson* [1992] IRLR 440 EAT; *Associated British Ports* v. *Palmer* [1993] IRLR 63 EAT; *Wilson* v. *Associated Newspapers, Palmer* v. *Associated British Ports* [1993] IRLR, 336 CA. For the position of the government and its critics, see Hansard (1993). For a discussion of personal contracts, see Evans and Hudson (1994).

REFERENCES

Ackers, P. and Black, J. (1991) 'Paternalist Capitalism: An Organisation Culture in Transition', in M. Cross and G. Payne (eds), *Work and the Enterprise Culture*, London: Falmer.

Applebaum, E. and Batt, R. (1994) *The New American Workplace*, New York: ILR Press.

Armstrong, P. (1986) 'Work Supervisors and Trade Unionism', in P. Armstrong *et al. White-Collar Workers, Trade Unions and Class*, London: Croom Helm.

Atkinson, J. (1985) 'Flexibility: Planning for an Uncertain Future', *The IMS Review* **1**: 26–9.

Auerbach, S. (1988) 'Injunction Procedure in the Seafarers' Dispute', *Industrial Law Journal* **17**: 227–38.

Bain, G. S. (1970) *The Growth of White-Collar Unionism*, Oxford: Clarendon.

Bain, G. S. and Price, R. (1983) 'Union Growth: Determinants and Density', in G. S. Bain (ed.), *Industrial Relations in Britain*, Oxford: Blackwell.

Bassett, P. (1987) *Strike Free: New Industrial Relations in Britain*, London: Macmillan.

Beaumont, P. B. (1987) *The Decline of Trade Union Organisation*, Beckenham: Croom Helm.

Beer, M., Spector, B. and Lawrence, P. R. (1984) *Managing Human Assets*, New York: The Free Press.

Berggren, C. (1992) *The Volvo Experience*, London: Macmillan.

Black, J. and Ackers, P. (1988) 'The Japanisation of British Industry? A Case Study of Quality Circles in the Carpet Industry', *Employee Relations* **10**, 6: 9–16.

Black, J. and Ackers, P. (1994) 'Voting for Employee Involvement at General Motors: A Case Study from the United States', in T. Elger and C. Smith (eds), *Global Japanization? Transnational Transformation of the Labour Process*, London: Routledge.

Blackburn, R. M. (1967) *Union Character and Social Class*, London: Batsford.

Blyton, P. and Turnbull, P. (1992) *The Dynamics of Employee Relations*, London: Macmillan.

Blyton, P. and Turnbull, P. (eds) (1992) *Reassessing Human Resource Management*, London: Sage.

Bratton, J. (1992) *Japanization at Work*, London: Macmillan.

Braverman, H. (1974) *Labor and Monopoly Capital*, New York: Monthly Review Press.

Brown, W. (1981) *The Changing Contours of British Industrial Relations: A Survey of Manufacturing Industry*, Oxford: Blackwell.

Brown, W. (1986) 'The Changing Role of Trade Unions in the Management of Labour', *British Journal of Industrial Relations* **24**: 161–8.

Buchanan, D. and Preston, D. (1992) 'Life in the Cell: Supervision and Teamwork in a "Manufacturing Systems Engineering" Environment', *Human Resource Management Journal* **2**, 4: 55–76.

Carter, R. (1979) 'Class, Militancy and Union Character: A Study of the Association of Scientific, Technical and Managerial Staffs', *Sociological Review* **27**, 2: 297–316.

Chandler, A. D., Jr (1990) *Scale and Scope: The Dynamics of Industrial Capitalism*, Cambridge, Mass: Harvard University Press.

Clegg, H. A. (1976) *Trade Unionism under Collective Bargaining*, Oxford: Blackwell.

Clegg, H. A. (1979) *The Changing System of Industrial Relations in Great Britain*, Oxford: Blackwell.

Crompton, R. and Jones, G. (1984) *White-Collar Proletariat: Deskilling and Gender in Clerical Work*, Basingstoke: Macmillan.

Cross, M. and Payne, G. (eds) *Work and the Enterprise Culture*, London: Falmer.

Daniel, W. and Millward, N. (1983) *Workplace Industrial Relations in Britain*, London: Heinemann.

Dawson, P. (1991) 'Flexible Workcells: Teamwork and Group Technology on the Shopfloor', *Labour Process Conference*, UMIST, April.

Dawson, P. and Webb, J. (1989) 'New Production Arrangements: the Totally Flexible Cage', *Work, Employment and Society* **3**, 2: 221–38.

Department of Employment (1988) *Employment for the 1990s*, Cmnd 540, London: HMSO.

Department of Employment (1989) *Removing Barriers to Employment*, Cmnd 655, London: HMSO.

Department of Employment (1991) *Industrial Relations in the 1990s*, Cmnd 1602, London: HMSO.

Dickens, L. and Hall, M. (1995) 'The State: Labour Law and Industrial Relations', in P. K. Edwards (ed.), *Industrial Relations Theory and Practice in Britain*, Oxford: Blackwell.

Donovan, Lord (1968) *Royal Commission on Trade Unions and Employers Associations: Report*, Cmnd 3623, London: HMSO.

Dunn, S. (1990) 'Root Metaphor in the Old and the New Industrial Relations', *British Journal of Industrial Relations* **28**, 1: 1–31.

Edwardes, M. (1983) *Back from the Brink*, London: Pan.

Edwards, P. (1985) 'Myth of the Macho Manager', *Personnel Management*, April: 32–5.

Edwards, R. (1979) *Contested Terrain*, London: Heinemann.

Elger, T. and Fairbrother, P. (1992) 'Inflexible Flexibility: A Case Study of Modularisation', in N. Gilbert, R. Burrows and A. Pollert (eds), *Fordism and Flexibility*, London: Macmillan.

Elger, T. and Smith, C. (eds) (1994) *Global Japanization?*, London: Routledge.

Employment Gazette (1994) 'The Flexible Workforce and Patterns of Working Hours in the UK', July: 239–48.

Evans, S. and Hudson, M. (1994) 'From Collective Bargaining to "Personal Contracts": Case Studies in Port Transport and Electricity Supply', *Industrial Relations Journal* **25**, 4: 305–14.

Ewing, K. (1993) 'Swimming with the Tide: Employment Protection and the Implementation of European Labour Law', *Industrial Law Journal* **22**, 3: 165–80.

Ewing, K. and Napier, B. W. (1986) 'The Wapping Dispute and Labour Law', *Cambridge Law Journal* **45**, 2: 285–304.

Fairbrother, P. (1994) 'Privatisation and Local Trade Unionism', *Work, Employment and Society* **8**, 3: 339–56.

Felstead, A. (1993) *The Corporate Paradox*, London: Routledge.

Ferner, A. and Colling, T. (1991) 'Privatization, Regulation and Industrial Relations', *British Journal of Industrial Relations* **29**, 3: 391–409.

Fine, B. and Harris, L. (1987) 'Ideology and Markets, Economic Theory and the "New Right"', in R. Miliband *et al.* (eds) *Socialist Register*, London: Merlin Press.

Flanders, R. (1961) *Management and Unions*, London: Hutchinson.

Florida, R. and Kenney, M. (1991) 'Organisation versus Culture: Japanese Automotive Transplants in the US', *Industrial Relations Journal* **22**, 3: 181–96.

Fosh, P., Morris, H., Martin, R., Smith, P. and Undy, R. (1993) 'The "Wellsprings" of Conservative Employment Legislation', *Industrial Law Journal* **22**, 1: 14–31.

Fox, A. (1966) 'Industrial Sociology and Industrial Relations', Royal Commission on Trade Unions and Employers' Associations, *Research Paper* 3.

Freemantle, D. (1985) 'Comment: An End to the Art of Compromise', *Personnel Management*, May.

Friedman, A. L. (1977) *Industry and Labour*, London: Macmillan.

Gardner, M. and Palmer, G. (1992) *Employment Relations: Industrial Relations and Human Resource Management in Australia*, Melbourne: Macmillan.

Garrahan, P. and Stewart, P. (1992) *The Nissan Enigma: Flexibility at Work in a Local Economy*, London: Mansell.

Gill, K. (1981) 'Reply', in Jacques, M. and Mulhern, F., *The Forward March of Labour Halted?*, London: Verso.

Graham, L. (1994) 'How Does the Japanese Model Transfer to the United States? A View from the Line', in T. Elger and C. Smith, *Global Japanization?*, London: Routledge.

Gregory, J. (1992) 'Equal Pay for Work of Equal Value', *Work, Employment and Society* **6**, 3: 461–73.

Guest, D. (1987) 'Human Resource Management and Industrial Relations', *Journal of Management Studies* **24**, 5, 503–21.

Guest, D. (1989) 'Human Resource Management: Its Implications for Industrial Relations and Trade Unions', in J. Storey (ed.), *New Perspectives on Human Resource Management*, London: Routledge.

Guest, D. (1990) 'Human Resource Management and the American Dream', *Journal of Management Studies* **27**, 4: 377–97.

Guest, D. and Hoque, K. (1994) 'The Good, the Bad and the Ugly: Employment Relations in New Non-Union Workplaces', *Human Resource Management Journal* **5**, 1: 1–14.

Hall, S. and Jacques, M. (eds) (1983) *The Politics of Thatcherism*, London: Lawrence and Wishart.

Hansard (1993) Parl. db. HL 24 May, c 12–42.

Harrison, B. and Bluestone, B. (1988) *The Great U-Turn: Corporate Restructuring and the Polarizing of America*, New York: Basic Books.

Heery, E. and Kelly, J. (1994) 'Professional, Participative and Managerial Unionism: an Interpretation of change in Trade Unions', *Work, Employment and Society* **8**, 1: 1–22.

Hobsbawm, E. H. (ed.) (1981) *The Forward March of Labour Halted*, London: Verso.

Hunter, L., McGregor, A., MacInnes, J. and Sproull, A. (1993) 'The Flexible Firm: Strategy and Segmentation', *British Journal of Industrial Relations* **31**, 3: 383–407.

Hyman, R. (1994) 'Industrial Relations in Western Europe: An Era of Ambiguity?', *Industrial Relations* **33**, 1: 1–23.

Industrial Relations Review and Report (1994) 'Non-Standard Working Under Review', August, **565**: 10–15.

Katz, H. (1988) 'Policy Debates over Work Reorganization in North American Unions', in R. Hyman and W. Streeck (eds), *New Technology and Industrial Relations*, Oxford: Blackwell.

Katz, H. and Sabel, C. F. (1985) 'Industrial Relations and Industrial Adjustment in the Car Industry', *Industrial Relations* **24**, 3: 295–315.

Keat, R. and Abercrombie, N. (eds) (1991) *Enterprise Culture*, London: Routledge.

Keenoy, T. (1990) 'HRM: A Case of the Wolf in Sheep's Clothing', *Personnel Review* **19**, 2.

Keenoy, T. and Anthony, P. (1992) 'HRM: Metaphor, Meaning and Morality', in P. Blyton and P. Turnbull (eds) *Reassessing Human Resource Management*, London: Sage.

Kelly, J. (1987) 'Trade Unions Through the Recession', *British Journal of Industrial Relations* **25**, 2: 275–82.

Kenny, M. and Florida, R. (1993) *Beyond Mass Production*, Oxford: Oxford University Press.

Kessler, S. and Bayliss, F. (1995) *Contemporary British Industrial Relations* (2nd edn), Basingstoke: Macmillan.

Kochan, T., Katz, H. and McKersie, R. (1986) *The Transformation of American Industrial Relations*, New York: ILR Press.

Kochan, T. and Weinstein, M. (1994) 'Recent Developments in US Industrial Relations', *British Journal of Industrial Relations* **32**, 4: 483–504.

Labour Research (1994) 'HRM at Cadburys', 24 December.

Lane, C. (1989) *Management and Labour in Europe*, Aldershot: Edward Elgar.

Lane, T. and Roberts, K. (1971) *Strike at Pilkingtons*, London: Fontana.

Littler, C. R. (1982) *The Development of the Labour Process in Capitalist Societies*, London: Heinemann.

Lockwood, D. (1958) *The Blackcoated Worker*, London: Allen & Unwin.

MacInnes, J. (1987) *Thatcherism at Work: Industrial Relations and Economic Change*, Milton Keynes: Open University Press.

Marchington, M., Goodman, J., Wilkinson, A. and Ackers, P. (1992) *New Developments in Employee Involvement*, Sheffield: Employmemt Department, Research Series 2.

Marsh, A. and Cox, B. (1992) *The Trade Union Movement in the UK 1992*, Oxford: Malthouse Press.

Marsh, D. (1992) *The New Politics of British Trade Unionism: Union Power and the Thatcher Legacy*, London: Macmillan.

Martinez Lucio, M. and Weston, S. (1992a) 'The Politics and Complexity of Trade Union Responses to New Management Practices', *Human Resource Management Journal* **2**, 3: 77–91.

Martinez Lucio, M. and Weston, S. (1992b) 'Human Resource Management and Trade Union Responses: Bringing the Politics of the Workplace Back into the Debate', in P. Blyton and P. Turnbull (eds), *Reassessing Human Resource Management*, London: Sage.

Marx, K. (1976) *Capital Volume 1*, Harmondsworth: Penguin.

Metcalf, D. (1990) 'Union Presence and Labour Productivity in British Manufacturing', *British Journal of Industrial Relations* **28**, 2: 249–66.

Milkman, R. (1991) *Japan's California Factories: Labour Relations and Economic Globalization*, California: Institute of Industrial Relations, University of California, Los Angeles.

Millward, N. and Stevens, M. (1986) *British Workplace Industrial Relations 1980–1984*, Aldershot: Gower.

Millward, N., Stevens, M., Smart, D. and Hawes, W. R. (1992) *Workplace Industrial Relations in Transition: The ED/ESRC/PSI/ACAS Surveys*, Aldershot: Dartmouth.

Milsome, S. (1993) *The Impact of Japanese Firms on Working and Employ-ment Practices in British Manufacturing Industry: A Review of Recent Research*, London: Industrial Relations Services.

Mueller, F. (1994) 'Teams Between Hierarchy and Commitment: Change Strategies and the Internal Environment', *Journal of Management Studies* **31**, 3: 383–404.

O'Connell Davidson, J. (1993) *Privatization and Employment Relations: The Case of the Water Industry*, London: Mansell.

O'Connell Davidson, J. (1994) 'The Sources and Limits of Resistance in a Privatized Utility', in J. M. Jermier, D. Knights and W. R. Nord (eds), *Resistance and Power in Organizations*, London: Routledge.

Oliver, N. and Wilkinson, B. (1992) *The Japanization of British Industry*, Oxford: Blackwell.

Peck, F. and Stone, I. (1992) *New Inward Investment and the Northern Region Labour Market*, Sheffield, Department of Employment Research Series 6.

Pendleton, A. and Winterton, J. (1993) (eds) *Public Enterprise in Transition*, London: Routledge.

Penn, R. (1993) 'Changing Patterns of Work in the Contempoary British Engineering Industry', mimeo, Engineering Industry Research Group, Lancaster University.

Pollert, A. (1988) 'The Flexible Firm: Fixation or Fact?', *Work, Employment and Society* **2**, 3: 281–316.

Pollert, A. (ed.) (1991) *Farewell to Flexiblity?*, Oxford: Blackwell.

Purcell, J. (1989) 'The Impact of Corporate Strategy upon Human Resource Management', in J. Storey (ed.), *New Perspectives in Human Resource Management*, London: Routledge.

Purcell, J. and Sisson, K. (1983) 'Strategies and Practices in the Management of Industrial Relations', in G. S. Bain (ed.), *Industrial Relations in Britain*, Oxford: Blackwell.

Rinehart, J., Robertson, D., Huxley, C. and Wareham, J. (1994) 'Reunifying Conception and Execution of Work under Japanese Production Management?', in T. Elger and C. Smith, *Global Japanization?*, London: Routledge.

Roberts, B. C., Loveridge, R. and Gennard, J. (1972) *Reluctant Militants*, London: Allen & Unwin.

Saville, J. (1988) *The Labour Movement in Britain*, London: Faber and Faber.

Scott, A. (1994) *Willing Slaves? British Workers Under Human Resource Management*, Cambridge: Cambridge University Press.

Sisson, K. (1993) 'In Search of HRM', *British Journal of Industrial Relations* **31**, 2: 201–10.

Smith, C., Child, J. and Rowlinson, M. (1990) *Reshaping Work: The Cadbury Experience*, Cambridge: Cambridge University Press.

Smith, P. and Morton, G. (1993) 'Union Exclusion and the Decollectivization of Industrial Relations in Contemporary Britain', *British Journal of Industrial Relations* **31**: 97–114.

Smith, P. and Morton, G. (1994) 'Union Exclusion: Next Steps', *Industrial Relations Journal* **25**, 1: 3–14.

Snape, E. (1994) 'Reversing the Decline? The TGWU's Link Up Campaign', *Industrial Relations Journal* **25**, 3: 222–33.

Stopford, J. M. and Turner, L. (1985) *Britain and the Multinationals*, London: Wiley.

Storey, J. (ed.) (1989) *New Perspectives on Human Resource Management*, London: Routledge.

Storey, J. (1992) *Developments in the Management of Human Resources*, Oxford: Blackwell.

Storey, J. and Bacon, N. (1993a) 'Individualism and Collectivism: Into the 1990s', *International Journal of Human Resource Management* **4**, 3: 665–84.

Storey, J. and Bacon, N. (1993b) 'Individualism of the Employment Relationship and the Implications for Trade Unions', *Employee Relations* **15**, 1: 5–18.

Storey, J. and Sisson, K. (1993) *Managing Human Resources and Industrial Relations*, Buckingham: Open University Press.

Sunday Times (1992) 'Insight Report, Glittering Rises', 11 October.

Terry, M. (1994) 'Workplace Unionism: Redefining Structures and Objectives', in R. Hyman and A. Ferner (eds), *New Frontiers in European Industrial Relations*, Oxford: Blackwell.

Thompson, P., Wallace, T. and Flecker, J. (1995) 'It Ain't What you Do it's the Way that you Do it', mimeo, *Organisational Studies*, University of Central Lancashire.

Torrington, D. and Hall, L. (1987) *Personnel Management: A New Approach*, London: Prentice-Hall.

TUC (1988) *Meeting the Challenge: First Report of the Special Review Body*, London: Trades Union Congress.

Turnbull, P. (1991) 'Labour Market Deregulation and Economic Performance', *Work, Employment and Society* **5**, 1: 1–16.

Turnbull, P. and Delbridge, R. (1994) 'Making Sense of Janpanisation: A Review of the British Experience', *International Journal of Employment Studies* **2**, 2: 343–65.

Turnbull, P., Woolfson, C. and Kelly, J. (1992) *Dock Strike: Conflict and Restructuring in Britain's Ports*, Aldershot: Avebury.

Turner, H. A. (1962) *Trade Union Growth, Structure and Policy*, London: Allen & Unwin.

Turner, L. (1991) *Democracy at Work: Changing World Markets and the Future of Labor Unions*, Ithaca, New York: Cornell University Press.

Turner, L. and Auer, P. (1994) 'A Diversity of New Work Organization: Human-Centred, Lean and In-Between', *Industrielle Beziehungen* **1**, 1: 39–61.

Tyson, S. and Fell, A. (1986) *Evaluating the Personnel Function*, London: Hutchinson.

Walsh, K. (1995) 'Quality Through Markets: The New Public Services Management', in A. Wilkinson and H. Willmott (eds), *Making Quality Critical*, London: Routledge.

Webb, S. and Webb, B. (1921) *Industrial Democracy*, London: Longman.

Webb, S. and Webb, B. (1921) *The History of Trade Unionism, 1666–1920*, London: Longman.

Wedderburn, K. W. (1986) *The Worker and the Law*, 2nd edn, London: Harmondsworth.

Weekes, B. C. M., Mellish, M., Dickens, L. and Lloyd, J. (1975) *Industrial Relations and the Limits of Law: The Industrial Effects of the Industrial Relations Act 1971*, Oxford: Blackwell.

Whitaker, A. (1986) 'Managerial Strategy and Industrial Relations: A Case Study of Plant Relocation', *Journal of Management Studies* **23**, 6: 657–79.

Wickens, P.D. (1993) 'Lean Production and Beyond: The System, its Critics and the Future', *Human Resource Management Journal* **3**, 4: 75–90.

2

INDIVIDUALISM AND COLLECTIVISM AND THE CHANGING ROLE OF TRADE UNIONS

Nick Bacon and John Storey

INTRODUCTION

Over the past decade and a half managers have been involved in an ongoing reappraisal of the balance between individualism and collectivism in the employment relationship (Storey and Bacon 1993). Many managers have been reconsidering the role played by trade unions in their organisations (Purcell 1991). This role has been increasingly questioned at a time of some crisis in the trade union movement. A series of authoritative national surveys have charted the decline of union organisation throughout the 1980s (Millward *et al.* 1992). Trade unions stand at an important historical conjuncture, not for the first time in their history, and they have been involved in much internal soul-searching concerning their own future relevance and what strategies they should pursue. This review has been on-going throughout the 1980s, particularly on the issue of legislation, which has increasingly regulated trade union activity (Marsh 1992), and the issue of single union deals (Oliver and Wilkinson 1992). This review has also continued into the 1990s and has gathered pace, albeit in a less dramatic and headline-catching manner. There have been several important staging posts in this increasing pace. In September 1992, the Involvement and Participation Association (IPA) launched a consultative document (IPA 1992) indicating a new approach to management–union relations signed by some significant figures including David Sainsbury, deputy chairman of J. Sainsbury plc, David Cassidy, chairman of the Boddington Group, Sir Bryan Nicholson, Chairman of the Post Office, and for the trade unions Bill Jordan, Leif Mills, Allan Tuffin and John Edmonds, representing the AEEU, BIFU, UCW and GMB respectively. The UK government opted out of the

41

Social Chapter of the Maastricht Treaty in 1992, underlining its commitment to labour-market flexibility.[1] The Trade Union Reform and Employment Rights Act 1993 continued the trend of legislation restricting trade union activity. The House of Commons Employment Committee reported on its inquiry into 'The Future of Trade Unions' in 1994/5 (House of Commons Employment Committee 1995). Change has also been afoot in the TUC, which in 1993 felt the need to relaunch itself and establish an HRM Task Group which reported to the 1994 congress (TUC 1994). Proposals from the TUC representation-at-work task group published in January 1995 signalled a further potentially important shift away from traditional collective bargaining by backing legal rights of representation at work for non-union members (*Financial Times* 1995). One theme underpinning much of this activity is the notion that changes have taken place which fundamentally alter the basis for trade unionism in the UK. In the submission made by the Confederation of British Industry (CBI) to the House of Commons inquiry it was stated that employers:

> Suspect that the tendency for people at work to seek protection in collective strength may well be in secular, rather than cyclical decline. Higher skill levels, higher manning and the associated need to secure the full and free commitment and enthusiasm of individuals at work – both personally and as team members – point to a new relationship.
>
> (CBI 1994)

One important determinant for the future of trade unions will be how they respond to new employment strategies. The purpose of this chapter is to explore this response.

Several attempts have been made to clarify the types of response made by UK unions to new employment strategies (Bacon and Storey 1993; Beaumont 1991; Martinez Lucio and Weston 1992). The future alternative scenarios of 'ideal-types' of trade unions have also been outlined. A four-fold classification is offered by Hyman (1994) (friendly society, company union, social partner or social movement), a three-fold classification by Guest (1995) (semi-institutional, friendly society and union HRM), and the two dimensions of moderation and militancy are offered by Kelly (this volume). However, each of these authors has tended to present an either/or choice for national union strategies while acknowledging that at workplace level union actors need to be more pragmatic. There has been less research on the framework in which plant-level union negotiators have acted. Attempts to probe the assumptions behind various courses of action at this level and their implications have been more limited (see Storey *et al.* 1993 for one such attempt). In this chapter we explore the variety of responses at plant, divisional and national levels. In so doing, we are seeking to elucidate the underlying assumptions which support each response.

The central argument of this chapter concerns the *fracturing of collectivism*. Important structural changes in the labour market – the changing balance of manufacturing and service sectors (Institute for Employment Research 1987), the mixture of full-time, part-time and temporary workers (Jenson, Hagen and Reddy 1988), the decreasing size of business units (Purcell 1994) – all suggest that the collective mass upon which trade unions were built continues to slip away. Collectivism is also being fractured by management strategies, and it is on this aspect that we are concentrating here. Various modes of individualism and collectivism[2] threaten to alter the role of the trade unions as it has traditionally been perceived. The new emphasis upon the individual employee in management strategies suggests that any notion of a standardised group of workers pursuing similar interests has become increasingly difficult to sustain, whether or not it had been an accurate representation of a 'collectivist' past. All of these changes demand some response from trade unions. Some have responded by claiming that the unions face an old-fashioned threat and can deal with it by traditional methods (see Kelly, Chapter 3). But this has not been the predominant response or necessarily the most sensible. Various notable figures in the trade union movement have begun to articulate alternative trade union strategies (Storey *et al.* 1993). It is our purpose in this chapter to explore these too.

There have been a wide variety of responses by trade unions to these challenges and the issues have been subject to political infightings. Despite this complexity there have been some overall identifiable drifts. We shall argue that there has been a drift in trade union strategies towards both individualism and collectivism, but of particular types indicating a reorientation within the British labour movement, the style of which we have not seen previously. However, it is important to stress that this drift is at present cautious and unsecured and to become permanent has a long way to go. Nevertheless, unions have adopted more of an individualist agenda both in vocabulary and in seeking to identify the wishes of their members. In many ways the question 'what can the union do for me?' flows from the decline in union membership over the past decade. The collectivism increasingly being adopted by unions is one of closer institutional partnership (where possible) with employers. This is partly explained by the decline of collective action and resistance indicated by the falling incidence of strikes and industrial disputes (Edwards and Hyman 1994).

RESEARCH METHODS

This research is part of a broader study using the concepts of individualism and collectivism to explore the development of new employee relations strategies.[3] Fieldwork data have been collected using three main methods. The first has been case-study research in nine companies/sectors: InterCity, Royal Mail, NHS Trusts, local government, Unilever, banks, Ford, Cadbury and National Power. The second method has been conducting interviews and workshops with the major trade unions. This involved officials and representatives at all levels including general secretaries, regional officers and shop stewards. Finally, we have also conducted attitude surveys of employees in our major case sites to assess their responses to management strategies (Bacon *et al.* 1994; Travers *et al.* 1995). It is necessary to stress that our discussion of trade union issues in this chapter reflects our case companies, which are 'mainstream' organisations (Storey 1992) which recognise trade unions and have experimented with HRM. They are not representative of the problems unions face with anti-union employers who have rejected the HRM approach – the so-called 'Bleak House' companies identified by WIRS3 (Millward *et al.* 1992; Sisson 1993; Guest 1995), or in dealing with non-union companies (McLoughlin and Gourlay 1994).

THE CHANGING BALANCE OF INDIVIDUALISM AND COLLECTIVISM: THE TRADE UNION RESPONSE

In a previous article (Bacon and Storey 1993) we have summarised the challenge the unions face as being composed of a dual threat. On the one hand there is the threat of individualisation, where employers increasingly target their policies towards the individual rather than seeking to treat employees as a collectivity. On the other, there is the threat of a new collectivism. In the modern workplace many companies are placing an increased stress upon the collective aspects of employment policies such as teamworking and employee involvement to generate greater commitment and employee identification with the aims of the company (Guest 1995). In this chapter we continue to use the concepts of individualism and collectivism and we have accordingly grouped the responses trade unions have made to these challenges into three sets: those responses which are based upon the view that there are no great differences between past and current management strategies; those that seek to deal with individualisation; and those that seek to meet the challenge of management policies which emphasise the new collectivism.

We must emphasise at this point that no union or branch of which we are aware has viewed one response as the universal solution and at each stage trade unions have reappraised their reactions in the light of changing management strategies. It was not uncommon to find a plant-based union official with a variety of different positions, depending upon their views of the specific management policies 'on the table' and other strategic conditions. Nevertheless, it is useful to highlight the potential varieties of response if we are to understand the nature of trade unions in the workplace of the 1990s. It must be stated that overall the trade union movement remains cynical about the ability of HRM to deliver and the ability of companies to deliver HRM. To give but one representation of this view, USDAW have argued that HRM initiatives 'to date have not always been particularly well conceived or handled by management' (USDAW 1993). There are several reasons for this. Firstly, even where HRM is adopted, it may fail to meet some basic requirements. It does not necessarily provide security and protect companies. Rover has been widely cited by the TUC and other sources as a company that has adopted HRM techniques, but when it was sold to BMW in 1994 workers first heard of the sale on the television. Rover failed to carry out HRM in the most serious area and the application of HRM techniques did not protect the company from takeover. This has suggested to trade unions that while the HRM agenda needs to be met they should remain wary of being deluded that it is sufficient to protect their members in the company. A second key issue is the ability of UK managers to deliver HRM. Management training in the UK continues to lag behind that of its leading competitors (Storey and

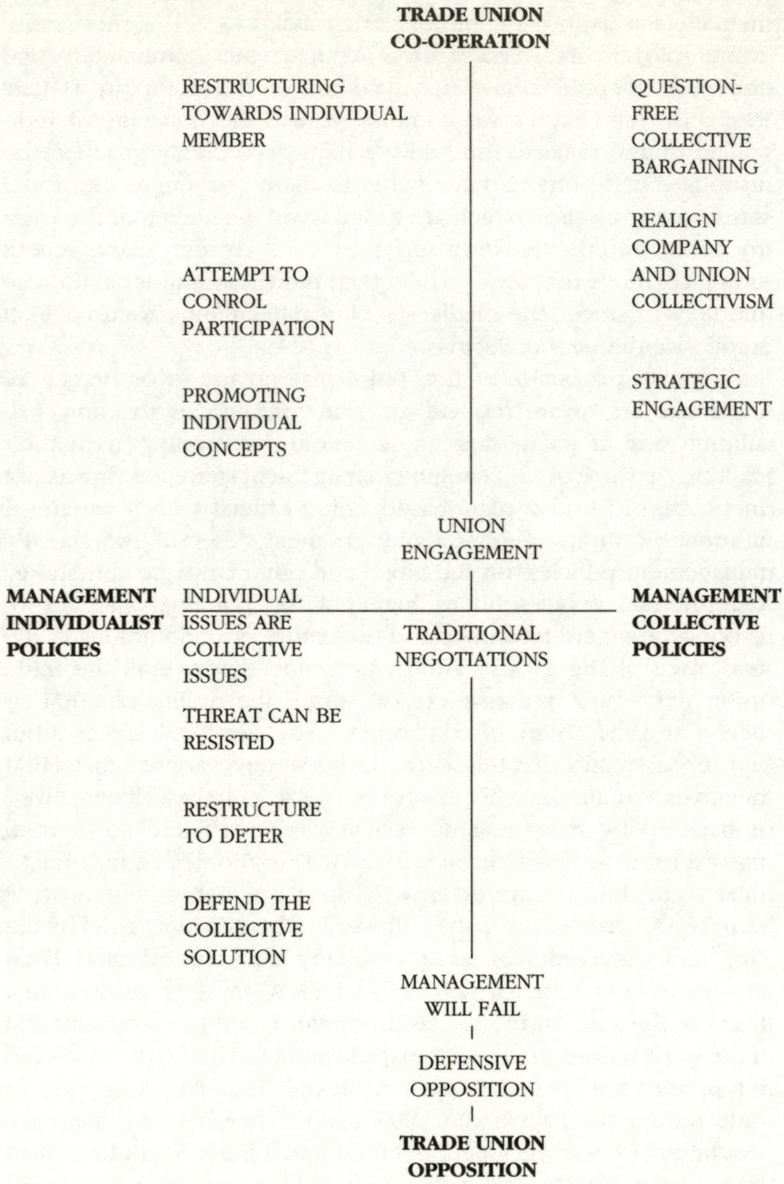

**TRADE UNION
CO-OPERATION**

RESTRUCTURING
TOWARDS INDIVIDUAL
MEMBER

QUESTION-
FREE
COLLECTIVE
BARGAINING

REALIGN
COMPANY
AND UNION
COLLECTIVISM

ATTEMPT TO
CONROL
PARTICIPATION

PROMOTING
INDIVIDUAL
CONCEPTS

STRATEGIC
ENGAGEMENT

UNION
ENGAGEMENT

**MANAGEMENT
INDIVIDUALIST
POLICIES**

INDIVIDUAL
ISSUES ARE
COLLECTIVE
ISSUES

TRADITIONAL
NEGOTIATIONS

**MANAGEMENT
COLLECTIVE
POLICIES**

THREAT CAN BE
RESISTED

RESTRUCTURE
TO DETER

DEFEND THE
COLLECTIVE
SOLUTION

MANAGEMENT
WILL FAIL

DEFENSIVE
OPPOSITION

**TRADE UNION
OPPOSITION**

Figure 2.1 Summary figure showing main findings on trade union

46

Sisson 1993). Trade unions have been critical of the ability of managers to address issues such as training and equal opportunities. While line managers may be more pro-active under HRM, the standard of management training is still inferior in many respects to the UK's leading competitors (Storey *et al.* 1993).

The wide variety of responses made by trade unions can be seen in Figure 2.1. The responses illustrated in this figure depict the situation at workplace level as we found it. Responses being made by union representatives at this level cut across national trade union policies and any separation of trade unions into militant and moderate categories. The horizontal axis distinguishes between trade union responses to those management policies emphasising individualism and those emphasising collectivism. The vertical axis indicates the extent of trade union co-operation with and opposition towards management policies. This dimension was selected as it represents a key demand of many managers we interviewed in our cases and has been taken by many union representatives as a key requirement of any effective response to HRM. Each of these trade union responses is based upon an interpretation of new management policies, the context and conditions. This, in turn, shapes the extent to which unions are willing to co-operate with managers. These linkages are set out more clearly in Figure 2.2.

Implicit within this figure is a dynamic which suggests that the degree of co-operation unions are willing to entertain is dependent upon the extent to which management policies are deemed to benefit the union and its members. This is modified by a strategic understanding of the context and conditions in which union representatives have to make such decisions.[4] The first set of trade union positions we discuss in more detail are not responses to either the individualistic or collectivistic aspects of management strategies but emphasise continuity of trade union response. These are located down the central axis of Figure 2.1. The second set are trade union responses to management policies emphasising the individual, found on the left-hand side of Figure 2.1. We shall then discuss those responses to management collective policies on the right-hand side of Figure 2.1. This will enable us to explore union responses to the fracturing of collectivism and the attempts by trade unions to discover a new role.

Trade union interpretation	Contex/ conditions	Trade union response
1. Employer commitment to HRM of real benefit	Employer willing to co-operate	Question-free collective bargaining
2. Individualism cannot be resisted	Weak unions	Restructure to individual members
3. Need to accept some of the HRM agenda	Trust managers, invited to participate	Realign company and union collectivism
4. HRM has some benefits	Union backed by members	Unions control participation
5. HRM has some benefits	Managers invite union participation	Strategic engagement with HRM
6. HRM has some benefits	Unions backed by members but don't trust managers	Promote individual concepts
7. Individual issues are collective ones	Cannot prevent individualisation	Deal with individual
8. HRM is essentially no different from past management strategies	Strong union	Negotiate in a traditional manner
9. HRM is a potential threat	Strong union	Control threat
10. HRM could weaken and outflank union	Effective union	Restructure to deter
11. Collective solutions are preferred	Unions strong	Defend the collective solution
12. HRM is detrimental but will fail anyway	Weak unions	Wait for managers to fail
13. HRM is anti-union and anti-employee	Unions strong/ company stable	Defensive opposition

Degree of co-operation increases

Figure 2.2 A ladder of trade union co-operation with HRM

Continuity and denying difference

The first three types of union response we discuss under this sub-heading are built upon the notion that unions do not need to change radically in order to meet the challenge of new management strategies. These positions, ranked in order of the amount of opposition with management they imply (see the central axis of Figure 2.1), are as follows: when unions oppose the initiatives by exercising collective strength; when unions are waiting for management to fail; when unions seek to negotiate the issues in a traditional manner. We suggest that each of these positions is subject to slippage in practice. When faced with managers who are determined to introduce new policies it is difficult for trade unions to resist, regardless of the strategic position taken by the union representatives.

Defensive opposition

In many cases unions have simply opposed policies which they deem to be against their members' interests or primarily motivated by anti-unionism. The first attempt by managers at Royal Mail to develop a new employee relations system was to produce a mission and values statement without consulting the union and then to refer all policies to these principles. The UCW moved to remove all reference to it in any negotiations. By 1988, one in six working days were being lost to strikes. The union has also opposed policies by scuppering them if agreements were broken after implementation. When Royal Mail used quality circles to encourage employees to vote against the union recommendation in a ballot, the union advocated non-participation. A direct position has also been adopted by the TGWU Vehicle Building and Automotive Trade Group. A wide variety of new management techniques have been grouped together by this trade group as inevitably leading to lean production, judged to be against both trade unions and the interests of workers. Thus all initiatives are to be regarded sceptically. Although the threat is deemed to be different from those posed by previous management policies, the response from the unions continues along traditional lines. In the words of the National Secretary:[5]

> Nothing has changed – it's business as usual for the unions. We have to educate and agitate. We must maintain our principles and maintain contact with our members. They may

not appreciate it at the moment but we need each other as much as ever.

The TGWU has also extended this analysis to developments in the oil industry.[6] It has argued forcefully that 'for the most part, moves away from collective bargaining have tended to increase the exploitation of, and discrimination against, individual employees' (TGWU 1993: 165). Given this experience, opposition and militancy appear to be rational solutions.

Waiting for management to fail: our time will come again

A second response has been to argue that managers are able to implement policies at a time of increased management prerogative which will be reversed in a different political and economic climate. Frequently, this was adopted where the unions had been unable to resist policies they did not like. In the privatised National Power, managers had introduced a new framework agreement involving individual performance pay and devolving many links with the unions to plant level. The response of the EETPU was a pragmatic one. The union had been forced along a path it did not want, but it was 'just like dealing with a private-sector employer'. While such developments were radical as compared to the Central Elecricity Generating Board, it was rather more like the engineering industry for senior union officials. Biding their time on new initiatives enables unions to maintain their organisational integrity and continue with traditional policies. The success of such a strategy presumes that new management techniques are little more than fads, that they will fail and that unions will eventually regain a more powerful position. If neither occurs, then it is possible that trade unions may face a bleak future hoping for a return to industrial militancy and running the risk of 'withering on the vine'. Neither of these alternatives may prove to be attractive.

Unions negotiate the issues in a traditional manner

Among many union representatives we interviewed at plant level the common response was that new initiatives being pursued by managers did not require a particularly innovative response. The importance of negotiating agreements and rules was still deemed central for any type of initiative. Implicit in this position is the view that new initiatives in managing human resources and work re-organisation are not substantially different from past initiatives. Consequently, if the rules and procedures surrounding the introduction of a new policy are not tightly agreed, then it is likely to fail in practice. By way of example, this approach was taken by the craft union at Lever Brothers. The union recommended its members to reject a new package (termed 'Horizon 2000') containing teamworking, individual appraisals and annualised hours because it would operate with sparse guide-lines replacing extensive agreements between management and unions. Underpinning this position was the view of stewards that HRM was a misguided ideology. The advantage of opposing change in this manner for the unions was the realistic and uncomplicated refusal to read anything deeper into new initiatives. It allowed the unions to oppose the 'manner' in which initiatives were implemented while not opposing the ideas contained in the initiative per se. The unions were also able to maintain that voluntary collective bargaining was the tool for management–union relations. However, one potential disadvantage of this position was that at a time when managers clearly felt that they had a more strategic view of employee relations the unions ran the risk of being marginalised. The unions were offering a traditional solution to what many managers have interpreted as a new set of problems and issues. By remaining overly dependent upon collective bargaining procedures unions may be selling a service managers and (possibly) their members no longer wish to buy.

Responses to individualisation

A minimum of seven different responses have been made by unions to the threat of individualism in management strategies. Each of these seeks in a different way to meet the challenge posed by the fracturing of collectivism. Ranked in order of the amount of opposition towards management moves to individualise the employment relationship, these are: defending the collective solution; restructuring as a deterrence; recognising a threat which can be resisted in that particular context; regarding individual issues as collective ones writ small; promoting individual concepts; attempts to control participation; and restructuring towards the needs of individual members. Each of these seven responses is shown on the left-hand side of Figure 2.1. The most important feature about this list of responses is that there has been a shift towards individualism in union strategies. The number of unions able to sustain the first few responses on the above list has been diminishing. They have drifted from insisting solely on previous collective forums and towards embracing and seeking to redefine individualism. This represents an important reorientation by trade unions towards the needs of their members as individuals and an increasing use of the vocabulary of individualism.

Defending the collective solution

One strategy in response to individualisation is to maintain that collective solutions are available for most individual problems, thereby rejecting the emphasis upon the individual. This response confronts the issue of fracturation in the most seemingly straightforward manner. It was advanced thus by a UCW Area Representative in the South-East:

> There are collective solutions for most individual problems. For example, if the Postal Worker Higher Grade cannot achieve what they should, then rather than attack individuals we would suggest that the aptitude test should be made more difficult . . . we can live with these new channels. We can get everyone involved and show just how many issues they are trying to deal with on an individual basis are actually collective issues that affect everyone.

The question as to what are collective and what are individual issues goes to the very heart of trade unionism, as unions have always had to deal with both types of issues. However, this tension has been thrown into particular relief by management strategies to alter this balance. In defending the collective solution the logic of collective action is being reasserted. If such a logic is upheld as *the* priority, then it offers an answer to most new management strategies – individualisation can be supported where it undermines neither the individual nor the collective. Such a response can be deemed unsatisfactory if factually incorrect and individual problems cannot be solved by collective policies, or where individual members or smaller groups reject the collective policy.

Restructuring as a deterrence

Where individualisation is perceived as a threat, a second type of response has been to restructure in order to be better placed to deal with the new agenda. Restructuring has occurred between unions by merging and within unions by internal reform. In the NHS, the merger of COHSE, NALGO and NUPE to form UNISON was a strategic rather than a purely defensive response to the political agenda of organisational restructuring in the NHS and the implications for bargaining structures. The pressure for bargaining to move to the level of the business unit threatened to duplicate union activities and waste resources. Unison provided unity in negotiations helping to overcome traditional rivalries and released important resources to support local bargaining. The merger has prevented the possibility of NHS Trusts playing unions off against each other. The second important aspect of this restructuring has been the information battle the unions have conducted to combat decentralised pay bargaining. The creation of NHS Trusts raised the possibility of local bargaining, and COHSE responded by devolving resources to regions and branches to help create self-sufficient bargaining units and decentralising the computerised pay database to the regions. This restructuring has helped to deter local pay bargaining to date. Organisational restructuring can also help groups to realign and enable unions to develop and pursue more pro-active strategies. By organisational restructuring, unions are able to reposition and modernise their structures in a way which may be management-sponsored. Among the potential costs of such a strategy is the possibility that management may respond by seeking alternative strategies which may be more explicitly anti-union. Organisational change can also be very painful for the staff and representatives of a trade union as power relationships are disturbed. Nevertheless, reorganisation remains a popular response among trade unions, although its cost- effectiveness has been questioned (Willman and Cave 1994).

HRM is a threat, but not so much here

A third position adopted has been to regard individualisation as a potential threat, but one that can be dealt with in a specific context. This was the position of the Joint Works Committee at Ford's Engine Plant at Bridgend. HRM was regarded as a threat to the trade unions, but more of a threat in the newer plants. At Bridgend it was felt that traditions and attitudes could not be changed overnight and the unions could maintain their influence by 'horse trading'. Leading shop stewards felt that a negative response to new ideas would threaten the future of the plant and that it was vital to negotiate changes to retain an influence. In so doing they were relying upon the organic nature of shopfloor trade unionism and its traditions, which would prevent any individualisation having unduly negative effects on the union.

Individual issues are collective issues writ small

Another response to individualisation has been for unions to restructure themselves in line with managerial strategy. Rather than focusing primarily on collective strategies and principally collective bargaining, it may be possible to direct the union's resources and attention towards providing for the individual member. This has occurred more where unions are not able to resist individualisation but are seeking to find a form of collectivism which is compatible with the new managerial emphasis on the employee. At National Power, the EETPU was flirting with this line as managers relied less on making agreements. A union official explained that the union's response to the issue of individual appraisals was to work around the problem:

> It's OK if people talk to the boss and it can still be collective. . . . We'll have to see how it goes . . . as they will do it anyway. If the individual appeals, we can support them. I think there will be wholesale problems. Individual issues are just collective issues writ small. We can deal with the same case twenty times instead of as a collective issue.

Although it is more expensive for trade unions to represent each individual in a separate manner, there are clearly economies of scale where the issues each individual faces are similar.

Promoting individual concepts

A complementary strategy is also possible because many of the 'soft' aspects of HRM are not necessarily anti-union; many have even previously been advocated by trade unions. Rather than opposing an initiative it previously supported, it is possible for a union to defend the concept with a managerial interpretation and promote the implications into areas managers are not prepared for. This differs from the last response in that rather than seeking a collectivism which is compatible with individualism, it seeks an individualism which is compatible with collectivism. This position was one advocated by the General Secretary of the GMB, John Edmonds, who has argued that HRM promises a new relationship and some ideas unions can use. Its vague and ambiguous nature allows unions to choose the aspects of it that they like. For Edmonds:

> I'm just taking the language of HRM and playing it back. It requires a different attitude to management. The good thing about HRM is that it gives us a handful of high cards to play. We can say, 'OK, we recall the HR Director's last speech, and we intend to play it back to you. That bit means job security, that bit means training' . . . . Let us use some of the attractive ideas of HRM. But let us also run them fully through and expose any inconsistencies between the underlying principles and the actual practice.
>
> (Storey *et al.* 1993: 65)

The UCW has been able to do this with the issues of employee involvement and the strategic engagement of the union in Royal Mail. In many divisions of Royal Mail, managers have an instrumental view of the new agreement and only want to use it when they see advantages in doing so. The response of the union has been to regard the agreement as 'the holy grail', seeking involvement at every level.

Unions control participation

Where unions believe it is wrong simply to oppose initiatives (or after unsuccessful opposition), one alternative has been to use an initiative in a way which shapes it to the union's ends. This is possible because many of the new initiatives are inherently 'power neutral', favouring neither managers nor trade unions in the abstract, but the key to their effects lie in the ends to which they are employed. There is scope to delimit the extent to which the forms of individualism conflict with collectivism. One such example of this has been the response of the UCW to the introduction of quality circles into Royal Mail in the early 1990s. The trade union representatives became fully involved, selecting the people who took part and the issues which were discussed. The aim of the union was to prevent members from undermining its position and, in the estimation of one union official, in three out of five cases the issues being discussed were health and safety and the attitudes of supervisors. Hence the input of members served to reinforce the union's position. Such a response can have a variety of effects: it puts unions on the offensive; it can lead to an increase in power; it helps prevent the involvement of the individual employee replacing trade union representation; and it addresses the issue on its own terms, threatening to reveal any other motives behind such schemes. The UCW used this policy because it has retained sufficient strength to prevent a unilateral imposition by management.

Restructuring towards the individual member

It is also possible for unions to accept the logic of individualism and rely less on the collective context for union activity and more on services that can be provided to individual members and allow individualisation to flourish. Here we are less interested in the broader ranges of services now on offer to invite union membership[7] and more in services directed towards work-related issues. ACAS has recently signalled this trend with large increases in individual requests for advice and information in contrast to its more traditional service to unions and employers.[8] A report by the Citizens' Advice Bureau claimed that it receives 800,000 complaints against employers each year (Monks 1993). Key growth areas are in legal and contract advice. Despite the growth of individual contracts one EETPU official covering the power supply industry noted:

> Although the old Area Manager posts have gone . . . by and large we keep them as members: there has been no great exodus. Partly this is because of tradition and partly because we provide very cheap services. We provide defence for the individual. Trade unions are giving individual advice much more on legal issues and dismissals. We are supporting the individual rather than the collective. We have the same members, we are just servicing smaller groups. It does make our job harder because we have an increasing number of

calls on our time, but increasingly we are selling our services to the individual. . . . For example, if you read our membership services document, we are recruiting the individual. It is all about convincing the individual we provide for them.

To emphasise the point that trade unions are changing their vocabulary, the above quotation the 'individual' is referred to six times. If providing services for individual members does appeal to employees not covered by collective bargaining or feelings of loyalty derived from workplace culture, such a response has much to recommend it to trade unions in the 1990s. The leadership of MSF have been promoting an upwardly mobile, individualistic image. In its submission to the House of Commons Employment Committee, MSF revealed survey findings that 27 per cent of its members are part of the professional and managerial class, and 56 per cent are clerical workers. The General Secretary Roger Lyons has commented: 'as skilled and professional people they have not acted out of a traditional notion of solidarity, but believe union membership offers them protection and rights at work' (*Financial Times*, 18 October 1993). The strategy adopted by MSF to meet the needs of its members involves seeking the quality kite-mark, BS5750, a strategic redirection described by Roger Lyons as highlighting the individual member:

> We shall be highlighting individual representation as a priority for trade unionism. We have developed expertise in individual rights and representation. An increasing number of our members have individual contracts and profit or performance-related pay and they can turn to us for individual advice.[9]

Servicing individual members is a sophisticated response relying less on company sponsorship and may provide the genesis of a better model for servicing the needs of 'new' and 'periphery' workers. The need for unions to change to cope with any shifts from collective bargaining to individual contracts has been recognised by the RCN, which has stated:

> Currently individual contract negotiation is likely to be one-sided where the employer presents . . . an individual contract and asks for it to be signed and returned as an acceptance of the employment terms and conditions contained within it . . . the opportunities for bargaining around them by individuals are not very strong. Unions can assist individuals by setting up

computer systems which can advise on standard forms of contract clauses and potentially the total contract value implications of choosing particular terms and dropping others. Unions may also need to try and negotiate with employers about the forms of such contracts even in cases of senior managers.[10]

An important aspect of this type of response has been its pro-activity. To combat a decline in the 'collective voice' role of the unions whereby managers communicate directly with individual employees, it is also possible for unions to do likewise. One EETPU official saw this as a 'paper war' where 'we can't stop the company communicating and we have to put the union view rather than the National Power view'. Individual communication strategies can be made to work for trade unions as collectivities as they can for employers. Communicating with individual members in the workplace has also become important, and with team briefings it is important that individuals are aware of wider issues such as previous assurances and the full range of policy options.

In addition to organisational restructuring, reorientation towards the individual member is also taking place in the political sense. The vocabulary of the individual is now much more prominent among trade unionists than in the past. Within the local government section of the GMB, HRM issues have been viewed as an indictment of trade unions which have failed to address the interests of their members fully and have failed to pressurise employers into giving individuals more information and access. The National Secretary commented at a 1994 GMB Conference:

> Unless trade unions adopt the correct agenda, employers may start to do it themselves and communications may start to by-pass local stewards and national officers. HRM can neuter trade unions unless we grasp the nettle at a time of financial constraint, where satisfaction is in the provision of quality services, managers will by-pass us. . . . In local government we have been traditionally highly unionised but now we are below 50 per cent in many areas and we need to ask why. Yes it is because of redundancies and Government policies but a key element was that we didn't address the issues our members wanted us to address.
> (GMB/TGWU/UNISON/Friedrich Ebert Foundation Seminar, 23–25 March, 1994)

This has led to some revision of the collective bargaining agenda. In three MORI polls (1985, 1988 and 1991) interesting work, job security and worthwhile work were all ranked above pay (GMB 1994). In a local government survey pay ranked as a lower priority for women than men despite the sector containing 540,000 part-time manual workers, 90 per cent of whom are women, who are the lowest paid (GMB 1994). These results are similar to those being discovered by employers, and if trade unions retain a traditional bargaining agenda and HRM policies are delivering teamworking and greater job satisfaction, employers may meet the interests of union members better than the union. A survey of new members conducted by MSF to establish more effective recruitment and retention policies revealed that the three most persuasive reasons for joining were the facility for representing individuals in difficulty, free legal assistance and the negotiation of terms and conditions. As the following extract shows, these results were interpreted by the union as pointing towards a limit on the threat of individualism given the imbalance of power in the employment relationship:

> This survey reinforces the fact that people still join trade unions for the same reasons they always have, given the potential imbalance of power between employers and employee. This will remain the case even with the trend in some sectors towards 'individualisation' of employment contracts. It is a mistake to think that an individual employee on a personal contract will no longer have need of . . . trade union membership. . . . On the contrary, there is a potentially huge demand for advice on contract terms, working conditions and pensions, and for individual representation.[11]
>
> (HMSO 1995)

Opinion poll data tend to support this view that trade unions are still regarded as essential to protect workers' interests (GMB 1994) despite, or because of, a renewed emphasis by managers on the individual employee.

Responses to a managerial emphasis on collective identification

The increasing emphasis managers have placed on the commitment of employees to organisational aims has posed a challenge for trade unions (Guest 1995; Guest and Dewe 1991). Here we shall chart three responses by unions to this challenge from a 'new collectivism': strategic engagement with HRM; realigning company and union collectivism; and questioning free collective bargaining. They are in order of the likely degree of opposition they imply towards management policies. What is most striking about these responses is that they are all forms of collectivism which emphasise co-operation rather than opposition. These are all located on the right-hand side of Figure 2.1. In many UK industries (for example, footwear and textiles) this has a long tradition. In Figure 2.1, the bottom right-hand side of the axes illustrates how we discovered no union responses based on opposition to the new managerial emphasis on managing the collective culture of the workforce. There was healthy scepticism about the extent to which manage-ment were serious in these attempts, and conflict culminated in industrial action in InterCity, Co-op Bank and Cadbury. However, in each of these cases conflict occurred not because the unions were opposed to the idea of 'partnership', but because they were being denied this opportunity. We therefore draw the conclusion that unions are meeting the challenge of companies' attempts to win the 'hearts and minds' of their members by predominantly seeking a partnership with management. There is less evidence that unions feel they can survive as the permanent opposition on all issues, although conflict over some issues was regarded as inevitable. Where we encountered rank and file militancy it was because union officials felt that managers were not serious about partnership and it was therefore necessary to defend their members' interests via industrial action.[12]

Strategic engagement with HRM

In the post-war period UK unions have dealt with new initiatives (such as new technology) by insisting that change be subject to collective bargaining. However, a more pro-active response can be to engage with what managers are trying to achieve in a more positive fashion than purely negotiating a financial return (although this aspect is important). This can involve unions jointly participating in attempts to increase employee involvement, introduce TQM programmes, increase productivity and improve the organisational culture in a manner which adds value to the management process. This approach has been advocated by, among others, John Edmonds and the General Secretary of the TUC, John Monks, who has written:

We do not fear the agenda of the human resource development manager. We prefer a people-oriented system to a
money-oriented one with the accountant in the driving seat –
as is the case in far too many British companies. I believe that
unions can have their own distinctive agenda with the human
resource development company; it is not a traditional agenda
but lies, for example, in the areas of ensuring that training is
linkable to external qualifications, of ensuring that women at
work receive special attention, of reducing working time, of
pointing up single-status issues, of keeping an eye on executive pay (which has reached obscene levels in some cases)
and of raising questions about pay systems, management
styles and future plans. In all these, there is a rich and fertile
territory for the creative union.

(Monks 1993)

The trade union leader who has perhaps gone furthest in
embracing the new techniques has been Bill Jordan, who has
argued that the single union deals signed with Japanese companies
are the result of the 'compatibility' of the AEU's traditions and lean
production. This stands in stark contrast to the TGWU view of lean
production referred to earlier in the chapter. Three aspects of this
compatibility have been pointed out by Jordan:

First, the system puts a higher value on the individual
employee, unlike the old mass production system that
regarded people as being as replaceable as the parts they
manufactured. . . . Second, the strength of the system comes
from the involvement and participation of the union and all
employees in the process of continuous improvement of the
methods of work and in the products they make. Third, the
new system has a seeming obsession with the quality of the
product which was at the heart of the craft tradition.

(Jordan 1992)

In some companies pursuing the people-orientated approach
this has involved unions in a more genuine joint relationship with
management. At Cadbury's Mouldings Factory and Rowntree
Nestlé the TGWU Convenors have become involved in the new
agenda. At Cadbury's Mouldings stewards felt that new initiatives
which benefited members could not be opposed. They chose to
ignore much of the rhetoric from both management and union

sides (including those at the Assortments Factory at Bournville) and assessed proposals entirely on their merits, believing that 'it is not really about HRM but about people'. This position had given the unions a seat at the table and influence on decisions at an early stage in working parties and quality groups. The potential danger of company unionism is union acquiescence allied to the threat that it may be the intention of the company in the longer term to de-recognise the union eventually, as appears to be the case at Cadbury (*Financial Times* 1994). Officials of the UCW party to the new framework agreement signed with Royal Mail had an opportunity for strategic engagement but also recognised a threat. This problem was explained by the UCW Divisional Organiser in the Midlands as the threat of incorporation was present:

> We see strategic involvement as being about consultation, not negotiation. We are worried about being forced into a position whereby we are just rubber stamping and legitimising plans without being given any opportunity to change them. We want the opportunity to insert trade union reservations and to produce our own industrial plan as opposed to accepting given business policy. We accept the need to split consultation and negotiation, and if we are allowed to make serious inputs at an earlier stage then we will inevitably, if they are taken on board, adopt a less oppositional stance as the plans reflect our views more closely.

Another key problem raised by strategic engagement is the distinction between consultation and negotiation. The difficulties which can be caused by trying to balance the consultation and negotiation role were further outlined by one Executive Committee member of the UCW:

> Basically I am a negotiator and it's difficult to switch to strategic involvement as the two roles are quite different. For example, I have recently been involved in a management authorisation focus group. We sat there and made our input, but it is very difficult not just to be raising problems. It is difficult to just look at the theory and the methods. I have found myself at the cross-roads of being an extension of the management system. I've found myself voting for things in meetings which are likely to compromise me at a later date. I would accept proposals at the planning stage which as a

negotiator with a brief I would oppose. It is difficult to ride the two horses. If we can clear up our role in the strategic framework then it may become clearer.

While this can be viewed as 'Donovan by a different means' whereby unions secure some level of effective influence, most solutions to the dilemma of riding two horses focus on bringing the policies advocated in different types of forums closer together. In the opinion of one UCW official in the Midlands:

> Getting involved in consultation will have some real impli-cations. We would need to make sure that our policies at the consulting stage are the same as those at the negotiating stage. We need more time to go away and decide upon our policies in order for our input to be real, representative and something we could deliver. I don't really think we would ever go in with a completely blank sheet as managers could not do so. . . . The big advantage would be that we could point out our opposition and our case earlier on, and make management more aware of the problems and faults in their policies. As I see it strategic involvement is about modifying views in order to avoid in-surmountable problems at a later stage.

In some instances trade unions have negotiated new framework agreements including changes in work organisation and human resource policies as companies felt that they would have to impose the new agenda with or without the trade unions. Strategic engage-ment, however, is difficult in some multi-union environments where groups of employees and trade unions have different interests. The new staff agreement signed at ICI in 1991 involved managing a 'hazardous mix' of trade union aims: the TGWU and GMB sought the elimination of lower grades, and improvement of promotion opportunities and career development; the AEU sought to reduce working time; the EETPU the removal of the 'glass ceiling' preventing promotion from the shop floor; and UCATT job security and guarantees on contractors. In many cases it can be difficult for trade unions to provide a collective response.

Realigning company and union collectivism

One response to the competitive environment and need for change in the past decade has been for unions to discover a 'common cause' or 'shared objective' with management. This trend reflects to a lesser extent developments reported in the USA (Kochan *et al.* 1986). Unions have been able to support new initiatives making it possible for employees to possess dual commitment to the company and the union. This enables different forms of collectivism to work in unison rather than threatening to replace each other. Although it would be fair to say that the search for partnership is not a new issue for UK unions, it has been given a renewed emphasis in recent years. The General Secretary of USDAW, Garfield Davies, has claimed that 'my union has always adopted a partnership approach wherever the employer has been able to initiate it' and Leif Mills, the General Secretary of BIFU, that 'we are seeking partnership, not from a position of on our knees but of genuine partnership of interest'.[13] A good example of this has been at Ford, where rejuvenating joint consultation at plant level has laid the foundation for major improvements in industrial relations and productivity, with major changes in working practices on a jointly agreed basis. As such it presents an Anglo-American model of social partnership between unions and managers at plant level to win future investment.

Key union actors listing the advantages of this approach pointed to the continued logic of collective action in overcoming the anti-union elements in management change programmes and doing so in a management-sponsored fashion. The limitations of such a strategy outlined by those we interviewed were that the partnership may be limited by the dangers of incorporation and the broader need of independence. At plant level, it is worth quoting the views of the Joint Works Convenor at Ford Bridgend at length on this topic:

> Yes, we are ready for a changed role, but we can only achieve so much in one plant. . . . We have been involved in a lot of change. . . . At the end of the day, however, our changed role is fixed to the extent we trust management and we don't trust management any more now than we did previously. We cannot be convinced to trust them. There is nothing they could do. Even if they offer Japanese-style job security we have to realise that job security has its limits and employment remains a market transaction. . . . The management of this plant do not hold the purse strings. . . . If

management can't deliver their side of any new deal, then how can we be prepared to just give from our side? Investing in people and training are good things, but the only reason they are invest- ing in individuals is to reduce the overall numbers, so it has a down side.

The extent to which partnership is possible can have real limitations. As the Convenor at Ford's Dagenham plant explained, if managers regarded it as an alternative to collective bargaining, then it would be regarded as an anti-union device:

Being a more pro-active partner is unthinkable really. They don't want jointism on that basis. They don't want to share power. . . . From a trade union perspective it is still Ford that is placing the blocks in our way to becoming a different type of trade union. We don't have jointism as yet. My definition of jointism would be to have an influence on strategic thinking and corporate strategy. But the company is still thinking that brown-field sites have to close. That they can compete is still not really accepted by Ford . . . the Personnel Manager's definition of jointism is not about collective bargaining. Recently, we were coming back from Nissan and he asked how we could get some of that. I said by a job security agreement, but he said that we were just reverting back to a collective bargaining solution. But that's my job and the company has still not come to terms with it. The jury is still out.

Again the danger of incorporation was high on the agenda of the union representatives we interviewed. To prevent this, much store was set by national-level negotiations to pursue broader issues such as investment. However, many plant-based actors, because of the pressures placed on them, have accepted arrangements which pull along other plants at a faster rate. As the Convenor at Bridgend explained, in agreeing a new collective stance locally, the logic of broader collective alliances is thrown into question:

Ford would like to have bargained locally, but we can resist that. We would feel vulnerable if we were localised. This is not to imply that a collective stance is easy and that iso-lationism and protectionism are not prevalent between plants. There is a splintering of national agreements as many of them are quite open. The company tends to 'best ball' us with the Colognes of this world. . . . We need to get more involved on the European stage . . . however, we still have problems in how far we can throw the collective net as trade unions. I would rather see other plants in Europe close than UK plants, other UK plants close before we do. As to which collectivism we identify with, it is stronger the closer to this plant you get. So there is a question of who we are seeking to defend by collective organisation, who are the 'us'. Inevitably, we can't keep the transplants at bay indefinitely as the 'them' because they are employing UK workers.

The question of collectivism for trade unions contains within it a distinction between those who are to be included in the community of interests and those who are not.

Question-free collective bargaining

Finally in this section, in response to the conditions and experience of the 1980s, some continental models of industrial relations have grown in popularity among trade unionists. This has taken two quite different forms and both promise to secure on a more permanent footing the compatibility of collectivism as commitment to the company and the union. First, several unions have agreed to 'do business' with employers using a Japanese-influenced model of single union deals, company advisory boards and implicit restrictions on independent collective action by the union. Second, the legal protection offered unions by the German works council model, for a long time rejected as inappropriate for Britain, now appears to be more attractive. At the national level important union leaders, including John Edmonds and Bill Jordan, have been making the case for the bankruptcy of the British industrial relations system (Storey *et al.* 1993). The submission of the AEEU to the House of Commons Employment Committee concerning the future of trade unions argued for legally based works councils on the German model (*Financial Times 1993*).[14]

These themes are reflected at plant level; for example, the TGWU Convenor at Cadbury's Mouldings Factory argued:

As far as I am concerned the sole concern is the factory management. Since 1987 there has been mutual trust and respect. Union membership is voluntary so they need to deal with us in order to gain the trust of our members. . . . If I had the option I would buy the Japanese system as a whole tomorrow. It is very similar to the initial ideas of Quakerism and very close to the tradition of Cadburys. If the company can provide good pay and job security then I would accept that.

One of the three main demands made of trade unions by the group of managers who participated in the IPA Document *Towards Industrial Partnership* (IPA 1992) was the acceptance of forms of consultation which include the whole workforce, not just union members. Although in many of our cases individual employee involvement has been accepted, trade union representatives were still not prepared to accept the creation of formal consultation bodies with worker representation as distinct from union representation. At the Co-op Bank, a staff council was established which added fuel to a debate about union recognition. It involved workforce representatives elected on a constituency basis discussing performance and corporate plans. From the point of view of the union it was not an attempt to build partnership but an attempt to match senior managers in a negotiating position with lay union representatives to circumvent existing procedural agreements. At Lever Brothers, a similar development had occurred with local factory-based consultation groups being devised with members elected within each factory. Factory managers felt that 'the traditional forms of consulting with people were insufficient'. The AEU Convenor was seeking to control such developments by arguing for the new groups to be composed of one-third trade union representatives, one-third management and one-third from the workforce in general who could be trade unionists. The main worry of the Convenors was that the company council would attract people seeking to develop their own careers rather than stewards who are more democratic and accountable. To date the issue of a European-wide consultation body for Unilever is also a contentious issue. The union position was that they would not accept sub-Maastricht standard agreements. In many of our cases the success of a works council model for delivering benefits for members was viewed positively (albeit pragmatically) following the UK experience of the 1980s.

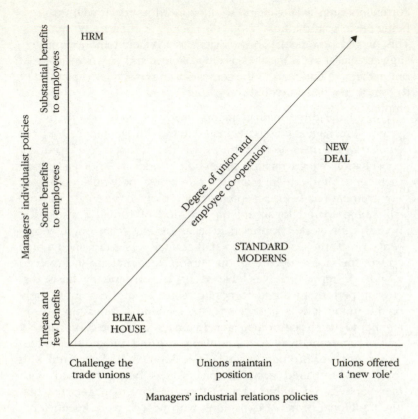

Figure 2.3 Explaining the trade union response to management strategies

UNDERSTANDING THE RESPONSE OF TRADE UNIONS TO DEVELOPMENTS IN EMPLOYEE RELATIONS

In seeking to explain why there has been such a variety of responses by trade unions it is necessary to take into account the traditions and political orientations of different unions. This is evident in the vastly different responses to lean production made by the TGWU and the AEEU. National union policies are also an important governing factor. Responses are also shaped by the nature of the new management strategies themselves. Under current banners such as 'HRM' a wide variety of initiatives are being introduced in ways which differ from company to company. This suggests that even if it were desirable (as Kelly in this volume suggests that it is), it would be difficult for unions to maintain just one response. Figure 2.3 offers a model of trade union responses to changing management strategies which again seeks to emphasise workplace reality rather than national union policies.

The vertical dimension suggests that where companies are introducing schemes which offer real benefits to individual employees in terms of career enhancement, promotional opportunities, skill development, increased autonomy and control over work, trade unions are more likely to co-operate with policies. If they offer none of the above but increase management control and encourage discretionary/discriminatory management, they are likely to be opposed by unions. The horizontal dimension of management collective strategies suggests that where policies pursue teamwork, employee involvement and a positive role for the unions, co-operation is more likely to be forthcoming. Management strategies which seek to deliver on both the individual and collective dimensions are likely to bring the greatest degree of co-operation.

By way of illustration we have labelled three positions. Where managers have sought to challenge trade unions and are not investing in their workforce, then we have the 'Bleak House' scenario (Sisson 1993). In this instance trade unions find it difficult to co-operate with management. Where the unions are being challenged but employers are significantly seeking to invest via sophisticated HRM policies, then we have a scenario with which trade unions find it difficult to co-operate. The 'New Deal' position allows more union co-operation as employers sanction trade union activity and are also seeking to train and invest in employees. The Rover deal would be a good example of this. In addition to this figure being used as an analytical tool we also suggest that it has practical policy implications for trade unions. In reality, trade unions do offer 'a ladder of co-operation' to managers, but we suggest that for both the purposes of seeking to win the support of managers and for propaganda purposes this could be made more explicit.

CONCLUSIONS ON THE FRACTURING OF COLLECTIVISM

In concluding this chapter we wish to be prescriptive and comment on the basis for effective trade union strategies to deal with the fracturing of collectivism. At the workplace/organisational level the research suggests a need for trade unions to tackle both individual and collective rights.

Trade unions and individualism

The wide variety of responses to the thread of individualism in current management strategies are testimony to the difficult nature of the problem for trade unions. It is not easy for trade unions to adopt a more individualist strategy. Nevertheless we have suggested that there are moves in that direction. This is occurring despite the fact that developing a vocabulary of the individual requires some revisionism. In seeking to identify the wishes of their members trade unions are, implicitly at least, accepting that their traditional methods for democracy are insufficient. A union member faced with the option of a trade union with an agenda from which they feel alienated and an employer offering career development opportunities may well choose the latter. The real challenge of HRM in 'mainstream' companies for trade unions is that it threatens to deliver for the individual what the trade union does not. Trade unions need strategies and policies whereby they are seen to be pushing for individual development. One possible way forward for trade unions is to grasp the nettle of individualism and separate out those aspects which are acceptable for trade unions and beneficial for members. Unions need a method of promoting the beneficial aspects of individualism within HRM, and one solution to this is via a legal programme of rights on the substantive issues of employment. This has recently been advanced by trade unions of different political hues. John Edmonds has explained the GMB's 'New Agenda' as one that is:

> about rights of individuals – training rights, equal opportunity rights, having a worthwhile satisfying job through work restructuring, and job security. These are the issues IR should be about and not just pay and strikes which people think trade unions are about. . . . We, the Executive, wrote a Purpose Statement which talked about widening horizons, developing individual talent, striving for a more satisfying work life, and so on.
>
> (Storey *et al*. 1993: 66–7)

As Edmonds recognises, individual rights for employees would cover the whole workforce, not just the highly organised. The logic of supporting individual rights, even at the risk of giving rights to individuals who do not participate in trade union activity, must be properly addressed. In its memorandum to the House of Commons inquiry on trade unions the TGWU submitted the following case:

> The TGWU believes that an improved legal framework of employment rights is necessary to give effective protection to people at work. Employment rights should apply as soon as employment commences and should apply equally to full-time and part-time workers, and to temporary and contract workers as well as permanent staff. The framework of employment rights should cover a wide range of issues including a statutory minimum wage, protection from unfair dismissal, sex and race equality, maternity and paternity rights, a right to paid holidays and the right to belong to and participate in a trade union, rights to union recognition, and the right to take industrial action without fear of dismissal or intimidation.
>
> (TGWU 1993: 165)

The right to be represented by a trade union has been closely linked to the relaunch of the TUC in 1993, explained by the General Secretary of BIFU, Leif Mills, as the attempt 'to make the TUC and the unions a natural home for those who are concerned about the quality of their life and their conditions of life'.[15] This was taken even further in January 1995, when the TUC proposed legal rights to representation at work for all, extending democratic rights into the workplace (*Financial Times* 1995).[16]

Trade unions and collectivism

The challenge employers are now making to trade unions as the source of collective loyalty and identification has gained a new vigour through quality programmes, direct communication methods, management de-layering and teamworking. However, where partnership models of industrial relations have been developed, we would suggest that this has eased one of the difficulties of collective action for the unions. If a 'shared objective' can be developed between management and unions, then the tendency for workers to identify their interests as identical to those of capital (Offe and Weisenthal 1985) is less of a challenge for the unions. There is a strong possibility that employees could display dual commitment to both the union and the company. The need for partnership has been strongly advanced by the TUC in recent years (Monks 1993) and alongside the right to representation by a trade union formed the centre-piece of the TUC's submission to the House of Commons inquiry into the future of trade unions. It would seem that without a social relationship for co-operation, trade unions will be unable to pursue effectively the interests of their members without management sponsorship.

It is this linkage between collective representation and individual rights that marks out the territory of trade union responses. Whereas the Institute of Directors (IOD) envisages the future of trade unions as providing individual services to their members rather than conducting collective bargaining in large industries, for the unions a stronger framework for individual rights and trade union recognition is necessary. As the NUCPS has put it:

> We do not draw a sharp distinction between the individual and collective interests of our members: we have always pursued both and will continue to do so. The balance between them is not dictated by us in practice, because we take up issues regardless. . . . Nonetheless we think of trade unions as essentially collective organisations in the sense that what is distinctive about us is our ability to improve the lot of members through collective representation. The whole point about trade unionism is that the individual worker will always be weak, confronted by the power of employers – and nowhere more so than now in Britain, with its traditional insistence on treating the employment contract as if it were some kind of commercial contract entered into by equal parties . . . . We offer workers the possibility of combining together, and achieving collectively what they could never achieve individually.[17]

NOTES

1 This appears to be far from the end of the story. Successive European legal judgements have had a direct effect on labour law in the UK despite the opposition of the UK government. The successor to Jacques Delors as European Commission president, Jacques Santer, who was strongly backed by the UK government over more 'federalist'

candidates, called in his investiture speech in January 1995 for the UK government to sign the Social Chapter of the Maastricht Treaty (*Financial Times* 1995: 22).

2 'Individualism' and 'collectivism' are rich and suggestive terms and have been used in a wide variety of ways. In a previous article (Storey and Bacon 1993) we have clarified the manner in which we use the terms. In short, we have argued for a multi-dynamic use of the terms, which have different meanings depending on whether we are referring to individualism in industrial relations (non-unionism), individualism in work organisation (task fragmentation and a high division of labour) or individualism in human resource management (tailored and competitive systems of recruitment, reward and retention). These issues are conceptualised in greater depth in our forthcoming book *New Employment Strategies: Towards Individualism or Collectivism?*.

3 This chapter arises out of an ESRC-funded project on Individualism and Collectivism, grant number R000233263. The financial support of the ESRC is gratefully acknowledged.

4 Whereas Kelly in this volume starts from a theoretical conception of militancy and moderation, we have taken as our starting point the qualification to his argument: that despite the ideological strategy of a trade union, a given policy may not be feasible in a given context.

5 GMB/TGWU/Unison/Friedrich Ebert Foundation Seminar, 23–5 March 1994.

6 See the debate between the TGWU and Shell in evidence given to the House of Commons Employment Committee Inquiry, 1 December 1993 (TGWU 1993: 164).

7 These may be important to recruitment, although in one study by Sapper (1991) membership services were not at the forefront of the expectations and requirements of potential members.

8 ACAS conciliated in over 72,000 individual cases in 1992 – an increase of 19 per cent over 1991. Of these individual complaints over employment rights, complaints of unfair dismissal still accounted for the majority with 44,000 cases (Employment Department 1994).

9 The MSF memorandum to the House of Commons Employment Committee Inquiry on 1 December 1993 (p. 136) stated: 'Our members are predominantly people who have chosen trade union membership and see it as relevant to their working lives. They also see a clear link between being members of a union that emphasises industrial autonomy and decentralised decision-making and their own professional development.'

10 RCN submission to the House of Commons Employment Committee Inquiry, 'The Future of Trade Unions', 7 December 1993: 207.

11 MSF written memorandum to the House of Commons Employment Committee Inquiry, 'The Future of Trade Unions', 1 December 1993: 140.

12 It is important to state that the pursuit of partnership in no way implies a surrender of the right to adopt a more militant position if this becomes necessary. Nor does it imply an end to shopfloor unionism and high member participation.

13 Oral evidence to the House of Commons Employment Committee Inquiry, 23 November 1993, 32.i: 108.
14 The memorandum from MSF to the inquiry argued: 'UK industry needs to develop a system of social partnership to allow business to prosper while at the same time ensuring a proper balance in the employment relationship between employer and employee. This may well involve the establishment of new structural arrangements such as works councils' (1 December 1993: 136).
15 Oral evidence to the House of Commons Employment Committee Inquiry, 23 November 1993: 117.
16 In 1991 the CGIL in Italy also started to campaign for a programme of rights to integrate workers' interests as employees and citizens (Hyman 1994: 132).
17 Submission to the House of Commons Employment Committee Inquiry (1 December 1993: 175).

REFERENCES

Bacon, N. and Storey, J. (1993) 'Individualisation of the Employment Relationship and the Implications for Trade Unions', *Employee Relations* **15**, 1: 5–17.

Bacon, N., Travers, C. and Storey, J. (1994) 'Individualism and Collectivism and Employee Responses', *British Academy of Management 1994 Annual Conference Proceedings*, 12–14 September, The Management School Lancaster University: 393–4.

Beaumont, P. B. (1991) 'Trade Unions and the HRM', *Industrial Relations Journal* **22**, 4.

CBI (1994) Memorandum submitted to the House of Commons Employment Committee Inquiry, 'The Future of Trade Unions', 25 January: 323.

Edwards, P. and Hyman, R. (1994) 'Strikes and Industrial Conflict: Peace in Europe?', in R. Hyman and A. Ferner (eds), *New Frontiers in European Industrial Relations*, Oxford: Blackwell.

Employment Department (1994) *Departmental Report*, Cmnd 2505, March, London.

Financial Times (1994) 'Cadbury Set to Weaken Trade Unions', 24 November.

Financial Times (1995) 'TUC Calls for Fresh Workplace Legislation', 17 January.

GMB (1994) MORI Polls for GMB, Head Office, London.

Guest, D. (1995) 'Human Resource Management, Trade Unions and Industrial Relations', in J. Storey (ed.), *Human Resource Management: A Critical Text*, London: Routledge.

Guest, D. and Dewe, P. (1991) 'Company or Trade Union: Which Wins Workers' Allegiance? A study of Commitment in the United Kingdom Electronics Industry', *British Journal of Industrial Relations* **29**, 1: 75–96.

HMSO (1995) House of Commons Employment Committee (1995) *The Future of Trade Unions*.

Hyman, R. (1994) 'Changing Trade Union Identities and Strategies', in R. Hyman and A. Ferner (eds), *New Frontiers in European Industrial Relations*, Oxford: Blackwell.

Institute for Employment Research (1987) *Review of the Economy and Employment*, Coventry: University of Warwick.

IPA (1992) *Towards Industrial Partnership: A New Approach to Management–Union Relations*, London: Involvement and Participation Association.

Jenson, J., Hagen, E. and Reddy, H. (eds) (1988) *Feminization of the Labour Force: Paradoxes and Promises*, Cambridge: Polity Press.

Jordan, B. (1992) 'Lean Production – The New Manufacturing Techniques', *AEU Journal*, January: 10.

Kochan, T. A., Katz, H. and McKersie, R. B. (1986) *The Transformation of American Industrial Relations*, New York: Basic Books.

McLoughlin, I. and Gourlay, S. (1994) *Enterprise Without Unions*, Buckingham: Open University Press.

Marsh, D. (1992) *The New Politics of British Trade Unionism*, London: Macmillan.

Martinez Lucio, S. and Weston, S. (1992) 'Human Resource Management and Trade Union Responses: Bringing the Politics of the Workplace Back into the Debate', in P. Blyton and P. Turnbull (eds), *Reassessing Human Resource Management*, London: Sage.

Millward, N., Stevens, M., Smart, D. and Hawes, W. (1992) *Workplace Industrial Relations in Transition*, Aldershot: Dartmouth.

Monks, J. (1993) 'A Trade Union View of WIRS3', *British Journal of Industrial Relations* **31**, 2: 227–33.

Offe, C. and Weisenthal, H. (1985) 'Two Logics of Collective Action', in *Disorganized Capitalism*, Cambridge: Polity Press.

Oliver, N. and Wilkinson, B. (1992) *The Japanization of British Industry*, 2nd edn, Oxford: Blackwell.

Purcell, J. (1991) 'The Rediscovery of Management Prerogative: The Management of Labour Relations in the 1980s', *Oxford Review of Economic Policy* **7**, 1: 33–43.

Purcell, J. (1994) 'Corporate Strategy and its Link with Human Resource Management Strategy', in J. Storey (ed.), *Human Resource Management: A Critical Text*, London: Routledge.

Sapper, S. (1991) 'Do Members' Services Packages Influence Trade Union Recruitment?', *Industrial Relations Journal*, Winter, **22**, 4: 309–16.

Sisson, K. (1993) 'In Search of HRM', *British Journal of Industrial Relations* **31**, 2: 201–10.

Storey, J. (1992) *Development in Human Resource Management*, Oxford: Blackwell.

Storey, J. and Bacon, N. (1993) 'Individualism and Collectivism: Into the 1990s', *International Journal of Human Resource Management* **4**, 3: 665–84.

Storey, J., Bacon, N., Edmonds, J. and Wyatt, P. (1993) 'The "New Agenda" and Human Resource Management: A Round-table Discussion with John Edmonds', *Human Resource Management Journal* **4**, 1: 63–70.

Storey, J. and Sisson, K. (1993) *Managing Human Resources and Industrial Relations*, Buckingham: Open University Press.

TGWU (1993) Memorandum submitted to the House of Commons Employment Committee Inquiry, 'The Future of Trade Unions', 1 December.

Travers, C., Bacon, N. and Storey, J. (1995) 'Individualism and Collectivism: Women, Men and Changes at Work', *Book of Proceedings: British Psychological Society, Occupational Psychology Conference*, 3–5 January, University of Warwick, Leicester: BPS.

TUC (1994) *Human Resource Management: A Trade Union Response*, London: Trades Union Congress.

USDAW (1993) Memorandum submitted to the House of Commons Employment Committee Inquiry, 'The Future of Trade Unions', 23 November: 112.

Willman, P. and Cave, A. (1994) 'The Union of the Future: Super-Unions or Joint Ventures?', *British Journal of Industrial Relations* **32**, 3: 395–412.

3

UNION MILITANCY AND SOCIAL PARTNERSHIP

John Kelly

INTRODUCTION

As the post-1979 decline of trade unionism gathered pace and showed few signs of letting up, academic and other commentators increasingly turned their minds from the analysis of decline to the prognosis for growth. A significant number of them concluded that union survival and recovery turned on the willingness of unions and their members to behave 'moderately' and to offer concessions to the employer (Bassett 1986; Crouch 1986; Kern and Sabel 1992; Leadbeater 1987). Labour–management co-operation, or 'social partnership', was to be the order of the day, and the old 'adversarial' industrial relations was castigated as destructive and irrelevant in the current era of intensified world competition. In extreme cases, unions were exhorted to abandon the strike weapon, icon of the 'trench warfare' of the 'old industrial relations' (to use the terminology of Dunn 1990), or (in the American case) to reconcile themselves to the near-total disappearance of collective bargaining (Edwards 1993: 97; Heckscher 1988).

In Britain, the start of this trend can be located in the early 1980s: on 2 April 1981 the EETPU announced a new type of collective agreement with the Japanese manufacturer Toshiba, embodying single unionism, binding pendulum arbitration, flexibility between work roles and other components of what later came to be known as 'new-style deals'; and in September 1983 the TUC General Secretary outlined the case for unions to improve their relations with government and employers in the wake of Labour's electoral defeat just three months earlier, foreshadowing what soon became known as the 'new realism' (Bassett 1986: 125, 46–52; TUC 1984). The EETPU's new-style deals and their

77

underlying principle of greater co-operation with employers were praised by numerous commentators, such as the *Financial Times* correspondents (Bassett 1986, Leadbeater 1987 and Lloyd 1986; also Adeney and Lloyd 1986),[1] and academics such as Colin Crouch, who described them as the 'wisest course' for the future of the trade union movement (1986: 15; see also Rico 1987).

In the early-middle 1980s commentary on the so-called no-strike deals placed more emphasis on the putative reduction in conflict than on the growth of co-operation, but the continued decline in strike activity into the 1990s has probably devalued the 'no-strike' agreement in the eyes of many employers. They have become increasingly interested in the rhetoric of 'human resource management' and its agenda of competitiveness, flexibility and commitment (Guest 1989). Whilst unions such as the TGWU were alarmed at what they saw as the anti-union implications of HRM, others were either enthusiastic or felt that the HRM agenda could be exploited by unions in their own favour (see Bacon and Storey, Chapter 2; Beaumont 1991: Martinez Lucio and Weston 1992; Oliver and Wilkinson 1992, Chapter 10). In 1990 John Edmonds and Alan Tuffin (GMB and UCW respectively) wrote a much-discussed document called *A New Agenda* which extolled the importance of a 'partnership' with employers built around issues of 'common interest' such as productivity growth, training, and health and safety (GMB/UCW 1990 and Edmonds 1994).

The TUC's Interim Report on Human Resource Management (1994a) pursued a similar theme of social partnership, understood as a relationship in which

> employers and trade unions seek . . . to build consensus to find the common ground on issues that are best tackled through joint action . . . those conflicts that do occur could be worked out in an atmosphere of mutual respect, trust and goodwill.
>
> (TUC 1994a: 24)

The idea of labour–capital partnership has increasingly been promoted in recent years by influential writers such as Robert Taylor (1994) and Alan Cave (1994) as well as by academics both in Britain and abroad (Bacon and Storey, Chapter 2; Blanchflower and Freeman 1992; Kelley and Harrison 1992; Kern and Sabel 1992; Kochan *et al.* 1986; Storey and Sisson 1993: 217–21, 233–34; Turner 1991).

The purpose of this chapter is critically to review these arguments for union co-operation and partnership with employers and to suggest that militancy is likely to prove a better guarantor of union survival and recovery. I first clarify and define the plethora of terms that can be found in discussions on union policy and then set out, in turn, the case for union 'moderation' and the counter-arguments for union militancy before ending with some qualifications to the argument as a whole.

DEFINING TERMS

Discussion of union policy is littered with bipolar terminology: conflict and co-operation, militancy and moderation, co-operative and adversarial industrial relations, accommodation and resistance. Sometimes these terms refer to union action, sometimes to union policy, often to the relations between unions and employers. Attempts to categorise union policy are often pitched at a very high level of abstraction (e.g. Martin 1989) and are therefore likely to report that only a handful of unions (such as the NUM and the old EETPU) have coherent policies whilst most are pragmatic (Towers 1989). It is clearly unsatisfactory to deploy three categories of union policy (militant, moderate and pragmatic) and find that the vast majority of unions fall into just one of them. Vic Allen attempted many years ago to define militant trade unionism in terms of aims and method: a militant union would exploit market advantages to the full and would refuse to accept an unsatisfactory price for the labour power of its members (Allen 1966: 41). This definition has the advantage of focusing on concrete union goals instead of the sometimes nebulous resolutions of union policy, but it has nothing to say about the types of power resources that unions might use or the ideologies they disseminate amongst their membership, both of which might be thought to have some bearing on militancy.

For the purpose of this discussion I want to propose that the distinction between militant and moderate unionism is sensible provided we define these concepts in a multi-dimensional way and use them to describe properties of the parties to industrial relations, not their relationships (although the former have implications for the latter).[2] We can think of militancy and moderation as having five dimensions: goals, methods, institutional resources, membership resources and ideology, and shifts to moderation (shown in

Table 3.1 Components of union militancy and moderation

Component	Militancy	Moderation
Goals	Ambitious demands (scale and scope) with few concessions	Moderate demands with some or many concessions (Accommodation)
Membership resources	Strong reliance on mobilisation of union membership	Strong reliance on employers, third parties or law (Demobilisation)
Institutional resources	Reliance on collective bargaining and/or unilateral regulation	Willingness to experiment with/support non-bargaining institutions (Subordination)
Methods	Frequent threat or use of industrial action	Infrequent threat or use of industrial action (Quiescence)
Ideology	Ideology of conflicting interests	Ideology of partnership (Incorporation)

brackets) have been labelled for each of these dimensions (Table 3.1). The goal component reflects Allen's (1966) distinction between different degrees of union ambition in bargaining (measured by scale and scope of demands), but is in any case a fairly familiar and conventional distinction.

Second, we can argue that a militant union is likely to emphasise membership mobilisation as part of a strategy of confronting employers and the state with collective power and seeking to impose costs on them. For Offe and Wiesenthal (1985: 185) the membership's 'willingness to act' is the necessary foundation of effective trade unionism, even where the union's role is institutionalised and underpinned by legal rights and employer support. Membership here refers both to the union's own membership and that of other unions. A moderate union, by contrast, will place more reliance on resources such as employer sponsorship or goodwill, collective agreements and external rules such as legislation in order to achieve its objectives. (In the extreme case a union would offer a package of benefits to an employer in return for union recognition before any 'membership' has even been hired by the employer.) A militant union is likely to insist on a single, union channel of representation, whereas its moderate counterparts will actively support non-bargaining channels such as consultative committees, company councils or works councils. Reliance on the threat or use of industrial action (in its many forms) contrasts with an infrequent threat or resort to action and a preference for peaceful methods of conflict resolution such as third-party intervention. Finally, a militant union can be thought of as one whose leaderships (at various levels) stress conflicts of interest between workers and employers and promote a corresponding adversarial ideology. The language of common interests, partnership and collaboration is, by contrast, the language of the moderate union.

Although Table 3.1 depicts two polar types, it is clear from the continuous nature of the goal and method components that militancy and moderation are best understood as two ends of a continuum. It is also true that unions are not free agents when it comes to goals, methods or resources: other parties, particularly employers and the state, can constrain or suppress particular types of union behaviour. Any observed degree of union militancy and moderation therefore results from an interaction between unions and their environments and cannot necessarily be regarded as a true measure of the preferences of the union and its constituent elements (rank and file, shop stewards, officers).[3] Moreover, the significance of particular policies or actions will vary historically. For instance, the idea of a single, union channel of representation was commonplace in the 1970s, but in the climate of the late 1980s/early 1990s and amidst the growth of non-union and non-bargaining institutions it has increasingly been called into question and has therefore now assumed a more militant character (McCarthy 1988; Storey and Sisson 1993: 231). Finally, there is no implication that union militancy (or moderation) is a stable or coherent attribute, since unions clearly do change (cf. the EETPU in the 1950s with that of the 1960s) and unions may display contradictions between the different elements of militancy (e.g. militant ideology and modest bargaining demands).[4]

Let us briefly consider some of the implications of the multidimensional approach before we turn to the arguments for and against militancy. First, unions may be militant on some dimensions, e.g. bargaining demands, but moderate on others, e.g. reliance on legal resources rather than membership mobilisation. Militancy (moderation) may therefore take different forms and it may be useful to think of the five dimensions (Table 3.1) as arranged in a hierarchy of depth and pervasiveness, with goals at the top and ideology at the bottom. As we descend the table, the adoption of a moderate orientation becomes increasingly significant in terms of the range and time-scale of implications. Goal concessions in one bargaining round may have only short-term significance because the union can catch up in the next round. Institutional changes are more far-reaching since the adoption of, let us say, works councils may freeze the scope of collective bargaining for a significant period of time. The disavowal of industrial action and the dissemination amongst a union's members of an ideology of partnership may be more far-reaching still.

Second, we can see that the unions which once figured heavily in policy discussions – the EETPU and the NUM – are perhaps unique in being apparently moderate and militant respectively on all five dimensions and having national leaderships strongly committed to these respective orientations.[5] Third, because militancy can express itself in different ways, the use of a single dimension, e.g. strike action, can therefore be misleading. Fourth, the meaning of particular non-membership resources – the law, public opinion, etc. – can only be judged in relation to the other resources (if any) that unions deploy and to the accompanying goals, methods and ideology of the union. Relying on public opinion to the exclusion of industrial action (as the RCN has done from time to time) would be the hallmark of moderation, but mobilising public opinion in conjunction with action (as shown by the schoolteachers in 1993 and the ambulance workers in 1989–90) would indicate militancy.

Finally, the militancy–moderation axis can also be applied to the other industrial relations actors, especially employers and the state. The militant employer would be distinguished by ambitious demands, e.g. pay cuts implemented unilaterally, perhaps with elements of coercion. We would also expect to find attacks on union resources through bypassing of shop stewards, resort to the law and derecognition of unions; and the promotion of a unitarist ideology attacking trade unionism as an unnecessary disruption of harmonious industrial relations.

THE CASE FOR UNION MODERATION AND PARTNERSHIP WITH EMPLOYERS

I have already noted that different levels of a union may be characterised by variations in militancy and moderation (see also Muller-Jentsch 1988). The argument in this chapter turns on whether the overall emphasis within a union should be towards militancy or moderation. An orientation towards one, say moderation, does not entirely preclude the other, but we assume that it implies the other is less desirable and is something to be avoided if possible. Five arguments have been advanced in the academic literature and amongst trade unions themselves for an orientation towards moderation and social partnership, and in no particular order, they are as follows.

The balance of power and competitive pressures

The shift in the balance of power towards employers since 1979 is one of the most basic and frequently used arguments for moderation. Both its causes – recession, unemployment, restructuring, government policy and legislation – and its expression – declining union membership and industrial action – are well known (Kessler and Bayliss 1992). It has exposed workers more fully than in the past to the pressures of highly competitive product and labour markets and to the employers' priorities of productivity improvements, labour intensification and cost reductions. In unionised plants, it is claimed, unions have to moderate their demands and offer concessions to the employer or face the risk of job loss, derecognition or plant closure (Oliver and Wilkinson 1992: 305). Militant opposition to new management techniques has also been criticised on the grounds that unions are unlikely to deter an employer from pursuing such initiatives and will succeed only in contributing to their own marginalisation within the system of workplace industrial relations (cf. Storey 1992: 277, who notes that the evidence on this point is unclear and Bacon and Storey, this volume). In non-union plants it is argued that the prospect of militant trade unionism would discourage employers from granting recognition. The choice in these plants is between moderate unionism or no unionism at all (cf. Lloyd 1990). Faced with such powerful pressures, more and more union leaders have sought to legitimise unions by arguing that they can, and do, contribute to competitive success (Cave 1994: 175–7, 183–4; Taylor 1994: Chapter 5; TUC 1994a: 30–42).

Strikes don't pay

During the heyday of 'no-strike' deals some leaders of the EETPU argued that strike action costs workers so much in lost wages that it was extremely difficult, if not impossible, for them to make up the loss (Sanderson quoted in Bassett 1986: 84–5; Lloyd 1990: 644–8). This suggestion has been reinforced by Metcalf *et al.*, (1993), who have calculated that wage strikes lasting more than about four days will probably result in net losses for the workers who participate in them. The failure of the miners' strike of 1984–5 to prevent job losses in the coal industry is often cited as an illustration of the parlous consequences of militancy in a climate of employer and state power (e.g. Adeney and Lloyd 1986; Coates and Topham 1986; Taylor 1993: 293–8). As the level of strike activity declined while competitive pressure continued through the 1990s, the possibility of even organising a strike, let alone winning it, seemed increasingly remote to some union leaders.

Militant unionism is fragile

Muller-Jentsch has argued that militant trade unionism is extremely fragile and that, while it may achieve short-term gains for its members, there will be a longer-term price:

> It is noticeable that where it [militant trade unionism – J.K.] is practised it has unleashed massive counter-offensives on the part of the employers (in the form of wide-scale lockouts) but also on the part of the State (one extreme case being Thatcherism).
>
> (1985: 30)

Militant unionism in the car industry came under counterattack from BL Chief Executive, Michael Edwardes (1983); schoolteachers suffered the withdrawal of their collective bargaining rights by the Conservative government following industrial action in the mid-1980s; whilst the National Union of Mineworkers was subject to a veritable assault by the Coal Board, the Conservative government, the police and the security services (MacGregor 1986; Milne 1994). The Conservative government has encouraged recognition of 'moderate' unions such as the Professional Association of Teachers, the Union of Democratic Mineworkers and the Association of Professional Ambulance Personnel (see Kerr and Sachdev 1992: 137). The fate of militant trade unionism in strike-prone sectors of foreign industry could also be cited as examples (see, e.g., Golden 1995 on FIAT).

Scope of union influence

Several unions have pursued the argument that they can extend their influence at the workplace by engaging employers in dis- cussions on issues that are of common interest (or at least, less contentious) such as training, health and safety, and productivity (GMB/UCW 1990; TUC 1991, 1994a). These issues, it is argued, also fall outside the normal range of items handled by collective bargaining and this may be an additional reason for their less divisive character. Some unions have suggested that these types of issue could be pursued through non-bargaining channels such as company councils, works councils or the more familiar and tra- ditional consultative committees (Bassett 1986; Lloyd 1990; TUC 1991, 1994b). The significance of company and works councils is that membership would normally be open to all employees and not confined to trade unionists (although in practice unions might come to dominate them as in the works councils in larger German establishments). In view of the contraction of the scope of collec- tive bargaining and the employer's control over the structure and scope of bargaining, a policy of moderation and partnership through new institutions, it is argued, offers the prospect of some influence rather than none at all.

Storey and Sisson (1993) have supported this view, noting that

> The insistence on the 'single channel' whereby negotiations, consultations, communication and participation could be handled through the medium of the trade unions is unlikely to be viable . . . . If trade unions want to extend their influence, they will also certainly have to compromise in this regard.
>
> (1993: 220, 231; also Bacon and Storey, Chapter 2)

In addition it has been argued that moderate unions can elicit substantive benefits for their members such as single-status terms and conditions of employment and job security (cf. Oliver and Wilkinson 1992: 257–62). The 1992 Rover agreement, for instance, embodied a clause stating that anyone who wanted to continue working for Rover would be able to do so, although the company retains the right to request voluntary redundancies (Taylor 1994: 122–6).

Moderate union growth rates

The full 'new-style agreement', including compulsory and/or binding arbitration, single status, various forms of flexibility, participation machinery and sole union recognition was pioneered as a recognition strategy by the EETPU and the AEU (Bassett 1986: 86–122). The available evidence shows, not surprisingly, that the lion's share of these recognition agreements has indeed been signed by the two most supportive unions (Table 3.2 and see Milner 1993 for similar findings).

Table 3.2 New-style agreements 1988–94 by union

EETPU	37
AEU	16
TGWU	7
GMB	6
Others	15
Total	81

Source: Gall and McKay (1994)

Gall and McKay estimated that these 81 recognition agreements provided collective bargaining coverage for about 29,000 employees, though they gave no data on the numbers who actually joined the relevant unions. Most of the EETPU and AEU agreements were with Japanese companies and we know from Oliver and Wilkinson's survey of such companies that average union density in those which recognise unions was 62 per cent in 1987 and 75 per cent in 1991 (1992: 267–9). Assuming overall union density in such plants (the average, weighted by plant size[6]) is now approximately 65–70 per cent, then the post-1988 new-style agreements would have yielded about 20,000 union members.

Although the pioneer of new-style agreements, the former EETPU, did lose members after 1979, it lost significantly fewer than many other unions. Between December 1979 and December 1991 EETPU membership fell by 19 per cent, but total union membership (TUC and non-TUC) fell by 28 per cent (Certification Office, *Annual Reports*). The avowedly moderate RCN whose pre-1995 constitution forbade its members from striking, grew by 85 per cent over the 1979–92 period, whilst its more militant nursing rival COHSE (now UNISON) saw its membership fall by 8 per cent. The anti-strike Professional Association of Teachers, formed in 1970, had approximately 40,000 members in 1992, while its more militant rival, the NUT, declined over the same period from 310,356 to 213,656 (Certification Office, *Annual Reports*). Two of the most militant unions, on the other hand, the NUM and the TGWU, have seen their memberships dramatically fall since 1979, by 75 per cent and 50 per cent respectively.

These five arguments and the associated evidence are the grounds most frequently cited to support union moderation, and to criticise militancy. As we noted earlier, there are different forms of moderation and militancy and the general arguments outlined above do not, as a whole, lead to any particular form. Union leaders such as John Edmonds have criticised the demobilisation of union membership entailed in strict 'no-strike' deals but have advocated the pursuit of new institutional resources such as works councils. Whilst 'no-strike' deals dominated debates in the 1980s, the decline of strike activity since then has led to a shift in the dominant forms of moderation. It is now the institutional and ideological dimensions which are very much to the fore, epitomised by the TUC documents calling for a fresh look at works councils and for a social partnership with employers (TUC 1994a, b). There is considerable debate therefore about the most appropriate forms of moderation, and objections to one form do not necessarily damage others. Nonetheless these different forms do rest on a common substrate: conflicts of interest between workers and their employers have been played down and supposedly common interests played up.

THE CASE FOR UNION MILITANCY

The case for union militancy falls under four broad headings, viz:

- the growing hostility of employers to any form of unionism
- the beneficial consequences of industrial action
- the meagre consequences of moderation
- the continuing antagonism of interests between workers and employers.

Employers and unions

Employer hostility to union recognition

There is a wealth of evidence (examined below) that employers are becoming increasingly hostile to trade unions per se and increasingly willing to think of life without unions, an idea that not so long ago would have been almost inconceivable (Dunn 1993). Since it is difficult, if not impossible, to achieve a partnership with a party who would prefer that you didn't exist, the growth of employer hostility is a major objection to the case for union moderation. Government antagonism to unions in its capacity as employer has been carefully documented by Smith and Morton (1993, 1994), and there is also mounting evidence for private employer antagonism.

First, there is clear evidence of growing hostility by employers to unionisation amongst their workforces, as Table 3.3 shows.

Table 3.3 Union success rate in recognition cases handled by ACAS 1976–93

	1976–82	*1983–6*	*1987–93*
Success rate	45%	32%	27%
Average number of total cases per annum	426	207	145

Source: ACAS, *Annual Reports*

ACAS Reports have documented the hostility implied in the declining success rate: 'Even when ballots established that membership levels were high, recognition for full collective bargaining proved most difficult to secure' (ACAS 1988: 20).[7] Second, a number of large, unionised corporations such as BT have adopted a policy of starting up subsidiary businesses on a non-union basis, and private companies that have taken over unionised public-sector activities such as hospital cleaning or catering have often been non-union (Beaumont 1992: 95).

Third, there is the evidence on union derecognition. At the time of Claydon's (1989) study it was reasonable to conclude that derecognition was a relatively small-scale phenomenon confined to specific sectors (newspaper publishing and coastal shipping in particular) and often to particular grades such as white-collar workers. Since then the position has changed significantly. Where Claydon reported 25 cases per annum in 1987–8, Gall and McKay (1994) found that from 1988 to 1994 the incidence of derecognition nearly trebled and by 1994 was running at almost 70 cases per annum. It is true that many of these cases involved white-collar workers and some involved groups with low and/or declining density and organisation, but derecognition has now spread to some of the best-organised groups of manual workers. The derecognition of the printing unions by the News International company at the time of its move to the Wapping plant in 1986 was widely publicised (Kessler and Bayliss 1992: 81–2). Less well known was the fate of the main dockers' union at Tilbury (the TGWU), which was derecognised towards the end of the 1989 strike against the abolition of the National Dock Labour Scheme. Shortly afterwards other unions in the port suffered a similar fate (Turnbull *et al.* 1992: 240). There was very little publicity about derecognition in the oil industry, where collective bargaining rights over pay have been withdrawn for some or all manual workers (production, craft and transport) by all of the major oil companies – BP, Esso, Shell and Mobil (Higgs 1994a). Union organisation in the oil industry goes back over fifty years, and 100 per cent density was the norm amongst manual workers. Yet in a relatively short period of time a combination of redundancy threats, large severance payments and attacks on union organisation has transformed industrial relations in the industry. Derecognition has now afflicted almost every major union and has hit both the strong (printing, docks, oil) and the weak (magazine publishing) (Gall and McKay 1994). This is a highly significant piece of evidence because it suggests that what employers object to is not a particular form of trade unionism but the very fact of its existence.

Employer hostility to collective bargaining

For the first time since the late 1930s collective bargaining now covers a minority of the workforce (47 per cent in 1990, according to Brown 1993: see also Milner 1995). A growing number of unionised employers have moved towards unilateral imposition of new terms and conditions of employment. Performance-related pay has been imposed in local government (Kessler 1995); Saturday opening was imposed by the clearing banks; and more classroom contact hours have been imposed by the new universities and by further education colleges. WIRS3 confirmed that the scope of collective bargaining contracted between 1984 and 1990 (Millward *et al.* 1992: 253). The main employers' organisation, the CBI, has called into question the continued relevance of collective bargaining. According to its Director of Employment Affairs, writing about WIRS3,

> Collective bargaining no longer presents itself as the only or even the most obvious method of handling relations at work; and fewer employees – and employers – feel the need of union mediation in their dealings.
>
> (Gilbert 1993: 252)

The Advisory, Conciliation and Arbitration Service, once obliged to promote collective bargaining, is no longer required to do so, following the passage of the Trade Union Reform and Employment Rights Act 1993.[8]

Proponents of social partnership have seriously underestimated employer hostility to collective bargaining, a fact that is apparent from their descriptions of actual 'partnership' initiatives. The TUC Report on HRM described Royal Mail's jointly agreed quality circle programme but failed to mention the widespread cutbacks in union facility time carried out by local Royal Mail managers (Darlington 1993). The TUC document also described the 'New Dialogue' between unions and management in BT but failed to mention that BT's plan to impose radical changes in working practices was only withdrawn after the threat of industrial action (*NCU Journal*, various issues). Likewise Taylor (1994) described the persistence of collective bargaining in the privatised utilities with- out mentioning the derecognition of unions by several water companies or the determined employer efforts to intensify labour and cut jobs (O'Connell Davidson 1993: 103–5).

Employer attempts to bypass or marginalise unions

According to proponents of social partnership the growth of HRM does not pose a significant threat to trade unionism, a claim based on the fact that HRM practices are most likely to be found in large, unionised companies rather than in non-union firms (TUC 1994a: 12–16). Yet this statistical association is open to precisely the opposite interpretation: if HRM *were* anti-union in effect, if not intent, then one would *expect* to find it concentrated in unionised firms since there would be no need for it in non-union firms. On this interpretation HRM is a sophisticated attempt to bypass or marginalise unions, and the first piece of evidence in support of this view comes, paradoxically, from the same TUC Report which downplayed the threat of HRM:

> the experience of many trade unionists is [that] . . . HRM is about nothing more than implementing redundancies, casualising the workforce, reducing wages and re-asserting management' s 'right to manage'. It is often associated with intensification of work and a deliberate strategy to de-recognise or limit the influence of trade unions.
>
> (TUC 1994a: 10)

Second, case studies of HRM have shown that the companies involved have almost all tried to reduce the range of issues over which unions exert influence. According to Storey's study of fifteen major British private companies and public corporations, fourteen of them had made some attempts to 'marginalise' shop stewards (1992: 82–3). There was

> a generally more aggressive stance towards the unions but without any apparent agenda (hidden or otherwise) to displace them. . . . Union leaders at both national and work-place level were left on the sidelines of most of the managerial initiatives during the period.
>
> (Storey 1992: 246, 250; see also Marchington and Parker 1990)

Indeed one large company – Cadbury Ltd – produced a confidential document stating that, 'the role of the trade union needs to be marginalised by greater focus on direct communication and consultation, but without an overt statement to this effect' (Labour Research 1994: 24).

The incidence of direct communications between junior managers (or supervisors) and their subordinates has in fact significantly increased, especially in unionised settings, a change interpreted by Millward as,

> one designed to supplement or partially replace trade unions as one of the principal channels of communication between management and employees.
>
> (Millward 1994: 88)

Third, unions are also being marginalised within non-bargaining institutions where they have traditionally enjoyed representation. In 1984 unions chose some or all of the employee representatives on 62 per cent of functioning consultative committees in unionised plants, but by 1990 this figure had fallen to 48 per cent (Millward 1994: 81).

All of this evidence demonstrates a wide-ranging hostility to union presence, activity and organisation on the part of employers, and also suggests that the scale and intensity of such hostility has gathered pace in recent years (Geroski *et al.* 1995). There is little sign here that employers are seeking out forms of moderate unionism, or are open to partnerships with unions: more and more they appear not to want unions at all. In this context union survival must depend on the willingness of the membership to defend the union against attack, if necessary by collective action. The offer of 'partnership' to a hostile opponent is likely to confirm to employers that unions are unwilling to mobilise their own memberships and that union exclusion is therefore feasible. Far from blunting anti-union hostility, any such offer will only perpetuate it.

The consequences of industrial action

Union growth rates

It is true that the RCN was Britain's fastest growing union in the 1980s and early 1990s and that it also adhered to a no-strike policy (now abandoned), although as it happens many of the health service professional associations recorded impressive growth rates in the same period without the aid of such a policy (Burchill and Seifert 1993). But the second fastest growth rate was recorded by the Fire Brigades Union, a militant left-wing union, whose membership climbed from 30,000 (1979) to 51,881 (1992), a rise of 73 per cent (Certification Office, *Annual Reports*). Next came BIFU, an organisation that became increasingly militant in this period in the face of authoritarian employers and severe job losses. Its membership rose by almost 22,000 (17 per cent) between 1979 and 1992. And although the EETPU showed a smaller rate of decline than the union movement as a whole since 1979, its rate of loss (19 per cent) was matched by the union most similar to it in terms of membership composition and industrial location. Over the same period, MSF lost 14 per cent of its membership. It is also the case

Table 3.4 Mining union membership 1986–92

| | NUM | | UDM |
	TUC figure	CO figure	CO figure
Dec. 1986	104,941	211,422	27,947
Dec. 1992	32,947	94,000	11,357
Decline (per cent)	68.6	55.5	59.4

Source: Certification Office, Annual Reports 1987, 1993; TUC Statistical Statements, 1987, 1993

that some anti-strike unions have failed, surviving only as tiny rump organisations (e.g. the Association of University and College Lecturers, formerly the APT), or have been forced into merger because of non-viability (e.g. the Institute of Journalists, which transferred engagements to the EETPU) or have disappeared altogether (e.g. the Federation of Professional Railwaymen). If we compare the traditional, militant approach to union recognition with the gains from new-style agreements, based on co-operation with employers, we find that between 1988 and 1994 traditional (i.e., non-new-style) recognition agreements extended collective bargaining coverage to approximately 29,000 employees, exactly the same estimate as for the new-style agreements (see above) (Gall 1993a, b). On the face of it there is little to choose, then, between these two different routes to recognition.

But what about the case of militant union decline most frequently cited, namely the NUM? Here we are able to make a direct, controlled comparison with its moderate rival, the UDM, formed during the Great Strike but issued with a certificate of independence only in 1986 (see Table 3.4).

The UDM lost almost 60 per cent of its membership in the relevant period, close to the NUM's 68.6 per cent loss of actual members (the NUM Certification Office figure includes many retired miners). When we allow for the UDM's concentration in the central coalfields, where job losses were fewer than in the NUM-dominated peripheral fields, then it is reasonable to conclude that the militant NUM and the moderate UDM have lost jobs and members at practically the same rate since 1986, contrary to popular myth.

Finally it is worth reminding ourselves that the periods of most substantial union growth in Britain have been periods of exceptional industrial militancy: 1889–92, 1910–20, 1935–45 and 1968–79. Cronin (1979) has argued convincingly that growth and militancy are causally connected and that the willingness of unions to launch strikes and the capacity to win them have proved historically to be the most effective recruiting weapons at their disposal, contrary to the proponents of union moderation. A similar conclusion has been reached using disaggregated data, although at this level the militancy–growth relationship is more complex: in the 1970s strike action by NALGO, NUBE and UCATT led to membership gains, but the militancy of the NUT led to membership losses (Undy *et al.* 1981: 162).

The pay-off to strikes

We can reject at the outset the argument that strikes per se do not pay. There is plenty of evidence that short strikes often involve no loss of pay or that pay losses are quickly made up with additional overtime working (Batstone *et al.* 1978). The issue, as Metcalf *et al.* (1993) make clear, is what types of strikes lead to payoffs for workers, but their own conclusion that only short strikes (up to four days) are sensible is open to serious question. The caveats set out at the end of their article are in fact highly damaging criticisms of their methodology. First, comparison of wage settlements with and without strikes probably underestimates the gains from industrial action because a successful wage strike in one firm could well lead other employers to pay the same or make a similar settlement without a strike. Second, there may be future gains from striking if an employer settles higher than would otherwise have been the case because the strike threat comes to be seen as credible. Third, the authors evaluate the cost of a strike as the loss of average wages, but this assumes (wrongly) that strikers always do lose wages, that they have no other sources of income (social security, tax rebates, union strike pay, donations or casual work) and that any lost wages will not be made up with additional overtime. Finally, the authors refer briefly to non-wage gains, but simply note that there are no data on them (Metcalf *et al.* 1993: 190).

We can think about non-wage gains using the multi-dimensional approach to union militancy. The substantive gains (measured by the degree of goal achievement and the cost) and membership gains from strike action have already been referred to, but workers and their unions could gain under the three other headings of militancy.

Institutionally, strike action can consolidate union organisation in a variety of ways: through the defence of shop stewards against victimisation, by enhancing the authority of the steward body or by enhancing members' commitment to the union (Stagner and Eflal 1982). Successful strikes can encourage future militancy and finally they can strengthen an ideology of conflicting interests amongst a union's membership (for recent examples of all these gains see Fantasia 1988; and for more general discussion see Kelly 1988).

There is little merit in the idea that industrial action is sufficiently ineffective to be discarded or downplayed and that unions should be seeking to cultivate a more co-operative relationship with employers. Historically workers have joined unions in order to gain effective protection at work against their employers, and the most visible demonstration of such effectiveness has been the successful strike (or other form of collective action).

The consequences of moderation

The fruits of new-style agreements

What of the putative gains from new-style agreements, such as job security, single status and union influence? Japanese companies in Britain frequently offered job security to 'core workers' (73 per cent of one sample claimed to do so in 1987: Oliver and Wilkinson 1992: 258). However, the same study noted that in 1991 50 per cent of the sample protected their core workforce by the use of temporary workers, a much higher figure than for manufacturers as a whole in 1990, where the incidence was just 9 per cent (Millward et al. 1992: 338).[9] In any case the job security provisions for core workers were statements of general policy and were not written, into contracts or agreements (Oliver and Wilkinson 1992: 258).[10] Single status for staff and non-staff grades was reported in 65 per cent of Japanese companies in 1991 but by 49 per cent of British manufacturing firms, a significant difference though not a huge one, suggesting that moves to single status are fairly widespread (Millward 1994: 113). Finally, the small amount of data on union influence under new-style agreements shows workers believing the union to be weak and ineffective (Grant 1993). Overall, then, the benefits for workers from new-style agreements have been distinctly unimpressive, particularly when compared with the claims of some of their proponents.

The fragility of moderate unionism

Full-blown moderate unionism involves the adjustment of worker demands in order to meet the employers' interests, support for non-bargaining institutions, opposition to industrial action, an ideology of partnership, and reliance on the employer, rather than membership mobilisation, for the continued existence of the union. The best-documented example of this phenomenon is Nissan's Washington plant, where union density was around 15 per cent in the late 1980s and 30 per cent in the early 1990s.

> The reasons for employee apathy towards the union are obvious . . . it is accurate to say the union does not play a significant part in what goes on at Nissan presently because it has no really independent role.
> (Garrahan and Stewart 1992: 68)

Oliver and Wilkinson claimed that average union density does not differ between Japanese firms with and without company councils of the type used to marginalise the AEU at Nissan and suggested that what made the difference amongst firms was the degree of employer encouragement for unionism (1992: 270–1, 298). Whether unionism in such plants depends on the activities of a company council or on managerial sponsorship is less significant than the fact that both of these explanations identify the goodwill of the employer as the key to union survival and high membership density. It is the extreme dependency of the union on the employer which is truly alarming about these cases, a dependency reinforced by the absence of the normal countervailing powers of trade unionism such as the collective bargaining process and a body of shop stewards with an adversarial ideology and the willingness and the capacity to mobilise the membership for various forms of action. It is this dependency which renders moderate trade unionism so vulnerable to an employer's counter-offensive in the event that they ever wished to dispense with unionism altogether, particularly when faced with even faint stirrings of worker discontent. Consistent with this argument is the fact that derecognition has largely been targeted at weak rather than strong unionism (although the position is beginning to change following the de-recognition of manual unions by the big oil companies, noted earlier).

Common interests?

Advocates of moderation rarely deny that there are conflicts of interest in employment. Redundancy versus job security, pay rises versus pay freezes, and intensification of work versus maintenance of existing effort levels: these are the traditional areas of conflict between workers and their employers, and all have persisted throughout the 1980s and 1990s. What they claim is that there is a set of issues on which unions, workers and employers have common interests and around which they can build more co-operative and less adversarial relations. The most frequently cited examples are training, health and safety, equal opportunities, work organisation and working time (GMB/UCW 1990; Monks 1993). However, recent reviews of developments in these areas paint a very different picture. They suggest that there are serious conflicts of interest in all these areas, notwithstanding the fact that every-body would agree, in general, on the desirability of training, health and safety, equal opportunities, flexibility and efficiency.

On training, the demand for skilled workers continues to be weak as many employers pursue a product-market strategy based on price competitiveness and low wages (Keep 1994: 325). Whilst the scale of training provision has improved since 1979, it is still poor by international standards and is significantly poorer in non-union firms. The focus of company training programmes is heavily slanted towards groups that are already well trained such as managers, professionals and skilled manual workers (Rainbird 1994: 337–41). Streeck (1992) has warned against the idea that training is a non-conflictual issue, pointing out that strong, militant unions are essential to impose training rules and obligations on recalcitrant employers and close off low-skill, low-wage adjustment policies (*pace* Kern and Sabel 1992).

In the area of health and safety Bach (1994) reported that the overall fatality, accident and injury rate worsened during the 1980s (and stagnated in the early 1990s) in part because of the declining numbers of health and safety representatives and union presence in workplaces, and also because of the growth in numbers of the types of firms, such as subcontractors and small firms, that have poor health and safety records. Grunberg (1983, 1986) has shown that the shift in the balance of power during the early 1980s recession allowed employers to increase the intensity of labour, thereby resulting in an increase in the accident rate. Enhanced labour productivity in response to competitive pressures was therefore achieved at the expense of workers' safety. On equal opportunities there has been some progress since 1979 in the erosion of occupational segregation and in the adoption and implementation of equal opportunities policies. On the other hand, the government policy of labour-market deregulation has been working in the opposite direction. The government has therefore vigorously opposed successive European draft directives improving women's rights, and has progressively dismantled legal protections for low-paid workers (many of whom are women). Within companies, equal opportunities policies have often been pursued in a half-hearted and limited manner. As one author noted, equal opportunities (EO) prescriptions 'assume unitary interests where divergent interests exist, [and] pay inadequate attention to the resistance EO generates' (Dickens 1994: 289). On work organisation there is case study and survey evidence to suggest that employers intensified labour in the 1980s, both by increasing effort levels and by tightening up on 'gaps' in the working day, such as shift starts and finishes and teabreaks (Edwards and Whitston 1991; Nichols 1991; Richardson and Rubin 1993). Finally, on working time, Blyton (1994) has noted that many of the 'flexibility' initiatives in recent years have actually provided employers with more control over employees' hours of work or provided employees with choice, but on the employers' terms.

I have reviewed developments in these areas at some length because they have been advanced frequently by advocates of 'partnership' as prime examples in support of their case. In fact the evidence only serves to reinforce the pervasiveness of the antagonistic interests of employers and workers and strengthen the case for militant, not moderate, trade unionism.

For all the reasons set out above the general case for militancy is more compelling and persuasive than the case for moderation. Before summing up the arguments of the chapter we need first to consider two final counter-arguments against the case for militancy and then to outline some critical qualifications to the argument as a whole.

COUNTER-ARGUMENTS AGAINST MILITANCY

Proponents of social partnership might argue that the evidence assembled here does indeed show the growth of employer hostility towards unionism but contend that this hostility is in part a temporary (and unfortunate) product of economic adversity, a *contingent*, not a *necessary* feature of current industrial relations. Second, they might argue that militant unionism would only intensify employer antagonism rather than ameliorate it.

Against this case I would argue that the growth of employer antagonism to unions is an expression of the inevitable conflicts of interest that pervade the employment relationship. The major piece of evidence in support of this claim is the fact that employer antagonism is to be found in practically every sector of the economy and has touched almost every trade union of any significance. The shift in the balance of power towards employers since 1980 has provided them with a significant increase in their freedom of manoeuvre. Actions pursued by employers under conditions of freedom offer a far more reliable guide to their interests than actions pursued under the constraints of union power and pro-union legislation. What we observe is that employers have sought to reassert power over their workforces to enable the pursuit of profit-restoring measures. The misleading rhetoric of human resource management and social partnership should not blind us to the continuing antagonism of interests that characterises the employment relationship (Blyton and Turnbull 1994: 28–35).

It is true that militancy may well exacerbate the *desire* of employers to marginalise or derecognise unions. But successful membership mobilisation on the basis of an adversarial ideology is likely to inhibit their *capacity* to act on this desire by significantly raising the costs of anti-unionism. In any case the alternative strategy of moderation, based on raising the benefits to the employer of staying (or becoming) unionised, has little to recommend it and runs the serious risk of eroding the only reliable foundation of unionism, the membership's willingness to act collectively against the employer.

QUALIFICATIONS

The first and most obvious qualification to the argument for union militancy is that unions are not free agents: the overall balance of power has shifted in the employers' favour, for economic, legal and other reasons. Even if a militant orientation on any or all of the five dimensions (Table 3.1) is thought desirable, it simply may not be feasible. The TGWU policy on employee involvement in new management techniques provides the text book illustration of constraints in action. In 1985 the TGWU adopted a policy of uncompromising hostility towards the emerging range of new management techniques, stressing their damaging impact on employee interests and their anti-union character (TGWU 1985). Union representatives were urged to oppose these techniques and avoid involvement in them. This position was tenable in settings where the union was well organised and powerful and where managements were half-hearted and divided over their initiatives. Where these conditions did not apply TGWU stewards faced a dilemma: should they defy union policy, get involved with management techniques and risk 'incorporation', or should they adhere to union policy, stay outside and risk marginalisation? (cf. Bacon and Storey, this volume). In the run-up to the 1987 and 1989 Delegate Conferences the issue was fought out between rival factions of the union and the result was a revised edition of the union's pamphlet which took a distinctly less hostile approach.

This example shows that external constraints and pressures on unions may force a change in policy despite the preferences of the union's own leaders. It could also be used to argue that it is not sensible for unions to choose between militancy and moderation in general because they must tailor their orientations to specific situations. In other words a contingent and pragmatic response is required, not an all-embracing and dogmatic choice. Every union negotiator would accept that there is a case for pragmatism and recognise the necessity to adjust general policies to particular situations (Kelly and Heery 1994). But there is a distinction between policy-*neutral* contingency and policy-*based* contingency. In the former, each case is decided on its merits and the union has no preference either for militancy or moderation, though its officers are likely to have minimal outcome criteria such as preservation of bargaining relationships. On the other hand, it is perfectly feasible to adopt a strong orientation (let us say towards militancy) and recognise that the application of the policy in concrete settings may prove difficult and that compromises may be unavoidable. Even if a union does compromise on a policy of refusing to negotiate on certain new management techniques, it can still retain an ideology of antagonism towards the employer and preserve the capacity to mobilise its members for industrial action. Policy-based contingency dictates that you pursue a parti- cular orientation whenever you can and implies that one orientation (say, militancy) is positively valued over and above the alternative (of moderation).

CONCLUSIONS

Labour–management co-operation has been at the centre of trade union agendas for the past fifteen years across the capitalist world (see contributions in Regini 1992). In Britain the proposals have taken a variety of forms from the new realism of the TUC, through the new-style deals of the EETPU and AEU, to social partnership and collaboration in HRM initiatives, and most recently to works councils as an adjunct to collective bargaining. Underlying the debates on these issues has been a dichotomy between militant and moderate trade unionism, a distinction that is useful provided we use the terms clearly. I therefore defined the militancy–moderation axis along five analytically separate dimensions, *viz.*, goals, membership resources, institutional resources, methods (industrial action) and ideology. This conceptualisation allows us to envisage different forms of militancy and moderation and to recognise that the distinctiveness of unions like the EETPU and the NUM lies in the fact that they were (and are) moderate and militant respectively on all five dimensions set out in Table 3.1.

Evaluation of the arguments for moderation and militancy showed that the gains from moderation were meagre, whether measured by membership increases or union influence, and in any case were not significantly greater than the results of more traditional policies involving militancy. Indeed, the more radical forms of moderation can seriously weaken trade unions, and leave them vulnerable to employers' attacks, because they erode both the willingness and the capacity of members to resist and to challenge employer demands. Ideologies of partnership and co-operation can damage the perception of conflicting interests, although the evidence on this point suggests that such perceptions are deep-seated and actually very difficult to erode (Kelly and Kelly 1991). Reliance on employer sponsorship and co-operation with consultative and advisory institutions can weaken or inhibit the growth of workplace union organisation and of any capacity to mobilise the union's membership for action against the employer. Advocates of moderate unionism have seriously underestimated the antagonism of employers to union presence, to union organisation at the place of work and to collective bargaining. For many employers, unionism stands in the way of the 'reassertion of their prerogatives' (Purcell 1991) and the continued restoration of profitability, often at the expense of workers' terms and conditions of employment. Hence the steadily growing tide of derecognition, resistance to new recognition, marginalisation of shop stewards and contraction of the scope of collective bargaining.

Militant unionism, as defined in this chapter, embodies a recognition of the antagonism of interests between workers and employers of which these various actions are the latest expressions. Consequently, militant trade unionism quite rightly seeks to defend the right to strike and to maintain the willingness and capacity of the membership to take collective action. Trade unionism without these attributes depends on employers and the state for its survival, whereas militant trade unionism builds on the only reliable foundation, namely its membership and their willingness to act. Militant trade unionism does not preclude collective bargaining relations with employers, nor for that matter is it incompatible with political exchange with governments. It can take different forms according to circumstances and therefore embodies an element of contingency. Ultimately it is sustained by the hostility of employers to independent trade unionism and by the antgonistic interests of workers and employers, an antagonism that pervades even ostensibly joint-interest issues such as training and equal opportunities.

ACKNOWLEDGEMENTS

I would like to thank the following people for helpful comments on a first draft of this chapter: Paul Smith, John Storey and Alan Tuckman.

NOTES

1 The EETPU merged with the AEU in 1992 and the new union – AEEU – was readmitted to the TUC in September 1993 after its expulsion in 1988.
2 Peter Fairbrother's 'theory of union renewal' operates with an apparently similar distinction, between militancy and accommodation, but the stress in his work is very strongly on the structure of union organisation (or what he calls the 'form'), conceived as three-dimensional: centralised–decentralised, hierarchical–non-hierarchical, reformist–non-reformist. It is true that some of the literature on social movements has hypothesised a connection between organisational structure and organisational goals (see Ferree 1992: 45–7), but other dimensions of collective action – goals, methods and ideology – have received as much attention as organisational structure. It is also true

that in practice Fairbrother's case studies often involve concrete discussions of union goals, mobilisation for action and ideological debates amongst activists about relations with management. So whilst Fairbrother's explicit theory has a structural bias that I do not share, his implicit theory, evident in his texts, appears to be much closer in content to the five-dimensional framework laid out here (see Fairbrother 1990; this volume; Fairbrother and Waddington 1990).

3 The labels of militant and moderate can be applied to unions as a whole but also to super-union bodies (federations) and to intra-union bodies (factions, regions, etc.).

4 While militancy is often taken to entail 'adversarial industrial relations', management also has a part to play in shaping the character of relations with its unions and workers. It is also important to stress that militant unions do have bargaining relations with management and do seek to reach agreements.

5 Characterising the industrial politics of the old EETPU is far from straightforward because outside the well-publicised greenfield sites and single-union deals, the EETPU organises some very traditional and fairly militant manual workers (see Lloyd 1990).

6 Overall density will be particularly depressed by low density in large establishments such as the 30 per cent figure for Nissan's Washington plant in a workforce of about 3,000 (Garrahan and Stewart 1992).

7 According to WIRS3 management were hostile to unions in just 31 per cent of private-sector non-union establishments in 1990, a figure which led the authors to conclude that, 'management antipathy cannot be the major reason for over a third of private sector workplaces having no union members' (Millward *et al.* 1992: 69). How can this claim be reconciled with ACAS data? The vast majority of non-union firms have had little or no experience of trade unionism. According to WIRS3, only 12 per cent reported union recruitment activity in the past six years, so managerial attitudes to unions are likely to be fairly general and not formed in the context of union recruitment activity. The important question is what do managers think about unions when they are actually faced by a union organising their employees and about to demand recognition? On that question the ACAS data should be taken as a more reliable guide.

8 This growing hostility to collective bargaining was foreshadowed some years ago in a pamphlet by the influential right-wing think tank, the Institute of Economic Affairs. The authors proposed the abolition of all legal protection for strikes and urged the replacement of collective bargaining and collective agreements by individual contracts, reducing unions to the status of friendly societies (Hanson and Mather 1988).

9 Oliver and Wilkinson (1992: 258) claimed that the use of temporary workers was more common amongst large British manufacturing companies than amongst their Japanese sample, contrary to the claim of Millward *et al.* But Oliver and Wilkinson's figures are based on *national* surveys of large companies which produced very low response rates – 18 per cent in 1987 and 14 per cent in 1991 – so the

WIRS3 data, based on an 83 per cent response rate, is to be preferred (Millward *et al.* 1992: 376).

10 American data show that even when employers involved in 'labour–management co-operation' do offer guarantees of employment (and many have refused to do so: Schuster 1985), there are plenty of loopholes in the agreements. When sales volume declined or employment security funds ran out, the big three car companies, for instance, were no longer bound by their employment security guarantees (Turner 1991: 87–8). There is now a considerable critical literature on the broader impact of new management techniques on American workers see Fucini and Fucini 1990, Parker 1985, Parker and Slaughter 1988, Yates 1992, Wells 1987).

REFERENCES

ACAS (1988) *Annual Report 1987*, London: Advisory, Conciliation and Arbitration Service.

Adeney, M. and Lloyd, J. (1986) *The Miners' Strike 1984–5: Loss without Limit*, London: Routledge & Kegan Paul.

Allen, V. L. (1966) *Militant Trade Unionism*, London: Merlin.

Bach, S. (1994) 'The Working Environment', in K. Sisson (ed.), *Personnel Management: A Comprehensive Guide to Theory and Practice in Britain*, 2nd edn, Oxford: Blackwell.

Bassett, P. (1986) *Strike Free: New Industrial Relations in Britain*, London: Macmillan.

Batstone, E., Boraston, I. and Frenkel, S. (1978) *The Social Organisation of Strikes*, Oxford: Blackwell.

Beaumont, P. B. (1991) 'Trade Unions and HRM', *Industrial Relations Journal* **22**, 4: 300–8.

Beaumont, P. B. (1992) *Public Sector Industrial Relations*, London: Routledge.

Blanchflower, D. G. and Freeman, R. B. (1992) 'Unionism in the United States and Other Advanced OECD Countries', in M. F. Bognanno and M. M. Kleiner (eds), *Labour Market Institutions and the Future Role of Unions*, Cambridge, Mass.: Blackwell.

Blyton, P. (1994) 'Working Hours', in K. Sisson (ed.), *Personnel Management: A Comprehensive Guide to Theory and Practice in Britain*, 2nd edn, Oxford: Blackwell.

Blyton, P. and Turnbull, P. (1994) *The Dynamics of Employee Relations*, London: Macmillan.

Brown, W. (1993) 'The Contraction of Collective Bargaining in Britain', *British Journal of Industrial Relations* **31**, 2: 189–200.

Burchill, F. and Seifert, R. (1993) 'Professional Unions in the National Health Service: Membership Trends and Issues', Paper for the Cardiff Business School Conference, 'Unions on the Brink', 28 September.

Cave, A. (1994) *Managing Change in the Workplace: New Approaches to Employee Relations*, London: Kogan Page.

Certification Office *Annual Reports*, 1980, 1987, 1992, 1993.

Claydon, T. (1989) 'Union Derecognition in Britain in the 1980s', *British Journal of Industrial Relations* **27**, 2: 214–24.

Coates, K. and Topham, T. (1986) *Trade Unions and Politics*, Oxford: Blackwell.

Cronin, J. E. (1979) *Industrial Conflict in Modern Britain*, London: Croom Helm.

Crouch, C. (1986) 'The Future Prospects for Trade Unions in Western Europe', *Political Quarterly* **57**, 1: 5–17.

Darlington, R. (1993) 'The Challenge to Workplace Unionism in the Royal Mail', *Employee Relations* **15**, 5: 3–25.

Dickens, L. (1994) 'Wasted Resources? Equal Opportunities in Employment', in K. Sisson (ed.), *Personnel Management: A Comprehensive Guide to Theory and Practice in Britain*, 2nd edn, Oxford: Blackwell.

Dunn, S. (1990) 'Root Metaphor in the Old and New Industrial Relations', *British Journal of Industrial Relations* **28**, 1: 1–31.

Dunn, S. (1993) 'From Donovan to . . . Wherever', *British Journal of Industrial Relations* **31**, 2: 169–87.

Edmonds, J. (1994) 'Trade Unions: At Last the Revolution Begins', Paper to BUIRA Conference, Oxford, 1–3 July.

Edwardes, M. (1983) *Back from the Brink*, London: Collins.

Edwards, P. K. and Whitson, C. (1991) 'Workers are Working Harder: Effort and Shop-floor Relations in the 1980s', *British Journal of Industrial Relations* **29**, 4: 593–601.

Edwards, R. (1993) *Rights at Work: Employment Relations in the Post-union Era*, Washington: Brookings Institution.

Fairbrother, P. (1990) 'The Contours of Local Trade Unionism in a Period of Restructuring', in P. Fosh and E. Heery (eds), *Trade Unions and their Members*, London: Macmillan.

Fairbrother, P. and Waddington, J. (1990) 'The Politics of Trade Unionism: Evidence, Policy and Theory', *Capital and Class* **41**: 15–56.

Fantasia, R. (1988) *Cultures of Solidarity: Consciousness, Action, and Contemporary American Workers*, Berkeley: University of California Press.

Ferree, M. M. (1992) 'The Political Context of Rationality: Rational Choice Theory and Resource Mobilization', in A. D. Morris and C. M. Mueller (eds), *Frontiers in Social Movement Theory*, New Haven, Conn: Yale University Press.

Fucini, J. and Fucini, S. (1990) *Working for the Japanese: Inside Mazda's American Auto Plant*, New York: Free Press.

Gall, G. (1993a) 'What Happened to Single Union Deals?', *Industrial Relations Journal* **24**, 1: 71–75.

Gall, G. (1993b) 'Unions not Beyond all Recognition', *Labour Research* **82**, 9: 15–16.

Gall, G. and McKay, S. (1994) 'Trade Union Derecognition in Britain 1988–94', *British Journal of Industrial Relations* **32**, 3: 433–48.

Garrahan, P. and Stewart, P. (1992) *The Nissan Enigma: Flexibility at Work in a Local Economy*, London: Mansell.

Geroski, P., Gregg, P. and Desjonqueres, T. (1995) 'Did the Retreat of UK

Trade Unionism Accelerate during the 1990–1993 Recession?', *British Journal of Industrial Relations*, **33**, 1: 35–54.

Gilbert, R. (1993) 'Workplace Industrial Relations 25 Years after Donovan: An Employer View', *British Journal of Industrial Relations* **31**, 2: 235–53.

GMB/UCW (1990) *New Agenda: Bargaining for Prosperity in the 1990s*, London: General, Municipal and Boilermakers' Union and the Union of Communication Workers.

Golden, M. (1995) *Heroic Defeats: The Politics of Job Losses*, in press.

Grant, D. (1993) 'New Style Agreements at Japanese Transplants in the UK', Paper for the Cardiff Business School Conference, 'Unions on the Brink', 28 September.

Grunberg, L. (1983) 'The Effects of the Social Relations of Production on Productivity and Workers' Safety: An Ignored Set of Relationships', *International Journal of Health Services* **13**, 4: 621–34.

Grunberg, L. (1986) 'Workplace Relations in the Economic Crisis: A Comparison of a British and a French Automobile Plant', *Sociology* **20**, 4: 503–29.

Guest, D. (1989) 'Human Resource Management: Its Implications for Industrial Relations and Trade Unions', in J. Storey (ed.), *New Perspectives on Human Resource Management*, London: Routledge.

Hanson, C. G. and Mather, G. (1988) *Striking Out Strikes*, London: Institute of Economic Affairs.

Heckscher, C. (1988) *The New Unionism*, New York: Basic Books.

Higgs, F. (1994a) 'Briefing Report on Shell Haven UK', in House of Commons Employment Committee Third Report, *The Future of Trade Unions*.Volume 11, Minutes of Evidence, 154–5, London: HMSO.

Higgs, F. (1994b) 'HRM at Cadbury's' *Labour Research*, **83**, 12: 24.

Keep, E. (1994) 'Vocational Education and Training for the Young', in K. Sisson (ed.), *Personnel Management: A Comprehensive Guide to Theory and Practice in Britain*, 2nd edn, Oxford: Blackwell.

Kelley, M.R. and Harrison, B. (1992) 'Unions, Technology, and Labour–Management Cooperation', in L. Mishel and P. B. Voos (eds), *Unions and Economic Competitiveness*, New York: M. E. Sharpe.

Kelly, J. (1988) *Trade Unions and Socialist Politics*, London: Verso.

Kelly, J. and Heery, E. (1994) *Working for the Union: British Trade Union Officers*, Cambridge: Cambridge University Press.

Kelly, J. and Kelly, C. (1991) '"Them and Us": Social Psychology and "the New Industrial Relations"', *British Journal of Industrial Relations* **29**, 1: 25–48.

Kern, H. and Sabel, C. F. (1992) 'Trade Unions and Decentralized Production: A Sketch of Strategic Problems in the German Labour Movement', in M. Regini (ed.), *The Future of Labour Movements*, London: Sage.

Kerr, A. and Sachdev, S. (1992) 'Third among Equals: An Analysis of the 1989 Ambulance Dispute', *British Journal of Industrial Relations* **30**, 1: 127–43.

Kessler, I. (1995) 'Reward Systems', in J. Storey (ed.), *HRM: A Critical Text*, London: Routledge.

Kessler, S. and Bayliss, F. (1992) *Contemporary British Industrial Relations*, London: Macmillan.

Kochan, T. A., Katz, H. C. and McKersie, R. B. (1986) *The Transformation of American Industrial Relations*, New York: Basic Books.

Leadbeater, C. (1987) 'Unions go to Market', *Marxism Today* **31**, 9: 22–7.

Lloyd, J. (1986) 'The Sparks are Flying', *Marxism Today* **30**, 3: 12–17.

Lloyd, J. (1990) *Light and Liberty: The History of the Electrical, Electronic, Telecommunications and Plumbing Union*, London: Weidenfeld & Nicolson.

McCarthy, W. (1988) *The Future of Industrial Democracy*, London: Fabian Society Tract 526.

MacGregor, I. (1986) *The Enemies Within: The Story of the Miners' Strike 1984–5*, London: Fontana.

Marchington, M. and Parker, P. (1990) *Changing Patterns of Employee Relations*, Hemel Hempstead: Harvester Wheatsheaf.

Martin, R. (1989) *Trade Unionism: Purposes and Forms*, Oxford: Clarendon.

Martinez Lucio, M. and Weston, S. (1992) 'Human Resource Management and Trade Union Responses: Bringing the Politics of the Workplace back into the Debate', in P. Blyton and P. Turnbull (eds), *Reassessing Human Resource Management*, London: Sage.

Metcalf, D., Wadsworth, J. and Ingram, P. (1993) 'Do Strikes Pay?', in D. Metcalf and S. Milner (eds), *New Perspectives on Industrial Disputes*, London: Routledge.

Millward, N. (1994) *The New Industrial Relations?*, London: Policy Studies Institute.

Millward, N., Stevens, M., Smart, D. and Hawes, W. R. (1992) *Workplace Industrial Relations in Transition*, Aldershot: Dartmouth.

Milne, S. (1994) *The Enemy Within: MI5, Maxwell, and the Scargill Affair*, London: Verso.

Milner, S. (1993) 'Dispute Deterrence: Evidence on Final-offer Arbitration', in D. Metcalf and S. Milner (eds), *New Perspectives on Industrial Disputes*, London: Routledge.

Milner, S. (1995) 'The Coverage of Collective Pay-setting Institutions in Great Britain, 1895–1990', *British Journal of Industrial Relations* **33**, 1: 69–91.

Monks, J. (1993) 'A Trade Union View of WIRS3', *British Journal of Industrial Relations* **31**, 2: 227–33.

Muller-Jentsch, W. (1985) 'Trade Unions as Intermediary Organizations', *Economic and Industrial Democracy* **6**: 3–33.

Muller-Jentsch, W. (1988) 'Industrial Relations Theory and Trade Union Strategy', *International Journal of Comparative Labour Law and Industrial Relations* **4**, 3: 179–90.

NCU Journal (1993) April, May, June.

Nichols, T. (1991) 'Labour Intensification, Work Injuries and the Measurement of Percentage Utilization of Labour', *British Journal of Industrial Relations* **29**, 4: 569–92.

O'Connell Davidson, J. (1993) *Privatization and Employment Relations: The Case of the Water Industry*, London: Mansell.

Offe, C. and Wiesenthal, H. (1985) 'Two Logics of Collective Action', in C. Offe, *Disorganized Capitalism*, Oxford: Polity.

Oliver, N. and Wilkinson, B. (1992) *The Japanization of British Industry*, 2nd edn, Oxford: Blackwell.

Parker, M. (1985) *Inside The Circle: A Union Guide to QWL*, Boston: Southend Press.

Parker, M. and Slaughter, J. (1988) *Choosing Sides: Unions and the Team Concept*, Boston: Southend Press.

Purcell, J. (1991) 'The Rediscovery of the Management Prerogative: The Management of Labour Relations in the 1980s', *Oxford Review of Economic Policy* **7**, 1: 33–43.

Rainbird, H. (1994) 'Continuing Training', in K. Sisson (ed.) *Personnel Management: A Comprehensive Guide to Theory and Practice in Britain*, 2nd edn, Oxford: Blackwell.

Regini, M. (ed.) (1992) *The Future of Labour Movements*, London: Sage.

Richardson, R. and Rubin, M. (1993) 'The Shorter Working Week in Engineering: Surrender without Sacrifice?', in D. Metcalf and S. Milner (eds), *New Perspectives on Industrial Disputes*, London: Routledge.

Rico, L. (1987) 'The Electricians' New-style Agreements', *Industrial and Labour Relations Review* **41**, 1: 63–78.

Schuster, M. (1985) 'Models of Co-operation and Change in Union Settings', *Industrial Relations* **24**: 382–94.

Smith, P. and Morton, G. (1993) 'Union Exclusion and the Decollectivization of Industrial Relations in Contemporary Britain', *British Journal of Industrial Relations* **31**, 1: 97–114.

Smith, P. and Morton, G. (1994) 'Union Exclusion in Britain – Next Steps', *Industrial Relations Journal* **25**, 1: 3–14.

Stagner, R. and Eflal, B. (1982) 'Internal Union Dynamics during a Strike: A Quasi-experimental Study', *Journal of Applied Psychology* **67**: 37–44.

Storey, J. (1992) *Developments in the Management of Human Resources*, Oxford: Blackwell.

Storey, J. and Sisson, K. (1993) *Managing Human Resources and Industrial Relations*, Buckingham: Open University Press.

Streeck, W. (1992) 'Training and the New Industrial Relations: A Strategic Role for Unions?', in M. Regini (ed.), *The Future of Labour Movements*, London: Sage.

Taylor, R. (1993) *The Trade Union Question in British Politics*, Oxford: Blackwell.

Taylor, R. (1994) *The Future of the Trade Unions*, London: André Deutsch.

TGWU (1985, 1989) *Employee Involvement and Quality Circles*, London: Transport and General Workers' Union.

Towers, B. (1989) 'Running the Gauntlet: British Trade Unions under Thatcher 1979–1988', *Industrial and Labour Relations Review* **42**, 2: 163–88.

TUC (1984) *TUC Strategy*, London: Trades Union Congress.

TUC (1991) *Towards 2000*, London: Trades Union Congress.

TUC (1994a) *Human Resource Management: A Trade Union Response*, London: Trades Union Congress.

TUC (1994b) *Employee Representation*, London: Trades Union Congress.

Turnbull, P., Woolfson, C. and Kelly, J. (1992) *Dock Strike: Conflict and Restructuring in Britain's Ports*, Aldershot: Avebury.

Turner, L. (1991) *Democracy at Work: Changing World Markets and the Future of Labor Unions*, Ithaca, N.Y.: Cornell University Press.

Undy, R., Ellis, V., McCarthy, W. E. J. and Halmos, A. M. (1981) *Change in Trade Unions*, London: Hutchinson.

Wells, D. M. (1987) *Empty Promises: Quality of Working Life Programs and the Labor Movement*, New York: Monthly Review Press.

Yates, C. (1992) 'North American Autoworkers' Response to Restructuring', in M. Golden and J. Pontusson (eds), *Bargaining for Change: Union Politics in North America and Europe*, Ithaca, N.Y.: Cornell University Press.

4

WORKPLACE TRADE UNIONISM IN THE STATE SECTOR

Peter Fairbrother

INTRODUCTION

The state is the major employer in Britain, comprising three principal components, the civil service, local authorities and the health service. In each of these areas during the 1980s, successive Conservative governments initiated a major restructuring and re-organisation, which in the case of the civil service has been transformed from a traditional bureaucracy to a managerial employer (Fairbrother 1994). A range of policies have been introduced aimed at challenging the uniform and standardised conditions of civil service work and employment, not least to remove the basis for collective organisation and action by civil service workers. Management structures and approaches have been recast in terms of the mirage of human resource management and customer care. Equally dramatic changes have been introduced in the local authority and health care sector, where governments have placed legislative requirements on service delivery, achieving a move towards more decentralised and devolved forms of managerial organisation. In the case of local authorities this has not only meant increased budgetary restrictions and restraint but also resulted in the modification of the previously department-based and consensual bargaining relationships.

It is in this context that unions in the state sector face a crisis, where these traditionally centralised and hierarchical unions have proved inadequate in the late 1980s and 1990s. This is a form of unionism where the workplace has not been the prime focus of concern, either organisationally or in terms of policy formulation and initiative (Drake *et al.* 1980). Nonetheless, these were relatively effective forms of unionism which in the 1960s and 1970s seemed to make some gains

110

(Undy *et al.* 1981; Fairbrother 1989). The problem they now face is that as managerial devolution and decentralisation have proceeded, in both privatised and non-privatised areas and with the associated introduction of market-type relationships, there has been a shift in the locus of bargaining from the national to local level (although not yet on pay, Bach and Winchester 1994). In general, unions are ill-equipped to meet these changed circumstances of bargaining and negotiation, and the associated shifts in the exercise of managerial power in these sectors.

THE ARGUMENT

It is the argument of this chapter that unions in the state sector are in a position to begin to develop more active forms of workplace unionism than was the case in the past. The occasion for this has come about with the massive restructuring that has taken place in this sector, as well as the ongoing disillusionment with the pros-pect or benefit of national bargaining. With moves towards more decentralised forms of management, union members have taken tentative steps to generate more participative and active forms of unionism. This, however, is not a straightforward or inevitable process, being the subject of debate and contest about the best way to proceed in circumstances of uncertainty and unpredictability. Nonetheless, where union members exploit these structural cir-cumstances, there is the prospect that a process of union renewal will occur (Fairbrother 1989, 1991).

The argument about union renewal is not straightforward. A narrow version of the argument is that the restructuring of the public sector, towards decentralised and devolved managerial structures, provides the conditions for a resurgence or a discovery of local trade unionism and a frisson of local activity where there was none previously (Fosh 1993). This argument is developed by pointing to the way that there may be 'surges' of membership involvement in workplace trade unionism according 'to the impact of events or developments that disturb the local union context' (*ibid.*: 580–1). Such developments include 'changes taking place in management–union relations, changes in the wider political situa-tion or changes within the union itself' (*ibid.*: 581). The impact of such occurrences is, according to Fosh, 'mediated by several factors such as local leadership style, industrial relations atmos-phere, past experience of the workplace union and structure of the local union' (*ibid*), with most emphasis being given to leadership style. This is further developed to elaborate the features of such a leadership style, drawing attention to the collectivist and participatory aspects as critical to the process of union renewal, although overlooking political affiliation and involvement (cf. Darlington 1994).

While this type of account opens up the question of union renewal, the aim of this chapter is to present a more general version of the union renewal thesis, suggesting that unions, particularly in the state sector, are changing both structurally and ideologically, with the development of new forms of unionism becoming a distinct possibility. These are forms of unionism where the emphasis is on decentralisation rather than centralisation, egalitarian forms of organisation and operation rather than hierarchy, and involvement and participation rather than passivity and remoteness. Although there is often an unevenness in the articulation of these features of participative unionism, they nonetheless constitute a set of practices which define the possibility of union renewal. In the development of such forms of unionism, leadership, as noted by Fosh (1993), may play a central role in articulating and expressing these developments, although this is neither a defining feature nor the limit of such change. What is critical is the emergence of participative forms of unionism in sectors of employment where there has been a long history of remote, centralised and hierarchical forms of unionism.

This is an emergent form of unionism, one that is beginning to appear in the context of changes in management, the organisation of work, different negotiating and bargaining arrangements, and a disaffection with past union forms. The logic of the argument is that a rearticulation of class relations in the state sector is taking place, with implications for managerial organisation and activity as well as unionism in these sectors. Taking management first, the restructuring associated with privatisation, the fragmentation of the state sector, market testing, competitive compulsory tendering, appraisal, and performance-related pay are part of repositioning of management in the state sector. In its starkest form, a 'new' management is in place, concerned with reshaping the state sector in a devolved and decentralised way and securing the compliance of workforces with these changes, where the stress is on individualism and individualised social relations. However, this is not a straightforward process, as established managers often require convincing of the need to change and more committed managers are recruited to replace the more intractable traditional managers. Further, these initiatives do not involve the individualisation of the social relations of production as such, but the attempt to reorganise collective workforces on an individualistic basis. This has involved the introduction of employment and work arrangements aimed at defining workers as individuals rather than as part of a collective. It is thus a complicated and uneven process of change.[1]

The other side of the analysis is the framework of issues addressed by Hyman (1989: 149–65, 166–87), with his emphasis on the ongoing tension between bureaucratisation and democratisation. For him, bureaucracy comprises three sets of fragile, although ingrained relations: the separation of representation from mobilisation; a hierarchy of control and activism; and the detachment of formal procedures of policy formulation and decision-making from members' experiences (pp. 181–2). Unfortunately, this can lead to a rather pessimistic account of the prospects of union renewal and recovery, suggesting an inevitability about the persistence of bureaucratic relations (Heery and Kelly 1994: 16).[2] In contrast, without overlooking the validity of this analysis, it is argued in this chapter that in the circumstances of state restructuring there is a possibility of participatory forms of unionism emerging (see also Fairbrother and Waddington 1990: 47, n. 1).

This form of unionism has three aspects. First, this is a union form where there has been a reintegration of representations and the procedures associated with these relations, and that of mobilisation. In other words, representatives become part of the process of membership mobilisation as active participants. Second, unions embody more participatory forms of control and accountability, which emphasise the importance of membership involvement and activity. This means that local members can and do take decisions on issues and topics which directly concern their immediate work and employment relations, such as staff levels, cancer screening, or racism in the local community. Third, members articulate and express their experiences in ways that are central to the union mode of organisation and operation. Primacy is thus given to procedures whereby members participate in decision-making and policy-formulation, most obviously via the membership meeting, which becomes the leitmotif of union activity. More broadly, this may involve consultations with workplace stewards or other union leaders, membership surveys, conferences, and the like.

In the context of restructuring, with the fragmentation and decentralisation of management, the development of more participatory social relations of union organisation remains only a possibility, since union renewal takes place not only against the backdrop of restructuring but also in terms of the previously established centralised and hierarchical forms of unionism that characterise the state sector. The result is that it is not at all obvious how and under what circumstances members can begin to review their unionism, and decide on the different alternatives they now face. This in turn requires a reconsideration of their past unionism, their own involvement, position and activity (Darlington 1994: 260–92). It also involves a re-examination of the complex interaction of relationships between full-time officers, workplace representatives and members and what they might mean in a reconstituted union (Darlington 1994: 285–90; Kelly and Heery 1994: 114–16).

One neglected aspect of the way in which unions may begin to change and develop new forms of unionism is the importance of political affiliation and involvement of union members. In many accounts, it is almost as if there is a bland assumption that trade unionists are 'naturally' supporters of the Labour Party and nothing more need be said or that political affiliation always takes second place to the pragmatics of unionism and for this reason also requires little comment. This, however, misses the point that not only do members debate unionism and how it may develop, but they also look to their politics in developing approaches and understandings of their current situation. It also raises the question how should politics be understood and made part of an understanding of trade unionism. One way has been to suggest that political parties provide both the ligaments of cohesiveness between different workplace memberships and a framework for understanding the way changes can be achieved (Darlington 1994: 291–2). The social democratic version of this relation is that the political party (the Labour Party in Britain) becomes the partner of a trade union movement preoccupied with 'economic' issues while other parties become an irrelevancy, particularly the so-called revolutionary parties (Flanders 1970: 24–37). Even so, an understanding of the processes of union renewal require a direct engagement and consideration of the politics of trade unionism.

This chapter explores the dimensions of union renewal in the state sector through a detailed study of workplace unionism over the last three years as it is here that the crisis is most evident, where workers face the reality of meeting the challenges of the 1990s. The focus of the chapter is the public services, examining a number of branches of the National and Local Government Officers' Association (NALGO) and the National Union of Public Employees (NUPE), located in local government, specifically social services,[3] and the two main unions in the civil service Benefits Agency, the Civil and Public Services Association (CPSA) and the National Union of Civil and Public Servants (NUCPS). This is followed by an account of the ways in which managements have attempted to reinforce their control over production relations, thereby marginalising previous forms of workplace union organisation. How local union leaderships have attempted to meet these threats is then examined; the conclusion is that where unions have addressed the crisis of organisational representation there are indications that more innovative and imaginative forms of unionism are beginning to emerge.[4]

RESTRUCTURING

The conditions and circumstances under which unions operate changed decisively during the 1980s. A state-initiated restructuring of work and employment relations, supported by increasingly restrictive trade union legislation and the deregulation of employment law, has cumulatively recast employment relations in both the public and private sectors 'to deny workers access to resources of collective power' (Smith and Morton 1993: 100). A key aspect of the programme has been a reorganisation of the structures of management within the workplace and at a local level. In both local government and the civil service there has been a major decentralisation of operational managerial activities, as well as financial responsibilities, to the base unit of these bodies, such as the local district or office. This decentralisation of day-to-day operations has occurred within the framework of budgetary control and strategic decision-making at a corporate or headquarters level. It has involved the introduction and use of increasingly complicated financial indicators and controls.

The reforms in the state sector are part of a deliberate attempt to construct a market order, which has been accompanied by decisive shifts in the terrain of trade unionism (Stewart and Walsh 1992; Smith and Morton 1993: 98–9). There are three main aspects to this new 'order'. First, there has been a process of establishing

so-called 'internal markets', taking the form of procedures concerned with the separation of purchasers/clients and providers of
these services, the exchange of goods and services involving
monetary transactions, and the imposition of budgetary controls
and accounting procedures (on the health service see Reed and
Anthony 1993; on the civil service, see Greer 1994, Chapter 5; on
local government, see Cochrane 1993). Second, the boundaries of
the state sector have been redrawn via the policies of privatisation,
compulsory competitive tendering of state services, particularly in
local government, and market testing of sectors of state activity,
particularly in central government (Kessler 1991; O'Connell
Davidson 1993; Fairbrother 1994). Third, there have been concerted attempts to abolish the national determination of the terms
and conditions of employment in the state sector, with a view to
diluting standardised and uniform arrangements across substantial
areas of state-sector employment (Kessler 1989; Brown and Walsh
1991; Bailey 1994; Bach and Winchester 1994).

The autonomy of local management created by this restructuring is
circumscribed within clearly defined and prescribed parameters. This
involves both explicit and much more subtle processes of control, as
in multi-divisional corporations (Marginson *et al.* 1993). On the one
hand, there has been an overt and public decentralisation and
devolution of managerial authority throughout the state sector. This
has taken the form of reorganising management structures, so that
management have control over their budgets and are seen to be
responsible for the operational activities within their remit. On the
other hand, there has been a much more insidious and comprehensive reaffirmation of central control over the state sector. This has
been achieved via managerial systems and accounting procedures
which set limits on what is permitted, such as budget controls and
accountability. The point of these procedures is that they are part of
an attempt to structure relations in ways that achieve managerial and
government objectives. In this respect, moves towards performance-
related pay and the like become part of a raft of procedures for
achieving the compliance of workforces with managerial objectives.

The restructuring of the last decade, underpinned by state
policies, has resulted in a shift in the circumstances of union
organisation and operation, particularly at a local level. While the
precise form of the restructuring was driven by managements'
attempts to exploit market and technological imperatives, one
condition for the successful implementation of these policies was

a compliant workforce. It is in this sense that managerial policies were also aimed at both restricting the scope of union activity and denying workers ready access to collective power. In view of the different ways that unions organise as well as the locus of activity within unions, the challenges of the 1980s and 1990s have been responded to and experienced in different ways.

Local government: social services

There has been a move by central governments to extend their control over the organisation and operation of local government administration and provision of state services, and there has been a steady centralisation of control within local government structures (Bains Report 1972; Pattison Report 1973; Scottish Office 1977; Department of Environment and Welsh Office 1977; Department of Environment 1979; Exchequer and Audit Department 1981; Griffiths Report 1988). This has been accompanied by a shift in the forms of control in local government, from an explicitly administrative mode of organisation to more managerialist-based approaches to control. Over the last two decades, the administrative model of control has been qualified with the introduction of measures more typically associated with the private sector, such as personal appraisal, performance-related pay, and the reorganisation of work procedures so that financial costs are taken more explicitly into account. While this has been an uneven process, the general thrust of change has been towards the establishment of a managerial model of local government.

These recent developments are signified most clearly by the establishment of centralised structures for policy formulation as well as the organisation of local state work into managerially accountable departments, organised along functional lines (Cockburn 1977; Cochrane 1993). For manual workforces, as noted by Terry (1982), the early changes were accompanied by attempts to regulate and control the organisation of work, through such measures as work study and job evaluation. More recently, the emphasis has been on the decentralisation of line management and the introduction of managerial approaches associated with consultation rather than negotiation (Kessler 1991). Overall, the result has been a restructured local government organisation and operation.

These developments have been reflected in the social services departments within the two local authorities studied (see Table 4.1).

Table 4.1 Two social services departments compared

	Metropolitan council	County council
The councils		
Area	Metropolitan City	Rural: 764.37 square miles
Political control	Labour Party	Conservative Party
Largest services	Education, housing, social services	Education, social services, planning and transport
Social services		
Numbers (full-time equivalent)	6,666.1	1,487.5
Number of workplaces	250	102

In each authority, the workforce is principally organised in terms of departments, under the formal responsibility of a chief executive or director. The social services department is one of the major departments in each authority, with social services workforces spread over numerous workplaces, employed in such diverse places as children's homes, elderly persons' homes, social welfare centres, day nurseries and nursery centres, adult social education centres, social work teams, home care and central administrative activity. Over the last two years a number of these areas have become part of the private service sector, as these councils have relinquished control of residential homes for the elderly, under legislation requiring compulsory competitive tendering (Local Government Act 1988).

The major recent policy development in social services, with widespread implications for trade unionism, is the community care legislation and reorganisation. The first objective of this move has been 'to give clients a better quality of life in a less institutionalised environment', while the second objective is 'to achieve lower costs in service provision' (CIPFA 1989: 32). This policy has been subject to reviews, in particular by the National Audit Office and the Griffiths Report (1988). After some delay in responding to this, the government endorsed the broad principle that local authorities should have the primary responsibility for the co-ordination of social service provision (except for the mentally ill), although this will involve a wider range of agencies than local government.

Alongside this, there remains uncertainty about the extent to which there will be a shift of financial and related resources to local government to enable it to carry out these tasks (CIPFA 1989: 33).

The thrust of these changes, particularly in community care, has been to transform the character of social services work away from the provision of services to the administration and co-ordination of care work. This has involved a split between the purchaser and provider relation in social service work, under the community care legislation of the early 1990s (Child Care Act 1992). Overall, this has been part of a process of reorganisation whereby the provision of social services has been costed and financially evaluated, irrespective of the form of organisation, as neighbourhood centres or as support teams. This has reinforced managerial supervision, as managers themselves have been made more accountable for expenditure. These developments have had a major effect on the way in which work is organised in two respects. First, there has been a separation of assessment work from the provision of services and support. One consequence has been a move towards the provision of social educational services for adults and children by contract from local schools and colleges rather than from within the resources of the social services department. Second, care management divisions have been made coterminous with relevant health authorities. This also means new managerial structures and work relationships, with the aim being, in the phrase frequently used in the county council, 'to provide a mixed economy of care'.

These developments are part of a comprehensive restructuring of the provision of social services in both authorities, grounding decisions much more explicitly on financial grounds than in terms of social needs. This represents the beginnings of a rejection of Fordist methods of administration (Cochrane 1993). Previously the state individualised the provision of services, such as the entitlement to social service support, through centralised and hierarchical forms of organisation, on the assumption of standardised solutions to general problems. The problem with this approach is that the standardisation of work leads to routinised performance and conservatism; those who process claims and distribute entitlement have little or no responsibility for decision-making. Such procedures became an impediment to attempts to reduce and control public expenditure, and it is within this framework that governments during the 1980s sought to create the situation where managers became responsible for the delivery of services. Under the guise of individual responsibility, managers and their workforces were given the responsibility for the allocation of restricted resources. This required the development of managerial hierarchies in the workplace which would ensure decision-making according to financial criteria, not social need. It also required the organisation of work procedures and employment relations so that managers were in a position to ensure compliance with these procedures.

The Benefits Agency in the civil service

The developments in local government both anticipate and parallel the restructuring that has taken place in the civil service. During the 1980s and into the 1990s the civil service was transformed from a centralised bureaucracy, with standardised procedures and terms and conditions of employment, into a managerial administrative service, composed of a set of agencies (semi-autonomous managerial units) and small policy-making and supervisory departments. The governments of this period laid the grounds for this transformation through a series of reports which addressed different aspects of this process (HM Treasury 1984; Ibbs Report 1988; Fraser Report 1991; Cabinet Office 1994). As in local government, these reforms involved the decentralisation of management structures and the introduction of procedures designed to circumscribe and elicit compliance from civil service workforces.

Until well into the 1980s, the provision of social security was organised through a succession of departments, the most recent incarnation being the Department of Social Security (DSS), a typically centralised and hierarchical civil service department, under the responsibility of a Minister, advised by senior civil service staff. With the decision, in 1989, to establish agencies in the DSS – the Information Technology Services Agency, the Contributions Agency and subsequently the Benefits Agency – there was a planned process of change and reorganisation. In the case of the Benefits Agency, a new managerial structure was developed, comprising management personnel who had immediate responsibility for the provision of benefit services. The purpose was to remould the Benefits Agency in ways that signified a break from the past. As reported:

> the most important thing of all was to change ourselves from being a hierarchical bureaucratic organisation concerned

with our internal processes into one that actually began to think about everything from a customer point of view and customer perspective, so we did an awful lot of things right at the outset to get the customer focus right.

(senior manager, 1992)

This involved the redesignation of managerial responsibilities at a district level, with the creation of the post of customer service manager, as well as encouraging claimants to develop a customer's point of view.

The outcome of this process of change was a restructured service, drawing on commercial principles. As one informant observed: 'it's very much to do with having a sharper, more business, more commercial orientation and bringing in some kind of market principles' (senior manager, 1992). This ethos of change was embraced by those who planned the establishment of the Benefits Agency, and it was put into practice after the launch of the Agency in April 1991.

The key element in this restructuring was to enable a degree of discretion at a local level that hitherto had not been possible. As the Permanent Secretary of the DSS observed:

We have steadily delegated an enormous amount of tasks to them [District Managers] which they wanted to have, like local recruitment, the ability to run their own accommodation budget, repairs and things like that, the ability to organise their office. We have put them on a cash budget instead of a head count budget, so they have cash income and can deploy how many people in how many grades they want within the budget given to them. They have enormous freedoms.

(Social Security Committee 1991: 15, para. 8)

The ethos is to enable management to exercise power within the overall framework of a devolved and decentralised management structure.

The benefits offices are grouped into an area form of organisation, composed of District Management Units (DMUs). These units are organised hierarchically, typically with a District Manager and managerial support staff, and a graded workforce. The principle underlying this structure is that it allows larger numbers of benefit staff to be grouped together, thereby enabling a more comprehensive specialisation of task and service to be introduced (a Fordist mode of organisation in an oft-proclaimed post-Fordist world). These changes have heralded the reorganisation of local offices, involving elements of centralisation and devolution. On the one hand, offices were grouped together to create district offices, under the responsibility of a Principal Officer; on the other hand, senior staff were given greater discretion and responsibility for both staff and financial issues.

Each DMU is organised as a cost centre. This, at one and the same time, lays the foundation for a degree of financial independence that has been unusual in the former department, while also creating the conditions for variation between districts. Initially this has been reflected in a distinction between districts where managers have been willing to exercise their increased discretion, and those where managers have refused to accept responsibility for their own budget because they are unable to comply with the requirements indicated in them. This has led to a rather paradoxical development where the devolution of managerial responsibility has also led to increasing intervention from the area management as District Managers look for guidance on a range of issues for which they have acquired new responsibilities.

Implications

The implications of this restructuring of local government and the civil service for trade unions are threefold. First, there is a symmetry in the patterns of restructuring for both sectors, with marked decentralisation and devolution of managerial structures and practices. What is different between the two sectors is that the base unit of the managerial organisation and associated industrial relations is much smaller in the civil service than for local government. The DMU comprised two or three offices, depending on the locality, whereas the departments in the local authorities continued to cover large geographical areas. Nonetheless, in both cases a new devolved and decentralised structure has been established, with managers in a position to exercise a greater degree of discretion in the organisation and administration of the terms and conditions of work and employment in their respective areas of responsibility.

Second, managerial policies have been marked by an ambivalence in practice, although there have been relatively consistent and sustained attempts to individualise workforces.[5] The point is that while the initiative for this restructuring has come from the government and been embraced by sections within managerial groups, sometimes opportunistically, otherwise with a newly found conviction, it remains the case that there is division within the state sector as managers commit themselves to the new while retaining elements of the old. Managements are not all of a piece and different approaches have been followed, some retaining elements of the previous more co-operative approaches while others see themselves more clearly as managers, not administrators providing public services (Stewart and Walsh 1992). For unions, this means that the terrain of change is not simply in one direction, without qualification.

Third, there is evidence of work reorganisation involving an intensification of effort and a fragmentation of tasks and procedures in these sectors; with implications for the way workers experience their employment and the way they look to their unions. This is most clearly evident in local government, with the separation of the purchaser and provider roles, but is also seen in both sectors with the introduction of contractual and semi-contractual work procedures and arrangements. This has been accompanied by the introduction of a range of employment measures associated with employee accountability and control, in the form of staff appraisal, 'merit' pay and the like. The result is the qualification of the hitherto standardised terms and conditions of employment, drawing attention to the specificity of employment and work relations, both at workplace level and in terms of specific employers. Thus the terrain of unionism, where unions in these sectors came to prominence with their defence of standardisation of work and employment relations, no longer has the relevance it had in the past.

UNION ORGANISATION

In the main, unions were founded as staff associations, recruiting from within specific grades, occupations or areas of work (on clerical unions in the civil service, see Humphreys 1958; on NALGO, see Spoor 1967; and more generally Waddington 1995). They tended to mirror the structure of management in terms of organisation and the way issues were examined and considered. With the establishment of the Whitley system of 'consultation' (in the 1920s for the civil service and the 1940s for local government) they developed consensual approaches to bargaining, with both unions and management negotiating and developing procedures within this framework. Over the last two decades, there have been attempts to adapt this framework on the assumption that the interests of unions and management differ. Significantly, this has resulted in management and unions approaching the new employment circumstances in ways that draw upon past experiences and relationships as well as seeking opportunities to redefine the employment relation in distinct ways.

The second feature of Whitleyism was the focus on national agreements, with the consequence that workplace unionism almost non-existent, at least until the 1970s. The interests of workers, in so far as they were articulated through trade unionism, were represented by national leaders sitting on joint management–worker committees established on principles of consensus rather than difference. During the 1970s these forms of union organisation and negotiating practice came to be questioned within a number of unions (Fryer, Fairclough and Manson 1974; Drake *et al.* 1980 and Drake *et al.* 1982). These considerations have been given an added impetus with the restructuring of the state sector. In the 1980s a new emphasis was introduced, particularly the decentralisation of responsibility for service and conditions to department levels of management. For unions this represents a major challenge to traditional ways of organising and operating.

State-sector unions have been the subject of analysis in recent years, examining the traditional hierarchy of representation that has characterised them, although the principal focus has been on manual workers. Terry (1982) in a challenging article argued that local government manual union organisation was by and large based on the 'key' steward 'brought into existence, and probably in part sustained by, managerial initiative' (p. 16). Historically, the centrality of such stewards was based on their ability to provide the ligaments of union organisation for a dispersed workforce in circumstances where there was a limited place for local bargaining. Key stewards often became 'the union' for both management and membership. Nonetheless, Terry foresaw the possibility of members beginning to identify their collective interests in more direct and immediate ways in response to management strategies to establish authority-wide conditions and terms of employment, such as work study arrangements. In a complement to Terry, Kessler (1986) also focused on manual workers, noting the fragmented and dispersed character of local government employment. He pointed to the distinctiveness of local government unionism, suggesting that there was limited value in direct comparison with models of steward organisation in manufacturing. Further, he commented on the significance of employment arrangements based on occupational groups employed in discrete departments.

Local government unions in social services

The unions in social services at County Council broadly paralleled that in Metropolitan Council, although the steward system was relatively undeveloped. In the case of NALGO, it had taken the branches in County Council longer to recognise and accept the shift to department-level negotiating structures, resulting in an embryonic form of unionism at department level. Metropolitan Council, the union in social services at County Council was organised on the basis of a steward system, convened by a chief steward, or in this case, a union convenor. There were thirty-seven stewards in social services throughout the county, representing some 500 members (1993). Unlike Metropolitan Council there was no internal division, although social services was divided into five divisions. Stewards were assumed to represent particular work-places, or groupings of workplaces.

The social services representative structures were both part of branches which represented the different employment functions in the local authority. As such they were the most comprehensively organised sections of the two branches in the sense that each had developed steward structures, whereas other department sections elsewhere in both branches had minimal union representation, relying very much on lead stewards. Nonetheless, the steward organisation in each branch was centralised and reliant on the senior steward for each department, despite the relatively small representational ratio in County Council NALGO (one steward: 13.5 members). They operated as hierarchical representative structures in the sense that the only representative who became involved in negotiations was the senior steward, and the other stewards merely acted as ciphers referring items to the senior steward or distributing union material to members. This remained the case despite the changes that were under way in terms of managerial restructuring and reorganisation.

In each authority, NALGO organised almost half the total work-force in social services, and was the main union for non-manual staff, while NUPE was the principal union for the manual staff. In the case of NALGO, the social services membership was part of a larger multi-functional branch, covering all departments in each authority. The membership was organised within each department by embryonic workplace steward structures, reaffirming these workers' identities as employees within social services, and giving some substance to the more abstract notion of being NALGO branch members. A stronger version of this occurred in the NUPE Metropolitan Branch, where the membership was organised as an autonomous social services branch in the authority, thus affirming an identity between union membership and occupational position. In contrast, County Council social service workers eligible to join NUPE were organised in three geographically based multi-functional NUPE branches, with limited social services-specific organisation.

The steward system for the NALGO social services group in the Metropolitan Council was structured around a chief steward, acting as the convenor, three deputy senior stewards representing different geographical areas of the authority, and twenty-nine stewards for over 1,100 members (1993). They were grouped into three social services divisions, which were coterminous with the Department of Health boundaries, as well as the parliamentary constituency boundaries. Although stewards tended to come from and represent specific workplaces or locations, there was no necessary requirement for this or for such stewards to act as delegates for specified constituencies. There was a convenor for each divisional set of stewards. In addition, a deputy chief steward supported the chief steward, who effectively was the 'key' steward around whom the union organisation is structured (Terry 1982).

In contrast, the NUPE structure was different in both authorities in two respects. First, in the Metropolitan Council, as already indicated, the social services' NUPE membership had formed its own branch. This was very much a lay-member-led branch, keep-ing the full-time official at a distance. The branch was organised around an executive committee which represented different geo-graphical and functional areas in the department. Nonetheless, it remained a relatively hierarchical form of union organisation, with the senior steward taking the lead on most issues within the area and the stewards playing little active part in branch activity. Second, the NUPE organisation in social services in County Council was part of a multi-functional branch structure, not unlike that of NALGO. This meant that while the branch secretary was involved in social service activity he also had responsibility for education and other related areas in local government. The result was that he very much relied on the full-time officer to provide support and necessary resourcing to deal with the range of issues that came up in the branch. This was a branch that was very much built around the activity of the lead steward.

Nonetheless, the NUPE branch organisation in both councils was marked by subordinate functional groups. In the case of the Metropolitan Council this was illustrated by the establishment of a black steward group in the face of an increased recognition of sexual and racial harassment of black members. Often it was white male NALGO members, as line managers, who were being accused of harassment and intimidation, thereby raising the problem of inter-union (now intra-union) conflict. In these circumstances, it fell to the predominantly white stewards and senior branch officials to represent these black members, and although it was generally agreed that these representatives did their best, it also gave rise to additional charges from the black women members that the branch was failing to represent them effectively. After much argument, including an internal inquiry, the branch established a black stewards' committee, with the right of representation on the branch executive. In future, black members, irrespective of their area of work, have the right to black representation and the branch is constitutionally obliged to respond positively to the recommendations and claims of the black representatives.

In the County Council, with the hiving-off of twelve of the twenty-four residential homes for the elderly to the private County Care Services, NUPE established a committee composed of a steward from each of these privatised homes, with an elected negotiating committee of four. This committee assumed the lead responsibility for negotiating the terms and conditions of workers employed in these homes, initially responding to the proposals presented by the management committee which covered the privatised homes, but in turn developing a more pro-active approach to bargaining. They were able to do this because the management had conceded union recognition and a bargaining forum. The union was assisted in this respect by the support of the Labour-led County Council, which agreed to a continuation of union recognition in the homes. Nevertheless, the important points to note are that the membership remained committed to the union and individual members were prepared to take on the responsibility of stewardship, the majority for the first time. In this respect, the union membership took up the opportunity paradoxically provided by privatisation (Fairbrother 1994).

The evidence suggests that the union structures and the consultative arrangements, both within the departments and the authorities more widely, underwrite the centrality of the chief stewards and branch officers for negotiation and representation. In part, this occurs because it is a set of arrangements that suit the department managements as well as the authorities. It is also an arrangement that reflects the way the union organises in at least two respects: first, a focus upon the central authority within the council; second, a limited attempt to encourage membership participation across a dispersed and fragmented workforce. More particularly, there is a vibrancy of union activity and concern at a department level, which remains partly submerged. When asked to identify members' concerns and worries, the chief stewards in all authorities mentioned low grading, workloads, health and safety, accommodation, restructuring and job security. Discipline cases would probably be handled by the chief steward personally, although attempts were being made to spread the load.

When comparing the two social services union groups, it is apparent that the Metropolitan union is organised in a more comprehensive way than the County Council one, partly because of the different sizes of the two authorities and partly so as to connect with more complex managerial structures. If unions in this authority were to face the managerial restructuring that was taking place, then it was necessary for them to organise so that the union representative structures provided an opportunity for stewards to negotiate and represent on behalf of their memberships. One feature of these arrangements was that in Metropolitan Council it would appear that issues were more readily identified and dealt with as a department concern than was the case with County Council. In both cases, there was evidence that the restructuring in these departments was placing a wide range of issues on the union agenda. This has already facilitated the increased recognition and acknowledgement by these workers of their common and, in some instances, collective concerns. The task facing both union groups is to shape and mould these concerns in a collective fashion.

Civil service unionism

Following the establishment of the Benefits Agency in April 1991, the unions faced a new and in some cases aggressively confident management concerned to undermine what they saw as a privileged and difficult local union leadership. Facility time was restricted, managers were less forthcoming in their dealings with local union leaders, and the regional level of the Whitley structure was abolished, on the grounds that most, if not all, locally based problems would be settled at an office or district level. In the face of these challenges, local union leaderships sought to introduce policies aimed at reorganising their unions, often in novel ways, reflecting their diverse experiences as non-manual workers, women and men, who could no longer rely on past procedures and forms of organisation.

In effect, the creation of the Benefits Agency signalled a shift in the frontier of control between workers and management (Goodrich 1975 [1920]). Previously, the offices were organised in a bureaucratic form which meant that at a local or office level there were relatively few grievances or problems that could be or indeed were settled at this level. This meant that the union form of organisation in the DSS (and its forerunners) was also centralised and relatively remote for most members. There were exceptions to these arrangements, particularly where a small number of active union members in offices attempted to force a shift in decision-making from regional or national levels, on at least some issues, such as overtime working during the mid-1980s. This, however, was very limited and often notable because of its relative infrequency.

With the move to agency status, and the devolution and de-centralisation of managerial structures, there was a shift in the frontier of control as managers attempted to impose new pro-cedures and practices on an often reluctant and uneasy workforce. It is in these circumstances that unions at a local level, with limited support from their national leadership, began to look anew at their forms of organisation and practice at this level. The contradiction in these developments was that for both management and the unions nationally there remained strong pressures to retain control over the developments that were taking place. As a result, in the face of managerial devolution and local union renewal, there are still strong pressures towards control and centralisation.

For unions which had long been highly centralised, where branch executives were effectively the union at a local level, the restructuring of the 1980s raised a set of complicated problems about appropriate organisation. At a national level, the civil service unions very quickly developed critical assessments of the policies implemented during the 1980s to restructure the civil service. With reference to the DSS, both the CPSA and the NUCPS formulated policies about the operational strategies initiated in 1982 as well as the raft of policies which resulted in the establishment of agencies.[6] The dilemma for these unions was how to articulate grievances at a local level while at the same time attempting to retain a national role in the formulation and development of policy.

Before reorganisation, branches were composed of a number of offices, often seven or more, usually spread over a large geographical area or around a large city. The branch co-ordinated activity between offices, gave support to office secretaries, and provided an indirect link with the regional Whitley structures. On this last point, many branch secretaries, for example, were active on the regional Whitley committees and thus provided regular report-backs about regional activity to branch committees. With the establishment of the Benefits Agency, the DSS branches were reorganised, especially in the NUCPS, with a reallocation of offices to other branches and the creation of smaller branches based on contiguous District Management Units. These developments enabled the branch secretaries, in particular, to address the problems of organisation in the offices. In one large city the two formerly separate offices were described by an NUCPS branch secretary in the following terms.

In one office, where the Broad Left, including Militant Tendency, had a leading presence, the major question was the effectiveness of the unions in confronting what was seen by most members as a major assault on terms and conditions of employment. The NUCPS was the major presence, covering the executive officers and above (fifty-seven members) and the security and telephone staff (eight members), while the CPSA recruited the more numerous but less active clerical staff (125 members). The NUCPS played the lead role in the main negotiating forum, the Office Whitley, taking the initiative on most issues involving the two unions. In addition, the NUCPS had also been successful in establishing an effective representative structure in the office, unlike the CPSA. Between 1985 and 1988, the chairperson of the NUCPS committee, a member of Militant Tendency, had increasingly acted as the senior steward, on behalf of the CPSA as well as NUCPS members. It was acknowledged by most others on the committee that his activity in the office, and more generally in the branch, had laid the foundation for a union presence that was capable of meeting and surviving the challenge of the Next Steps programme to restructure and fragment the civil service. In effect, the local union presence in the office had been built up by politically active and committed leaders, prepared to develop a union presence via a traditional representative union structure.

Following the initial restructuring of the benefits offices, District Managers began to reform industrial relations procedures. Although it was not evident in all offices, many District Managers attempted to devolve industrial relations within their districts. In one office, the manager issued an instruction that problems should be dealt with in the first instance by HEO-grade staff, each of whom had functional responsibilities across the offices in the district, resulting in the somewhat farcical situation of the union officials negotiating with staff who had no authority whatsoever to decide issues involving the union. The union leaderships complained to the District Manager about these arrangements and, after some argument, there was some clarification and reallocation of responsibility so that the union officials dealt with more senior-grade staff on immediate work-related issues and the district management on the remaining items, generally those which concerned more than one section.

More generally, with the establishment of the agency, the management throughout the region attempted to restrict unions by resorting to the constitutional procedures of the Whitley arrangements. Existing agreements were reviewed by managements in the districts; agreements that were not wanted were dropped. This was most dramatically illustrated by the challenge to facility rights in these offices, when the overall amount of facility time available throughout the region was reduced dramatically. Facility time to pursue issues at a regional (subsequently area) level was ended on the official grounds that no issues would ever reach area management. A strict limit of twenty hours' facility time for all unions per district was then introduced. In one district this meant a reduction in the number of representatives on the trade union side: rather than four at Office One and six at Office Two there was an allowance of four trade union representatives across the two offices. Further, it meant that if the union representatives attended a Whitley meeting, then they had used a week of their allowance.

These developments provided the occasion for local union leaderships and their active memberships to begin a process of union renewal, in the sense that the decentralisation of managerial structures and the establishment of agencies faced local unions with both problems and opportunities. In the twelve months following the establishment of the Benefits Agency there was a general challenge by the District and Area Managers to union rights and prerogatives in all but one of the offices studied. In the first instance, this resulted in a loss of confidence in some sections of the unions which organise these workers. But, paradoxically, it also meant that there has been increased opportunity for local groups to begin to broaden the active base of the union. This has been a period when it became more likely that previously inactive members would become involved in office or branch union activity. Members of branch executives became more active, both at branch level as well as at office level on the newly established district negotiating committees. Alongside this, there are signs that individual members had become more likely to look to the collective membership to deal with the problems and grievances that were emerging during the process of restructuring.

One feature of this development of local-level trade unionism has been the greater willingness by union leaderships to dis-aggregate the concerns of their membership. This is illustrated by the move in a number of union committees to acknowledge and address the interests of women members. The unions successfully pursued a policy of extending the opportunities for part-time work, reflecting the interests of their many women members. While this policy was part of a government approach to dilute full-time employment in the civil service, the unions at local level nego-tiated the actual implementation at office level, taking into account the specific interests of women members. The result was that in one office there were no part-time workers a few years ago; by 1992 59 out of the 280 workers in the office were on a part-time basis, mostly on terms which reflected the particular concerns of women members. In this, the unions negotiated parity with full-time workers, and the part-time workers saw this initiative as a successful union action, with the result that these workers became very supportive of the union. More generally, members of the CPSA and NUCPS have been much more likely to refer issues and problems to their union representatives than was the case in the past. This might involve referring what seem like arbitrary managerial decisions to the union, such as allocation of work, or difficulties with maternity arrangements. In these cases the union representatives sought redress by negotiating with the newly responsible managers at district level. Often this involved working out procedures as they went along.

Such developments over bargaining procedures and negotiating issues were complemented by a much greater willingness for staff to meet and consider industrial action than at any other period that they could remember. In some cases, staff were prepared to walk out unilaterally and question the right of the management to behave as they did. More than this, union meetings were well attended compared to previous periods. There had been an increase in membership interest in union activity and the beginnings of a process of developing union activity in more participative and involved ways. Such developments did not occur overnight and were the result of debate and organisation by union members, particularly by local leaderships.

UNION RENEWAL

To varying degrees, a complicated process of union reorganisation has been taking place, from a form of unionism where bureaucratic effectiveness prevails and predominates to a more participative and involved form of unionism. This was made more difficult by the fact that the members of these unions comprised both dispersed, fragmented and isolated groups of members and large groupings in office blocks and the like. In the past, these unions had addressed the diversity of membership circumstances by centralised bargaining and representation, which did not place a premium on member involvement and activity. With the decentralisation of managerial structures, unions in both sectors began a process of reorganisation, although this was not a straightforward process; nor was it without contention and debate. Nevertheless, if this is part of a general process of reorganisation and reconstitution of unionism, in these and related sectors, then it is an important harbinger for the future.

The restructuring of the 1980s provided the occasion for a re-evaluation of the traditional form of unionism in the Benefits Agency. Both the CPSA and the NUCPS had long been centrally organised unions, providing the framework for local union activity, whereby branches were responsive to nationally initiated policies. Although these two unions continued to play an important part in developing a critique of these moves towards agencies and the associated decentralisation of managerial structures, for union members the restructuring at office level was an opportunity to recast their union membership at this level.

Such developments were clearly illustrated in the civil service, where local leaders and their members have begun to open up a range of issues that previously were not within their province. This includes issues relating to staffing levels, the allocation of overtime work, and the refurbishment of offices. While these are not startlingly novel areas of negotiation and bargaining, the local representatives were often involved in such negotiations for the first time in their working lives. In addition, partly at the initiative of previously non-active members and partly at the behest of local leaders, these union groups, with their large numbers of women members, have begun to move decisively to raise questions relating to equal opportunities and sexual and racial harassment, as well as the consideration of atypical forms of employment in terms of membership rather than employer interest. The opportunity for this has been provided by the reorganisation of bargaining arrangements from regional or national level to office level.

Bargaining levels

For much of their history, state-sector unions have been characterised by centralised and relatively remote forms of organisation and operation, sustained, at least in part, by particular forms of managerial organisation and operation. Nonetheless, over the last decade there has been a move in both local authorities and the civil service towards a devolution of managerial responsibility, in local authorities to departments and in the civil service to districts. In the main, this has been a move to locate negotiations concerned with operational activity at a more localised level. Such changes have important implications for union organisation and operation, both for the branches and the union beyond.

In the case of local government, the historical focus of negotiations at authority level served to sustain a centralised union
structure where the branch officers played their part as key actors
in the process of union representation in relation to local
authorities. This was the principal point of contact between union
representatives and managerial staff. Such an involvement meant
that these officials were likely to acquire the expertise, the experience and the familiarity to represent and negotiate on behalf of
their membership with management. The other side of these
procedures was that there were strong inhibitions on the emergence of actively involved and participative memberships, partly
because of the scale and scope of local authority employment as
well as the relative absence of local bargaining fora. Nonetheless,
there has been a relatively long recognition by local leaderships
and national activists in these unions of the importance of locally
based representative structures and there have been attempts in
both unions to establish such structures.

In the case of the local authorities the shift in bargaining and
negotiating arrangements has been from the level of the local
authority to that of the department. Both manual and non-manual
unions have long organised as relatively centralised and hierarchical bodies so as to connect with the local authority bargaining
structures. One consequence of this has been that these unions
have relatively ineffective steward structures, representing the
specific concerns of members either on a geographical or on a
functional basis. With the shift towards decentralised bargaining
arrangements, following on from budgetary and financial devolution to the departments, these unions have attempted to follow
suit and develop departmental forms of representation. To date,
such developments are at the beginning and are complicated by
the merger of the two major local government unions, NALGO and
NUPE, but it can be expected that these trends are likely to
continue and be developed in due course.

The profile of civil service unionism has likewise been that of a
centralised, relatively remote form of unionism, with both branch
secretary and other officials providing the active base of these unions.
While there were exceptions to this pattern, this was a form of
unionism which prevailed and to an important extent still appears to
characterise unions in this sector. This pattern of unionism was
sustained by the very achievements of the past, namely the winning
of standardised terms and conditions of employment during the early

135

and mid-part of this century. Unions, via national negotiations, defended these conditions and in the process sustained a form of unionism that did not rest on widespread membership activity and involvement.

The managerial restructuring of the civil service in the 1980s and the fragmentation in the 1990s with the establishment of agencies provided the opportunity for union memberships, and particularly branch leaders and activists, to move towards the development of more locally involved unions. The decentralisation of managerial structures was accompanied by a devolution and localisation of bargaining arrangements, which provided union memberships with the opportunity to negotiate over a range of issues which previously had been outside their remit. While there is an un-evenness in the way that trade union groups have addressed these circumstances, there is a general opening up of bargaining issues and questions at a local level.

Union organisation

These developments raise a number of questions about union organisation and activity in both industries. No longer is it possible for unions to organise on the assumption of relatively remote and inactive memberships, involved in union activity at the behest of national leaders or regional officers. This is a form of unionism which does not allow local activists readily to address the pressing problems that have begun to emerge through the restructuring of the 1980s. Instead, a premium is now being placed on forms of collective organisation that are rooted in the workplace in ways that were not necessary in the past. In uneven and hesitant ways, these union memberships have begun to consider these questions.

In the case of local authority unions, where there has been a long tradition of service and condition negotiations at an authority level, these changes have raised very acute problems for branch officials and full-time officers who attempt to service regions. Whereas in the past the branch officials were principally respon-sible for the majority of negotiations and consultations in the authority, often with some involvement from regional full-time officers, this had become increasingly impracticable. It was no longer possible for such officials and officers to retain a familiarity with the detail of such negotiations, although there were signs on the part of many of valiant but largely unsuccessful attempts to do so. As a result authority-wide union officials had to rely increasingly on department briefings to allow them to present adequate cases at the authority level. The problem was that many of the department representatives were inexperienced, and in the case of business units, unions found it very difficult to find members willing to become involved in negotiations with their 'new' managers, although as indicated there were exceptions to this general pattern.

Similar changes have begun to take place in the civil service unions, with the difference that the lead and focus of such changes is on the branch secretaries and their executives. In the past, it is fair to note, many branch secretaries acted as ciphers for national union policy, transmitting policies downwards and reporting membership responses upwards. While this oversimplifies what were more complicated relationships, it nonetheless captures one of the major dimensions of the traditional form of union organisation. With the decentralisation of managerial structures and the devolution of bargaining arrangements, these officials found themselves in a position to play a more active role in negotiations and representing members' concerns than previously. It is on the basis of these new-found opportunities that it has become possible to develop more participative forms of unionism than was the case in the past.

In these circumstances there are signs of pressure from members, as well as local activists, for the development of more responsive forms of unionism. These moves, however, have been very tentative, often confined to grumbles and complaints about the reorganisation and intensification of local authority and civil service work. The problem is that neither union had the mechanisms or the means whereby members could readily raise issues that stewards could begin to identify and collectively address. For this to happen a more participative form of unionism was required, but these unions, buried in the traditions of the past, with their large, fragmented and dispersed memberships, found it very difficult to transform rhetorical commitments to participation and involvement into concrete measures designed to enable such a transformation to take place.

Implications

The emergence of more active and broadly based forms of unionism at local level has occurred within the residual forms of these centrally organised unions. What is happening is that there is a shift in the locus of unionism, from the centre to the local level, although the paraphernalia of centralised union forms of organisation remain in place. The point is that for members the focus of their unionism is gradually shifting to the office level, while the national leaderships have barely begun to grapple with the task of providing support for these memberships in the changed environment of agencies and devolved managerial structures. The problem for these unions is how to co-ordinate the activity of the branch form of organisation while at the same time enabling unionism at the local level to develop and flourish. Thus, the form of unionism in this sector has begun to evolve in more participative and locally based ways, although in appearance they remain centrally organised and directed unions.

To the extent that this analysis is correct, as unions become embedded in these devolved and decentralised processes of representation and negotiation, the prevailing forms of centralised unionism will be difficult to maintain. However, at present, in spite of an affirmation of the centralised and hierarchical patterns of union organisation, there are increasingly desperate attempts to graft on the basis of more devolved and participative forms of unionism. The problem unions face is how to adapt and reorganise to reflect these different circumstances without pulling the union apart or demobilising it. One danger is that the reorganisation at a workplace level will take place in a relatively ad hoc and disconnected way, workplace by workplace. A second danger is that divisions could emerge within these unions, both horizontally and vertically, as different sections of the union attempt to map out what they regard as the best way forward. A further danger is the emergence of forms of 'enterprise' unionism where the union is dependent on co-operation from the employer and where the scope of trade unionism is defined by the enterprise management.

As if this is not enough, at this critical moment in local government, NUPE and NALGO have taken the decision to merge with each other, together with COHSE, to create UNISON. This union is now the largest in Britain and has some 1.3 million members in local government, gas, health, electricity, water, transport, and higher education, two-thirds of them women. In some ways this was particularly propitious, since one dominant theme in the rationale for the merger is the democratisation of the union at local level. The problem facing the members of this new union is how to achieve these aspirations, since it is no easy task to transform three differently organised unions, with distinct traditions and constituencies, into a unified structure within the workplace. Not only is there a question about class relationships within the workplace, since the social relations of work and employment in these industries remain intact and unaltered, but the very different traditions of the previous unions may also provide important barriers to the development of genuinely participative forms of unionism. On the one hand, the very real class differences between manual and non-manual workers, between those in managerial positions and those in routine clerical and related administrative positions, remain in place (Carter and Fairbrother 1995). How the concerns of different groups within the union, at both national and local levels, will be resolved in the new union structure remains unclear. Rhetorical utterances about the value of unity do not in themselves remove or overcome the profound differences rooted in the social relations of work and employment. On the other hand, the union at local level is very much a merger between a lay-led union (NALGO) and a full-time officer-led union (NUPE), with the third union (COHSE) somewhere in between. It remains an open question whether the union memberships will be able to maintain a commitment to more participative forms of unionism, especially if there is a move at national level to underwrite the centrality of the full-time officials, as was the case traditionally in NUPE. With the continued restructuring of the local state there are pressures both ways as members face a world where national bargaining becomes marginal, where local bargaining increases in prominence and importance, and where maintenance of membership levels and representation becomes more difficult.

The situation for the civil service unions is somewhat different. Here there have been moves towards more participative forms of unionism, but these developments have been within each union and the links that have been established between local union groups have often been unofficial and informal. At national level there is a long history of troubled relations between the leaderships of NUCPS and the CPSA, usually expressed around the political differences, although occasionally resting on a perceived class antagonism between the two unions. Nonetheless, class differences did not prevent the forerunners of the NUCPS, the Society of Civil and Public Servants (representing the middle grades of the civil service) and the Civil Service Union (representing principally the ancillary grades) from merging in 1988. One consequence of the maintenance of two independent unions and the uncertain relations between the national leaderships (also reflected at department and agency level, although to a lesser degree) is that the initiatives at workplace and local level, borne out of the importance of addressing the day-to-day, the here and now, are taking place in the absence of reforms elsewhere in the union. This leaves the local leaders relatively isolated within the wider framework of union politics. Thus while it may be possible to initiate change in the workplace, this will remain ad hoc and uneven if attempts are not made to establish the basis for horizontal links between different workplace union groups within the one union and between unions. One danger is that these tentative moves towards participation will be still-born as national leaders cling to the certitudes of the past and fail to address the opportunities provided by the present.

FINAL COMMENTS

The study raises the question of the conditions for union renewal in the state sector. In the case of local government there has been a reaffirmation of centralised and hierarchical forms of union organisation in the context of a decentralisation of managerial structures and organisation. This has placed increasing burdens on the full-time officer staff as well as the lay leadership in these unions. Where there have been attempts to develop more broadly based forms of union representation, advocates of change have often come up against the difficulty of developing representative structures in situations where there has been little tradition of local bargaining and where work and employment relations do not lend themselves to a ready identification of collective organisation and identity. In this respect the traditions of centralised and hierarchical forms of union organisation have prevailed and traditional forms of unionism have been affirmed. In this respect the relative stasis within these unions has been underwritten by managements which have continued to insist on centralised bargaining procedures and negotiations, even when the detail of restructuring was implemented locally.

In contrast, the civil service unions have begun to reorganise in more participative directions. This has been despite the preferences and concerns of the national leadership, who have attempted to maintain the semblance of nationally focused and organised union structures. In practice, the national leadership became irrelevant, as the restructuring of the civil service generally and the establishment of the Benefits Agency in particular proceeded. They were no longer in a position organisationally to do other than acquiesce in the developments that have begun to take place at local level. It is in these circumstances that more participative forms of unionism have begun to emerge in the unlikely circumstances of the civil service.

More generally, this study has wider implications for both the state sector and the private sector. It can be argued that in many industries, but particularly engineering, forms of participative unionism have long been in existence (for parallel arguments on road haulage see Smith 1995b). This certainly is one of the points made by Darlington (1994) in his recent study of three manufacturing plants on Merseyside, in north-west England. There, workplace union committees have maintained an active presence within their plants, despite the drastic effects of the restructuring that has taken place or the less than supportive stances of many full-time officials. This suggests that one of the key conditions for active and vibrant forms of workplace unionism is a work and employment circumstance that allows issues to be raised and settled at local level. Where this is not the case, it is very easy for solutions to be made outside the workplace, by national or full-time officials who do not work to the same imperatives as those in the workplace, a situation that has long characterised state-sector unionism, including unions in the recently privatised utilities.

The corollary of this argument is that a simple opposition between workplace or membership concerns and leadership interests, particularly those of national and full-time officer leaders, is not sustainable (Kelly and Heery 1994: 203–7).[7] This clearly is the case, but the question in all unions is the balance between the different levels of organisation. The issue is whether this balance can be achieved in a way that does not demean or subordinate the concerns and activity of the workplace membership. As Darlington points out (1994: 285–90), full-time officials, and by implication national leaders, are often in a position to define 'the contours within which any potential "renewal" and revitalisation of workplace unionism might take place' (p. 290). But it is equally necessary to note that the form this takes in relation to the possibility of members influencing the impact of such intervention depends on the very different traditions and forms of unionism in different sectors. The manufacturing unions that Darlington refers to are structured very differently, although in some respects no less hierarchically, than many public-sector unions. Whether the tensions 'between bureaucratically effective forms of unionism at a national level and collective participation at workplace level' (p. 290) can be overcome depends on whether workplace members can extend the types of initiatives identified in this chapter so that they take the lead in the determination of union policy and practice at both national and local levels.

The development of more vibrant and participative forms of union is something that must come from within the workplace, rather than from outside the union, from a political group (Darlington 1994: 291–2), or from above, at the national level. Where the impetus for change comes from outside, there is always the danger of an elitism emerging whereby external agents decide what is in the best interests of those in the workplace. The importance of political membership in the groups studied was that it provided a reference point for individuals in developing a critical stance on the way their unions had organised and operated in the past; nonetheless, they were effective trade unionists because they were both of and for the workplace. In other words, the question is not whether political groups should play a part in the development of active forms of unionism or whether national and regional officials have a part to play, but that the touchstone for active and democratised forms of unionism is the workplace and the workplace members, and not others.

These developments thus bring the question of union form and union renewal back into the centre of debates about trade unionism. In the context of restructuring, a reliance on centralised and hierarchical forms of unionism no longer suffices. However, there are dangers in only viewing the questions of union renewal as if they are confined to the workplace. This can lay the foundation for active forms of 'enterprise' unionism where workers in particular sectors and workplaces organise so as to pursue their own interests, irrespective of other sectors and workplaces. Thus there is still a role for centralised union organisation in representing and symbolising collective interests across and within the new decentralised and renewed forms of organisation that may be emerging. In practice, this means assisting in the organisation of the workplace and the associated network of relations, resourcing and assisting groups and networks, and acting as delegates of the workplace, rather than representative leaders who speak on behalf of the workplace in the abstract. It means looking at combine-type committees, both within industries and sectors and also within communities and regions. It is a reversing of the flow of the traditional relationships characteristic of most unions, particularly in the state sector, so that the national level resources and facilitates rather than represents and thus controls.

The difficulty for a union renewal based on the workplace is how to achieve a network of united rather than isolated union leaderships and activists. One solution is to begin to develop a network of activists both within and between different workplaces and unions. The rationale of such activity is that the key to workplace control of policies and initiatives outside the workplace, or involving more than one workplace, is that accountable leaders have both the means and the opportunity to create and control such networks. Of course, this brings workers into contact and involvement with union personnel and political activists who are located outside the immediate world of work and employment relations faced by the union membership. The point is that the relationship between the two must be one whereby 'outsiders', be they researchers or political activists, are subordinate and accountable to workplace representatives. The achievement of such a circumstance is unlikely to be an easy or indeed a straightforward task, as past history so amply illustrates. It is likely to be contested and challenged, but there is no real prospect of any alternative.

The strength, the basis and the rationale of unionism remains within the workplace. It is here that union membership for most members most of the time begins and ends. It is also here that the promise of more outward-looking and engaged forms of unionism will be built, where the rhetoric of many unions will be put into practice. It is the argument in this chapter that unions in the state sector have begun to take some of the preliminary steps towards a realisation of this promise. It is in this respect that unions once again return to the centre of debates about democracy both within unions and as part of broader concerns within the liberal democratic state.

ACKNOWLEDGEMENTS

An earlier version of this chapter was presented at the 12th International Conference on the Organisation and Control of the Labour Process, Aston University, 23–5 March 1994. The chapter reports some of the results of a research project financed by an ESRC Grant (R000232006). I would like to thank all those who participated in the research and gave me so readily of their time. I would also like to record the debt I owe to Ian Kessler, Paul Smith, Michael Terry, and Jeremy Waddington, who each read and commented on earlier drafts of the chapter, as well as all the participants in the conference session who argued about and debated an earlier version of the chapter, as well as Elain Bowers, Simon Clark, Anthony Ferner, and Jeremy Waddington, who read and discussed the chapter with me.

NOTES

1 This develops arguments by Carter and Fairbrother (1995) where the claim is that there is a remaking and rearticulation of class relations at the immediate point of production, with the result that a state middle and working class are becoming much more apparent.

2 The dangers of this type of analysis are clearly brought out in the recent essay by Heery and Kelly (1994) when they imply that the use of the terms 'bureaucracy' and 'bureaucratisation' locks the analysis within a Weberian framework and suggests a cyclical analysis of union forms of organisation. They claim that Fairbrother and Waddington (1990) are guilty of presenting an analysis predicated on the assumption of a separation between leaders and members (p.16). This, of course, is not what Hyman argued; there emphasis is on bureaucratised and democratised relations and probably points to a looseness in the analysis of such relations with the use of the term 'bureaucracy' and the associations it has with Weberian sociology. In an elaboration of their analysis Kelly and Heery (1994: 203–4) seem to concede the ambiguity surrounding the term 'bureaucracy'. The lesson from these confusions is that a much sharper conceptualisation is needed of the sorts of relations encapsulated by the term 'bureaucracy' (used by most writers) or by 'managerialism' (as used by Heery and Kelly). For further discussion, see the comment by Smith (1995a) and for an analysis which in its theoretical assumptions suffers from some of the problems identified by Heery and Kelly, despite working with reference to Hyman's analysis, see Darlington (1994).

3 NALGO and NUPE, together with the Confederation of Health Service Employees (COHSE), merged on 1 July 1993 to form UNISON.

4 The data for the research come from an ESRC-financed three-year longitudinal study of twenty-four workplace union committees in the West Midlands region, some of which were branch executives while others were steward committees and the like (R000232006). The committees were drawn from the public-sector bodies, utilities and manufacturing enterprises in equal numbers. Where possible I studied both the staff and the shopfloor committees in the same enterprise or

government body. Complementing this, I conducted less detailed studies on another five union committees, following up particular themes that had emerged in the core cases. I was also involved in leading ten union schools in the Midlands region which produced further information about workplace unionism. In each core case study I interviewed the leading representative(s) of each committee at least four times, twice in the first year and once in the two subsequent years, using semi-structured interview schedules. Where possible I also interviewed their managerial counterparts at annual intervals, altogether involving nine managers. The regional full-time officers of seven of the major unions in the region were also interviewed on an annual basis. These interviews were complemented by a questionnaire survey of the committee members each year. Where possible I attended union meetings (six) and visited workplaces (twenty-four). I also interviewed key commentators, in terms either of employer or union position in the region, such as the Secretary of the Regional TUC, thus providing an overview of union developments in the region. To further the comparative basis of the research I also carried out an annual postal survey of workplace unions in the three sectors, although the response rate was disappointingly low (overall 18.3 per cent) and uneven: 1991: ? senior union representatives (? per cent) and ? employer representatives; 1992: ? senior union representatives (? per cent) and ? employer representatives; 1993: ? senior union representatives (? per cent) and ? employer representatives. Nonetheless, the information generated does provide confirmation of the trends and patterns seen in the core case studies. The material reported in this chapter covers eight union branches, each of which was studied throughout the three-year period of the research. In the analysis and presentation of the data, note has been taken of the developments that took place in the other union committees studied, so as to provide a comparative reference point to the analysis.

5 These attempts have not always had the results hoped for by policy-makers, with one recent study on performance-related pay in the Inland Revenue concluding that the likely impact of such schemes has been employee demotivation; see Marsden and Richardson (1994).

6 The CPSA organised the clerical grades and the NUCPS the executive grades, although in the case of the DSS the unions unusually both recruited the boundary grade, Local Officer 1. This was an historical anomaly.

7 One of the weaknesses of the Kelly and Heery study (1994) is that they do not examine a union where there has been a clear tradition of full-time officer dominance or where the union was organised explicitly on the basis of centralised and hierarchical control over what was assumed to be passive and inactive memberships, such as the civil service or NUPE for much of its history. This, however, is a deficiency and not a negation of their otherwise important and fascinating account. Often critics of substantively focused research projects are too dismissive of the difficulties of access or vagaries of field research. After all, when texts or manuscripts are unavailable in other types of

research, there is often an air of sympathy about that which was unavailable; the same strictures should apply to substantively focused research. Nonetheless, it is incumbent on authors to draw to the readers' attention the limits of the research.

REFERENCES

Bach, S. and Winchester, D. (1994) 'Opting Out of Pay Devolution? The Prospects for Local Pay Bargaining in UK Public Services', *British Journal of Industrial Relations* **32**, 2: 263–82.

Bailey, R. (1994) 'Annual Review Article 1993: British Public Sector Industrial Relations', *British Journal of Industrial Relations* **32**, 1: 113–36.

Bains Report (1972) Study Group on Local Authority Management Structure, *The New Local Authorities: Management and Structure*, London: HMSO.

Brown, W. and Walsh, I. (1991) 'Pay Determination in Britain in the 1980s: The Anatomy of Decentralization', *Oxford Review of Economic Policy* **7**: 44–59.

Cabinet Office (Office of Public Service and Science) (1994) *The Civil Service: Continuity and Change*, Cmnd 2627, London: HMSO.

Carter, B. and Fairbrother, P. (1995) 'The Remaking of the State Middle Class', in T. Cutler and M. Savage (eds), *The New Middle Class*, London: University College London Press.

Chartered Institute of Public Finance and Accountancy (1989) *Local Government Trends* – CIPFA.

Cochrane, A. (1993) *Whatever Happened to Local Government?*, Buckingham: Open University Press.

Cockburn, C. (1977) *The Local State*, London: Pluto Press.

Darlington, R. (1994) *The Dynamics of Workplace Unionism: Shop Stewards' Organization in Three Merseyside Plants*, London: Mansell.

Department of Environment (1979) *Organic Change in Local Government*, Cmnd 7457, London: HMSO.

Department of Environment and Welsh Office (1977) *Local Government Finance*, Cmnd 6813, London: HMSO.

Drake, P., Fairbrother, P., Fryer, B. and Murphy, J. (1980) *Which Way Forward? An Interim Report of Issues for the Society of Civil and Public Servants*, Coventry: Department of Sociology, University of Warwick.

Drake, P., Fairbrother, P., Fryer, B. and Stratford, G. (1982) *A Programme for Union Democracy: The Final Report for the Society of Civil and Public Servants*, Coventry: Department of Sociology, University of Warwick.

Exchequer and Audit Department (1981) *The Government's Expenditure Plans, 1981–82*, Cmnd 8175, London: HMSO.

Fairbrother, P. (1989) 'State Workers: Class Position and Collective Action', in G. Duncan (ed.), *Democracy and the Capitalist State*, Cambridge: Cambridge University Press.

Fairbrother, P. (1991) 'In a State of Change: Flexibility in the Civil Service', in A. Pollert (ed.), *Farewell to Flexibility?* Oxford: Blackwell.

Fairbrother, P. (1994) 'Privatisation and Local Trade Unionism', *Work, Employment and Society* **8**, 3: 339–56.

Fairbrother, P. and Waddington, J. (1990) 'The Politics of Trade Unionism: Evidence, Policy and Theory', *Capital & Class* **41**: 15–56.

Flanders, A. (1970) *Management and Unions: The Theory and Reform of Industrial Relations*, London: Faber & Faber.

Fosh, P. (1993) 'Membership Participation in Workplace Unionism: The Possibility of Union Renewal', *British Journal of Industrial Relations* **31**, 4: 577–92.

Fraser Report (1991) *Making the Most of Next Steps: The Management of Ministers' Departments and their Executive Agencies*, London: HMSO – Fraser Report, Efficiency Unit.

Fryer, B., Fairclough, A. and Manson, T. (1974) *Organisation and Change in the National Union of Public Employees*, Coventry: Department of Sociology, University of Warwick.

Goodrich, C. (1975 [1920]) *The Frontier of Control: A Study in British Workshop Politics*, London: Pluto Press.

Greer, P. (1994) *Transforming Central Government: The Next Steps Initiative*, Buckingham: Open University Press.

Griffiths Report (1988) 'A Report to the Secretary of State for Social Services by Sir Roy Griffiths', *Community Care: Agenda for Action*, London: HMSO.

Heery, E. and Kelly, J. (1994) 'Professional, Participative and Managerial Unionism: An Interpretation of Change in Trade Unions', *Work, Employment and Society* **8**, 1: 1–22.

HM Treasury (1984) *Progress in Financial Management in Government Departments*, Cmnd 9297, London: HMSO.

Humphreys, B. (1958) *Clerical Unions in the Civil Service*, Oxford: Blackwell & Mott.

Hyman, R. (1989) *The Political Economy of Industrial Relations: Theory and Practice in a Cold Climate*, Basingstoke: Macmillan.

Ibbs Report (1988) Jenkins, K., Caines, K. and Jackson, A. *Improving Management in Government: The Next Steps*, London: HMSO – The Ibbs Report.

Kelly, J. and Heery, E. (1994) *Working for the Union: British Trade Union Officers*, Cambridge: Cambridge University Press.

Kessler, I. (1986) 'Shop Stewards in Local Government Revisited', *British Journal of Industrial Relations* **24**, 3: 419–41.

Kessler, I. (1989) 'Bargaining Strategies in Local Government', in R. Mailly, S. Dimmock and A. Sethi (eds), *Industrial Relations in the Public Services*, London: Routledge.

Kessler, I. (1991) 'Workplace Industrial Relations in Local Government', *Employee Relations* **13**, 2: 1–31.

Marginson, P., Armstrong, P., Edwards, P. and Purcell, J. (1993) *The Control of Industrial Relations in Large Companies: An Initial Analysis of the Second Company Level Industrial Relations Survey*, Industrial Relations Research Unit, School of Industrial and Business Studies, University of Warwick, Coventry: Warwick Papers in Industrial Relations, No. 45, December.

Marsden, D. and Richardson, R. (1994) 'Performing for Pay? The Effects of "Merit Pay" on Motivation in a Public Service', *British Journal of Industrial Relations* **32**, 2: 243–61.

O'Connell Davidson, J. (1993) *Privatization and Employment Relations*, London: Mansell.

Pattison Report (1973) *The New Scottish Local Authorities: Organisation and Management Structures*, Edinburgh: Scottish Development Department, Working Group on Scottish Local Government Management Structures.

Reed, M. and Anthony, P. (1993) 'Southglam: Managing Organizational Change in a District Health Authority', in D. Gowler, K. Legge and C. Clegg (eds), *Case Studies in Organizational Behaviour and Human Resource Management*, London: Paul Chapman.

Scottish Office (1977) *Local Government Finance in Scotland*, Cmnd 6811, Edinburgh: HMSO.

Smith, P. (1995a) 'Change in Trade Unions since 1945', *Work, Employment and Society* **9**, 1: 137–46.

Smith, P. (1995b) 'The Road Haulage Industry: from Statutory Legislation to Contested Terrain', in C. Wrigley (ed.), *Industrial Relations in Britain 1945–79*, Aldershot: Edward Elgar.

Smith, P. and Morton, G. (1993) 'Union Exclusion and the Decollectivization of Industrial Relations in Contemporary Britain', *British Journal of Industrial Relations* **31**, 1: 97–114.

Social Security Committee, 1990–1 (1991) *The Organisation and Administration of the Department of Social Security*, HC550–i, London: HMSO.

Spoor, A. (1967) *White-Collar Union: Sixty Years of NALGO*, London: Heinemann.

Stewart, J. and Walsh, K. (1992) 'Change in the Management of Public Services', *Public Administration* **70**, Winter: 459–518.

Terry, M. (1982) 'Organising a Fragmented Workforce: Shop Stewards in Local Government', *British Journal of Industrial Relations* **20**, 1: 1–19.

Undy, R., Ellis, V., McCarthy, W. E. J. and Halmos, A. (1981) *Change in Trade Unions*, London: Hutchinson.

Waddington, J. (1995) *The Politics of Bargaining: The Merger Process and British Trade Union Structural Development, 1892–1987*, London: Mansell.

5

EMPOWERMENT VERSUS INTENSIFICATION

Union perspectives of change at the workplace

Jeremy Waddington and Colin Whitston

There is a widely held view in the UK that managements have held the upper hand in workplaces throughout the 1980s and early 1990s. Supported by the Thatcherite political project of the period, managers have sought increases in competitiveness. Associated with this programme, and intended to facilitate its achievement, managements have also introduced a range of measures at the workplace designed to alter the character of workplace relations. This chapter explores some of the workplace effects of these measures. Based on a survey of active union members, it argues that managerial attempts to increase worker involvement and participation have been overwhelmed by the effects of labour intensification. In particular, the pattern of grievances pursued by active union members suggests that work intensification remains at the core of workplace relations rather than forms of workers' empowerment.

Advocates of management-initiated workplace reform argue that recent practice has led, or will lead, to workers being more committed to the objectives of their employers; and that new approaches indicate the extent of the shift in management attitudes away from adversarial relations towards more collaborative arrangements (for example, see Hanson and Mather 1988). Empirical evidence of such a fundamental shift in employment relations is more difficult to uncover than some of the more prescriptive commentators would suggest, and casts a further critical light on a wide range of debate and practice in the area of workplace change. Survey evidence is drawn not from management sources, but from active trade union members in unionised firms. The evidence suggests that changed labour-management practices are increasingly in evidence. However, their introduction does not constitute a coherent pattern, nor do they indicate worker empowerment. Rather, they indicate extended managerial authority, closer control of labour, and a pattern of individual grievances which belie a reformed employment relationship.

These findings have direct implications for union policy. Several recent union policy statements have argued that unionists should move towards a 'social partnership' at the workplace, established around issues of 'common interest' such as productivity growth, training and health and safety (GMB/UCW 1990; Monks 1994; MSF 1994; TUC 1994). It is also argued that unions are unable to resist employers' challenges for the collective loyalty of workers. Advocates of this position argue that unions will have to accept a 'dual commitment' on behalf of workers to both union and company if they are to pursue their members' interests effectively (Bacon and Storey, this volume). Implicit in these positions is the assumption that management attitudes have changed to the extent that they are prepared to work more co-operatively with workers. The case of Rover is often cited as an exemplar of the 'social partnership' approach (Cave 1994: 127; Bacon and Storey, this volume). The extensive survey data of this chapter fail to find any widespread substantive evidence of such a shift in management attitudes. Instead, it shows that 'them and us' attitudes are firmly rooted among managers. These are likely to restrict opportunities for 'social partnership' schemes in the same way as the 'them and us' attitudes found among workers exposed to 'new industrial relations' practices (Kelly and Kelly 1991). In other words, union policies directed towards 'social partnership' will need to address opposition from management as well as that from within if they are to achieve their stated objectives.

The chapter comprises three sections. The first identifies some of the key features of workplace change in the UK context. This enables us to locate the analysis of trade union perspectives on workplace change within the debate on managerial practice. The second section presents evidence from active trade union members of changed management practices. This section shows the extent of practices intended to change methods of pay determination and to reorganise work. Workplace measures to promote participation and involvement are most pronounced at unionised workplaces (Millward *et al.* 1992; Millward 1994). By surveying active trade union members we thus focus attention on those workplaces where change is supposedly most developed. The third section examines the grievances pursued by trade union activists on behalf of their members. It shows that management attitudes are the most frequent source of grievances. In other words, the possibility, or the effectiveness, of a 'social partnership' approach on the part of the trade unions may be thwarted by opposition from management as well as from workers.

THE CURRENT POSITION: EVIDENCE FROM SURVEYS OF MANAGERS

This section isolates some of the principal features of workplace change examined in the later sections of the chapter. Whether these features of workplace change constitute a break with past practice we leave for discussion after presenting the data. A series of Workplace Industrial Relations Surveys (WIRS) identified some of the key elements of workplace change since 1980 (Daniel and Millward 1983; Millward and Stevens 1986; Millward et al. 1992; Millward 1994). Two features are shown to be central to developments in the UK. First, workplace change is rarely implemented as a single coherent package of measures; specific measures are more often introduced piecemeal. Second, workplace changes are more likely to be found in unionised rather than non-unionised workplaces; and to operate in conjunction with existing procedures rather than as their replacement. These features are reviewed below in order to establish the principal parameters of workplace change in the UK and to situate the survey of active trade union members on which this chapter is based.

Although workplace change is rarely introduced as a single coherent package, three elements are central to its development in the UK: commitment strategies; measures to increase flexibility; and approaches intended to individualise aspects of the employment relationship. There is some overlap between these categories. However, in order to highlight their character, they are treated separately here. These elements of workplace change are regarded as a means to improve competitiveness by raising employees' commitment and by involving workers in the continuous improvement of the production process (Collard and Dale 1989; Guest 1987, 1988).

In broad terms there are two forms of commitment strategies, both of which incorporate some features of participation and involvement; those that are 'soft on power' (Clegg et al. 1978) such as team briefings and quality circles, and those that may allow more substantial shifts in authority such as team working and single-status arrangements. There are also distinctions within these two forms of commitment strategy. For example, quality circles are regarded as promoting more direct participation than team briefings and may involve changes in the traditional patterns of authority relations (Collard and Dale 1989). Similarly, while team briefings are means whereby communications can be transmitted downwards through a company, quality circles necessitate some element of problem-solving which is directly related to the workplace. Where these soft forms of commitment have been introduced, managers report increases in effective decision-making, productivity rises and improvements in employee job satisfaction (IRS 1993). In addition, opinion-poll evidence collected by MORI shows that such schemes promote greater commitment to the company and support for its management (Industrial Society 1989). However, a survey of employees showed no increase in commitment following the introduction of team briefings (Marchington *et al.* 1992: 35).

In contrast to workplace changes that are soft on power, team working and single-status arrangements may involve more widespread changes to workplace authority relations. Team working, for example, is associated with workers' empowerment, increased job controls, and the shifting of informal disciplinary functions to within the team rather than relying solely on instructions from supervisors (Marchington and Parker 1990: 108). Similarly, single status or 'harmonisation' is regarded as a central pillar of a comprehensive commitment strategy as it removes some vertical demarcations (Oliver and Wilkinson 1988: 123–5). In the UK managements have tended to rely more on forms of commitment that are soft on power (Marchington *et al.* 1992; Millward *et al.* 1992: 165–80). This chapter sets out to establish whether forms of commitment, irrespective of their implications for power relations, are associated with significant changes in management attitudes.

A second element of workplace change examined here is measures to increase flexibility. There is now a vast literature which attempts to isolate the different features and implications of flexibility (Atkinson and Meager 1986; Pollert 1991). The purpose here is not to review this literature, but to identify those features which are operationalised in the part of the survey used for this research. Three features are used: two forms of functional flexibility, multiskilling and task flexibility; and flexible working time. Functional flexibility refers to the range of jobs a worker can undertake. Multiskilling is usually applied to horizontal functional flexibility; that is, the capacity to transfer between jobs at the same skill level. Task flexibility refers here to the mobility and interchangeability of labour within the workplace. A key difference in practice between multiskilling and task flexibility is that the former usually requires extensive training (for example, to provide an engineer with electrical skills), whereas the latter is achieved through the reorganisation of work rather than through additional training, such as the creation of a generic assistant grade in health to replace specific portering and catering grades. Finally, flexible working time incorporates measures that allow workers to have some limited control of the specific hours that they work, although the total hours are not necessarily affected.

The third element of workplace change highlighted in the UK is approaches intended to individualise aspects of the employment relationship. Attempts to individualise the employment relationship are intended to alter its character, allowing managers to raise commitment through the setting of individual goals which the employee can directly link to those of the organisation. In particular, pay systems have been revised to incorporate more individualised approaches. Four specific pay systems are considered here: performance pay/appraisal, plant/site/company bonus, group payment by results (PBR), and individual PBR. The WIRS3 study showed that by 1990 almost half (45 per cent) of all establishments had a variant of individual incentive pay, and about one-third (34 per cent) operated merit pay schemes. Compared to these individualised systems, group-based incentive pay systems were far less common; they were found at only 12 per cent of establishments (Millward et al. 1992: 260–1). Underpinning the introduction of all PBR schemes is the intention that they act 'as an incentive to work harder, or with less supervision' (Brown 1989: 261). Growth of such schemes may thus be associated with work intensification (Nichols 1991; Edwards and Whitston 1991). The hours of those working on individual PBR systems were less likely to be monitored than were the hours of those working on other systems (Millward et al. 1992: 261), suggesting that management were less reliant on direct supervision where such schemes operated.

In addition to this range of payment systems, two methods associated with pay determination are also included in the survey, job evaluation and work study. In recent years job evaluation has been associated with union involvement in the setting of pay differentials (Millward *et al.* 1992: 266–9). It thus incorporates some aspects of collective involvement in pay setting. Work study is associated with PBR schemes as a 'measure' of the link between the pace of work and the level of output. The growth of PBR schemes and work study are often commensurate, as work study is used to break down tasks into their component parts for measurement and pricing.

The location of these elements of workplace change is also a feature of its development in the UK. Contrary to the position in the USA, where wide-ranging HRM practices are more a feature of non-unionised workplaces (Foulkes 1980; Kochan *et al.* 1986), workplace change incorporating measures intended to raise commitment are concentrated in unionised rather then non-unionised workplaces in the UK (Sisson 1993; Millward 1994: 129). Some managements in the UK have been unable to dispense with unions in the short run, particularly the role of the shop steward in the 'negotiation of order', and have relied on a workplace dualism that incorporates aspects of individualism and collectivism (Hyman 1989: 32; Storey 1992: 242–62). While the piecemeal introduction of workplace change may qualify its effects, elements of recent workplace changes are nevertheless often intended to exclude or weaken the position of unions at the workplace (Smith and Morton 1993). Paradoxically, a union presence is shown to promote the incidence of forms of commitment, participation and involvement (Leighton 1992). By basing our sample on the responses of active trade union members, we focus on those workplaces where change is thought to be most advanced. In other words, if there is evidence of a fundamental shift in workplace relations and management attitudes, it is most likely to be found at the workplaces from which our sample is drawn.

In summary, the position in the UK is mixed. An extensive range of commitment, involvement and individualising practices have been introduced, and the introduction of these practices is concentrated in unionised workplaces. This pattern of introduction leads to a key hypothesis of this chapter. For if recent workplace changes promote employee commitment and support for managers' actions, as surveys of managers suggest, and practices directed towards these goals are concentrated in unionised workplaces, we would anticipate the pattern of grievances pursued by trade unionists to indicate a shift in management attitudes. Evidence would be expected to show that the attitudes associated with traditional collective bargaining are diminished in their effect as the influence of the different elements of workplace change assume greater significance in the transformation of workplace relations. Furthermore, as the introduction of workplace change is concentrated in unionised workplaces, the responses of active trade union members should indicate 'the best case' in the UK. These propositions are examined in the following section.

CHANGE IN THE WORKPLACE: THE TRADE UNIONISTS' VIEW

The data used in this chapter are drawn from the Trade Unions into the 1990s Project conducted at the Industrial Relations Research Unit, University of Warwick. This project involves twelve major trade unions whose membership covers the entire industrial and occupational spectrum of employment in the UK. More than 70,000 postal questionnaires were distributed during 1991 and 1992 to new union members, active members and workplace representatives, and full-time union officers. Preliminary results from eight unions are presented here. The responses of more than 4,500 activists are examined; however, since not all activists answered every part of the questions, the numbers of those who answered each question are provided in each figure below. While there are some instances where responses were collected from more than one union activist in a single workplace, the number of these is relatively small. The data, therefore, record active unionists' perspectives on developments at more than 4,500 workplaces in the UK. The data are presented in two sections: the first section examines aggregate data; the second examines the data disaggregated by sector.

The national picture

Figure 5.1 shows responses from active members on the extent of selected management practices covering a significant number of the members they represent. For each management practice two measures are provided: the first indicates the coverage three years prior to the survey; the second shows the coverage at the time of the survey. The difference between the two measures thus illustrates the perceived extent of growth of each management practice. Two groups of management practice are identified here:

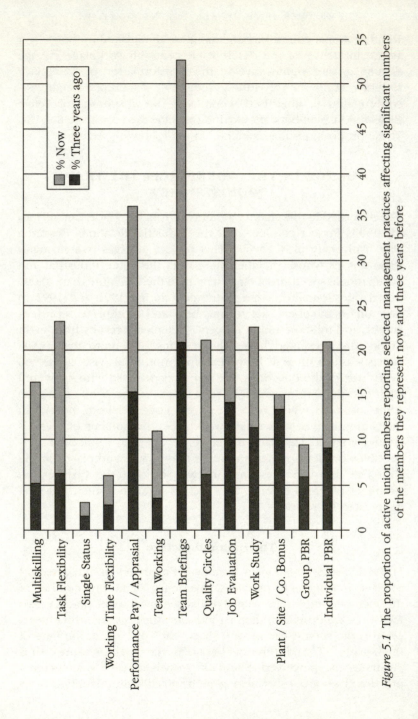

Figure 5.1 The proportion of active union members reporting selected management practices affecting significant numbers of the members they represent now and three years before

pay determination issues comprising performance pay/appraisal, plant/site/company bonus, group PBR, individual PBR, work study and job evaluation; and features of work organisation including multiskilling, task flexibility, team working, flexible working time, single status, team briefings and quality circles. Each of these groups is considered separately for ease of explanation.

Pay determination

Active union members recorded considerable variation in the coverage and growth of the different methods of pay determination. At the time of the survey performance pay/appraisal covered more than 35 per cent of workplaces. The incidence of performance pay/appraisal had grown by 21 percentage points, indicating growth of a managerial practice essentially unrestricted by industrial or occupational boundaries. While appraisal is not always used directly as part of a payments system, the incidence of this category does indicate a growing trend towards a closer monitoring of individual effort, and, by extension, individual job content. However, job evaluation, long identified as a procedural tool for collectively determining demarcation and differentials in unionised workplaces (Millward *et al*. 1992: 269), was also reported by over 30 per cent of activists, and its incidence had grown by 19 percentage points. This may indicate that individualisation occurs within an institutional framework which limits its impact for many workers.

Forms of individual incentive payments were reported by over 20 per cent of activists. Furthermore, such payment systems had increased in coverage by twelve percentage points in the three years prior to the survey. In contrast, the growth rates of collective systems were minimal (group PBR, + 3 percentage points; plant/site/company bonus, + 2 percentage points). Group PBR systems were reported at only 9 per cent of workplaces and plant/site/company bonus schemes at 15 per cent of workplaces. These data confirm the evidence of managers who report 12 per cent of workplaces as covered by group PBR and 17 per cent of establishments with some form of group or whole establishment/organisation incentive pay scheme (Millward *et al*. 1992: 261). Where incentive systems operate, there is little evidence of the development of team working or other forms of work organisation which depart from traditional cash-nexus motivators. However, the incidence and growth of work study, the basis of traditional incentive schemes, matches closely those of individual PBR systems.

Work organisation

Increases were also recorded in each of the work reorganisation practices. However, it is clear that task flexibility and multiskilling are more common, and are growing more rapidly, than team working, flexible working time arrangements or single status. Task flexibility was reported by 23 per cent of respondents and had grown by almost 17 percentage points, while multiskilling was reported at 16 per cent of workplaces and had increased by nearly 9 percentage points. Given the wide occupational spread of respondents, these figures suggest extensive gains by employers in the field of labour utilisation. It remains an open question whether these gains in labour utilisation have been 'sold' to management by workers or have been extracted from workers by managements, although Ingram (1991) suggests that the higher rate of wage settlements associated with changes in working practices indicates the former rather than the latter. The higher incidence of task flexibility compared to multiskilling also suggests that gains in labour utilisation are being achieved through the reorganisation of work more frequently than through retraining programmes. The relatively low incidence and growth of team working provide a notable contrast to the growing incidence of forms of task flexibility and multiskilling. Team working covered fewer than 12 per cent of workplaces and had increased by less than 8 percentage points. This result is quite consistent with the low levels and growth of group PBR systems reported above. Similarly, flexible working time was reported by only 7 per cent of respondents and showed only moderate growth from a low level.

Single status was even more infrequent: it was found at fewer than 4 per cent of workplaces and had grown by less than 2 percentage points. These results duplicate those recorded from management surveys (Millward 1994: 104–13). While this practice is often associated with Japanese-owned manufacturing sites, it is claimed that it is not exclusive to them (Oliver and Wilkinson 1988), and that it is a key element in encouraging flexibility and commitment (IRS 1993). Given the claims made about the drive for flexibility and commitment, it is surprising that the coverage of the measure is so limited. This limited coverage suggests that work-place relations remain hierarchically demarcated. This result confirms case study evidence from greenfield sites where even the most ambitious attempts failed to achieve a single-status employment environment (Newell 1993).

Among the commitment practices, team briefings covered the largest number of workplaces and were the fastest growing. They were reported in no fewer than 53 per cent of workplaces and had grown in coverage by 31 percentage points. This figure is broadly comparable with management surveys which reported such arrangements in 44 per cent of establishments in industry and commerce, although they were more numerous at unionised establishments (Millward 1994: 127). As they entail only a one-way channel of communication, team briefings are not part of direct participation or worker empowerment under any definition. Quality circles, for which more claims are made as forms of direct participation and as mechanisms for changing workplace authority relations (Collard and Dale 1989), were reported at a relatively low 22 per cent of workplaces, and had been growing at half the rate of team briefings. Given that quality circles tend to exist for only short periods and have relatively high rates of decay, this figure is likely to exaggerate current incidence. The low rate of growth of quality circles may also reflect the opposition of many middle managements to their introduction and a growing preference for Total Quality Management approaches (Marchington *et al.* 1993; Hill 1991). However, the relative emphasis on team briefings suggests that managements are opting for those elements of work-place change that have the least effect on workplace power relations.

Sectoral differences

This section highlights the marked differences in management practices between sectors and how these differ from the national situation. Three sectors are identified for the analysis. The private sector comprises 2,380 responses from active members concentrated in manufacturing. Public services include 1,294 responses from activists working primarily in the National Health Service and local government. Finally, the exposed sector is made up of 961 active members working in privatised utilities, government agencies and other areas subject to 'marketisation'. There are some occupational differences within these samples: responses from the private sector are concentrated among manual occupations; responses from the public services are primarily drawn from those working as technical and health professionals or in personal and protective service occupations; and exposed-sector responses are from those working in managerial, professional and technical occupations. In order to remain consistent with the data presented earlier, the distinction between pay determination and work organisation practices is retained.

Pay determination

Figure 5.2 presents data on the six items more or less directly concerned with pay determination. In order to highlight the different patterns of sectoral development the graph shows only the index of growth of each item over the three years prior to the distribution of the survey.

Performance pay/appraisal grew in coverage throughout each of the sectors. Growth was fastest in the public services and, particularly, in the exposed sector. This may reflect the occupational differences in the samples, with managerial, professional and technical staff being most affected. It may also be associated with the extensive de-layering among such staff in the exposed sector. Whatever the case, in each of the three sectors it is clear that there were marked increases in the monitoring of individual effort. Job evaluation has recently been associated with unionised establishments and has represented a significant source of collective influence on work organisation and reward. Its continued growth in the public services suggests that much of this collective influence still remains. It would appear that many of the institutional changes in public services, for example, the creation of hospital trusts, has proceeded at a faster rate than has the rejection of more traditional forms of collective influence. If this argument is correct, managerial reliance on traditional practices affords unions some opportunities to exert a workplace influence. However, this position may change rapidly with increased managerial autonomy, 'marketisation' and the rejection of national or framework agreements (for example, see Bach and Winchester 1994).

Job evaluation is also growing rapidly in the exposed sector. The points regarding the public services thus also retain some force in the exposed sector. There is also evidence of more widespread use of personal contracts among the managerial and professional

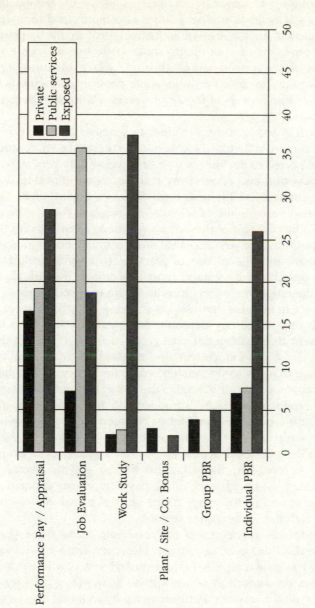

Figure 5.2 The growth of pay determination issues by sector

groups from which the exposed-sector sample was drawn. The increased usage of personal contracts is likely to reduce the influence of job evaluation. This point is also quite consistent with the rapid growth in the use of individual PBR in the exposed sector. In other words, although some collective influence is retained in the exposed-sector through job evaluation, this influence would appear to be under some pressure as methods to individualise more aspects of the employment relationship become commonplace.

The growth in work study was almost exclusive to the exposed sector and is more difficult to explain. *Ceteris paribus* work study would be expected to decline, or at least increase only very slowly, as new production and supervisory techniques are introduced to replace the rigidities of Taylorist forms of work organisation. The growth of work study in the exposed sector suggests that it is being 'Taylorised' after the rest of the economy. In combination with the growth of performance pay/appraisal these results seem to indicate more extensive managerial use of practices to ensure workplace control, coupled to the establishment of more individualised aspects of the employment relationship in the exposed sector.

Figure 5.3 extends this analysis by showing both the coverage and growth of selected pay determination practices. It is immediately apparent that managerial change of methods of pay determination is most pronounced in the exposed sector. Given the wide-ranging changes to ownership, company structure and bargaining arrangements in this sector, this pattern is not surprising. While the range of practices introduced in the exposed sector suggests that there is little consistency between the 'marketisation' initiatives being taken, the rate of growth of some of these practices in the public services suggests that a similar evolution is underway. In contrast, the situation in the private sector is relatively sedate. Although each of the pay determination practices increased in coverage, the range in the rates of increase is narrow compared with that in the other sectors.

Work study was concentrated in the private sector three years prior to the distribution of the survey. However, from a low base, work study has grown rapidly in the exposed sector, where it now covers a greater proportion of workplaces than either the private sector or the public services. Performance pay/appraisal is growing in each of the three sectors. Given the occupational composition of the exposed sector the results from this sector may not be a

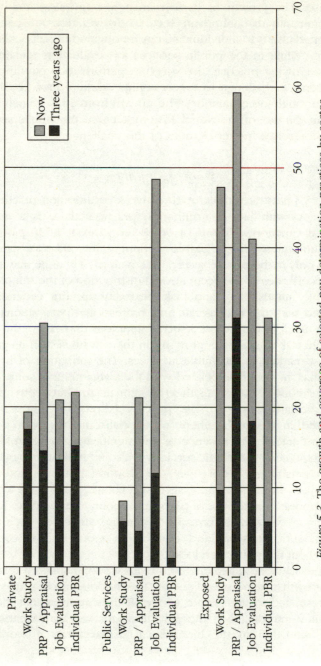

Figure 5.3 The growth and coverage of selected pay determination practices by sector

surprise. The growth of performance pay/appraisal among the predominantly manual private sector, however, does suggest more concerted efforts to individualise pay among traditionally collective groups. While in the public services job evaluation remains the fastest growing practice, the surge in performance pay/appraisal represents a challenge to the restraints workers may be able to exert through job evaluation. The growth from an extremely small base in the use of individual PBR systems in the public services may represent a further element of this challenge.

Work organisation

Figure 5.4 illustrates the growth of work organisation practices by sector. As with pay determination practices there is a marked sectoral variation in forms of work reorganisation. In particular, growth in multiskilling, flexible working time and single status are found only in the private sector. This pattern of change may reflect the peculiarities of the occupational distribution of the sample. For example, multiskilling and task flexibility are not generally associated with the managerial and professional occupations from which much of the exposed-sector sample is drawn.

While task flexibility is growing in the private sector, its growth is most marked in the public services. The formation of hospital trusts has thus been associated with the dismantling of some of the demarcations between health professionals and between auxiliary and ancillary workers. This process is probably most clearly reflected in the replacement of specialist grades with generic assistant grades. The absence of any significant growth in flexible working time in the public services is also an indicator of managements' retaining control over the working hours of individual employees. Preliminary analysis of a separate question on working time suggests that the use of part-time labour, temporary and fixed-term contracts, and all forms of 'distancing' strategies, such as the use of subcontractors and contracting work out, is common throughout the public services.

Single-status arrangements and team working showed relatively little growth, irrespective of sector. The introduction of single status was restricted to the private sector. It thus appears that the task flexibility introduced in the private sector was accompanied by some reduction in the hierarchical demarcation of workplace

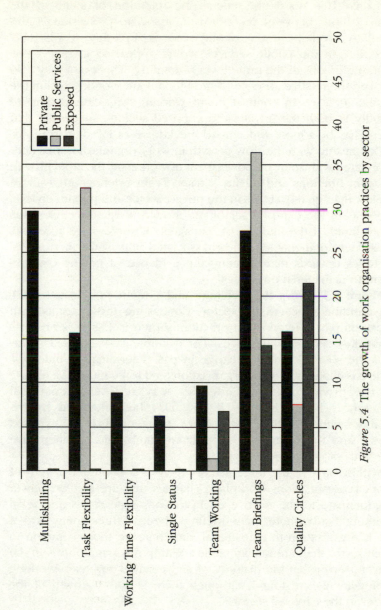

Figure 5.4 The growth of work organisation practices by sector

relations, whereas in the public services hierarchical demarcation remains. This no doubt reflects the retention of some of the demarcations between professionals, associate professionals and auxiliary workers in the public services. In other words, task flexibility in the public services would appear to involve those working in jobs at the same level of training. This point may also explain the relative absence of growth in team working within the public services. In contrast, team working was extended more rapidly in both the private and exposed sectors, suggesting that there may be a more widespread breakdown of job demarcations.

Contrasting with the slow growth in work organisation practices associated with some empowerment of workers is the rapid growth of team briefings and quality circles. Team briefings grew more rapidly than quality circles in the private sector and public services, whereas in the exposed sector the growth in quality circles was more rapid. If the findings of management surveys are accepted, these developments should be associated with shifts in workers' attitudes towards management and evidence of greater commitment to managerial objectives.

Figure 5.5 shows the coverage and growth of selected work organisation practices by sector. Contrasting these results with those on pay determination practices shown in Figure 5.3 reveals some key sectoral differences. For example, the exposed sector was the source of much change in pay determination practices, whereas changes in work organisation tend to be more of a feature in the private sector. While this may reflect occupational differences in the sample, it may also be influenced by the abandonment of national bargaining arrangements in the exposed sector and the failure to establish any uniformity in alternative methods of pay determination.

Within each of the three sectors there is a common pattern of work reorganisation: workplace changes that are soft on power predominate to the relative exclusion of single status and team working. Furthermore, team briefings, the least threatening form of work organisation to managerial authority, are more common in each sector than are quality circles. Within this pattern, it is in the private sector that the majority of single-status and team-working arrangements are found, although there is some growth of the lattter in the exposed sector.

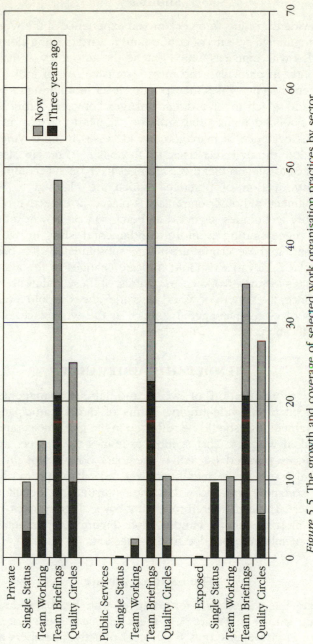

Figure 5.5 The growth and coverage of selected work organisation practices by sector

Summary

The evidence points to a very mixed experience at the workplace, with traditional systems of control and reward existing alongside or blended with practices which extend the autonomy of managerial authority. In particular, the more extensive use of individualised payment systems which incorporate closer monitoring of performance and which involve direct linkages between output and pay have extended managerial authority. Similarly, across all sectors there is evidence of management successes in improving labour utilisation through increases in flexibility. There is also some evidence to suggest that these changes have been accompanied by the introduction of practices which are claimed to improve commitment, although emphasis is placed, irrespective of sector, on those techniques regarded as being soft on power rather than those necessitating a more fundamental shift in workplace relations. If these claims are to be substantiated, the pattern of workplace grievances should indicate changes in the attitudes of managers towards workers. In contrast, if these claims are without substance, the pattern of workplace grievances should indicate the effects of closer managerial control at the workplace and work intensification.

MEMBERSHIP GRIEVANCES

If the reorganisation of work and labour management has produced more wide-ranging forms of direct participation and involvement, this should be reflected in the grievances pursued by individual workers. This section examines the subject matter of grievances pursued by active members both nationally and at sectoral level. Active members were asked to specify the three most common grievances that they pursued on behalf of their members. The data, therefore, do not cover all grievances, but only those most frequently handled (see Figure 5.6). In total, 4,635 active members responded to the question.

The national picture

Despite the widespread reporting of task flexibility and multi-skilling shown in Figure 5.1, these practices were not a major source of grievances; only 8 per cent of active members reported these forms of work organisation as the source of one of their three most popular grievances. Changing these elements of work organisation does not thus produce widespread opposition and lends some weight to the arguments that these aspects of flexibility may be 'sold' by workers in exchange for higher rates of pay (Ingram 1991) or a greater awareness among employees of the commercial pressures on firms (Marsden and Thompson 1990). In contrast to the latter argument, staffing levels and workload are also reported among the three most commonly pursued grievances by over 20 per cent of active trade unionists. The effort bargain, rather than work organisation, thus remains at the heart of disputes concerning the employment relationship. The emphasis placed on staffing levels and workload points to work intensification as underpinning the pattern of workplace grievances. Furthermore, the citing of discipline as a source of grievances by 22 per cent of active trade union members is further evidence of tight workplace controls enforced by line management. In addition, almost 20 per cent of activists mention the interpretation of agreements, and a further 20 per cent grading issues, among the top three individual grievances. These results indicate a continued attachment to collective controls over labour organisation and effort. All these factors exceed pay as causes of individual grievances.

Similarly, for individual workers the working environment remains central to day-to-day relationships at work. No fewer than 34 per cent of active members reported health and safety as being one of their three most common sources of grievances. As work intensification endangers physical and psychological health, this result is consistent with the argument that work intensification is at the core of workplace relations. Health and safety remains one of the few areas where active members are in a position to draw upon an extensive case law and specialists in health and safety employed by their unions in support of grievances. The high prevalence of health and safety grievances may thus reflect the impact of legal support and the coverage of formal health and safety procedures. A further contributory factor to this high incidence may be the 'redefinition' of grievances as health and safety issues, thereby enabling recourse to a legal procedure that is familiar to active members.

Given the claims for the new labour management practices, it is a surprise that 42 per cent of activists placed management attitudes or behaviour among the top three individual grievances. This result

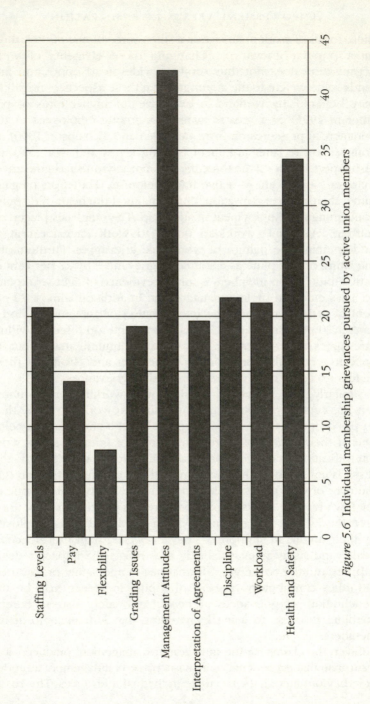

Figure 5.6 Individual membership grievances pursued by active union members

belies a fundamental change in workplace relations. Management attitudes were the most significant source of grievances reported by active members. It thus appears that there is a critical mismatch between policy formation and aims and the daily experience of work. This mismatch may be explained in terms of the prevalence of commitment measures that are soft on power rather than more wide-ranging measures. Put starkly, any increase in worker commitment accruing from team briefings or quality circles appears insufficient to overcome differences in the workplace between managers and workers when labour intensification is underway. It may also indicate the extent of differences between levels of management. The design of such policies by senior managers is relatively easy, but it is more difficult for middle and line managers to accept and operationalise these policies. This result, therefore, may indicate a failure to operationalise at workplace level policies formulated by senior managers at corporate level. Similar evidence of a mismatch between policy and practice, with roots in competitive pressures, have also been noted in a number of case studies (Edwards and Whitston 1993). In other words, while managers claim that recent workplace change is associated with greater workforce commitment to management objectives, the centrality to the pattern of grievances of management attitudes suggests that this commitment is, at best, qualified.

Sectoral differentiation

Earlier sections of this chapter showed considerable variation by sector in the form of workplace change. If, as we assume, the pattern of grievances reflects the peculiarities of workplace change, the incidence of grievances should also vary across sectors. This section examines this proposition using the same sectors as identified above. Figure 5.7 presents the results in the form of the most frequently cited grievances in each sector.

It is clear from Figure 5.7 that there are quite marked sectoral differences in the pattern of grievances. Management attitudes and health and safety were prominent sources of grievances in each of the three sectors. In the private sector other principal sources included interpretation of agreements, discipline and workload; in public services staffing levels, workload and grading issues; and in the exposed sector staffing levels, pay and the interpretation of agreements.

171

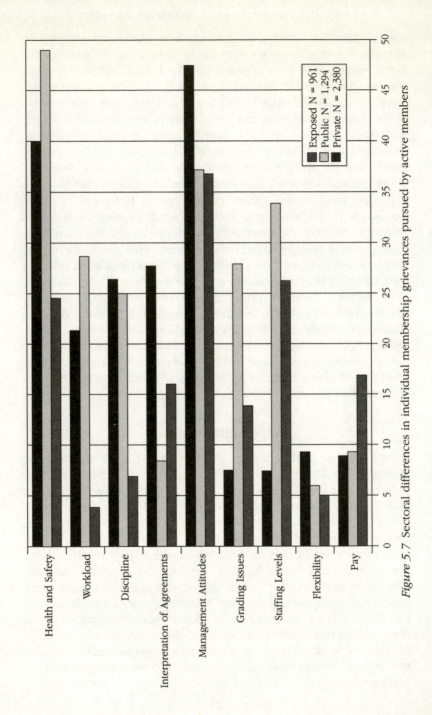

Figure 5.7 Sectoral differences in individual membership grievances pursued by active members

Management attitudes and health and safety were sources of grievances common to all sectors. In other words, the shift in management attitudes claimed to accompany recent workplace changes was absent throughout. Furthermore, management attitudes remained the single most cited source of grievances in the private sector, where both soft and hard forms of change to workplace organisation were reported (see Figure 5.5). In other words, even where team working and single status were most prevalent, they did not mitigate the effects of management attitudes. This would seem to suggest that other elements of management change are more prevalent in their effect on grievances than are measures to increase employee commitment, participation and involvement.

The appearance of health and safety as a key source of grievances in all sectors reflects the impact of legal support and the coverage of formal health and safety procedures. However, variation between sectors is also apparent. For example, the relatively low level of health and safety grievances taken in the exposed sector no doubt reflects the occupational composition of the sample; in particular, its bias towards senior white-collar grades. The particular emphasis on health and safety in the public sector may result from the large proportion of respondents from the National Health Service, where workplace health and safety issues are closely associated with professional medical practice.

The case for labour intensification remaining at the heart of workplace relations can be made for all sectors, although there are peculiarities to each. In the private sector and public services, workload issues are a key source of grievances, whereas staffing levels are central in both the public services and the exposed sector. The appearance of workload issues and staffing levels in public services suggest that issues concerned with the intensification of work are at the forefront of workplace relations. It seems likely that the labour shakeout in the private sector during the recession of the early 1980s accounts for the absence of staffing levels as a source of grievances.

Turning to the other issues peculiar to each of the sectors also reveals consistencies with the changes in workplace organisation and pay determination reported earlier. For example, the wide-ranging series of changes in pay determination practices within the exposed sector (see Figure 5.3) is accompanied by a relatively high level of grievances over pay issues. Similarly, in the two sectors where the most active moves towards bargaining decentralisation have occurred, the private and exposed sectors, the interpretation of agreements remains a central issue. It also appears that the sharp increase in job evaluation in the public services (see Figure 5.3) was accompanied by a similar increase in grading issues as a source of grievances. This relationship is quite consistent with the maintenance of some forms of collective influence over pay determination and differentials in public services.

CONCLUSIONS

The picture of the world of work as experienced by a broad spectrum of active union members underlines the need for caution when estimating the pace and direction of change in the employment relationship. Whatever innovative features may be found within particular organisations or workplaces, other developments in the same workplaces ensure that change is more uneven, more muddled, and less radical than many supporters of recent practice would lead us to believe. A more cautious assessment is required of workers' experience of commitment, participation and involvement. In particular, the effects of measures intended to enhance employee commitment are undermined by those arising from measures to increase competitiveness through work intensification. The centrality of management attitudes as the principal source of grievances also suggests that the introduction of measures to raise employee commitment has not been accompanied by a fundamental shift in management behaviour. This may indicate differences between the practices of managers at the workplace and the intention of their senior colleagues in formulating some of the workplace changes. However, the reluctance to move away from the elements of workplace change that are soft on power, and the more widespread adoption of pay systems which incorporate the monitoring of individual effort, suggest that tightening control remains the overarching objective of management practice at the workplace, irrespective of the intention of senior managers.

Recent management practice does not represent a substantial basis on which to establish a 'social partnership' between workers and managers at the workplace. Indeed, the mismatch between the intention of senior managers and the practices of line managers is not dissimilar to that between the statements of intention at the national level of unions in support of social partnership and the persistence of 'them and us' attitudes among workers (Kelly and Kelly 1991). The evidence presented here cannot by itself show that 'social partnership' is unobtainable, but it does cast doubt on the underlying assumption of such a policy, namely, that the labour process and the employment relationship have evolved in a more consensual direction. This is not to argue that new work organisation and management practices cannot be modified by collective bargaining; on the contrary, the evidence tends to suggest the continuing importance of independent collective action.

ACKNOWLEDGEMENTS

The authors thank Paul Marginson, Helen Newell, Keith Sisson and the editors of this volume for their helpful comments on earlier drafts of this paper.

REFERENCES

Atkinson, J. and Meager, N. (1986) *Changing Working Patterns: How Companies Achieve Flexibility to Meet New Needs*, Report prepared by the Institute of Manpower Studies for the National Economic Development Office, London: NEDO.

Bach, S. and Winchester, D. (1994) 'Opting Out of Pay Devolution? The Prospects for Local Pay Bargaining in UK Public Services', *British Journal of Industrial Relations* **32**, 2: 263–82.

Brown, W. (1989) 'Managing Remuneration', in K. Sisson (ed.), *Personnel Management in Britain*, Oxford: Blackwell.

Cave, A. (1994) *Managing Change in the Workplace*, London: Kogan Page.

Clegg, C., Nicholson, N., Ursell, G., Blyton, P. and Wall, T. (1978) 'Managers' Attitudes Towards Industrial Democracy', *Industrial Relations Journal* **9**, 3: 4–17.

Collard, R. and Dale, B. (1989) 'Quality Circles', in K. Sisson (ed.), *Personnel Management in Britain*, Oxford: Blackwell.

Daniel, W. and Millward, N. (1983) *Workplace Industrial Relations in Britain*, London: Heinemann.

Edwards, P. and Whitston, C. (1991) 'Workers are Working Harder: Effort and Shop-floor Relations in the 1980s', *British Journal of Industrial Relations* **29**, 4: 593–601.

Edwards, P. and Whitston, C. (1993) *Attending to Work: The Management of Attendance and Shopfloor Order*, Oxford: Blackwell.

Foulkes, F. (1980) *Personnel Policies in Large Non-Union Companies*, New Jersey: Prentice-Hall.

GMB/UCW (1990) *New Agenda: Bargaining for Prosperity in the 1990s*, London: General, Municipal and Boilermakers' Union and the Union of Communication Workers.

Guest, D. (1987) 'Human Resource Management and Industrial Relations', *Journal of Management Studies* **24**, 5: 503–21.

Guest, D. (1988) 'Human Resource Management: A New Opportunity for Psychologists or Another Passing Fad?', *The Occupational Psychologist* **2**.

Hanson, C. and Mather, G. (1988) *Striking Out Strikes: Changing Employment Relations in the British Labour Market*, Hobart Paper 10, London: Institute of Economic Affairs.

Hill, S. (1991) 'Why Quality Circles Failed but Total Quality Management Might Succeed', *British Journal of Industrial Relations* **29**, 4: 541–68.

Hyman, R. (1989) 'Trade Unions, Control and Resistance', in R. Hyman *The Political Economy of Industrial Relations: Theory and Practice in a Cold Climate*, London: Macmillan.

Industrial Relations Services (1993) 'Employee Involvement – The Current State of Play', *Industrial Relations Review and Report*, October, 545: 3–11.

Industrial Society (1989) *Blueprint for Success: A Report on Involving Employees in Britain*, London: Industrial Society.

Ingram, P. (1991) 'Changes in Working Practices in British Manufacturing Industry in the 1980s: A Study of Employee Concessions Made during Wage Negotiations', *British Journal of Industrial Relations* **29**, 1: 1–24.

Kelly, J. and Kelly, C. (1991) '"Them and Us": Social Psychology and "The New Industrial Relations"', *British Journal of Industrial Relations* **29**, 1, 25–48.

Kochan, T., Katz, H. and McKersie, R. (1986) *The Transformation of American Industrial Relations*, New York: Basic Books.

Leighton, P. (1992) *Employee Involvement: The East Anglian Experience*, Chelmsford: Anglia Business School.

Marchington, M., Goodman, J., Wilkinson, A. and Ackers, P. (1992) *New Developments in Employee Involvement*, Research Series No. 2, Sheffield: Employment Department.

Marchington, M. and Parker, P. (1990) *Changing Patterns of Employee Relations*, Hemel Hempstead: Harvester.

Marchington, M., Wilkinson, A., Ackers, P. and Goodman, J. (1993) 'The Influence of Managerial Relations on Waves of Employee Involvement', *British Journal of Industrial Relations* **31**, 4: 553–76.

Marsden, D. and Thompson, M. (1990) 'Flexibility Agreements and their Significance in the Increase in Productivity in British Manufacturing since 1980', *Work, Employment and Society* **4**, 1: 83–104.

Millward, N. (1994) *The New Industrial Relations?*, London: Policy Studies Institute.

Millward, N. and Stevens, M. (1986) *British Workplace Industrial Relations 1980–1984*, Aldershot: Gower.

Millward, N., Stevens, M., Smart, D. and Hawes, W. (1992) *Workplace Industrial Relations in Transition*, London: Dartmouth.

Monks, J. (1994) 'Working Up to Recovery', *New Statesman and Society*, 18 November: 34–5.

MSF (1994) *New Management: An MSF Guide*, London: Manufacturing, Science and Finance.

Newell, H. (1993) 'Exploding the Myth of Greenfield Sites', *Personnel Management* January: 20–3.

Nichols, T. (1991) 'Labour Intensification, Work Injuries and the Measure-ment of Percentage Utilization of Labour', *British Journal of Industrial Relations* **29**, 4: 568–92.

Oliver, N. and Wilkinson, B. (1988) *The Japanization of British Industry*, Oxford: Blackwell.

Pollert, A. (1991) 'The Orthodoxy of Flexibility', in A. Pollert (ed.), *Farewell to Flexibility?*, Oxford: Blackwell.

Sisson, K. (1993) 'In Search of HRM', *British Journal of Industrial Relations* **31**, 2: 201–10.

Smith, P. and Morton, G. (1993) 'Union Exclusion and the Decollectiv-ization of Industrial Relations in Contemporary Britain', *British Journal of Industrial Relations* **31**, 1: 97–114.

Storey, J. (1992) *Developments in the Management of Human Resources*, Oxford: Blackwell.

TUC (1994) *Human Resource Management: A Trade Union Response*, London: Trades Union Congress.

6

'TEAM WORK' ON THE ASSEMBLY LINE

Contradiction and the dynamics of union resilience

Anna Pollert

INTRODUCTION

Despite the widespread interest in new or revamped management practices[1] to increase employee involvement and commitment to company aims, there is comparatively little qualitative research on workplace responses to complement surveys such as that of Marchington on employee involvement (1992) and Guest and Dewe on worker commitment (1991). As Morris and Wood (1991) have argued, techniques which circumvent institutional structures of industrial relations are best grasped by processual, case study analysis, which can illuminate substantive changes in working practices, trade union and worker response. The impact of new management techniques on pluralist industrial relations (Guest 1989; Beaumont 1991; Martinez Lucio and Weston 1992a and b; Storey 1992) is now of particular concern since the findings of WIRS3 (Millward *et al.* 1992: 176) that management worker involvement initiatives were more common in unionised than in non-unionised workplaces (48 as against 36 per cent). One current issue to probe further is whether the individualised approaches of new management techniques can co-exist with traditional collective bargaining systems, running in parallel as dual structures (Storey 1992; Sisson 1993: 208), or whether the latter will 'wither on the vine' in the long term.

The present study is of team working in a food manufacturing factory, within the framework of a hardening of management approach, tightening market competition, the turn to employee involvement as a mode of improving productive performance, and a multinational take-over. The approach is a top-down, vertical slice through the organisation, from senior management to the shop floor, in which experiences and perceptions of the new management practices are explored. Team working as an ideo-logical construct of worker involvement and as a mode of organising the shop floor is analysed in terms of its artificiality in the context of the repetitive, routine nature of continuous process and assembly production. Its real economic significance, as a system of budgetary control over labour costs devolved to first line managers, is set against its participatory rhetoric, while problems of organisational politics, between economic team fragmentation and overall hierarchic corporate control, are revealed in complex sets of contradictions. The resulting tensions and ambiguities have unanticipated implications for those who manage the new system, and those working within and against it. Their significance for the survival of workplace trade unionism is paradoxical: for in spite of the management-stated rationale for team working as a means of marginalising the shop steward from shop-floor control, the in-adequacies of team working as a means of managing production and promoting shop-floor consent opens spaces for the union to retain a foot-hold. However, how far the opportunities for union controls afforded by the contradictions of management's new techniques are also dependent on managerial tolerance of shop stewards' intervention, either for short-lived pragmatic reasons or because of positive support for the efficacy of pluralist industrial relations, is a further factor of analysis. The balance between these two dimensions of union survival in an increasingly unitarist, anti-union climate of management, will only emerge with longi-tudinal analysis.

The case study of Choc-Co, a large site of a multi-establishment, unionised company in the food processing industry, is based on several weeks in 1992, and a follow-up of developments in 1994. Union membership was close to 100 per cent for craft and pro-duction workers, the first organised by the Amalgamated Engineer-ing and Electrical Union, the latter by the General, Municipal and Boilermakers' Union. The research method comprised semi-structured, recorded interviews with company and factory senior managers, middle and first-line managers, production workers and shop stewards. Employees were interviewed individually and in groups, depending on circumstance and preference, while inter-views with shop stewards were supplemented by attendance at a monthly shop stewards' meeting.[2] Observation on the shop floor and company and union documentation also inform the analysis.

The importance of the labour process, skill and gender division for analysing the impact of new management techniques is a feature of the approach.

NEW MANAGEMENT TECHNIQUES IN CONTEXT

The food manufacturing industry and Choc-Co

The choice of researching a food manufacturing company is a deliberate attempt to move 'mainstream' analysis of new management techniques into gender-mixed sectors. Most research on new management focuses on male-dominated industries or is gender blind, and even recent analysis on this subject in the food industry chooses to exclude the gender dimension from analysis (Scott 1994: 33). The Food, Drink and Tobacco sector (Standard Industrial Classification) has a gender composition of 59 per cent male and 41 per cent female, more feminised than manufacturing as a whole (70.3 per cent male, 29.7 per cent female), but exhibiting the feature of sexual division neglected in the much-researched but far from typical Motor Vehicles and Parts sector (88.5 per cent male). The combined Food, Drink and Tobacco industries also comprise the single largest British manufacturing group, producing 17.8 per cent of gross manufacturing output (*Business Monitor* 1989), and the second largest employer after mechanical engineering, with 500,800 workers (and food by far the largest part). It is a relatively successful part of the UK economy and despite the recession, expanded from 9.9 per cent to 11.4 per cent of manufacturing employment between 1974 and 1992 (*Employment Gazette* 1993). As a highly concentrated sector dominated by multinationals driven by the dynamics of acquisition, rationalisation, and cost competition (Pollert 1993), it is also illustrative of the endemic conflict between capitalist restructuring and the espoused ideological aims of cultivating company commitment and developing human resources (Legge 1989; Ramsay 1991).

Historically, however, in Britain the sector is also significant for its progressive Quaker employers and the early use of new systems of labour management. As well as applying Taylorist modes of work control and work study, concerns at Choc-Co in 1918 with 'the careful choice of overlookers and managers, who should be able to both lead and to inspire' (Child 1969: 50) attest its pioneering role in personnel management. The company also established a paternalist, welfare tradition, a pluralist industrial relations framework with early union recognition,[3] and a system of participative management with a works council in operation since 1919 (IR-RR 1985). It thus provides an example of a mature organisation in which the 'new' management techniques of the 1980s and 1990s can be compared with the legacy of the earlier innovations of welfare paternalism, and how this contrast was perceived by those whose consent was being sought by management.

Finally, the case study site was distinctive as the largest flag-ship of the British blue-chip company, employing 3,400 production workers in 1992[4] and manufacturing the company's best-selling chocolate lines, which cushioned it from the worst of the recession as well as conferring benefits in major capital investment. In the late 1980s Choc-Co was taken over by Food-Co, a major multinational, which invested £125 million over five years and made this site its confectionery division headquarters. The relative advantage of this site within the company arguably made it a 'best-case' scenario in terms of stability and success for nurturing employee commitment. Compared with this, several other factories had not been so fortunate; before the take-over, Choc-Co as a British multinational company had itself been a major rationaliser, and several factories suffered redundancies and even closures in the Factory Redeployment Plan.[5] The case study site thus concentrates on those who remained among the employed in a wider process of restructuring. But, such relative advantage can never be permanent when 'reorganisation is always on the agenda as a possible response to intensified competition' (Armstrong 1988: 156: viz. the need to regard the individual case study of labour process change in the wider context of capitalist dynamics). Here, competitive pressure was ever-present in cost cutting, both before Choc-Co became part of a larger multinational company and after, when, following a few years' investment, Food-Co's cost recouping led to major employment reductions even in this flag-ship site in 1994.

The introduction of team working

New management techniques were introduced in Choc-Co while it was an independent company, well before its take-over in 1988. As elsewhere in Britain, these were introduced as instruments to improve employee performance in the context of heightened competitive pressure. Management during the booming market of the 1970s, when the brand-leader, Countline, permitted continuous expansion and industrial relations bargaining to 'milk the cocoa-cow dry', was depicted by the factory manager as: 'A benevolent dictatorship – very gentlemanly and very inefficient. In terms of strategy there was no long-term plan, and in industrial relations, there was anarchy' (see, for sector parallels, Smith *et al*. 1990: 177).

The recession of the early 1980s changed all this. In the highly price-sensitive chocolate market (also hit by the Conservative government's doubling of VAT), both profitability and volumes declined, only recovering to 1979 levels in 1989. In the context of this crisis, the Factory Redeployment Plan restructuring exercise was initiated and a company high-flier was brought in from abroad as Operations Manager for the UK business, with a brief to review both the company's cost structure and its industrial relations approach. Team working and worker involvement were seen as the new vehicles of improvement, set, however, within a new strategy of rationalisation and 'the reduction of man-hours per ton'. Where the rationalisation process met resistance the management response was to reiterate its hardened stance towards 'obstructive' unions; it 'Would consult and inform the workforce, but it would assert its right to manage and *in extremis*, do things it would not have done before' (Factory Manager).

With this toughened industrial relations climate as one dimension of change, the other was a range of employee involvement techniques: Quality Circles were launched in 1986, and a new Training Department established in 1987 to improve communication and train staff for the new participatory structures. Some harmonisation initiatives conferred advantages on employees and were partly driven by union pressure: single-status dining arrangements were introduced in 1987 and holidays and working hours were equalised for production and white-collar staff with the introduction of the 37 hour week in May 1993. But for management, the agenda was to promote a 'culture of business improvement' (Production Service Manager) and shift from a paternalist 'we'll look after you, but don't think' and 'doing things for you' to a participatory but unitarist 'It's a cold, hard world, we'll sink or swim together' (Factory General Manager).

Team working was central to the new 'involvement culture' and introduced with a new supervisory structure of team leaders in 1989. This was part of a flattening of the supervisory structure common to British management throughout the 1980s (IDS 1991):

the previous system of assistant managers, production assistants, overlookers (in two grades) and chargehands was simplified into three managerial levels: departmental managers, section managers and team leaders.[6] In line with the general trend of conferring greater importance on first-line managers in new management techniques (Storey 1992), the team leader was to be the first rung of management, as well as the chief diffuser of team working to the shop floor. Team leaders' 'knowledge requirements' of reporting and disciplinary and industrial relations procedures were to complement 'skill requirements' of team leading and building, basic skills in all operations in the team, communication, instructional training, training requirement assessment, accounting and interviewing skills (factory training department documentation). The 1992 team leader training programme of five months on the job and five one-week training modules reflected this range of requirements:

- Role of team leader; motivation and team work.
- Planning, organising and quality.
- Identifying training needs and developing staff.
- Work performance measures, finance, costs and budgets.
- Standard setting, performance discussions.
- Communications, interviewing, discipline and grievance problems.

The role was to combine the 'soft' and 'hard' facets of 'people' and 'process' management (Legge 1989), the first, including motivation and involvement, underpinning the 'hard' financial accountability of the team on all budgets in terms of labour cost-control systems.[7] As the ensuing analysis illustrates, team working was a label for pushing down to the shop floor management accounting controls by making the line manager 'before all else, a *budget holder*' (Armstrong 1989: 164, italics in original; Storey 1987).

The corollary of the financial agenda of the team leader was his or her replacement of union workplace controls and channels of communication. Fortnightly team briefings (the downward flow of management information) and three-weekly team reviews (internal team discussions) were held. With 150 teams and only twenty-nine shop stewards across the whole factory, it was difficult for the union to maintain vigilance over every aspect of change introduced via these routes. As observed in other studies of team working, the aim was for greater group cohesion, but also the accompanying team competition and peer pressure (Garrahan and Stewart 1992).

Team performance score boards, some with liquid-display messages, were put up throughout the factory.

The union strategy

Unlike the introduction of similar 'involvement' techniques in a non-union chocolate multinational company where the shop-floor response was fragmented and ineffective (Scott 1994), Choc-Co's distinguishing characteristic was its mature unionised tradition. The GMB understood team working as aimed at weakening collective controls of the shop floor. At Choc-Co, union strategy was shaped by national union policies and the local industrial relations history as well as market circumstances (Martinez Lucio and Weston 1992b). A tradition of co-operative industrial relations, together with the national GMB policy of working with the new management initiatives in order to influence them and widen the scope of collective bargaining (p. 82), set the tone for close union involvement in the implementation of team working. However, this broadly co-operative approach (endorsed both by the TUC and the International Union of Food Workers) was partly facilitated by the advantaged position of this site of Choc-Co; at nearby sites experiencing greater product and employment instability, relations with the union (here, the Transport and General Workers' Union) were more antagonistic. Nevertheless, over the 1980s, closer inter-plant union communication meant that the GMB adopted more of the TGWU's 'holding on to independence' approach (p. 84). The case study factory convenor was more active than his predecessor and, together with a willingness to negotiate new initiatives, there was opposition to attempts to erode collective union regulation of working practices, in terms of both team working and other incrementally introduced changes. While union co-option by management was always a danger here because of the site's earlier privileges, toughened economic circumstances in the 1990s arguably began a levelling of circumstances between plants. The evidence put forward here largely supports earlier research (Heaton and Linn 1989; Scott 1994), that, where workplace trade union organisation is already strong, it is resilient in the face of new management techniques and indeed, may even find opportunities for shoring up union legitimacy and power. Later developments of the 1990s, however, place a question-mark over long-term optimism.

THE TENSIONS OF TEAM WORKING AND THE UNION ROLE

Team working and its limits among craft workers

As this chapter emphasises, the concept of 'team working' is notoriously ambiguous. In its connotation of skill versatility and task flexibility within the 1980s pre-occupation with removing 'Fordist' decomposition of tasks, it has failed to gain union endorsement where it threatens either craft or production jobs by removing demarcations between them. Management inability to cross the production–craft divide, as well as inter-craft demarcations (Cross 1985) is common in the food industry (NEDC 1990; Storey 1992: 87). Some cross-trade flexibility already existed at Choc-Co, with both engineers and electricians trained in information technology, and electricians possessing engineering skills. But engineers' lack of electrical skills were regarded as a major cause of machine down-time and an obstacle to long-term change. The company had originally proposed a multi-skilling initiative to create a craft-trained engineer with electrical skills – an Advanced Engineering Craftsman (AEC). Negotiations continued from 1984 to 1986, were resumed after the concept of AEC was dropped, reached deadlock with Choc-Co's Maintenance Joint Council in 1990, and were restarted back with the AEC concept in 1994. However, management had in the mean time incrementally introduced maintenance teams to the shop floor.

Team working and production workers

Only in production work, which has long been semi- or unskilled in the food industry, did the company succeed in negotiating something called 'team working'. The labour flexibility rationale of teams, however, had few consequences for the production process (see Storey 1992: 90 on the limits of HRM in de-skilled work environments). Indeed, despite the rhetoric of 'involvement', the fact that the 'Fordist' production system of specialised machinery, task fragmentation and standardisation of components was not challenged by management's enthusiasm for new work group labels testifies to the preference for the efficiency and profitability of cheap, unskilled labour in mass production (see Clarke 1992: 16 on the flexibility of Fordism). The account here signals how the

185

physical layout and process of flow-line mass production conflicts with the arbitrary fragmentation team organisation imposes, where teams are supposed to be finite, identifiable groups of workers. Within this overall framework, it also emerges that the gendered bifurcation of continuous process production between the 'making' and the 'packing' ends, and between capital- and labour-intensive manufacture, creates different conditions for the operation of team working for men and women.

In the mass food production industry, jobs have increasingly become the routine adjuncts to mechanised and automated process technology. Employees are responsible either for the smooth running of continuous flow and automated linked machinery or the routine loading and packing of goods. Work is repetitive, machine-paced, with few opportunities for direct participation in terms of influencing production. For the majority of employees the 'flexibility' of team working is limited to job rotation, greater integration of quality control into production, cleaning-up around the production area and work intensification (Garrahan and Stewart 1992; Scott 1994). Too much individual flexibility among production workers has been found to mar stability and predictability in flow production, as Storey (1992: 87) found at Birds Eye, where initial enthusiasm for the panacea of 'functional' flexibility was revoked for its inefficiency. The introduction of microprocessor and other new technology has had little impact on the overall routine nature of overseeing the production line: new skills involve greater numeracy and information-gathering ability which, if anything, replace operators' previous judgemental skills with the role of monitoring automated process control equipment (NEDC 1990). The view that technological dynamism in this sector introduces upskilling to the line is thus questionable; different skills are not necessarily greater skills, and there may be a polarisation of skills between operators, whose discretion is diminished, and maintenance/problem solving, which demands specialist equipment and information technology expertise. At Choc-Co, as elsewhere in the industry, it was less sophisticated lines which afforded some opportunity to detect faults and make some mechanical adjustments to technology; generally, the more micro-processor self-regulation, the less scope for production workers' manual intervention (*ibid.*). Adjustments would be numerically dictated, needing no judgement of the production process, while faults required specialist expertise in the dedicated equipment.

Production work and gender division

The division of confectionery production, as in most process industry, between the 'hot' or 'wet' end of manufacture and the 'dry' or 'cold' end of packing is accompanied by a clear sexual division of labour. Men dominate in the first – often called the 'kitchen' (*sic*); this is usually capital-intensive, computer-controlled production, although there remain some heavy manual mixing jobs, and a few specialised ingredient preparation jobs which require the experience of tacit skill rather than formal craft training. Women are concentrated in the routine, repetitive labour-intensive occupations (see Glucksman 1990 on the transition from female hand-packing to mechanised assembly).

The perpetuation of gender segregation within semi- and unskilled work is a complex phenomenon. One theory suggests that the division between capital-intensive jobs as male and labour-intensive jobs as female is associated with management's drive to maximise the return on capital investment with twenty-four shift work (Armstrong 1982: 32). Not only was there the push factor of 'protective legislation' excluding women from night work, but there was the pull for men of shift premium rates. At Choc-Co, this logic applied both to the 'wet' end of process work and to the high-volume packing departments of the flag-ship brand, which had attracted heavy capital investment and twenty-four-hour operation run on rotating day and night shifts. Although the legal basis for women's exclusion from these areas disappeared when the 1986 Sex Discrimination Act removed restrictions on women's night work, this only slowly altered the pattern of sexual division. Women found it hard to enter 'high technology' areas even though the jobs themselves required only routine monitoring and recording; the machines and their operation had become male-gendered, exclusionary and socially constructed as more skilled than fast, dextrous jobs (Cockburn 1985; Phillips and Taylor 1980; Coyle 1982).

At Choc-Co, the highly automated section producing the best-selling Countline also remained 'the lads' area', even though the work was just as, if not more, routine and boring as other packing departments. In spite of an espoused management policy of bringing women into these areas (partly because of their allegedly more 'sensible' attitudes to industrial relations), women entered only the older, less technically sophisticated section. Interviews revealed that where men were habituated to single-sex work, they devised

ANNA POLLERT

a range of exclusionary excuses, from 'not being able to use bad language in front of women' to women allegedly 'getting away with more' with team leaders, and not being willing to do the 'filthy' cleaning jobs underneath the machinery (*sic*). Otherwise management and workers blamed each other for lack of progress in sex equality: the first claimed (with some justification) that men did not want women, while the latter claimed (again with truth) that management refused to install 'facilities' for women. First-line managers regarded the whole 'problem' as a 'sensitive area', and with the male labour supply plentiful, there was arguably no pressure to rock the boat by altering the status quo.

While there is nothing intrinsic, permanent or inevitable in the gendering of jobs, it remains a key dimension of the structuration of workplace relations. At Choc-Co, the perpetuation of the sexual division of labour, with men concentrated in capital-intensive and women in labour-intensive production, meant that team working, even in its limited form for all semi-skilled production workers, was an even more artificial construct for most women than for most men. In the making end, mixing and other machines were usually computer-controlled, and with very few men in the area, they could at least form small teams which rotated between machines. In the (male) Countline automated assembly lines, tasks involved watching, levelling and quality assurance as wafers were fed into the chocolate covering machinery, and at the packing end, monitoring the automatic wrappers, and occasionally changing reels of foil and plastic film. Thus, while the tasks themselves were highly repetitive, they required only monitoring and attention, not hands-on continuous work. This permitted certain freedom to rotate tasks, move around the shop floor and communicate. Hence, 'team working', while not involving new skills, at least encouraged more social exchange, co-operation and variety than before.

The majority of women, on the other hand, were on the automated packing machines at the end of lines, with little task variation, or in the labour-intensive 'Assortments' department, where they were tied to the speed of the moving belt, and engaged in the minute subdivision of manual tasks of assembling boxes of assorted sweets, each assigned to placing one or two chocolate shapes in the passing moulds, covering the layers with paper, closing the boxes and feeding them to the wrapper. Of course, the collective nature of the line already defined it as a team, as many workers repeated. But the detailed division of labour meant that even the minimal change of job rotation meant nothing more than moving from one point on the line to another and repeating broadly the same operation – perhaps with a different sweet.

Differences in production unit size and structure also distinguished capital- from labour-intensive work; in the more automated areas, there were only between five and ten operators, some grouped and others spread across the shop floor, but in small enough numbers for some group identity. In Assortments, a line comprised some forty workers – far too many for a team in the Training Manager's optimum model of ten to fifteen people, yet nevertheless called one. Production unit stability also differed between the two types of production areas and affected teams: work in automated machine monitoring usually required the same employment levels whatever the output levels, hence 'team' integrity could be maintained. However, volume variation in labour-intensive assembly work meant sudden rushes of work and the need for more assemblers when products from the making-end accumulated, or the need to redeploy superfluous workers when machines ran at under-capacity and delivered fewer sweets for boxing (cf. Armstrong 1982: 32). Hence, 'teams' would frequently alter in size as workers were moved on and off. This fluctuation – or the need for *factory and departmental-wide flexibility* – undermined the rigidity of the team structure (and vice versa) and created industrial relations complexities in terms of rules for transferring people across teams to where they were needed. But there was a further consequence for 'teams' in the gendering of occupations; in Assortments and several other areas where packing was constituted as female employment, variation in labour requirements had become traditionally structured as part-time employment (Beechey and Perkins 1987). The complexity of four- and five-hour shift management, combined with other restructuring processes, such as the shortening of the working week to thirty-eight hours, created logistical jigsaws which both cut across teams and went beyond individual team leaders' competencies.

Team working: contradictions and the space for shop stewards' intervention

So far, the spuriousness of the notions of skill 'flexibility' and 'involvement' in the context of semi- and unskilled repetitive work, and particularly in feminised labour-intensive operations, has been highlighted as a contradiction inherent in 'team working' in mass production. This clear mismatch between managerial aims of cultural change and the reality of production was a basic factor in maintaining a lucid shop-floor view of work as the wage-effort bargain, in which trade unionism retained an essential role. But there were further strains within the definition of team working as a practice which undermined it and created spaces for trade unionism.

Choc-Co's essentially unitarist definition of 'involvement' as a vehicle for a 'culture of business improvement' meant that the team working system adopted bore no resemblance to the participative, democratic Swedish model, but corresponded most to the hierarchically dominated Japanese version (Berggren 1992: 9; Mueller 1994). The team leader was selected by line management, not elected by the team; control and communication were supposed to by-pass the union, rather than be jointly regulated with shop stewards; and although suggestions by workers were encouraged through Quality Circles and team reviews, these were confined to efficiency issues.

While some explanations of management's inability to put its 'new industrial relations' rhetoric of devolved control into practice have been posited in normative terms, as a reluctance to break with past norms of maintaining managerial prerogative (Scott 1994: 150), here assessment Choc-Co's adherence to hierarchical control, beneath the veneer of participation, is grounded in a materialist analysis of financial controls. Cost saving was the foremost imperative for senior management in this company, and human resource initiatives were subordinated to management accounting controls, as in most large British companies (Armstrong 1989; Marginson *et al.* 1993). After its take-over by Food-Co, the multi-plant company, Choc-Co, became a profit centre in the parent company's confectionery division, with operating units, including the case study factory, as cost centres whose performance was measured in terms of cost saving within the budget given by the company. This cost-saving drive trickled down to departments and then to teams, each obliged by its own budget to reduce labour costs per ton.

The combination of top-down financial disciplines and the principle of devolved budgets to teams was translated into the compromise of team leaders being no more than supervisors under a new label, but with greater responsibility for production costs than before. But this ambiguity created its own tensions, and arguably also backfired on the cost-control system itself. Departmental and section managers had lost some of their former control and problem solving functions to the team, while the intended autonomy of team leaders was curtailed by eventual dependence on departmental budgetary limits. These factors meant that for both departmental managers and team leaders, the new system contained built-in strains between independence from and accountability to those above them. Further, the cost-saving culture undermined the very instruments to advance further savings – the team leaders – by skimping on their training. Team leaders, as we shall see, were frequently ill-equipped to perform their function of managing the shop floor.

The accumulation of conceptual and organisational difficulties of team working in this traditionally unionised environment meant that, for the time being at least, the shop stewards retained their importance in workplace regulation despite the aims to reduce it, precisely because they were capable of negotiating change where team working stalled. Middle managers *and* team leaders consulted them over employment levels, procedures for changing work loads, health and safety issues, new working hours and a host of every-day issues. Inevitably, this placed the union in an ambiguous position: its shop-floor control was maintained, yet it was 'propping up the system' which was designed to undercut it.

The wider issue raised, however, is that while previous analysis of the relationship between 'new' and 'traditional' industrial relations has posited a model of the two systems running separately but in *parallel* (Storey 1992), the analysis of the 'new' as largely *dependent* on the 'old' suggests a more complex process of interweaving, rather than dualism. This is partly to be explained by the inner contradictions of the system, and partly by the manner of its joint development between management and unions – the most likely course in an organised environment. For the union, its indispensability as a prop to team working heightened the inevitable contradictions of its regulative function in the 'negotiation of order' (Hyman 1989: 32): 'jointism' both gave a measure of control and implicated it ideologically and practically. At Choc-Co, this double role was highlighted in negotiating the new team working pay structure.

Union ambiguity in the negotiation of order in the new pay structure of team working

The new pay structure was a central plank of team working. Some job enlargement was visualised in the form of training in additional

191

knowledge or skills 'units': varying combinations of units could provide 'credits' which produced three levels of Additional Skills Payments (ASPs), some conferring roles of responsibility within the team.[8] The union considered that it had a major input into the training units, had given production workers some added interest in their work, and had forced financial concessions from the company. The Additional Skills Payments were, indeed, disliked by the Company Industrial Relations Manager as inducements to wage drift.

But while the union may have won some kudos from the details of the agreement, it had no control over its broader purpose. For the company's intentions of producing a culture of business awareness, the ASPs were potentially ideological vehicles. First, as shop stewards were aware, the concept of 'personal' rates was a habituation to individual pay rates outside collective bargaining arrangements. Second, because of the limits to change in the production process itself, the training modules provided few new technical or transferable skills and were mainly socialisation in managerial and commercial values. Beside knowledge units such as 'hygiene' and 'safety', units such as 'confectionery procedures', 'cost' and 'quality' awareness were solely aimed at business performance. In addition, stewards had no control over the distribution of training, which was in the remit of team leaders, and hence lost control over this aspect of pay.

Team working at Choc-Co, then, produced difficulties in its own terms, which encouraged reliance on the very institutions of trade unionism it was supposed to supplant. It provided spaces for the union in the 'negotiation of order' which maintained its shop-floor role, but in a double-edged manner. To what extent were the tensions of the system recognised by senior managers?

THE VERTICAL SLICE THROUGH THE COMPANY

The senior management view

As the Company Director of Personnel recalled, the Operations Manager in the late 1980s encouraged all management teams to 'go and find out about JIT, TQM and the like'. Factory General Managers and the senior company management team went to seminars and visited other Choc-Co factories in Europe and other 'leading-edge' new techniques companies such as IBM, Hewlett-Packard, Proctor & Gamble, Kodak and Rothmans. Evangelical zeal to go forth and seek the latest fashions in management bred more enthusiasm than clarity (see Ramsay 1991: 3). In 1992, there appeared no senior management consensus about where team working was going; some, including the General Manager, visualised TQM as the ultimate goal; others, including the Training Manager, saw TQM as a very different strategy, and team working as about involvement and cultivating an education 'culture'. The many phrases bandied about characterising the new direction, from 'We'll tell you our strategy, we want you to participate' to 'We want you to think for yourself ', revealed the vagueness about whether team working was about 'involvement' in the unitarist sense of assuming managerial goals, or a wider agenda of employee 'participation' (c.f. the distinction by Marchington *et al.* 1992).

The evaluation of the contribution of team working to company performance also lacked the precision good practice requires (Ramsay 1991: 16). 'You only look at overall performance; if the bottom line is OK, this gives confidence in the changes' (Production Service Manager[9]).

In his view, the many measures of production versus the plan, in terms of operational efficiency, monthly figures on hours per ton, fixed and variable costs and general budgetary performance, all showed improvement, and this was considered enough to confirm that change was in the right direction. A 'commitment based' scheme and a long-term culture of 'involvement in improvement' could not, it was felt, be quantified. Another interpretation of the reported confidence in the productive efficiency of team working was that managers were aware that whatever else happened, a long-established 'hard' system of work study remained in operation. As mentioned earlier, Choc-Co had been deploying these techniques since the 1920s, and following the multinational's take-over, this was supplemented with Food-Co's systematic deployment of 'Productivity and Quality' teams at local, national and international level.

Imprecision concerning the evaluation of new management techniques also extended to a lack of senior management consensus about the precise meaning of union marginalisation via team working. The Factory General Manager envisaged a 'drawing back and giving the teams more space' and the unions adopting a 'higher-level, more strategic role'. The Factory Personnel Manager put this more strongly as 'throwing away the rule book'. Others, however, placed greater emphasis on the continuing role of negotiated shop-floor change. This ambiguity is explained by the pragmatism which in reality underlay the rhetoric of a new culture: collective union channels were utilised to support or legitimate management initiatives, and a range of opinions co-existed regarding the longer-term desirability of this situation.

Middle management: departmental and section managers

Compared with their seniors, middle managers appeared to have fewer illusions about the efficacy of an 'involvement culture' and had their feet more firmly rooted in economic reality:

> When Thatcherism was in a growth phase, it [the new 'involvement' techniques] was OK. Now there is fear of a downturn – it's harder to convince people of their role. There's fear of putting forward ideas – it might lose them their overtime – or something like that.
>
> (Mint/Beans Departmental Manager)

Others offered blunt explanations for change: 'Before, there had been many more people, so one needed more supervisors. Now there are fewer, with a consequent need for fewer managers' (Departmental Manager).

They were at the sharp end of the conflict between a cost-cutting, budgetary control production culture and a quality and involvement employment policy. While they were generally enthusiastic about less bureaucratic management, an improvement in communication and the general features of shop-floor accountability and initiative, for them, the 'bottom line' was meeting the departmental budget.

Matching the weekly product plan with shifts and different employment levels was a normal part of food manufacturing management. Fewer problems with finding a balance between departmental needs and the inflexibility of team structure occurred in the more automated (and mainly male) areas: here, teams were identifiable units around particular groups of equipment, and production was less variable. Even so, the management task of fine-tuning production and employment was still complex, particularly where there were several stages in the production of a sweet, and accumulations or shortages interrupted a smooth flow of production, causing labour shortages or plant down-time. Beans production, for example, operated on a three-shift system creating an accumulation of sweets in the mornings

194

for the packers, who worked only days. The solution was to match *packing* with *making* by introducing three-shift working to packers too, an increase in capital usage which resulted in labour rationalisation. Organisational and industrial relations issues required careful negotiation with shop stewards; the extra complication of re-forming teams to match the new situation merely added to their problems.

The Assortments department (female) posed the most difficulties for the co-ordination function of middle management with a number of part-time shifts, and all new workers recruited on temporary contracts. Seasonal and temporary workers had been used here since the 1970s and in the 1980s, agency temps too: yet casualisation and team working were meant to co-exist. Constant difficulties also lay in the requirement for some slack in the system to allow for 'spares' to meet production and packing bottle-necks. Continuous plant in chocolate enrobing had insufficient reliefs and had 'to go and beg, borrow and steal' from packers (factory union convenor – male). But the packing teams, which needed a minimum of thirty-two, were themselves fully stretched and could not afford to lose workers. The 'solution' was to recruit temporaries to the enrobers in the high season, and in packing, to create a 'spares' team! This contradiction in terms referred to a group who had to work anywhere they were sent and were predictably discontented. Middle management also dealt with important changes frequently forgotten in debates on new management practices. Even the shortening of the working week to thirty-eight hours had implications for teams. Different shift patterns for part-timers to maintain employment protection agreed by the Joint Negotiating Council agreement (for which the minimum threshold was thirteen hours per week) had to be created. This necessitated new start times and again, a restructuring of teams.

Logistical balancing apart, there was a further, fundamental tension in the role of middle management in the new devolved structure; although responsible for the overall departmental budget targets, middle managers were not supposed to be involved in the teams' weekly budgets and costings. Departmental and Section Managers were not always clear where production problems were located – whether in manufacturing or packaging – and were presented with financial, not manufacturing information. As one put it, 'Before we used to record machine down-time; now, we only get the budget.'

With this limited knowledge, they were left guessing, with the suspicion that team leaders were often fire-fighting, with neither the time to develop their skills, nor the ability to delegate responsibilities.

In the context of team working complicating an already complex managerial task, there was some ambivalence for middle managers in having to turn to shop stewards for help. At one level they were committed to endorsing the power of the team leader, and resented interference from shop stewards. But pragmatism meant increasing reliance on stewards for smoothing over inexperienced team leaders' problems. At another level, departmental managers recognised the value of union involvement in the regulation of conflict in complex changes in working patterns and employment numbers. Maintaining collective bargaining channels allowed a number of critical changes to pass with minimum disruption, such as preparing for further decline in the assortments market through staff redeployment, voluntary redundancy and natural wastage.

Team leaders

More and more gets pushed down to us – and it's going to get worse. (Male team leader, Beans)

Don't call us team leaders, call us mushrooms. (Male team leader, Countline)

The teams can't get together; there's too many different sizes to have their own budgets. (Female team leader, Assortments)

You must believe in team working – understand why you need to be more aware. With me, I get some respect – because I've done their jobs. (Female team leader, Assortments)

Within the organisational shortcomings of team working, team leaders were arguably the weakest link (Storey 1992: 221). The fact that the team leaders were little more than supervisors with intensified work loads meant that they were often unable to live up to their formal job requirements. Their experience varied individually and between departments and generalisation is difficult, but the broad impression was that only a small minority of mainly young men relished the challenge of the new 'mini-manager', while the majority were overworked and dissatisfied. The management 'ideal-type' in the sample were either already on a fast upward track through the supervisory system before team working was introduced, or recruited from outside. One recounted his enthusiasm for using personal computers, his drive to get to grips with the budgetary system and improve attendance, and his ability to get two or three other young team members 'who can delve into things and to go as high as they want to get things done'. What was not clear, however, was whether he would remain as team leader, or aim higher; he was already dissatisfied with management assessment of individual pay-rates, and felt his special effort was under-rewarded.

Team leaders were dissatisfied with their ambiguous status: although the team leaders' individual pay contracts were comparable to middle managers', their total earnings depended on shift and overtime premiums, as for the shop floor. Those who missed out on the latter, particularly women in non-shift areas such as Assortments, were disadvantaged. As 'managers', none felt wholly accepted, their lower status reflected in the absence of managerial holidays and other fringe benefits. They were also torn between the individualism fostered by their new management status and individualised pay contracts, and an awareness of their limited upward mobility chances. Finally, the experience of the early process of internal selection from chargehand to team leader left a bitterness and sense of insecurity; this was not groundless, since by 1994, there had been team leader redundancies.

Even in the Countline departments, where team working suffered fewer organisational tensions than elsewhere, the metaphor of 'mushrooms' – 'keep 'em in the dark and feed them shit' – was used. Rationalisation of first-line management, the formal demands of the job, insufficient training and work intensification were frequent complaints. Difficulties in terms of not being 'backed up' by their seniors echo findings elsewhere (Storey 1992: 240). Management communication downwards was generally considered to have improved (although some were sceptical that it was 'all for show'), but communication upwards and being 'listened to' depended on middle managers' receptiveness. Here, in spite of talk (and training) about a new culture of involvement, it seemed that variation depended, as ever, on individual idiosyncrasy. Some team leaders valued 'a good relationship' with Departmental Managers, and some wanted 'to be asked more', while others cited the obstructive middle manager whose drive to beat the budget 'bled the system dry', meaning that it took six years to get a problem plant repaired – at a cost, it was pointed out, of £100,000 in a department with an estimated £163 million annual turnover. Short-termism and pre-occupation with volume production at the expense of quality and preventative maintenance had not, it seemed, been eradicated.

Nor were the tasks of 'people' and 'product' management reconciled. Besides the job of deploying labour, team leaders had to check wages, clocking-in, overtime, holidays, absenteeism – not to mention team budget accounts, making use of the personal computers, Lotus spread sheets (and any other information systems they chose to use), and organising team-training and team-building. Few had time to mingle on the shop floor, as they were supposed to do, and as the old chargehand, who had been 'more one of the boys' (*sic*) had done. A common remark that 'there's no time to talk to the shop floor' (male team leader, Countline) was endorsed by workers, shop stewards and craftsmen, who all mentioned that they 'could never find the team leader'. Quality, according to some team leaders, had consequently dropped: 'That used to be the charge-hand's job. Now, quality should be in our own control – but it's hard to motivate people.'

If this was the situation for first-line managers in departments where teams were small and stable, it was doubly the case in Assortments, where 'teams' were too large and unstable to merit the term, and where 'team leaders' were effectively chargehands presiding over a patch-work of part-time shifts throughout the day.

There was also the fundamental, systemic contradiction between the social demands of team building and a productivity strategy of labour intensification. Senior management's exhortation for greater team leader delegation to the team as a resolution to work overload was in vain. There was insufficient labour slack to do this. Removing team members into administration from direct production was a luxury few could afford: 'you have to justify to yourself when you can take staff off' (male team leader, Countline). Similarly, cost constraints reduced the time available for team reviews and training.

The obsession with budgets confused team leaders as well as middle managers. Training in accountancy was considered too short and 'way over our heads'. Only one very young male team leader seemed to positively enjoy this aspect of the job; others, particularly older leaders, were sceptical about the accounting system used:

Before I was a team leader, I was turning out the same tonnage per week, and I was always on target for tons; now, with exactly the same tonnage, we're in the red. I've been to team leaders' meetings every four weeks, they've had someone in from factory accounting for a low-down, but we still scratch our heads.

(Male team leader, Beans, chargehand since 1977)

Budgets as justification for labour rationalisation were disparaged:

I'm told to take people out, but I don't worry if I know everyone's working. If I was told I had spares or the team wasn't working, I'd say 'rubbish'. I don't ask for blood, I ask for a 100 per cent effort. What the company expects, I don't know.

(*ibid.*)

Team leaders were a disenchanted group. Although they had accepted union de-recognition as a condition for becoming team leaders, they now looked to some kind of collective union representation. In 1992, the company balloted team leaders over union re-recognition and arrived at a 50–50 result. However, in 1994, the GMB conducted its own ballot, with an overwhelming 80 per cent of team leaders wanting recognition (probably remaining within the GMB), and a subsequent company ballot arrived at a similar result. Paradoxically, the very people who were meant to lead to shop-floor union exclusion were now asking for bargaining rights. Something about team working had backfired.

The workers' view

Perceptions of team working

'We've always worked as a team' was the refrain for many for whom the 'new' system was simply a change of label. Women, particularly in Assortments, were the least impressed and the 'spares team' most disheartened. At best, the system had made no difference and many resented the disruption caused by splitting teams, the lack of stability within them and their large size. For those with years of service, the arbitrariness of team composition and the loss of organically built groups was demoralising, and inter-team competition, it was felt, had served to nourish mistrust, rather than improve commitment. Quality had been better internalised in the old system than now: 'Everyone's watching everyone else – we didn't used to do that. Before, we used to care, now we couldn't care less. We let anything go' (woman worker, Assortments).

Supervisory relations had also been built up on mutual understanding, length of service and experience, and the new managerial style sometimes offended:

> The team leader's attitude is all wrong. She doesn't even say 'good morning, ladies', she's unhelpful, doesn't explain anything. It was lovely with our chargehand – a nice, happy team [sic]. I hate coming in now.
>
> (Woman worker, Assortments)

The assessment of team working in the more automated, mainly male areas was more positive. Individual difference between team leaders as people was seen as the overarching factor of success, but some approved of a general change in supervisory style:

> I prefer the team leaders, they listen to suggestions, they'll discuss more – makes you feel you've got more responsibility, more say in how you run things.
>
> (Male worker, Countline)

> Managers are more polite. They notice things. The old chargehands would come along and point to you like children.
>
> (Male worker, Beans)

What of team working creating a new culture of business improvement? Only 206 workers – fewer than 10 per cent of the workforce – were in forty-six Quality Circles and, as the Training Manager pointed out, it was these same people who were active in other team-based initiatives, such as Quality Advisers. Some had managed to effect changes, mainly in the areas of health and safety and hygiene, and other small improvements to production, and where this had occurred, considerable satisfaction was voiced. Many more workers, however, referred to Quality Circles as 'brain-picking' or 'brain-washing' and while not averse to involvement and influencing production as a principle, had not forgotten the cash nexus: ideas should be paid for, and the old suggestion-box was fairer. As for the team training courses, a considerable number had taken some, approved of the idea of training, but could not see much relevance, either to the job or their approach to work: 'I haven't done any courses; I think they're a good idea, but a bit pointless' (woman worker, Beans). 'I like the training courses; but they don't alter repetitive jobs' (woman worker, Assortments).

Those who had trained as team advisers were clearer about how they could apply their knowledge to the job, but were often frustrated at not being able to get anything done. And while some said that 'training might take off on the extra money', they also pointed out that extra effort would only be commensurate with the limited extra pay. In general, there seemed still to be two sides in a factory: 'You're told you can talk to management as one of us. But it's always "them and us"' (woman worker, Assortments).

In sum, although the workforce was a loyal one to the extent that there was a historical identity of interests between Choc-Co and the welfare of the city, there was no indication of a change from a primarily instrumental orientation to wage labour. Men in Countline worked as much overtime as possible, with hours varying between 50 and 70 per week, and referred to the company's tradition of paying low basic rates, and their dependence on overtime working. Part-time women workers valued the relatively good pay-rates compared with other, mainly service-sector, employment, but were keen to forget about Choc-Co when they left work. If anything, good-will had been lost with the modernisation of the company and the loss of its welfare tradition. Interviews with women workers in particular revealed how the abandonment of 'family-friendly' policies, such as the special works buses and trains, the 8.30 a.m. to 12.30 p.m. shift suitable for women with young children and the facility to take off school holidays, were resented.

Perceptions of trade unionism

In an era of alleged new individualism and declining collectivism, card-carrying union membership even in a 100 per cent unionised factory is no guarantee of ideological support for shop-floor union activists. Survey evidence, however, suggests that companies have not won over unions in terms of hearts and minds (Guest and Dewe 1991). This case study attempts to probe this further. One interview revealed an interesting paradox:

Since the new system, it's weakened the union – taken away 'them and us'. You need unions to negotiate, but the

confrontation has gone. You don't have a united workforce.
But you want the union or steward there.

(Woman worker, Beans)

This seems to register both a recognition of a more com-
promising stance at the level of general negotiation *and* the
continuing importance of shop-floor representation. Most workers,
however, stressed the latter as increasingly important. The tighter
the team leader control the more there were calls for shop stewards
to be present (cf. the Canadian Auto Workers survey which found
increasing worker support for 'the need for a union' after several
years of having team leaders: IRS 1992: 10). In Assortments, for
example, workers wanted direct information on the line speed
(which was in fact to be provided in a digital display) because they
felt 'conned' when the leader increased the speed without informing them, especially as they no longer received Payment by Results.

Whether or not employees supported the new team working
system, there was general consensus on the 'need for a shop
steward on every shift'. This indicates the continuing legitimacy of
trade unionism, and a view that support for new management
practices would only be given if collective representation were
maintained. If anything, more rather than less union support was
required to match the fragmentation of team structure and as a
defence against attacks on working conditions.

The trade union view

If you talk to people here, they've always wanted teams;
they've never done anything else; nothing's changed for the
ordinary people; they're still working in the same job; all
they're seeing is layers of supervision going out of the system.

(Male shop steward, 1992)

Going back to the history of the company I don't think it's
about team working, I think it's all about saving; I reckon
they've saved £4 million on the supervisory structure alone.

(Male shop steward, 1992)

It's [team working] made the union closer together – a better
understanding of the role of shop steward and team leader.

(Factory union convenor, 1994)

Interviews with the factory convenor and shop stewards demonstrated a clear understanding of the aims of the new management techniques. The mention of 'budgets' caused hoots of derisory and bitter laughter. Stewards saw through the system of teams charging each other costs for 'lending out' a spare worker as a ploy to manage with existing numbers through work intensification. Team briefings were unequivocally seen as 'indoctrination', and some areas of the new team roles, such as team 'safety adviser', were feared as usurping the better-trained union safety officers. Shop stewards endorsed middle managers' and team leaders' view that the union role was indispensable, because of the failings of the system:

> They train team leaders on what they want them to know, not on what they need to know.
>
> (Male shop steward)

> Often, team leaders try to get management help with a problem, can't get an answer, so end up going to a steward.
>
> (Woman shop steward)

The union was particularly involved in areas of the factory where team working was, in the convenor's words, 'floundering', mainly in Assortments. The management defence that the many problems encountered were merely teething troubles was dismissed thus:

> That's nonsense, it's been going for three years. If the company goes to the unions and asks them to sit down in a committee to look at team working, it means they're searching for something that isn't there.
>
> (Factory union convenor)

This was a reference to a joint working party set up in 1992 to discuss the operation of teams, and regarded as confirmation that management was using the union to prop up its new techniques.

Attendance at a stewards' monthly meeting in 1992 highlighted the importance of setting team working in the context of a barrage of new issues and challenges. Repetitive Strain Injury, itself a product of increasing line speeds and intensity of work in labour-intensive packing areas, occupied a major part of this meeting. (Berggren 1993 similarly notes the consequences of increased work pace and intensity in the 'new management strategy' of 'lean production' in Japanese car plants both in Japan and in the USA.) In general, the new management techniques demanded constant vigilance over subtle moves in the frontier of control. Even though experienced stewards were used to this, the pace of initiatives had increased. For example, in 1992, stewards were losing track of Quality Circle projects, which might have serious implications for employment levels and safety, and reported being told that if they wanted to know more about them, they should join one or start one. The mounting of electronic score boards with personalised peer-group pressure displays such as 'Sean – late again' and 'Team such-and-such so many tons, team so-and-so *only* so many' was discovered and stopped. A further issue was a hidden problem in the proposed 'equalisation' of weekly pay to monthly salaries, in which salary slips would integrate numerous components of pay, such as the hourly rate, overtime and shower allowance of time, making them less transparent for checking.

Follow-up research in 1994 indicated how the pressure on the union continued to mount. The new Choc-Co General Manager had instigated another factory reorganisation, this time changing from a departmental to a more specialised 'plant' structure. The purpose was to further tighten controls on output and productivity. The opening of a more efficient Countline plant had created 100 redundancies, and general 'downsizing' brought to a total of 600 job losses through voluntary redundancy and natural wastage in early 1994, with a further 400 planned for later in the year – leading to a loss of around a third of the factory workforce in a year. This radical employment reduction was the multinational Food-Co's response to a stagnating market combined with the drive to reduce costs sharply in order to gain the desired returns on its acquisition of and investment in Choc-Co. Over the two years from beginning the research in 1992 to follow-up in 1994, the industrial relations climate for trade unionism had become tougher. Vigilance over management ignoring agreements, contracting out work, and communicating directly with the workforce was ever more difficult. As the convenor put it, the pressure 'Makes you more on your toes, more acute . . . makes you work harder' (factory union convenor, 1994).

In 1994, the double-edged nature of union involvement in team working and new management practices continued, with the relationship between new techniques and traditional collectivism still indeterminate.

CONCLUSIONS

The slice through Choc-Co has demonstrated that team working as a system of work organisation and of employee involvement was not working. Senior managers appeared confident that these were teething problems, but as we got closer to the shop floor, line managers, workers and shop stewards indicated the complexities and tensions of the system. Which view is closer to the truth? Considering that at the time of research, team working had been running for over three years, 'teething' does not seem a very convincing argument. Rather, it appears that there are structural contradictions at the heart of the strategy: between worker alienation in a production system which still depends on unskilled, repetitive jobs and the aims of winning hearts and minds to the objectives of business improvement; between the needs of wider production units in the collective labour process and the narrow needs of the team; between a management culture dominated by accountancy controls and the investment needed in equipment, training and pay, all of which contribute towards employee motivation; and between the wider dynamics of capitalist restructuring involving work intensification, employment reduction and insecurity and the aims of building worker commitment to the company.

At Choc-Co, with its tradition of welfare management and a mature, stable workforce, it further appeared that the imposition of new strategies had weakened good-will among sections of the workforce, rather than created a new type of commitment. The conflicting dynamics in the new system, and the risk that the baby had been thrown out with the bath water in terms of replacing welfarism with 'modernism', did not seem to have been registered by senior management.

The evidence put forward here is further confirmation of the critiques of the incoherence and short-termism of new management strategies in the industrial relations literature. What is of further significance for the discussion of trade unionism is the highlighting of a familiar theme: that management policies may backfire on themselves and create spaces for trade unionism to retain a niche in organisation despite attempts to displace it. A second development of previous discussion of a dual system of individualised employment relations and traditional forms of collective bargaining systems existing in parallel is the suggestion that the negotiation of order at shop-floor level leads to the two systems *intertwining*, rather than operating in tandem.

One prediction from this is that such 'jointism' will succumb to the imposition of a unitarist management, once the usefulness of union negotiation can be dispensed with. Much, of course, depends on management style and market conditions, and on union power. Where unions do become incorporated into 'propping up' the system, this creates a double edged opportunity for them: they can be co-opted by management to do their 'dirty work', but they can also intervene in terms of collective representation of workers' interests. They can do both at once, as the case of Choc-Co illustrated. In a sense this situation is nothing new, but merely sharpens the ambiguity of trade unionism as the management of conflict and order. Much also depends on the labour market, unemployment, shop-floor and local morale and traditions; continuing support from the shop floor at Choc-Co for trade unionism as a defence of employees' interest came across in the repeated refrain 'you need the shop steward there'.

In 1994, the situation for trade unions remained indeterminate; one scenario could be that shop stewards might be more systematically excluded from the shop floor, and team leaders forced to 'manage' on their own. Should this happen, it is likely that the tensions previously handled through collective union channels would not disappear, but would be swept under the carpet. Instead, there would be a more coercive system of control, jettisoning any pretence of cultural change, and arguably endangering even the modicum of consent found in the field in 1992. Such speculation can only be answered by further follow-up research.

NOTES

1 This chapter does not intend to enter the debate about the existence of HRM, not least because the term was never used by research respondents. I refer, therefore, to new management practices or techniques. This is not ideal, since it fails to address the problem of 'newness' – but it reflects a common perception of new fashions. I refer to 'employee involvement' broadly to include not only the typology of Marchington *et al.* (1992), but also 'direct participation' such as team working.
2 Ideally, I would have preferred my own random selection from a list of employees. However, since production pressure meant that the only criterion for releasing a worker for interview was whoever could

be spared from the line, there was little chance of managerial hand-picking which would bias the sample.

3 Choc-Co continued (in 1994) company-level pay bargaining with a Joint Negotiating Council for the production workers' unions, and a company-wide Maintenance Joint Council formed in 1982 for craft workers. It left the national sectoral bargaining system of the Cake and Biscuits Alliance Joint Industrial Council in 1974.

4 On account of the capital intensity and high automation of this factory, only 34 per cent of workers were women, a gender ratio closer to the national manufacturing average than the sector as a whole. Rationalisation brought the 1992 production workforce to 57 per cent of the 1981 level (men 61 per cent, women 51 per cent of 1981 figures). De-feminisation occurred by more than halving the part-time female workforce (in 1992 39 per cent of the 1981 figure of 1,336). During the 1980s, between 400 and 600 of the total production workforce were seasonal casuals or on one- or two-year contracts (mainly women).

5 The Factory Redeployment Plan was a rationalisation and investment plan phased from 1984 to 1987, in which two factories were closed, a new chocolate-making factory was opened, and the company restructured to site brand specialisation. The company invested a total of £90 million, of which £25 million was capital investment and £45 million 'cost-saving investment'; the plan was estimated to have saved £7,900,000 per year as a result (Company Industrial Relations Manager and company documentation). Later in the period, individual rationalisations took place, with an Operational Review between 1987 and 1989 shedding 400 supervisory jobs across the company and 150 in the case study plant.

6 In 1993 this structure was further simplified to 'plant' managers (units which were smaller than departments) and team leaders.

7 The importance of cost saving is illustrated by an exercise in 1991, when all team leaders were involved in a budgetary process to examine ingredient usage on site, with a target of saving £400,000 per year for the next two years. This 'project-driven change' was then given to the section managers, and, via the team leaders, related back to the team so that the improvements would be 'owned by the team'.

8 In 1991 for a thirty-nine hour week, ASP 1 added £2.73, ASP 2 £5.45 and ASP 3 £8.18 to basic pay.

9 References for quotations for senior and middle managers are un-gendered, since they were all male apart from the Training Manager, who is not quoted here. However, since team leaders and workers comprised men and women, their gender is registered in quotations.

REFERENCES

Armstrong, P. (1982) 'If it's only Women it Doesn't Matter so Much', in J. West (ed.), *Work, Women and the Labour Market*, London: Routledge & Kegan Paul.

Armstrong, P. (1988) 'Labour and Monopoly Capital', in R. Hyman and W. Streek (eds), *New Technology and Industrial Relations*, Oxford: Blackwell.

Armstrong, P. (1989) 'Limits and Possibilities for HRM in an Age of Management Accounting', in J. Storey (ed.), *New Perspectives on Human Resource Management*, London: Routledge.

Beaumont, P. B. (1991) 'Trade Unions and HRM', *Industrial Relations Journal* **22**, 4: 300–8.

Beechey, V. and Perkins, T. (1987) *A Matter of Hours: Women, Part-time Work and the Labour Market*, Cambridge: Polity.

Berggren, C. (1992) *The Volvo Experience: Alternatives to Lean Production in the Swedish Auto Industry*, London: Macmillan.

Berggren, C. (1993) 'Lean Production – The End of History?', *Work, Employment and Society* **7**, 2: 163–89.

Child, J. (1969) *British Management Thought*, London: George Allen & Unwin.

Clarke, S. (1992) 'What in the F . . .'s Name is Fordism?', in N. Gilbert, R. Burrows and A. Pollert (eds), *Fordism and Flexibility: Divisions and Change*, London: Macmillan.

Cockburn, C. (1985) *Machinery of Dominance: Women, Men and Technical Know-how*, London: Pluto Press.

Coyle, A. (1982) 'Sex and Skill in the Organisation of the Clothing Industry', in J. West (ed.), *Work, Women and the Labour Market*, London: Routledge & Kegan Paul.

Cross, M. (1985) *Towards the Flexible Craftsman*, London: Technical Change Centre.

Garrahan, P. and Stewart, P. (1992) *The Nissan Enigma*, London: Mansell.

Glucksman, M. (1990) *Women Assemble: Women Workers and the New Industries in Inter-War Britain*, London: Routledge.

Guest, D. (1989) 'Human Resource Management: Its Implications for Industrial Relations and Trade Unions', in J. Storey (ed.), *New Perspectives on Human Resource Management*, London: Routledge.

Guest, D. and Dewe, P. (1991) 'Company or Trade Union: Which Wins Workers' Allegiance? A Study of Commitment in the UK Electronics Industry', *British Journal of Industrial Relations* **29**, 1: 75–96.

Heaton, N. and Linn, I. (1989) *Fighting Back: A Report on the Shop Steward Response to New Management Techniques in TGWU Region 10*, TGWU Region 10 and Northern College, Barnsley.

Hill, S. (1991) 'Why Quality Circle Failed but Total Quality Management Might Succeed', *British Journal of Industrial Relations* **29**, 4: 541–68.

Hyman, R. (1989) *The Political Economy of Industrial Relations*, London: Macmillan.

IDS (1991) *Supervisors: A Leading Role in Managing Change*, London: Income Data Services, Study 479.

IR-RR (1985) 'Employee Relations at Rowntree Mackintosh', *Industrial Relation Review and Report* **349**, August, London: Industrial Relations Services.

IRS (1992) *Trade Union Responses to New Management Techniques*, IRS Employment Trends 511, London: Industrial Relations Services.

Legge, K. (1989) 'Human Resource Management: A Critical Analysis', in J. Storey (ed.), *New Perspectives on Human Resource Management*, London: Routledge.

Marchington, M., Goodman, J., Wilkinson, A. and Ackers, P. (1992) *New*

Developments in Employee Involvement, UMIST, Research Management Branch, Employment Department.

Martinez Lucio, M. and Weston, S. (1992a) 'Human Resource Management and Trade Union Responses: Bringing the Politics of the Workplace back into the Debate', in P. Blyton and P. Turnbull (eds), *Reassessing Human Resource Management*, London: Sage.

Martinez Lucio, M. and Weston, S. (1992b) 'The Politics and Complexity of Trade Union Responses to New Management Practices', *Human Resource Management Journal* 2, 4: 77–91.

Marginson, P., Armstrong, P., Edwards, P. K. and Purcell, J. with Hubbard, N. (1993) 'The Control of Industrial Relations in Large Companies', *Warwick Papers in Industrial Relations*, No. 45, Coventry: IRRU, School of Industrial and Business Studies, University of Warwick.

Millward, N., Stevens, M., Smart, D. and Hawes, W. R. (1992) *Workplace Industrial Relations in Transition*, Aldershot: Dartmouth.

Morris, T. and Wood, S, (1991) 'Testing the Survey Method: Continuity and Change in British Industrial Relations', *Work, Employment and Society* 5, 2: 259–82.

Mueller, F. (1994) 'Team Between Hierarchy and Commitment: Change Strategies and the "Internal Environment"', *Journal of Management Studies* 31, 3: 383–403.

NEDC (1990) *Jobs and Technology in the Food and Drink Manufacturing Industry*, National Economic Development Council Food and Drink Manufacturing Sector Group, London: NEDC.

Phillips, A. and Taylor, B. (1980) 'Sex and Skill: Notes towards a Feminist Economics', *Feminist Review* 6: 79–88.

Pollert, A. (1993) 'The Single European Market, Multinationals and Concentration: The Case of Food Manufacturing', *Journal of Public Policy* 13, 3: 77–96.

Ramsay, H. (1991) 'Reinventing the Wheel? A Review of the Development and Performance of Employee Involvement', *Human Resource Management Journal* 1, 4: 1–21.

Scott, A. (1994) *Willing Slaves? British Workers Under New Management*, Cambridge Studies in Management, Cambridge: Cambridge University Press.

Sisson, K. (1993) 'In Search of HRM', *British Journal of Industrial Relations* 31, 2: 201–10.

Smith, C., Child, J. and Rowlinson, M. (1990) *Reshaping Work: The Cadbury Experience*, Cambridge: Cambridge University Press.

Storey, J. (1987) 'Developments in the Management of Human Resources: An Interim Report', *Warwick Papers in Industrial Relations*, No. 17, Coventry: IRRU, School of Industrial and Business Studies, University of Warwick.

Storey, J. (ed.) (1989) *New Perspectives on Human Resource Management*, London: Routledge.

Storey, J. (1992) *Development in the Management of Human Resources*, Oxford: Basil Blackwell.

7

THE DIFFERENT EXPERIENCE OF TRADE UNIONISM IN TWO JAPANESE TRANSPLANTS

Carol Stephenson

INTRODUCTION

During the 1980s and 1990s the sociological study of work and employment in Britain has been dominated by debates concerning industrial restructuring towards flexibility, 'lean' or 'waste-free' production and the 'Japanisation' of industry. There has been much discussion about the consequences for workers of the restructuring of industry. Claims for the positive implications of flexible working practices have faced growing criticism, as more and more research indicates that such practices present workers with a deterioration in working conditions, work intensification and, typically, the marginalisation of trade unions (Williamson 1989; Parker and Slaughter 1988; Garrahan and Stewart 1992). However, the question of how and why workers have come to accept these practices and restrictive trade union agreements deserves more attention. It is this question of worker consent to flexible work practices which this chapter aims to address.

The nature of worker consent in two Japanese-owned transplants based in Washington, near Sunderland, Tyne and Wear in the North-East of England, will be examined. They are Nissan Motor Manufacturing (UK) and Nissan's part-owned supplier plant Ikeda Hoover. As these companies operate a 'Just-in-Time' (JIT) production system an insight into the impact of the JIT relationship on worker consent in the supplier company is possible. This investigation will reveal the factors which have influenced the development of differing responses within the plants to flexible mass production. Within Nissan, thus far at least, there has been little co-ordinated resistance to the logic of flexible working, while at Ikeda Hoover the development of a trade union base has led to effective opposition to flexible, 'lean', mass production.

RESEARCH METHODOLOGY

The routes previously taken by sociologists to make contact with workers, such as through the company or trade union, were not open in this research. The recognised trade union, the AEEU, has little shop floor power in Nissan with which to extend invitations to sociologists, even if it wished to do so.[1]

Nissan managers have claimed that the promotion of the 'Nissan way of working' is a corporate goal (Nissan Community Relations Officer, November 1991). Consequently Europe's industrialists, academics and trade unionists are allowed to witness – if briefly – the Nissan way of working in action through well-organised guided tours of the plant. However, Nissan (thus far at least) has not been prepared to open the plant to comprehensive independent sociological investigation.

Consequently workers interviewed were contacted through informal networks.[2] As an active trade unionist and a native of the North-East of England the author has 'roots' in the working-class community. Those roots made possible contact with workers from the Nissan and Ikeda Hoover plants. Discussion of this research with working-class North-Eastern students also led to a number of useful contacts being made with workers from Japanese-owned companies.[3]

The method of making contact with workers differed between the two case study workforces. While some Ikeda Hoover workers volunteered the names of work mates and acquaintances, Nissan workers did not volunteer that information and they were not asked to do so.[4] By providing the names of others, workers were making their involvement in the research known to a third party. Some Ikeda workers were prepared to do this, and this may have resulted from the relative confidence of this group of workers.

In total forty-one research interviews were conducted with Nissan and Ikeda Hoover workers. Twenty interviews with Nissan workers and two interviews with Ikeda Hoover workers were conducted between 1988 and 1991. Between 1991 and March 1994 a further three Nissan and thirteen Ikeda Hoover workers were interviewed. One Nissan worker has been interviewed three times and one Ikeda Hoover worker has been interviewed twice. These interviews were conducted in the respondents' homes or in a neutral place of their choice. With the permission of interviewees, these discussions were taped and transcribed.

In addition to interviews with worker respondents, interviews were conducted with officers from the region's major manufacturing and engineering unions, representatives of development agencies and senior managers from the Japanese-owned sector.

The limitations of this research method should be recognised. A relatively small number of qualitative research interviews have been conducted to contribute to this work and consequently the views and perspectives which are presented here cannot be taken as representative of the workforce at large. Preferably this qualitative interview method should have been supported with other methods. Visits to Nissan are available, and this made possible some appreciation of the structure and atmosphere within the plant.[5] Qualitative interviews are a useful tool in the discovery of the meanings workers attach to their actions; however, the opportunity to observe the line and workers' activity in greater detail and talk to workers on the line about how they worked would have been valuable.[6] Workers may not be consciously aware of all of their actions or that certain aspects of their work is of interest to the sociologist, and the interview method is incapable of overcoming these problems.

WORKER CONSENT

The question of why workers consent to work within the capitalist system is not new to sociologists. Michael Burawoy conducted participant observation research among a group of mass production workers who were paid on a collective bonus, piece rate basis. He framed the question of consent thus:

> Why should workers push themselves to advance the interests of the company? Why co-operate with and sometimes even exceed the expectation of those 'people upstairs' who 'will do anything to get another piece out of you'? But it wasn't long before I too was breaking my back to make out, to make the quota, to discover a new angle, and to run two jobs at once – risking life and limb for that extra piece. Why was I actively participating in the intensification of my own exploitation and even losing my temper when I couldn't? That is the problem I pose.
>
> (Burawoy 1979: xi preface)

212

Burawoy's comments are of interest to this examination of flexible, 'lean', mass production as he claimed his actions involved him in the intensification of his own labour. Advocates of so-called post-Fordist work methods which are based on flexibility and the elimination of waste claim that the success of this philosophy rests on the fact that workers contribute more than the basic completion of work tasks: they participate in the development of the labour process and take responsibility for a range of tasks. The co-operative industrial relationships which make this possible come about because employers and employees recognise that they are mutually dependent for success and long-term security. It is claimed that workers central to the flexible, waste-free organisation are multi-skilled and their loyalty is underpinned by the respect this work organisation offers and by the employment security which emanates from the advantages won by these methods (Atkinson and Meager 1987; Hirst and Zeitlin 1989).

Recent commentaries on worker consent have demanded four things from an investigation of this type.

First, that worker consent must be understood in context of the political and economic environment within which work takes place (Maguire 1988; Nichols and Beynon 1977). In addition, the position of the workplace within the circuit of capitalist valor-isation will affect management style, labour process and industrial relationships, therefore the impact of that position must be appreci-ated. Burawoy failed to examine how the relatively protected position of the case study plant, Allied, influenced the level of worker consent apparent there (see Knights and Collinson 1985). Second, the impact of work process and organisation on worker consent and control must be examined. Third, as worker consent is a socially created phenomenon, the common understandings and rules and norms of social interaction must be uncovered. It is the task of the sociologist to identify those rules and develop an appreciation of how they came about and how they affect accept-ance or dissent within the working environment. Lastly, through an appreciation of the meanings workers attach to their actions the true level and nature of worker consent can be gauged (Knights and Willmott 1989).

BACKGROUND TO THE DEVELOPMENT OF THE CASE STUDY COMPANIES

The economic recession of the late 1970s and early 1980s, combined with government economic policy on the free market and for nationalised industries, had a catastrophic impact on employment in the Northern region. In 1981 alone there were more than 40,000 redundancies in the region, mainly in the manufacturing sector. The region's branch plants (some were established initially with financial assistance resulting from economic policy for the regions) retreated to more profitable environments (Robinson 1990: 9; Hudson 1989).

Manufacturing employment suffered the worst losses. Between 1979 and 1986, the South-East lost 25 per cent of its manufacturing jobs, the West Midlands 28 per cent and the North 34 per cent. In total 140,000 manufacturing jobs were lost. Only Wales suffered greater losses (Trade Union Studies Information Unit 1987).

Despite claims for economic revival during the 1980s, unemployment in the Northern region in December 1993 stood at 10.6 per cent of the working population. March 1994 saw the closure of the region's last deep shaft coal mine in Northumberland (*Labour Research*, January 1994).

In 1981 Nissan announced its intention to locate a plant in Europe, which it claimed would ultimately employ 5,000 workers.[7] The primary motive for the move was to break into the European market in advance of the development of further protectionist barriers. The need to establish bases in the USA and in Europe was intensified by the relatively unstable home economy in the 1980s. Nissan's domestic market share fell during the 1980s and they were more dependent than any other Japanese car manufacturer on exports. The strong yen apparent in the 1980s made Nissan's reliance on exports more problematic as it had a negative impact on the company's foreign currency transactions (Williamson 1989: 6–7).

Multinational Corporations (MNCs) in their quest for new markets and suitable production bases can act simultaneously as the purveyors of new relations of production. Garrahan has claimed that the consensus of approval in the local and national media and local government and development agencies which surrounds this new Japanese-owned sector emanated from the hope that it would play a proactive role in introducing new methods of work process and new industrial relations to established industries, thus rejuvenating a failing regional economy (Garrahan 1986; Crowther and Garrahan 1988; Garrahan and Stewart 1992).

The choice of Britain as a production site illustrates the imperative of an MNC in securing the most advantageous production site for the securement of profit. Nissan came to Britain because during the 1970s and 1980s the British market became Nissan's biggest export market in Europe. Since the informal agreement came into effect limiting Japanese imported cars to Britain to 12 per cent of total annual sales, Nissan has sold 6 per cent of that total, beating the combined sales of Toyota, Honda, Mazda and Colt (*Financial Times*, 1986). The North-East of England offered large areas of land at minimum cost and financial incentives were offered by both national and local government. Garrahan and Stewart claimed that the total incentives offered to Nissan were in excess of £100 million (see Garrahan 1986 and Garrahan and Stewart 1992).

In addition, legislation and recession had curtailed the power of British trade unions. In the North-East trade unions lost large numbers of members as a consequence of the recession and the decline in manufacturing and heavy industries, which had traditionally been strongly unionised. This decline made it possible for Nissan to negotiate the best possible agreement for trade union recognition. The nature and impact of that agreement will be examined in greater detail later.

Nissan has established linkages with 177 suppliers in Britain, although only eighteen of these are in the North-East. They claim to have created over 8,000 permanent jobs in the region, with over 4,000 employed directly by Nissan. However, in 1993 Nissan shed 400 jobs through voluntary redundancy and reduced working hours as that year saw the steepest fall in car demand in Europe since the Second World War. Despite this Nissan exported more than 182,000 Micra and Primera cars worth almost £1,000 million in 1993, making it the leading British-based car exporter (Nissan M. M. UK Ltd 1993; Gibson and Hogg *The Journal* 2 February 1994).

IKEDA HOOVER UK

Ikeda Hoover UK is the product of a joint venture between Ikeda Bussan Co. (of Japan) and Hoover Universal Ltd (of Britain). Ikeda Bussan is a major seat and interior trim manufacturer in Japan and has a yearly turnover of £400 million. Hoover Universal UK are part of the American-owned company Johnson Controls Inc., which turns over £600 million per annum. Ikeda Hoover UK is 51 per cent owned by Ikeda Bussan, and 49 per cent owned by Hoover Universal. Nissan has a stake in the Ikeda Hoover plant as it part owns Ikeda Bussan. Ikeda Hoover UK was launched in 1986 to supply Nissan UK with seats and interior trim on a JIT basis. Between 1986 and 1989 Ikeda was based in a warehouse in Washington where parts were stored before being fed when needed into Nissan. In 1989 Ikeda began production on a purpose-built site on the Nissan Trading Estate, the enormous piece of land which surrounds the Nissan plant and which was purchased by the car plant at minimum cost. Ikeda currently employs 444 workers and currently claims to be manufacturing solely for Nissan UK.

Ikeda use the term 'synchronous production' to describe the sophisticated precision form of JIT in operation. The two plants are computer linked, enabling Ikeda to manufacture the correct colour and style for the car body, which is simultaneously manufactured at Nissan. Ikeda Hoover supply Nissan with parts every fifteen minutes. Ikeda workers have responsibility for delivering parts at the very time they are required, directly to the point on the factory floor where they are to be fitted immediately to the car body.

Garrahan and Stewart recognise that in acquiring a large greenfield site Nissan were able to select component supplier plants and ensure their establishment on the trading estate, enabling a JIT production complex to develop. They recognise the fragility apparent in the JIT system, but claim that Nissan were able to choose suppliers with the same management style and labour process:

> Of additional importance in Sunderland is that Nissan can rely on management styles similar to its own in supplier companies on the Industrial Estate and elsewhere. A further uncertainty which needs eliminating to sustain the JIT method of production arises with respect to industrial relations: an industrial dispute in one part of the JIT system would bring the system to a halt in its entirety as no reserve stocks of parts are kept. Nissan's way of responding to this need to have complete control of the labour process is to place emphasis on loyalty to the company as an industrial ethos rather than loyalty to the union.
>
> (Garrahan and Stewart 1992: 45)

Garrahan and Stewart have assumed that supplier plants would maintain the same management style, work practices and industrial relations as the main manufacturer. They made the assumption that conditions at Ikeda and the experience of working for Ikeda would be comparable to that at Nissan and therefore that Ikeda management too would successfully place emphasis on loyalty to the company rather than to the union. However, in the following examination of worker consent these assumptions are found to be flawed, and consequently it can be argued that Garrahan and Stewart overestimate Nissan's control of the JIT industrial complex which surrounds it. Worker consent to flexible, 'lean' working has been maintained at Nissan, and the factors involved in that will be examined. The factors which differentiate Ikeda from Nissan, and which have prompted worker opposition within the supplier plant, will also be examined.

WORKER CONSENT AT NISSAN UK

In Britain Nissan has played a central role in the diffusion of ideas associated with flexible, 'lean' production. Peter Wickens, Nissan's former Director of Personnel, has claimed that the successful relationship with the Nissan workforce is not based on improvement of workers' experience of the labour process itself; rather it has been achieved because workers were involved in the development of that process; Nissan workers were able to 'own their own change' and therefore need not fear it:

> Control *by* the process can change to control *of* the process. Instead of Volvo's attempts to build job satisfaction into the very act of building the car via extended job cycles, satisfaction can arise from performing the short, repetitive cycle well, achieving high levels of productivity and quality, and at the same time being involved in changes to the process and a range of other tasks e.g. maintenance, housekeeping, problem solving.
>
> (Wickens 1993: 33–4)

Wickens has accepted that the goals of Taylorism, such as the elimination of waste, are intact. So too are some Taylorist methods, such as the standard operation. However, the method of attaining these has been to recognise that labour is not a burden on profit making, but an asset to it. Nissan recognise the advantage of using what is 'in workers' heads'. This sharing of knowledge is accepted as Nissan workers recognise that 'sharing knowledge, then profitability and security will accrue to all, it is the right thing to do'. The result is what Wickens has called 'lean, people centred, volume production' (Wickens 1993: 21 and 31).

Senior managers link Nissan's success to the adoption of a triad of work principles: flexibility, quality control and team work. That triad rests on three principles: first, that workers take individual responsibility for their work; second, that individual workers have knowledge and understanding of their work and should therefore contribute to the organisation of the work process and environment; third, that individuals work most effectively and achieve more as part of a team.

A number of factors are significant in the maintenance of worker consent within Nissan, and these will be examined in the following sections. These are the effective exclusion of an independent trade union, the political and economic environment and labour market, the labour process and the social and financial incentives associated with consent made available to Nissan workers.

NISSAN'S TRADE UNION AGREEMENT WITH THE AEEU

Nissan signed a single union agreement with the AEEU in April 1985, prior to recruiting a workforce for the Washington site.[8] The agreement left no meaningful role for the trade union; there was to be no shop steward representation and no role for the union in negotiation or in representation of its membership. Ikeda Hoover subsequently signed an identical agreement with the AEEU.

Full-time officers of the AEEU accept that these agreements were restricting but argued that they should be seen as 'a foot in the door'; a basis upon which unionists within the plants could work towards achieving a greater role for the union. To date there has been little progress in improving on the original agreement within Nissan. The one concession on the part of the company has been to allow a shop steward within the plant. However, that steward has no recognised role in terms of negotiation for, or representation of, AEEU members within the plant. None of the Nissan workers interviewed knew the shop steward or had any contact with him, although some did know that there was an AEEU steward within Nissan.

The AEEU currently place the figure for union membership at Nissan at 33 per cent; however, Nissan claim that 45 per cent of their workforce is unionised. While membership figures appear healthy, these are misleading as workers interviewed had a number of rationales for joining or not joining the recognised trade union.

Some pro-union workers had retained membership of trade unions recognised under previous employment and others claimed that they had taken a principled stand of not joining the AEEU because, as one worker put it, they had been 'sold down the river even before the factory was properly built'. As a consequence some Nissan respondents who claimed to have been pro-union (and who may, in other circumstances, have formed the basis for union organisation) rejected involvement with the AEEU.

Ironically some of those who had joined the AEEU were sceptical about trade unionism. Some had joined the AEEU as they hoped to get employment in engineering in the future. Others had joined at the request of managers. Two letters from Nissan to their staff urged them to join the AEEU.[9] These letters argued that Nissan and the AEEU had 'a joint commitment to success' and asked all workers to join the AEEU. A team leader claimed that he had decided to join as higher levels of membership would secure the agreement with the union and stave off any threat for recruitment rights from potentially more hostile trade unions.

Trade unions have traditionally played a part in industrial relations within mass car manufacture. Within Nissan the functions of communication and problem solving have been replaced by the team leader, the Company Council and the Kaizen meeting.

Team leaders gather information on the shop floor, pass it on to senior managers and in turn relay information down to shop floor workers.

The Company Council carries out a communication, negotiation and problem-solving role which traditionally would have been performed by trade union representatives in discussion with managers. There is a maximum of ten elected members from the plant's shop floor and offices on the Council. To qualify for candidacy for the Council, workers must have been employed by Nissan for at least two years and should not have gone past the verbal warning stage in the grievance procedure.

The position of a Company Council representative differs in a number of ways from that experienced by a shop steward in a mass production car plant in the 1960s or 1970s. S/he has no formal contact with, or support from, external sources (such as a wider trade union structure) or workers from other companies who may offer a different view from that of Nissan's management. A suggestion from the Council representative has none of the impact of a request from a shop steward who represents an organised trade union shop floor.

Five employer representatives to the Company Council are appointed by Nissan's Managing Director. Officer positions of Secretary and Chair are held by senior managers. Minutes are taken and circulated to staff by the senior Personnel Manager, and the Council sits twice a year.

The third structure which replaces the function of the trade union is the Kaizen meeting. Nissan argue that as part of the philosophy of flexibility, workers are encouraged to participate in 'creating their own change' (Wickens 1987: 46). 'Kaizen' (meaning continual improvement) is achieved by workers meeting in teams to develop projects to improve any part of the work process or experience of work. Managers evaluate the projects, and those judged to be the best are put into operation. Kaizen projects have related to such diverse matters as bus routes, sports facilities, the standard of canteen food and improvements in the production process itself.

The Kaizen meeting performed a number of both practical and ideological functions within Nissan. It allowed communication to occur between shop floor workers and senior managers, without the interference of a third party (i.e. a trade union) or the threat of stoppages. It therefore allowed workers to identify areas of potential unrest and dissatisfaction in a safe environment. Kaizen allowed managers to access workers' knowledge of the production process. Garrahan and Stewart noted that workers have suggested changes which have led to the speeding up of work.[10] Garrahan and Stewart also acknowledged that through Kaizen workers learn how to participate in the Nissan way of working in a way which is acceptable to their employers. In addition to this, it is important to note that the legitimacy of Kaizen has been maintained as projects are not narrowly defined or directed towards improvements in the labour process or other areas which directly affect the accumulation of profit. Workers interviewed were able to point to changes which had occurred as a result of Kaizen and which have improved their experience of work, even if those are as simple as changes to the local bus service. Changes of this nature have meant that workers have felt able to communicate with their managers and experience some of the benefits of that communication, therefore legitimating, thus far at least, the absence of the trade union and the new framework of communication and the resolution of problems.

THE EXTERNAL POLITICAL AND ECONOMIC ENVIRONMENT, THE LABOUR MARKET AND WORKER SELF-PERCEPTION

Economic vulnerability is a constant theme in discussions with workers. Nissan workers were relieved to be employed at what was perceived to be one of the region's last secure workplaces.

There was a greater propensity for Nissan workers (as opposed to counterparts in the supplier plant, Ikeda Hoover) to offer new realist explanations for the demise of the region's traditional industries which involved scepticism about the value of trade unionism: 'Where I used to work the blokes said "you have got to be in a trade union". What good did that do them? They are all unemployed now . . . what did the trade union do for me?' (Nissan manufacturing worker).

Several workers interviewed clearly enjoyed the public self-image associated with being a 'Nissan worker', and some enjoyed being associated with their employer outside work. For example, Managing Director Ian Gibson, during an interview, aware of the prestige many of his workers associated with working for Nissan, mentioned the instance of a team of Nissan workers who requested permission to wear Nissan shirts and logo while competing in the Great North Run. Workers gained prestige from being engaged in what was considered to be secure employment in a region of high unemployment, but also from their association with a company that has been portrayed as regional benefactor and champion of new and successful work methods. The public and internal propaganda of Nissan manufacturing and quality supremacy had clearly influenced the perceptions of some workers interviewed:

> we work harder than anybody at any of the other car companies, Leyland, Vauxhall – I know that for a fact. The quality we produce is that much better. . . . It is these type [sic] of work methods that means Nissan stays ahead of the opposition.
>
> (Nissan manufacturing team leader)

Nissan workers offered a new equation of mutual trust with their employer when describing their acceptance of new working practices. Their view was that as Nissan's work practices differed from those associated with 'failed' industries, their experience of employment security would also differ. They were consequently prepared to accept the new work practices and industrial relation-

221

ships as long as employment security was forthcoming. Worker consent at Nissan was clearly bound up with Nissan's ability to deliver relatively well-paid and secure employment and with it the public prestige of working for what has been widely perceived to be the region's 'best' employer.

Had the recruitment of large numbers of workers with specialist skills for the manufacture of cars been of primary importance, it is unlikely that Nissan would have chosen a greenfield site in a region with no history of car mass production. Nissan's preference for workers with appropriate attitudes towards flexibility and continual change rather than workers with previous relevant work experience has ensured that Nissan have been able to select a workforce from large numbers of applicants. Thirty thousand applications were received for 1,600 jobs created with the production of the Micra. Nissan recruited a young workforce: the average age of shop floor workers was 24 years.

Applicants go through a series of interviews during the selection process. However, Nissan managers accept that the process of selection is not 'watertight' in terms of identifying suitable workers and claim that there is a 9 per cent turnover rate among new starters within the first three months. This results from a management decision that a candidate is not suitable, or from self-selection on the part of the worker. The de-selection of probationary workers confirms in the minds of some Nissan workers interviewed that Nissan workers are 'special':

> Not everyone can be a Nissan worker: it wouldn't suit everyone. But we say that if you are at Nissan for three months, then you are a Nissan worker for life.
> (Nissan Community Relations Officer, plant visit, 1991)

SOCIAL AND FINANCIAL INCENTIVES TO WORKER CONSENT

Incentives to worker consent are both social and financial in nature.

The organisation of work at Nissan rests on the triad of flexibility, team working and quality control. Workers' responses to this triad indicate that flexibility is primarily numerical in nature, and involves multi-tasking. As Garrahan and Stewart note, workers are responsible for their own quality standards and for the surveillance of the quality of the work of others.

Workers interviewed attest to the existence of peer-group pressure within the team to maintain speed and quality standards. The failure of the individual has ramifications for the whole team. The awarding of VES (Vehicle Evaluation Scores) by Nissan managers to teams has formalised competition between groups of workers: 'They would love to find a quality fault made by another department' (Nissan maintenance engineer).

While Nissan claim that their workforce enjoy the same wages and conditions, individual workers are appraised annually by supervisors, and that carries financial reward. Appraisal was based not only on work performance but, as this team leader explained, on supervisors' judgements of:

Flexibility, your willingness to change . . . whether you agree with improvements, things like that. You see some people don't like them at all, but other people welcome improvements that make the job easier and some people don't want to know . . . [the supervisor] knows everyone like.

(Nissan manufacturing team leader)

The monitoring of workers' attitudes by shop floor managers is most clearly illustrated in what the team leader called 'willingness to change', i.e. to flexibility, to participation in Kaizen. In order to qualify for good appraisals workers have to make their attitude to the Nissan way of working *visible* through an active commitment to quality monitoring and Kaizen. It was not enough simply to accept change: that acceptance had to be made visible.

Workers were aware that their activities and attitudes were under scrutiny not only from managers, but from peers:

Eyebrows would be raised by work colleagues if I left any time before six . . . you know when it is OK to leave.

(Nissan design engineer)

you always have to impress someone, look good as well as be good. If you have a good idea you have to be careful who you tell or they will say it is theirs . . . then they are the good bloke.

(Nissan manufacturing team leader)

Interviews with workers revealed the existence of an expected code of social conduct within Nissan. The norms and rules of that conduct involved competitiveness, individualism, ambition and total commitment to the company, and even, at times, personal adversity. Sticking to that code meant anonymity, and/or reward:[11]

> I have seen people assembling cars on the line with their legs in plaster, which is just ridiculous, I mean just hobbling along the side of the track – but it goes down great, it gets them 'brownie points'. They come to work like that and it is just the ultimate dedication.
>
> (Nissan maintenance worker)

However, while some workers whole-heartedly entered into the Nissan way of working, others were prepared to 'give them what they want'. These workers felt that they must make visible the appearance of loyalty and commitment, even when they were sceptical about the value of the activities they were performing:

> There is a policy at Nissan of telling managers what they want to hear . . . they make it very clear what they think politically, so everybody makes out they are bluer than blue and I do too. I couldn't say well actually, Arthur Scargill is my favourite person.
>
> (Nissan quality control worker)

As there was a clearly set down code of acceptable conduct which involved making visible commitment to the Nissan way, there was opportunity for workers to 'cheat' at consent. As workers recognised that appearances were important, a number were willing to give the appearance of being 'true believers' in the superiority of the Nissan way, while harbouring doubts about its value.

Those workers keen to seize the opportunities of self-betterment Nissan offered set standards against which others were measured; as a result many workers felt they had to contribute in some way, or stand out as individuals:

> It looks good, for example, to be going for a promotion, whether you want one or not. It is expected that everyone wants to get on. So sometimes people put in for it knowing that they won't get it just to keep up a good appearance.
>
> (Nissan manufacturing worker)

Interviews reveal insincere compliance with the Nissan way on the part of some workers at least. Parallels can be drawn here between the identification of this insincere compliance, or what Knights and Collinson (1985) might have called a cynical compliance, and other accounts of conformity within organisations. For example, Goffman's (1968) study of the self-identity of inmates in a total institution illustrated a series of 'survival' responses.

Worker competition and visibility do not occur spontaneously on the Nissan shop floor: the harsh political and economic environment has left workers with few employment alternatives, and the organisation of work and the cultural and political ethos apparent within the plant set out clear guidelines for success, failure and reward. The cumulative effect of workers' strategies, to date, has been the effective suppression of a collective response to flexible working practices. This comment from a maintenance worker illustrated the impact of the absence of a collective approach to long-term employment with the car manufacturer:

> I think there is pretty much an atmosphere of people wanting to get on all the time. They can't survive on the shop floor for the whole of their working lives; it is too hard. It is go up [promotion] or get out.

The apparent level of worker consent in operation at Nissan does not represent an end to conflict within the 'lean', mass production car plant. Appearances, in this instance, are deceptive. Through an investigation of perceptions of workers and the mean- ings workers associated with their actions it can be seen that they have adopted a number of strategies for coping with their work in what is an economically vulnerable environment.

WORKER CONSENT AT IKEDA HOOVER

Ikeda managers claim their plant operates on the same triad philosophy of team working, flexibility and quality control as adopted by Nissan. The agreement reached between the AEEU and Ikeda Hoover is identical to that agreed by Nissan, and the two plants operate within the same depressed regional economy; however, at Ikeda a trade union base has developed which has taken an active role not only in problem identification and solving, but in the development of opposition to flexible, 'lean' production. There were three shop stewards for 444 workers, but only one for over 2,500 workers at Nissan.

Moreover, at Ikeda shop stewards play an active role in the identification and communication of problems to management and in communication between shop floor workers and management.

They represent workers at disciplinary hearings, and union activists have developed strategies with which to increase union membership and influence. For example, all workers would be represented by a steward at a disciplinary hearing. Non-union workers who were given support would be encouraged to join the union following the hearing. Pro-union workers noted during interviews that following union interventions (pay negotiations, negotiation for increased health and safety standards, the representation of workers during hearings) union recruitment increased.

The Company Council, in marked contrast to that of Nissan, is staffed predominantly by representatives who are members of the AEEU, three of whom were the plant's shop stewards. One steward, who was described by other workers as 'the union convenor', was said to take responsibility for briefing all Company Council worker representatives prior to meetings in order to ensure that 'we get what we want'.

The activity of shop floor workers at Ikeda had made it possible for AEEU officers to have access to the plant. Ikeda stewards had made contact with the wider union body outside the plant and that had enabled some Ikeda unionists to take in union and TUC education programmes. As a result, unionists have gained a wider perspective on the experience of flexible working practices and support for the development of the union through contact with other trade unionists.

Trade union activity had led to opposition to the 'lean' production strategy of continual change and improvement. Attempts to introduce 'standing' sewing throughout the sewing shop had been resisted.[12]

Despite managers claiming in 1989 that there were plans to introduce a Kaizen-style meeting, workers interviewed claimed that this had not been introduced at the Ikeda plant. There had also been an attempt to introduce an annual appraisal system, but that too had not been successful.

While Ikeda workers had accepted the principle of individual responsibility for quality (although a number were critical of quality standards), workers did not claim that their attitudes and actions were scrutinised by peers.

Workers interviewed were asked why the union had become active and influential within Ikeda. The following themes emerged.

THE LABOUR MARKET

Ikeda have faced recruitment difficulties, and workers and team leaders have testified to these. Had Ikeda's priority been to recruit to its shop floor workers with appropriate attitudes rather than skills and experience, as at Nissan, they would have had a large pool of applicants from which to select a workforce. However, the requirement for workers with specialised skills in almost one-third of the shop floor manufacturing workforce narrowed the field from which workers could be selected. In the sewing shop, where the fabric of seats and trim are constructed, women workers claim their work is specialised and skilled, requiring previous experience. Women interviewed described their work as machine tailoring or machine upholstery and claimed it could not be carried out by novice machinists. These women derived confidence from the fact that they could not easily be replaced:

> It is very hard and heavy work. We work with the foam as well as the material to make the whole seat – you have to put your whole body into it, all your arms up to the elbow have to be used to pull and move the foam and material [standing stooped to show how the work was done]. . . . It took me a while to pick it up; there is no way you could do it without experience . . . not reaching the quality standards they expect and the speed.
>
> (Ikeda sewing machinist)

Ikeda confirmed that all women employed in the sewing shop had previous experience and 90 per cent of the remainder of the workforce had experience of industrial/manufacturing employment.

An officer with the General, Municipal and Boilermakers' Union (GMBU) – of which the Tailors' and Garment Workers' Union is now a part – confirmed that there has been a shortage of skilled machinists in the region as there are few manufacturers which continue to provide training in machine tailoring. Skilled machinists were in such short supply that workplaces which recognised the GMBU had telephoned the union to ask if they knew of workers who were available for employment.

Ikeda workers in general were more willing to make unprompted comparisons between their current work and previous experiences of employment than were their Nissan counterparts.[13] Women interviewees claimed that Ikeda's flexible working did not offer 'something new' primarily because they had previously seen the introduction of flexible working practices. Several women workers had worked together prior to coming to Ikeda, typically in unionised workplaces. Women workers claimed that the develop- ment of the active union base began within the sewing shop and was the result of the camaraderie and confidence acquired from their skills and previous experience of machine work. 'They couldn't replace us easily; the job is highly skilled; even I struggled when I came' (sewing machinist).

A number of experienced workers set examples to other workers in their union activity and in their opposition to the implementation of new, and what were considered to be potentially damaging, work practices. Among those interviewed, three workers – two women sewing machinists and a male worker from seat assembly – argued that they had developed a social presence on the shop floor; they were able to 'take other workers with them'. For example, Ken did not take up a union position, but encouraged young workers to join by drawing parallels between previous work experiences and his present experience:

> I wouldn't say I was militant in any way: I have worked in so many places that it always seems to happen that it is me and my two mates, all about the same age, [who] do all the shouting and the kids just sit there. They just have not got a clue, you know. We say to them, 'look, they are trying to take two men off our line and we are going to have to walk out that door. We can't let them get away with it because they will do it to them first and then you will get your cards and you'll never get them men back', and they will say 'aye, aye', and I said 'look, it's your job I am talking about!' There is this lad bought a Toyota, he's a canny kid, I said 'I am talking about your car that you are up to your eyes in debt over and you are going to lose it.' They are starting to think a bit now, the kids: they are starting to get it together.
>
> (Ikeda seat assembly worker)

Ikeda interviewees claimed that shop stewards were experienced workers who 'carried clout', knew that management were encouraging competition between teams and orchestrated the activity of those around them: 'The shop steward said she knew what they [management] were doing and why. She said, [to shop floor workers] 'I am the shop steward: don't get involved in it' (Ikeda sewing machinist).

WOMEN WORKERS

Interviews with women workers illustrated that they drew confidence and status from their lives and experiences outside the immediate work environment. Women described themselves as 'mothers' and 'grandmothers' and as having 'grown up families'. Women workers had used this credibility and confidence to gain respect from those around them and to oppose the introduction of practices which they felt were potentially damaging:

> They have brought in this competition between the teams for a cup [trophy] – for 'Housekeeping'. The team with the cleanest work area gets it. Some of the younger ones get themselves worked up about it. They are young and daft. But that doesn't happen in my team. To most of us winning a cup has no appeal: there are more important things. I said to my supervisor [laughing], 'I am a grown woman with a grown up family. What do I want with a cup?'
>
> (Ikeda sewing machinist)

During interviews Ikeda workers displayed a greater concern for the welfare of colleagues than their counterparts at Nissan. A number of workers discussed the specific cases of colleagues they felt had received unfair treatment at the hands of managers. This might be explained in a number of ways. Awareness and concern for the welfare of colleagues at Ikeda were partly facilitated by the size of the factory and workforce. Nissan by comparison was a giant, and many Nissan workers interviewed knew of no one beyond those working in their immediate team. Within Ikeda, communication was facilitated by union stewards, mainly through verbal communication between union representatives and pro-union workers throughout the plant. Within Nissan, by contrast, no formal or organised communication network existed as a counter to the information circulated by management. In addition, it is important to note that women workers were more likely to express concerns about specific cases, frequently linking the plight of others to their own concerns for family members. For example, several mentioned their concern that young workers may be suffering the effects of repetitive strain injuries and worried at their long-term implications:

Some of them are only in their early twenties and have their whole lives in front of them. One lad was twenty-three. I have a son that age.

(Ikeda sewing machinist)

Two other factors were said to have stimulated the development of the union: the Ikeda management style and the use of time and motion study in the development of the labour process.

MANAGEMENT STYLE

The management style apparent at Ikeda among both shop floor and senior managers was described by the majority of workers interviewed as unsympathetic. This had increased hostility among shop floor workers. Workers claimed their managers had adopted confrontational tactics in an attempt to ensure worker co-operation:

Morale is low and absenteeism has been high. So if you are off three times over a three-week period you get a caution. But some people can't help being off if they are ill. There have been these stupid incidents where people have tried to come back before they are ready and then had to go off again and they end up with warnings! There was one girl who lost sight in one eye and she was brought in on a caution. The whole plant waited to see how she was treated. I would go as far as to say that they waited to see how she went on before accepting the wage agreement. People were really angry about that incident.

(Ikeda sewing machinist)

A number of factors are likely to have influenced this management style, such as the personal perspectives of senior managers or that union-led opposition to 'lean', flexible production had left managers with few choices but to take a more aggressive stance. However, Ikeda workers said that the JIT relationship with Nissan influenced their own manager's style. For example, union requests to improve health and safety conditions were not implemented immediately as Ikeda were unwilling to stop production. Workers claimed that supervisors reacted angrily when quality defects produced by Ikeda were discovered within Nissan, and that could lead to a management-led inquiry. Workers spoke of the involvement of senior managers in the management of the shop floor work, particularly where faults had led to delays at Nissan for which the company would be charged.

Garrahan and Stewart claimed that Nissan and Ikeda workers were treated in similar ways when quality defects were found. Indeed their account conflated the management of the two plants:

> Nissan defines a quality fault of this nature as relatively unimportant because it does not affect 'marketability'. Nevertheless, workers are sometimes spoken to like children where faults of this nature occur. Interviews with workers at Ikeda Hoover, Nissan's on-site supplier of seats, give many accounts of how quality, under the guise of consumer interest, is used to control rather than extend, employee discretion and dignity.
>
> (Garrahan and Stewart 1992: 72)

Garrahan and Stewart claimed, and I concur with this view, that Nissan workers are active in monitoring their own behaviour and that of their peers. However they also claim that Nissan workers wished to avoid being treated 'like children' by their superiors. However, Nissan workers gave no indication that the response of team leaders and supervisors was to humiliate, and I would argue that it is because Nissan workers were not treated (as one Ikeda worker described his experience) 'like you are wearing the dunce's cap' that the ideology of the 'Nissan way' has retained legitimacy in the perceptions of its workforce. Had Nissan taken a more interventionist or punitive approach, horizontal competition (between workers) might have been replaced – as it was at Ikeda – by vertical disagreement between workers and managers.

THE LABOUR PROCESS AND TIME AND MOTION STUDY

There is little to suggest that Ikeda had successfully used 'what was in workers' heads' to identify ways in which the labour process could be speeded up or time savings made, as had been possible through Kaizen meetings within Nissan. As a consequence, Ikeda relied on time and motion study to make improvements in efficiency. Workers across the plant witnessed this use of industrial engineering techniques, and this increased vertical antagonism towards managers.

They had one bloke on a machine with half a dozen managers standing over him with stop watches timing everything he did. He was shaking like a leaf, so much so he was dropping things and they were saying 'why has he dropped that?' and timing how long it took him to pick it up. It was terrible watching it.

(Ikeda seat assembly worker)

Ikeda workers recognised that the JIT relationship with Nissan increased their bargaining position as trade unionists. Those who had initiated the development of the union drew confidence from the knowledge that the JIT system ensured that any disruptive action they might take would have consequences for the whole Nissan production system. Threatened or actual stoppages 'brought results', as one worker put it.

We have not chosen to purposely go for stoppages. People have to be pushed to go that far. Any disruption there has been unplanned, but we realise it has big implications for the whole company – like when the roof was damaged in high winds and they wanted us to work. The women were nervous, justifiably so . . . in the end the steward led the women into the canteen. That wasn't orchestrated in advance by the union; it could have been avoided if they had properly fixed the roof. They are just so pushed all the time [that when] we want something they cannot stop the line to get things done properly. It was the same story with the [slippery] flooring. They estimated it would take three working days to do the flooring and they couldn't do that because Nissan works all the time. The tension goes right through the plant, but it comes from their [Ikeda management's] fear of Nissan.

(Ikeda sewing machinist)

The following comments illustrated this worker's perception that Ikeda management needed not only to satisfy Nissan's demand, but to retain credibility within Nissan. He claimed that rather than allowing Nissan workers to become aware of industrial disruption at Ikeda, a line break down would be 'organised' within Nissan:

If we have got a little bit of a dispute up there they know straight away there is trouble because we are supposed to do twenty-four [seats] an hour. Now, if we drop [in supply to the plant], they [Nissan] know there is something wrong and they say 'Oh they are starting'. . . . Now, if we get down to about sixteen, Nissan [production line] always has a break down! . . . Every time it happens they have got a break down at Nissan, so there is something in it, you know!

(Ikeda seat assembly worker)

The most significant factor in the development of union resistance at Ikeda Hoover, then, may not be that stoppages would bring the Nissan complex to a halt, but, as the above Ikeda worker made clear, that through such action Nissan workers would be made aware of the organisation of opposition within their nearest neighbour and supplier.

CONCLUSION

Work processes in the two case study companies were based on a combination of Taylorist and post-Fordist work practices. Both companies relied on standard operations and standard time calculations, and at Nissan workers were offered financial incentives through the yearly appraisal programme. Workers in both companies were involved in the intensification of their own labour through the monitoring of their own quality standards and those of others. However, at Nissan workers were involved in additional self-subordinating activities such as Kaizen and the monitoring of a variety of actions of their peers in accordance with the philosophy of active participation in corporate goals.

At Ikeda workers had resisted the introduction of new technologies and practices (e.g. the standing sewing machine) and some workers interviewed offered a critique of flexible work practices which indicated an understanding of the possible dangers associated with participation in continual improvement strategies. Kaizen meetings, through which more co-operative workers might have identified savings, were not in operation at Ikeda. As a consequence, time and motion study was relied upon, and that in turn increased tension between workers and managers.

Garrahan and Stewart recognised that in co-operating in Kaizen workers were involved in identifying time and labour savings. However, I have illustrated how Kaizen served other purposes which secured worker consent in Nissan. Kaizen, in part, usurped the function previously carried out by the trade union and in doing so legitimated the absence of the union, while securing the image

of Nissan as a responsive, listening employer. Savings were identified and made in the labour process without the intervention of
engineers or managers, and consequently the potential for
increased vertical conflict was avoided.

The style of management within the two companies was quali-
tatively different. The Ikeda management style was described by
workers as confrontational, and workers claimed managers had
adopted an interventionist approach; workers were aware of the
presence of senior managers on the shop floor and claimed they
became involved when the smooth running of JIT was interrupted,
attributing blame to groups and individuals. Burawoy argued that
the likely impact of the close scrutiny of workers by managers
would be vertical conflict. By contrast he claimed that a relaxed
management style in conjunction with an appropriate framework
of incentives may encourage social activity which secures worker
consent. This research confirms Burawoy's view as the interventionist management style apparent at Ikeda Hoover had led to
increased vertical antagonism, while at Nissan competition and
scrutiny occurred horizontally, between peers.

Garrahan and Stewart failed to theorise the possible implications
of JIT production for the management style and labour process of
the supplier plant. They assumed the two plants would be able to
maintain comparable industrial relations and labour processes
despite the fact that the advantages won by Nissan through JIT
were, to a great extent, at the expense of the supplier plant.
Knights and Collinson's (1985) critique of Burawoy illustrates the
importance of theorising on the impact of the position of the case
study company in the circuit of capitalist valorisation on management style and labour processes and workers' responses to these.
Garrahan and Stewart's failure to do so has led to an over-
estimation of the stability of the production environment: Ikeda
workers claimed that the JIT system had influenced management
style and consequently that it had been partially responsible for
stimulating the development of union opposition.

Research findings presented here confirm the impact of a
depressed economic environment on the confidence of workers
who feared unemployment. The economic environment influenced
worker consent in two other ways: in the availability and recruitment of a 'suitable' workforce and in the attitude of workers to
employment and to trade unionism. Nissan's choice of sites illustrates the imperative of a multinational company in selecting an

environment best suited to the attainment of worker consent. Garrahan and Stewart claimed that Nissan's ability to move suitable supplier companies on to their site limited the risk associated with JIT production. However, this research illustrates that it cannot be assumed that the advantages gained in the selection of a site will be equally shared by component suppliers which seek to operate a JIT production system. Indeed the choice of site resulted in recruitment difficulties for Ikeda as a result of the demise of the region's clothing sector. The shortage of skilled machinists and their necessity for the operation of the firm ultimately conditioned the supplier's ability to implement a flexible, 'lean' production system where management are firmly in the driving seat.

This research illustrates the potentially powerful position of groups of workers on the periphery of the JIT conglomeration. Research critical of the effects of JIT and 'lean' production practices has correctly identified the often female, semi- or unskilled and migrant workers as facing exploitation and poor working conditions on the periphery of the JIT system (see Rowthorn 1988). However, the research reported above illustrates the importance of the demand for skills and the condition of the labour market, the self-perception of workers, and previous employment and the effect of life experiences on workers' willingness and ability to develop union-based opposition to flexible labour processes. Skilled women workers had initiated the development of the workplace trade unionism at Ikeda. Women's self-perception and self-confidence had been affected by their external roles as family heads and mothers and by previous experiences as skilled workers.

Through an examination of the meanings workers associated with their actions, as opposed to simply recounting workers' accounts of actions, it was possible to identify the adoption of expedient behaviour towards the Nissan way in order to retain anonymity and/or win reward. Identifying the meanings workers associate with actions enabled an appreciation of the underlying strategy of Nissan workers consenting to 'lean' production. Nissan workers' commitment to the Nissan way was bound up with the promise that consent offered employment security; Nissan was 'different', and so too would be their experience of security. The impact of the employment losses of 1993 on workers' confidence in the Nissan way and the absence of trade union influence is not known as yet. These losses, in addition to the expedient attitude of some workers towards the rightness of the Nissan way of working and the effective trade union organisation at the supplier company, suggest that worker consent within the Nissan JIT production complex may not be as stable as earlier accounts suggest.

This research illustrates that workers have the ability to overcome restrictive trade union agreements and develop active and effective union opposition from within their own workplaces. There is a clear need for an action-based contingency approach to looking at trade unionism under new management, rather than an approach which seeks to predict, from outside, the likely behaviour and action of trade unionists within any given situation.

NOTES

1 Between 1988 and 1991 the author was employed to work as a research assistant with the Local Studies Unit (LSU) based at what is now the University of Sunderland. During that time she worked closely with Philip Garrahan and Paul Stewart on their project to study the Nissan Motor Company.That project led to a number of publications by Garrahan and Stewart, most notably *The Nissan Enigma*, published in 1992. The author's role as a research assistant during that period was to make contact with workers from the Nissan plant on behalf of Phil Garrahan and Paul Stewart. During that period she registered as a Ph.D. student. She chose Nissan as a case study plant as she had conducted and published research on Nissan prior to her employment with the LSU. The author has used the data gathered from the interviews in which she participated. As a consequence some of the data presented have been examined in other publications by Garrahan and Stewart. The author continued to make contact with workers at Nissan and Ikeda Hoover. Research following her employment at the LSU and much of the material presented here is new unpublished material.

2 A number of options for making contact with Nissan and Ikeda Hoover workers were considered. Advertising in the local press was considered as an option, but that was put to one side as a last resort if informal routes to making contact with workers proved untenable. That decision was taken for two reasons. First, workers might be understandably suspicious of such requests and therefore that approach may have been ineffective. Where possible personal contacts with workers were made and the author was able to give assurances of anonymity. Where personal contacts were made, greater success in securing co-operation was ensured in comparison to instances where contact was made via a third party. Second, press advertisements may have increased hostility among the company and the recognised union. That may have ended any co-operation they were prepared to offer and lead to warnings to workers not to speak to researchers outside work.

3 The informal route to contact was varied: through friends of friends, relatives of friends or of trade union colleagues, through students at what were Sunderland and Newcastle Polytechnics. While a number of trade union colleagues were able to provide contacts with family, friends and former work mates who were working for the Japanese-owned sector, the author was gratified to find that these workers did not all share the opinions of the 'go-between' with regard to trade unionism; trade union colleagues enabled her to gain contact with working-class people through their social networks and families and not only with a 'radicalised' group of workers.

4 The author was concerned to avoid interviewing cliques of Ikeda workers who may have become friends as their views were similar. Workers were asked to provide contacts with colleagues they did not know socially and whose views of the experience of working at the plant were not known to them.

5 Despite a number of requests the author has not been able to see the Ikeda line at work and has had to rely on detailed descriptions from interviewed workers. Ikeda Hoover does not place the emphasis Nissan does on publicising their method of working and industrial relations.

6 The author does not share Garrahan and Stewart's perspective on methods as laid down in *The Nissan Enigma*. Here they claim that interviewing workers in their own homes was a chosen method, preferable to other methods. In the light of Nissan's reluctance to allow access to workers within the plant, and therefore the opportunity to observe in greater detail the line at work, this research methodology resulted from necessity rather than choice.

7 The Nissan Motor Manufacturing Company has world-wide production of 2.6 million units, with twenty-four overseas assembly plants in twenty-one countries. (Nissan M. M. UK Ltd 1991). Nissan is the world's fourth largest vehicle manufacturer, after General Motors, Ford and Toyota respectively.

8 The union which has recognition within the two case study companies is referred to as the AEEU throughout this chapter, although the Amalgamated Engineering Union (AEU) originally signed the two agreements. Following the merger of the AEU with the electricians' union, the EETPU, the union adopted the name AEEU, the Amalgamated Engineering and Electrical Union.

9 One of these letters, which was sent to all manufacturing staff, is reproduced in Garrahan and Stewart (1992: 69). A second appeal was made to all team leaders and supervisors as it was hoped they could 'set an example' to other workers.

10 For example, one Nissan worker spoke of the Kaizen recommendation that rods be suspended above head height on heavy rubber ropes so that power tools could be hung, and picked off when necessary, rather than dropped to the floor, which had been the previous practice. Workers would no longer need to bend to pick them up.

11 One respondent commented on the origin of the term 'Liger Line', the in-house name for the main production line. That had been devised

by a keen worker during a Kaizen meeting to represent the Lion of England and the Tiger of Japan: 'he is a supervisor now'.

12 That involved workers standing over a sewing table resting their weight on one leg while operating the power pedal with the other. Workers claimed this constituted a threat to health and safety and therefore a deterioration in working conditions. One standing line had been established using temporary workers, but permanently employed women machinists had successfully resisted its wholesale introduction.

13 Nissan workers interviewed did not offer comparisons with previous workplaces in the way that Ikeda Hoover workers were willing to do. Only two Nissan interviewees had worked in the British car industry. They made unsolicited references to their previous workplaces and argued that what happened at Nissan would not have been allowed to happen in British Leyland or Jaguar. These were the only two Nissan workers interviewed who drew direct comparisons with previous work. The remaining Nissan interviewees had no previous experience of the car industry; some had none of mass production or manufacturing work and others had no work experience at all. Two Nissan workers argued that making cars (the task of Nissan workers) could not be compared with work not associated with the car industry. Ikeda Hoover interviewees were able to make comparisons between what they saw as their previous manual/semi-skilled/sewing employment and their current work, which they saw as being 'much the same'.

REFERENCES

Atkinson, J. and Meager, N. (1987) 'Is Flexibility just a Flash in the Pan?', *Personnel Management*, September: 25–9.

Beynon, H. (1973) *Working for Ford*, London: Allen Lane.

Burawoy, M. (1979) *Manufacturing Consent: Changes in the Labour Process under Monopoly Capitalism*, Chicago: University of Chicago Press.

Crowther, S. and Garrahan, P. (1988) 'Corporate Power and the Local Economy', *Industrial Relations Journal* **16**, 1: 51–9.

Financial Times (1986) 12 December, p.14.

Garrahan, P. (1986) 'Nissan in the North East', *Capital and Class* **27**: 5–13.

Garrahan, P. and Stewart, P. (1991) 'Nothing New about Nissan', in C. Law (ed.), *Restructuring the Automobile Industry*, London: Routledge.

Garrahan, P. and Stewart, P. (1992) *The Nissan Enigma*, London: Mansell.

Goffman, I. (1968) *Asylums*, Harmondsworth: Penguin Books.

Hirst, P. and Zeitlin, J. (1989) 'Flexible Specialisation and the Failure of Competitive UK Manufacturing', *Political Quarterly* **60**, 2: 164–78.

Hudson, R. (1989) *Wrecking the Region: State Policies, Party Politics and Regional Change in the North East of England*, London: Pion.

Knights, D. and Collinson, D. (1985) 'Redesigning Work on the Shop Floor: Consent or Control?', in D. Knights, H. Willmott and D. Collinson (eds), *Job Redesign, Critical Perspectives in the Labour Process*, Farnborough: Gower.

Knights, D. and Willmott, H. (1989) 'Power and Subjectivity at Work; From Degradation to Subjugation in Social Relations', *Sociology* **23**, 14: 535–58.

Knights, D., Willmott, H. and Collinson, D. (eds) (1985) *Job Redesign, Critical Perspectives in the Labour Process*, Farnborough: Gower.

Maguire, M. (1988) 'Work, Locality and Social Control', *Work, Employment and Society* **2**, 1: 71–87.

Nichols, T. and Beynon, H. (1977) *Living with Capitalism*, London: Routledge & Kegan Paul.

Nissan M.M. UK Ltd (1991) *Nissan Information Pack*, London: Press and Public Relations Department.

Nissan M.M. UK Ltd (1992) *Nissan Information Pack*, London: Press and Public Relations Department.

Nissan M.M. UK Ltd (1993) *Nissan Information Pack*, London: Press and Public Relations Department.

Parker, M. and Slaughter, J. (1988) *Choosing Sides: Unions and the Team Concept*, A Labour Notes Book, Boston, Mass.: Southend Press.

Robinson, F. (1990) *The Great North?*, Newcastle: BBC North.

The Trade Union Studies Information Unit (1987) *The Closures Campaign*, Newcastle upon Tyne: Trade Union Studies Information Unit.

Wickens, P. (1987) *The Road to Nissan*, London: Macmillan.

Wickens, P. (1993) *Lean Production and Beyond: The System, its Critics and its Future*, paper to the University of Sunderland, 29 January.

Williamson H. (1989) *Back in the Melting Pot? Rethinking Trade Union Perspectives on Japanese Motor Industry Investment in Britain and 'Japanese-style' Industrial Relations*, London: Centre for Alternative Industrial and Technological Systems, Mimeograph.

8

ORGANISING THE UNORGANISED

'Race', poor work and trade unions

John Wrench and Satnam Virdee

The combined effects of long-term economic restructuring, recession and new levels of structural unemployment have produced significant changes in patterns of inequality and the dynamics of the class structure in Britain. More specifically, they have contributed to a 'crisis' for trade unions and the labour movement (Hobsbawm 1981; Lane 1982). Groups whose employment circumstances have been most significantly affected by the developments of the 1980s and early 1990s are women and minority ethnic workers. This chapter looks at the attempts by two general unions to organise two groups of workers who consist mainly of ethnic minorities and women, and how the context of the 'crisis' impinged on these attempts.

Economic factors alone do not explain the fundamental changes in employment over the 1980s. For example, the particularly high level of unemployment experienced in Britain was not simply 'inevitable', but at least in part reflected the lack of commitment to the maintenance of full employment on the part of Britain's ruling elite (Ashton and Maguire 1991). Similarly the crisis facing trade unions is the product of both economic forces and political ideologies, the latter demonstrated in the political and legal assault by the Conservative government on trade union rights and functions in Britain. Between 1979 and the end of 1993 nine pieces of legislation, including five Employment Acts, had removed all barriers to the 'free and flexible' labour market lauded in new-right Conservative ideology.

The Conservatives' comprehensive programme of employment law reform comprised the removal of statutory and administrative supports for collective bargaining, partial

240

deregulation of the contract of employment, creation of statutory rights for members and non-members alike against unions . . . successive reduction of union tort immunity for industrial action . . . introduction of procedural rules for the initiation of industrial action, and tort liability of union funds.

(Smith and Morton 1993: 98)

In 1993 a clause was introduced by the government into the Trade Union Reform and Employment Rights Bill allowing employers to bribe employees to give up the right to trade union representation, and cut the pay of those who do not (*Guardian*, 27 May 1993).

The principal significance of Conservative employment legislation has been to deny workers access to resources of collective power (Smith and Morton 1993: 99). In February 1994 a High Court judgement ruled that employers are entitled to know the identity of all workers who are being balloted on industrial action. This development was described by a union organiser as 'an extraordinary attack on the civil liberties of trade union members', thus rendering them liable to be victimised by employers for considering such action (*Guardian*, 25 February 1994).

Secondary industrial action, the single most potent means of success in pursuing a strike, has been outlawed; while uniquely in Britain, majority decisions in unions are not binding on individual members. So demanding are the new rules that some lawyers consider it virtually impossible to organise a strike legally.

(*Guardian*, 18 October 1993)

The changes over the last fifteen years have eroded the sectors which have traditionally provided the mainstay of trade union membership, and have increased the proportional significance of sectors that are difficult to unionise. Unions need to target these new groups of workers for replacement membership at a time when government policies have made such recruitment immensely more difficult. Within this picture, minority ethnic[1] workers form an extra dimension. They are disproportionately concentrated in these 'poor work' sectors, and they raise a whole extra set of issues with regard to union policies. When these minority ethnic workers are women, a further range of issues are added to the agenda.

JOHN WRENCH AND SATNAM VIRDEE

WOMEN, EMPLOYMENT AND TRADE UNIONS

Recent decades have witnessed the increased participation of women in the labour force, and within this a greater proportion of *married* women (Morris 1991). The proportion of female employees increased from 25 per cent of those in paid employment in 1901 to 43 per cent in 1988 (Brown and Scase 1991: 7). A Department of Employment study in 1994 suggests that by the year 2006 almost 90 per cent of the increase in the labour force will be accounted for by women; in a broader context, women have been entirely responsible for the growth in employment in Europe in the last two decades (*Guardian*, 9 April 1994). As men in their forties and fifties are being steadily ejected from the labour force, they are being replaced by women in much inferior sectors of employment – the 'poor work' sectors.

Although the union membership rate of women has lagged behind that of men, history shows that this does not reflect an unwillingness to engage in industrial struggle, and women have been disproportionately figuring amongst new recruits to unions. Trade unions, however, have a record of neglecting issues which relate to specifically to their women membership (Phizacklea and Miles 1980: 97), and recent figures suggest that trade unions are now starting to lose women from membership after several years of stability in their female ranks (*Labour Research*, May 1994).

This chapter looks at two case studies where manual trade unions have attempted to organise groups of vulnerable workers who are mainly minority ethnic women. It concludes that the difficulties experienced by unions in these circumstances are of four related but different types:

- Difficulties arising from the broader context of economic restructuring, recession, and structural unemployment.
- Difficulties created for unions by the Conservative government's employment legislation.
- Difficulties relating to the relationship between trade unions and minority ethnic workers, and more specifically to minority ethnic women workers.
- Difficulties inherent in the contradictory nature of trade unions in a capitalist society and the conflict within the labour movement over the strategies and values they should adopt.

Before describing the two case studies, this chapter first considers some of the broader issues relating to trade unions, migrants and minority ethnic workers.

TRADE UNION RESPONSES TO MIGRANT LABOUR

It has been argued that trade unions face three dilemmas in terms of their response to migrant workers (Penninx and Roosblad 1994). The first is whether to resist immigration or co-operate with and try to influence state immigration policies; the second is whether to include migrant workers as trade union members once they have arrived, and the third is, once they have been recruited, whether special union policies should be established for migrant and minority ethnic members over and above those policies for white members.

To keep the price of labour from falling trade unions have traditionally tried to do two things: to limit the labour supply and to improve and equalise wages and conditions. In the aftermath of the Second World War European unions were unable to resist successfully the introduction of large numbers of foreign workers into the industrialised countries of Western Europe, mainly because indigenous workers were reluctant to take the low-paid, low-status jobs themselves (Vranken 1990: 55). If the first strategy – limiting the labour supply – had not been possible, then the second – organising these new workers and demanding equal pay and conditions – should have been given some priority. In reality this second strategy proved to be embraced less rapidly than it might have been.

Martens (1993: 3) writes that within the organised labour movement, workers find it hard to understand why they should first be mobilised against imported foreign labour, and then, when that demand has failed, to have to welcome those same workers with open arms and prevent them being singled out for exploitation, segregation and victimisation. The dilemma is expounded further by Castles: the fact that unions had originally opposed immigration would alienate migrant workers, who would then be less likely to join them. 'Thus there was a potential conflict between trade union policies towards immigration on the one hand, and policies towards migrant workers once they were in the country, on the other' (Castles 1990: 6).

Running through these dilemmas is the variable of racism, which in some instances was mobilised as part of union attempts to restrict the labour supply, and at other times ran counter to the principle of equalising wages and conditions. With regard to the first dilemma, racism could easily be drawn upon in the fight to keep out immigrants, and between and after the two World Wars, there were many quite blatant examples of this (Fryer 1984). However, with the post-war permanent settlement of new migrant-based communities in Britain, racism interfered with the second strategy – the need to get migrant workers organised and defended. In many industries white trade unionists insisted on a quota system restricting black workers to a maximum of (generally) 5 per cent, and there were understandings with management that the principle of 'last in first out' at a time of redundancy would not apply if this was to mean that white workers would lose their jobs before blacks (Fryer 1984: 376). In the 1950s transport workers banned overtime and staged strikes in protest against the employment of black labour, and others sent motions to annual conferences asking for black workers to be excluded from their sectors (Bentley 1976: 135). There was a 'determined effort' by the National Union of Seamen to keep black seamen off British ships after the war (Fryer 1984: 367).

Despite this treatment it remained a fact that in Britain (in contrast with many other European host countries) post-war black migrant workers had an *above average* propensity to join trade unions. For example, the Policy Studies Institute (PSI) survey showed that in 1982, 56 per cent of Asian and West Indian employees were union members, compared with 47 per cent of white employees (Brown 1984: 169). Although some of this difference was due to the over-representation of minority ethnic workers in those industrial sectors where trade union membership rates are higher for *all* workers, the PSI study reported that their greater inclination to join unions holds true even when allowing for the differences in occupational concentration, reflecting an ideological commitment to the principles of unionism. More than ten years later, another PSI study showed that employees from some ethnic groups still had higher rates of unionisation than white employees: Afro-Caribbean and Indian employees had 44 per cent and 38 per cent respectively, compared to 35 per cent of white employees. On the other hand, Pakistani and African Asian employees had slightly lower rates than whites (33 per cent and 28 per cent) and Bangladeshi employees significantly lower (14 per cent) (Jones 1993: 76).

EQUAL VERSUS SPECIAL TREATMENT

With the inclusion of migrant workers into unions, and the transformation of migrant workers into minority ethnic British workers, the third dilemma began to take precedence over the previous two: that of equal versus special treatment. Should a trade union concern itself only with issues common to white and minority ethnic members or should it in addition operate special policies relating to the specific interests of the latter? If minority ethnic workers suffer disadvantages not experienced by white workers, then 'equal treatment' will allow these disadvantages to remain. However, if a union devotes extra resources to issues specifically concerning minority ethnic members, this may cause resentment and resistance on the part of white workers who see minority ethnic members as getting favourable treatment (Penninx and Roosblad 1994).

Until the end of the 1960s the standard trade union position on this was exemplified by the Trades Union Congress (TUC) view that to institute any special policies would be to discriminate against the white membership. As one TUC official put it in 1966: 'There are no differences between an immigrant worker and an English worker. We believe that all workers should have the same rights and don't require any different or special consideration' (Radin 1966: 159). In 1970, Vic Feather, TUC General Secretary, argued 'The trade union movement is concerned with a man or woman as a worker. The colour of a man's skin has no relevance whatever to his work' (Wrench 1987: 165).

However, in the early 1970s the TUC began to adopt special policies against racism. This shift came about for a number of reasons. First, there was the increasing organisation on the issue by black and white trade union activists; second, there were a number of industrial disputes in the late 1960s and early 1970s which had highlighted union racism towards striking black members; and third, there was the growth of extreme right-wing groups such as the National Front, who played on the divisions between black and white workers and gave open support to the white trade unionists in some of these disputes (Phizacklea and Miles 1980: 93–4). Thus the TUC, having first dropped its opposition to race relations legislation, now started active campaigns against racism in the movement.

In the late 1970s and early 1980s the TUC began to produce educational and training materials on equal opportunities and racism for use in trade union education courses (e.g. TUC 1983a, 1983b). In 1981 the TUC published 'Black Workers: A TUC Charter for Equal Opportunity', encouraging unions to be more active on the issue. Seven years later the TUC reissued the Charter. The TUC also worked with the Commission for Racial Equality (CRE) in the production of a code of practice, and has encouraged unions to make use of this code. In recent years in the wider European forum the TUC has lobbied the European Trade Union Confederation to take on board issues of migrants' rights and racial equality, drawing attention to the UK experience of the important role of legislation in combating discrimination.

Increasingly in the UK, individual unions have set up separate committees or structures to deal with race relations and/or equal opportunities issues, and adopted equal opportunity policies and made anti-racist statements. Many have created national officers to take responsibility for issues affecting black members, for encouraging the participation of black members and furthering equal opportunities. A recent survey of twenty-one unions found that ten had a national-level committee dealing with race equality issues and nearly two-thirds had taken positive steps such as targeting workplaces, organising conferences for black members and producing recruitment literature in minority ethnic languages (Mason 1994: 307).

NEW PROBLEMS OF RECRUITMENT

Although the Asian and Afro-Caribbean migrants of the 1950s and 1960s were always good 'joiners' of unions, the above-average propensity of black workers to join unions now seems to be declining. This could in part be related to the disillusion experienced by some 'first-generation' migrant workers over their treatment by unions over the years, and the fact that the 'second generation' cannot be relied upon to have an automatic ideological sympathy towards unions. Then there is a growing category of black/migrant workers who are under-unionised. These are the workers in the expanding sector of low-paid, unregulated, marginal work – sweat-shop workers, part-time workers, cleaners, home-workers. Often they contain the most vulnerable groups, such as older Asian women who speak little English, and newer arrivals such as refugees, migrants and illegal workers, and these are the most difficult categories of workers to organise. Across Europe, as rules for work permits become tighter, more migrant workers become 'illegal' or unauthorised. Consequently 'they are particularly favoured by employers because of their restricted bargaining power' (*Labour Research*, February 1989).

> With no rights of settlement, rarely the right to work, no right to housing or medical care, and under the constant threat of deportation, the new migrants are forced to accept wages and conditions which no indigenous worker, black or white, would accept. They have no pension rights, no social security, the employers do not have to insure them – they are illicit, illegal, replaceable.
>
> (Sivanandan 1989: 87)

Many within British unions have realised the need to organise such workers. For example, in 1989 the Transport and General Workers' Union (TGWU) attempted to organise sweat-shop workers – including Kurdish refugees and illegal workers – in North London, with some success in recruiting membership and gaining compensation for unfair dismissal and payment of unpaid wages. As the chair of the local TGWU branch put it, 'This happens to illegal workers – they work for one or two weeks; when they ask for their wages the boss says "No way; if you stay here I am going to call the police"' (*Labour Research*, August 1989).

THE FIRST CASE STUDY: TGWU

To illustrate some of these difficulties in practice, this chapter will take a case study relating to the Transport and General Workers' Union (TGWU). The TGWU has over a million members and was, until 1993 and the merger between NUPE, NALGO and COHSE to form UNISON, the largest trade union affiliated to the TUC. As well as electing the first black general secretary of a trade union, Bill Morris, the TGWU organises more minority ethnic members than any other union, estimated at around 10–12 per cent, or 150,000–180,000 members (cited in *Equal Opportunities Reveiw* 1992: 22).

The TGWU has initiated at national level a number of special measures specifically related to its minority ethnic members. The issue of black participation in trade unions was initially raised within the TGWU in 1987 when growing concern from the members on this issue led the union's Biennial Delegates Conference (BDC) to decide that 'the union should set up a network of race advisory committees to promote the involvement of black and ethnic minority workers within the union' (*Equal Opportunities Review* 1992: 22). An Equal Opportunities Working Party comprising representatives from each of the eleven TGWU regions was established to implement the BDC decisions. This working party was able to provide concrete evidence on the extent of under-representation of black members among the union's officers, and among the membership of Regional and National Committees (TGWU 1989: 21). The General Executive Council accepted the recommendation of the Working Party to establish a structure of national and regional race advisory committees. These committees would be responsible for advising on initiatives to promote the recruitment, organisation and involvement of minority ethnic members. In addition, a National Equalities Officer was appointed to help establish these new committees and oversee their work.

THE SERVICE SECTOR

The first case study falls into the service sector. Since 1979 there has been an increasing shift of jobs from manufacturing industry into services. The number of jobs in manufacturing has fallen by about 2 million since 1979, whereas jobs in services have grown from 12.8 to 14.5 million during the same period. This change has important implications for trade union membership. As trade union organisation has traditionally been stronger in the manufacturing sector than the service sector, it is precisely in the areas where they are now most required that unions have least strength, and that unions experience greatest difficulty in retaining or increasing membership. John Edmonds, General Secretary of the GMB, set out the difficulties:

> We must accept that within the next decade the trade unions are not going to be in a position to force contract cleaners, for example, to pay reasonable pay and conditions through traditional trade union organisation. We are not going to have effective trade union organisation in every large hotel in the country. . . . The whole private service area, particularly leisure, isn't very well organised and is likely to remain significantly unorganised for all sorts of structural reasons. . . . If you have an industry where the workforce is highly mobile, where they are not attached to any particular

employer for any length of time, then the organisational difficulties are very substantial indeed. It is obviously more difficult to organise there than it is in a factory of 500 people who have relatively long service records.

(Interview in *Marxism Today*, September 1986: 17–18)

THE ORGANISATION OF CLEANING WORKERS

The case study concerns a TGWU branch and the local TGWU office responsible for servicing it. This was the Hillingdon (formerly Southall) TGWU office in Region 1 of the TGWU, encompassing Greater London and the South-East. The branch selected was a recently established cleaning branch, and made an interesting case for a number of reasons, including:

- A workforce that was located in a traditionally low-wage sector.
- A large female South Asian membership.
- A temporary South Asian local officer responsible for the organisation of the cleaners.
- A local office which serviced an area of high minority ethnic concentration, including the town of Southall, West London.
- The identification by the Race Relations Advisory Committee (RRAC) of Region 1 of the TGWU of the organisation of the cleaners at Heathrow Airport as being a priority task.

Heathrow is the world's busiest airport. In the financial year 1993/94 it handled 48,400,000 passengers, over 42 per cent of total passenger traffic through all UK airports. It is also the UK's premier air cargo handling facility, handling cargo in 1991 valued at over £34 billion. Its annual revenue for the year 1993/94 was £630.7 million, while its operating profit was £250.4 million. Heathrow handles ninety airlines from eighty-five countries, and offers direct flights to over 220 destinations (BAA 1992, 1994). Clearly, as one of the largest service complexes in Britain, it plays the role of a key institution in the British economy: dynamic and highly profitable, with the added glamorous image associated with international air travel. However, for many of the 54,000 people who work there, conditions of employment are anything but glamorous. One such group of workers are the contract cleaners.

Since the 1960s Heathrow Airport has been the largest employer of Southall's Asian women, who work in the cleaning and catering divisions (CARF/SR 1981: 18). These minority ethnic workers were recruited into the area originally to work at Woolf's rubber factory. The plight of the predominantly female South Asian cleaning workers at Heathrow Airport had been brought to the attention of the TGWU on many occasions in the past (see CARF/SR 1981). This was in the context of a heated debate within the West London trade union movement in the late 1980s which included allegations of racism on the part of the white hierarchy of local trade unionists. In particular there had been an incident in 1984 with a large cleaning contractor at Heathrow, where the union had been seen to be guilty of complicity in racial discrimination. In July 1984 it became known that Reliance Cleaners, a large contractor operating at Heathrow, had lost their contract, and they issued redundancy notices to all their staff. However, in order to avoid redundancy payments they tried to harass some of the Asian women workers into resigning, gave them false information about their entitlements, and tried to stop them from collecting their wages (Public Service Action No. 12, December 1984). Although many of the women had been paying subscriptions to the TGWU, they received more sympathetic assistance in their grievances from a local community-based organisation, Southall Rights. Indeed, the union's area representative commented to a local reporter that he hadn't made much of an attempt to organise the Heathrow workers because he 'couldn't be bothered to understand Indian names – they were difficult to pronounce'. He commented that 'if I know Indian people they always have two jobs' and observed that 'if you offer nuts you should expect monkeys'. Awaiting the outcome of an industrial tribunal (at which the women were eventually awarded compensation), he complained 'Asians are not willing to fight for themselves' (Workers Against Racism 1985: 8).

In 1988, after a report was published by the London Borough of Ealing, the TGWU undertook to review its organisational policies in relation to the cleaning workers. The 'Ealing Report' highlighted job insecurity, physically demanding work, low pay, unsocial hours, shift work, lack of training, and allegations of racism and sexism from employers' (London Borough of Ealing 1988).

A conference, convened jointly by the Borough and the TGWU and attended by the then General Secretary-elect, Bill Morris, agreed to make the organisation of the cleaners a priority task and implement a plan of action. This was based upon three measures that would, it was hoped, not only contribute to the effective organisation of the cleaners but also lead to a development of workplace cleaning representatives. The initiative undertaken by the union in organising the cleaners must be seen as being stimulated not only by the pressure from the cleaners and Ealing Council but also by the TGWU's national 'Link-Up' campaign, which formed the union's major recruitment initiative of the late 1980s and early 1990s (Snape 1994: 223).

At the time of this initiative, twelve interviews were carried out by one of the authors with cleaning workers and TGWU represen-tatives.[2] The experiences of one cleaner, summarised from just part of the interview notes, gives some insight into the cleaners' working conditions:

> Mrs A. is an Asian woman who has been employed as a cleaner at Heathrow Airport since 1975. She works a forty-hour week on a shift basis, for which she is paid £84 a week. Despite having to use hazardous chemicals and continually suffering from skin rashes and nausea she has received no health and safety instruction from her employers. No changing room facili-ties are provided; the company deducts a small weekly amount from her wages to clean her work clothing even though she does this at home. She gets a half-hour paid lunch break but is prohibited from using any of the airport's canteen facilities. When she first began work at Heathrow she was entitled to three weeks' paid leave, but this was recently reduced to two weeks without any explanation by the employers. There is no grievance procedure in operation in the non-unionised sector of the airport, and she believes that complaining about her conditions will risk dismissal from her job.

The first measure by the TGWU was to establish a branch solely for the cleaners in April 1990. Beforehand, the handful of cleaning workers who had joined the union had been forced to join the baggage handlers' branch at the airport. This had not been very successful, as a branch dominated by the problems of baggage handlers was clearly inadequate in servicing the needs of the cleaning workers. As a result, these cleaning workers had remained union members only a short time. The second measure was the appointment of a temporary local TGWU officer with the sole responsibility for organising the cleaners. This Asian officer had extensive knowledge of the cleaning and catering industry at

Table 8.1 Composition of cleaning branch: ethnicity and gender

	Asian members	White members
Women	35	4
Men	5	6

Heathrow Airport, having been a steward there for twenty years between 1965 and 1985. The third initiative was the production of recruitment literature in all the appropriate minority ethnic languages. This literature outlined the importance of joining a union and provided information on how the union could help in relation to health and safety issues, workplace grievances and dealing with racial and sexual harassment from employers and workers alike.

In terms of the previous discussion, these measures showed some recognition within the TGWU of the need for 'special measures' as opposed to 'equal treatment' for this sector of minority ethnic workers. Unfortunately the measures outlined to improve the rate of unionisation among cleaning workers proved to be relatively unsuccessful. Although the two-year recruitment effort increased membership from six to fifty, this was still only 5 per cent of the potential membership of 1,000 (see Table 8.1).[3]

WHY WAS THIS RECRUITMENT DRIVE UNSUCCESSFUL?

A key reason why the local TGWU office was unable to organise a larger number of cleaners was the constraint of the industrial relations climate and restrictive employment legislation, as set out at the beginning of this chapter. One major difficulty was the continual refusal of Heathrow Airport Ltd (HAL) to agree to a union recognition agreement. This meant the local officer was unable to organise the cleaners at their place of work – the most likely place where the cleaners would join a union. The main method of recruitment had to be one of home visits to those cleaning workers known to be working at the airport. This was a very time-consuming task which often had to be undertaken outside normal working hours, and the resulting rewards in membership were small in relation to the effort. The difficulties were exacerbated by shift-working, which meant that the officer would often have to make several visits to the homes of these cleaning workers before making contact with them. In addition, because the local officer was unable to organise the cleaning workers at their place of work, the recruitment literature which had been translated into the appropriate minority ethnic languages could not be distributed to them there. An attempt to distribute literature in places of worship also proved to be unsuccessful because few cleaners had time to attend such places, through the long and unsocial hours they worked and the need for many of them to undertake more than one job as a result of the poor wages paid by the cleaning companies. (None of the six cleaning workers interviewed in the study had ever seen the recruitment literature produced by the TGWU.)

Since 1979, the pay and conditions facing many low-paid workers have worsened as a result of the abolition of Schedule 11 of the 1974 Employment Protection Act (previously known as the 'Fair Wages Act'), which had been in existence in various forms for almost 100 years. Although the wages of the cleaners have always been relatively poor, this change has left them particularly vulnerable to unscrupulous employers wishing to erode their terms and conditions of employment further. It has given some employers in the cleaning sector at the airport the encouragement to force through further pay reductions by employing 'undocumented' or 'unauthorised' minority ethnic labour. These are often workers who entered the UK on a tourist visa, found work and have overstayed, which often forces them into part-time, casual, or short-term jobs on a cash in hand basis. Many of these left their own country for political reasons. Some of the cleaning employers used the threat of informing the authorities as a way to pacify all the cleaners working at the airport. Wage reductions are imposed in the knowledge that 'undocumented' workers will not seek redress from the union because of their precarious legal position. This has left the cleaners vulnerable to what one local officer referred to as 'an obscene level of exploitation'.

Finally, the traditional trade union strategy of defending jobs by undertaking industrial action and seeking support from fellow workers has been largely emasculated by recent government legislation. According to one local TGWU officer, not only were the stronger sections of workers at Heathrow Airport unwilling to defend the cleaning workers, but they themselves were under threat of redundancies by the employers. The effect was that most employees, including those who were union members, were working in a climate of fear at Heathrow Airport. For example, in September 1993 more than 100 porters at Heathrow Airport were sacked after going on strike in an attempt to persuade their employers to recognise the Transport and General Workers' Union (*Morning Star,* 7 September 1993).

UNION MISTAKES

This case study shows how the broader economic climate coupled with the political assault on union rights has had a direct effect on union recruitment attempts. This is not to say, however, that all the problems faced in this case were due to external forces. There were some problems that the local TGWU office was fully instrumental in creating for itself in this campaign. It may be going too far to say that by avoiding such mistakes, the local TGWU office would have recruited a far greater number of cleaning members, but at least the union would have managed to retain the full confidence and support of the existing cleaning members of the branch.

The first mistake related to the local TGWU officer's failure to call a single branch meeting of the cleaning membership in the two years that the branch was established. This officer argued that it had been difficult to arrange a time that was acceptable for those cleaners who worked unsocial shifts. As a result, even those fifty cleaning workers who had joined the union remained atomised, lacking an effective and fully working forum which would enable them to come together to articulate their grievances collectively. A second avoidable problem occurred when the local TGWU office (and also Region 1) terminated the contract of the local officer. Although another local officer assumed responsibility for the cleaning workers at Heathrow Airport, this task had to be undertaken in conjunction with his responsibility for the catering workers based there. This meant that even less time would be devoted to the servicing of cleaners and addressing their concerns. This new officer acknowledged that the cleaning branch had lost a number of members as a result of the disillusionment of the cleaners with the local TGWU office, and the perception that they would not receive the same quality of service as they had from the temporary local officer. Whatever the reason for this action, it seems to fall under the heading of our third dilemma – the unwillingness of the union to consolidate 'special measures' into a more permanent structure. It could be argued that the cleaners had special needs, yet the eventual outcome was to incorporate their organisation into the normal existing structures.

The very characteristics which made the cleaners easy to exploit – the fact that most were ethnic minority women with poor or non-existent English-language skills – also made them hard to recruit and organise, and yet many local union officials were unconvinced that special measures were necessary to allow for this. Many of the cleaners had previously favoured organising themselves outside rather than through the union because of the image of the union as an unsympathetic white organisation. The local TGWU office, in the heart of a large Asian population, had an all-white staff, with little knowledge of the local community. Some cleaners felt that local union officers had been racist in their attitudes, and that white stewards were likely to be unsympathetic to taking action against racist behaviour. Furthermore, there was still the local legacy of experiences such as the Reliance Cleaners dispute to overcome. Officials in the local TGWU office had no experience in servicing black members. As a black union officer explained, 'you're in Southall dealing with Asians and yet you have nobody on the counter who is Asian. . . . This is a problem nobody realises – Asians don't feel confident in turning up to an all-white office.' There was a particular need for an Asian equal opportunities officer at the local TGWU office as many of the older Asian women had difficulties with English.

INNOVATIVE APPROACHES

Although it was quite clear that traditional methods of organisation had proved to be unsuccessful in relation to the cleaning workers, there continued to be a marked reluctance on the part of some local TGWU officers to consider alternative and more innovative approaches to the problem. In particular, there seemed to be a great reluctance to involve local minority ethnic community groups such as the Indian Workers Association (IWA) and the Southall Trade Union and Employment Advisory Service (STUEAS) in their attempts to organise the cleaning workers. This was because some local TGWU officers viewed such groups as direct competitors for their role. One local TGWU officer argued the IWA was actually making the recruitment of cleaners more difficult for the union by 'using the problems faced by the cleaners to usurp the functions of the local TGWU office'. This officer refused to acknowledge that some cleaning workers had sought help from such groups because the local TGWU office was regarded as a 'white institution' which was removed from the problems facing the cleaners: 'There's a lot more to the problems facing the cleaners than the Southall [now Hillingdon] TGWU office being racist.'

However, after the failure of the cleaners' recruitment campaign the new local TGWU officer with responsibility for the organisation of the cleaners articulated a different view. He believed that co-operation with local community groups would help the local TGWU office in organising the cleaners. There was an acknowl-edgement that the local office had made mistakes in the past by attempting to organise cleaning workers in isolation from represen-tatives of local community groups such as the Indian Workers Association who were employed in other areas of the airport. An Afro-Caribbean shop steward in the car industry who was a member of Region 1's RRAC also felt that it was important to work with local community groups to bridge the gap between the local office and the cleaning workers, and recruit them to the union. He suggested that if a particular area of work such as the cleaning sector was unorganised, 'it should be down to the officer respon-sible to take the initiative to get amongst the community and sell the union in terms of what can be done'.

Some progress towards achieving a level of co-operation with local community groups has begun to happen. The local TGWU office in conjunction with the IWA has begun to devise ways of recruiting cleaning workers at their place of work by getting IWA and union members who work in other areas of the airport to inform and pass on recruitment-related information to the cleaning workers. However, at the time of writing this chapter it is too early to assess whether this has resulted in any tangible change in the organisation of the cleaning workers.

BROADER IMPLICATIONS

This particular case study indicates a number of broader points relevant to the relationship between minority ethnic workers and trade unions. At a time of declining union membership and growth in marginalised forms of work, trade unions will increasingly need to set up initiatives to recruit minority ethnic workers within these jobs. The above case study shows that for many such workers, barriers of isolation, language, low pay and anti-social hours make this task difficult. To help overcome these barriers unions need to take account of the special needs of minority ethnic workers. Extra time and resources will need to be made available; specific initiatives are needed which make full use of community networks and organisations, as well as using local ethnic minority newspapers and radio stations. Union recruitment literature and other material will need to be translated into community languages. Union officers from ethnic minority communities are necessary at a local level, with the appropriate insight into language and culture. Unions need to demonstrate to the minority ethnic communities that they will not only tackle traditional union matters on behalf of their minority ethnic members, but will also fight against racism on their behalf, and involve themselves in broader community issues, such as immigration injustice and racial harassment on the streets.

The issue of the relationship of trade unions to external community-based minority ethnic groups is a controversial one, which pricks a number of sensitive points in British trade union history. As stated earlier, post-war black migrant workers experienced white trade union racist exclusion in the 1950s and 1960s. For example, in the 1965 dispute at Courtaulds' Red Scar Mill, Preston, white workers and the union had collaborated with management in the attempt to force Asian workers to work more machines for proportionately less pay, and later that year a strike by Asian workers at the Woolf Rubber Company was lost through lack of official union backing (Sivanandan 1982). Partly as a result of such experiences, minority ethnic workers tended to organise themselves outside the factory walls, making such organisations more 'community-based' than 'work-based', and in subsequent industrial disputes they would draw upon such groups. In the late 1960s and early 1970s there occurred a number of strikes characterised by strong support for Asian workers by local community associations and an equally noticeable lack of support by a local trade union. In particular, three notorious disputes were those at the Coneygre Foundry in Tipton in 1967–8, Mansfield Hosiery in Loughborough in 1972, and Imperial Typewriters in Leicester in 1974. All three were precipitated by management and union collusion in discriminatory practices, such as paying Asian workers lower wages, barring them from promotion, or selectively making them redundant. In each case the strikers benefited substantially through the support of local community organisations and political groups, and Asian workers from other factories (Wrench 1987: 166–7).

One example of an external group which was associated with some of these disputes is the Indian Workers Association (IWA). The question of the relationship between the IWA and the union figures in both the case studies of this chapter, although there are significant ideological differences between the IWA in Southall and the IWA(GB) rooted in the West Midlands. The IWA in Southall, although involved in the Woolf's strike in 1965, is nevertheless much more 'moderate' and less trade union orientated than the IWA(GB) (Josephides 1991: 20). The IWA(GB) traces its origins back to organisations of Indians in Britain in the 1930s. These organisations were largely concerned with the independence of India, and after the political independence of India and Pakistan in 1947 went into decline. However, they became active again in the 1950s, one stimulus being the need to provide assistance to the newly arriving Indian migrants to Britain. It expects its members to belong to unions, and assists them in making representations at branch, district or TUC level on issues of importance to its members. The IWA(GB) has always had a distinctive political philosophy – it locates its work of fighting racism and discrimination within its overall mission of creating a strong and united working-class movement. It has had some success in its activities, initially in forcing specific unions to accept Indian members, and then in numerous campaigns on behalf of individual victims of racism and discrimination in the workplace. Members see themselves not as constituting an alternative to trade union organisation, but as strong trade unionists themselves, who welcome alliances with other multi-racial progressive groups (Josephides 1990).

THE SECOND CASE STUDY: GMB

The issue of a trade union's relationship with external community-based groups, and the IWA in particular, is central to the second case study. This concerns the attempts of the GMB union to organise a group of mainly South Asian women sweat-shop workers employed at Burnsall Ltd, a small metal finishing company in Smethwick, the West Midlands, in 1992–3.

The union described the situation at Burnsall:[4] 'Here, exceptionally low-paid workers were sweated and subjected to the whim of a capricious and autocratic management. Along with total mobility of labour, docking of wages and imposed overtime, we have the maximum extraction of value from workers in a highly competitive industry.' The women complained that they got less money than the men for similar work, but the main catalyst for the strike was the health and safety issue. Workers complained of skin rashes and dizziness from the tanks of heated chemicals. The management ignored the request of a pregnant woman who lifted metal pieces out of a degreasing tank to be moved to lighter tasks. In May 1992, when three months pregnant, she was rushed to hospital and suffered a miscarriage. The doctor who attended her said that the cause of her miscarriage was consistent with the lifting work she had been doing.

One of the women workers was docked an entire week's wages for missing one day at work. Another reported: 'We ate surrounded by filth – they treated us like animals.' In the three months before the strike, the union made many approaches to secure recognition, informing the management that 95 per cent of their workforce were now union members. On 1 May 1992 a white worker was dismissed for refusing to work overtime. On 11 June a secret ballot took place of the twenty-six of the twenty-nine workers who had joined the union. No votes were cast against the strike. On 15 June the strike began. The objective was union recognition, to combat low and unequal pay, imposed overtime and a hazardous environment.

There were twenty-six strikers, mostly Punjabi women who spoke little English. In the fifty-four weeks of the strike there was a daily picket, with a least one full-time union officer spending at least some time on the picket line each day. The strike was intermittently featured in newspaper articles and television news and documentary programmes, and attracted considerable public support. A London support group was formed, and later a local Birmingham support group too. Marches of solidarity were held, and concerts and social events organised to raise money for the strike fund.

Despite the general public sympathy, the strike failed. Legal restrictions on picketing and secondary action limited the impact of the strike on the company, who found it relatively easy to recruit scab replacement labour. Local jobcentres told women on the unemployment register to report to Burnsall's, otherwise their benefit would be stopped. The majority of Burnsall's customers were non-union, which made it impossible to organise boycotting of products treated by Burnsall. There were a few unionised companies which took their products, such as Jaguar. After pressure from a Jaguar shop steward and a sympathetic article in the *Guardian*, a manager at Jaguar instructed its suppliers to terminate their relationship with Burnsall. However, the success at Jaguar could not be repeated at Rover, Land Rover and other unionised companies which did business with Burnsall.

In May 1993 a scab who had been hired at Burnsall only that day attacked with a knife a young male striker on the picket, who later underwent emergency surgery for partially severed fingers. The union featured this vicious assault in a four-page leaflet calling for solidarity, distributed at all the unionised factories that do business with Burnsall. After twenty-six days without a single response to the leaflet, the union officials came to the conclusion that the strike was over. They argued that if other trade unionists were not going to take solidarity action for a fellow trade unionist mutilated on an official picket line, then they were unlikely to take action whatever further appeals were made. Other trade unions argued that they were unable to provide more substantial and effective support unless they were *officially* asked by the GMB; however, such action on the GMB's part would be seen to be unlawful. The GMB union officials had no further initiatives to propose, saw no prospect of victory, and recommended calling off the picketing. After a three-hour meeting with the strikers the strike was called off. It had lasted for just over a year.

THE ENDING OF THE STRIKE

The strike ended in a great deal of acrimony between the union, the external support groups, and the strikers. The union had committed itself to an official dispute, within the law, including compliance with the law on balloting, picketing and secondary action. This policy was criticised by the support groups who favoured a wider blacking of Burnsall work, and mass picketing. This was rejected by the union for legal and practical reasons – if the GMB broke the law it would leave itself open to raids on its finances. One full-time official argued that for a mass picket to be successful it must block all vehicles and all scab labour entering and leaving the factory, which would entail blocking off a road well used by local commercial traffic. 'Thus, for the union to defy the law would be no more than an invitation to countless inconvenienced companies to plunder, via the courts, the union's resources.' On top of this, he pointed to all the recent times that mass picketing had ended in defeat in recent years.

A leaflet issued by the London Support Group during the strike argued that it was precisely because of the new restrictive legislation that broader action was necessary:

> Historically, strikes by black workers have only been successful through the support of the community and mobilisation by black and anti-racist organisations. In the 1990s, with the ban on secondary picketing and other anti-union legislation making it harder than ever to mobilise through traditional trade union structures, community action is vital.

However, in this case, community mobilisation was problematic for the GMB. In January 1993, half-way through the strike, a support group external to the union was set up in Birmingham, and almost immediately relations between the union and the Birmingham support group broke down. The crisis seems to have been precipitated by the call by the General Secretary of the IWA(GB) at a meeting of the support group for mass picketing and secondary action, on the grounds that the strike could not be won by lawful means. A leading activist in the support group was reported to have told a union officer that 'the union now had to step aside. It had had over six months to win the strike and had failed. It was now time for the support group to take over and see what it could do.'

The GMB felt that if this action was taken on behalf of the union in an official dispute, it could place the union and its funds in extreme jeopardy. The courts and Burnsall could legally raid the union's finances. The GMB tried to get the support group to limit its role, which the support group was unwilling to do. Therefore the union issued a statement (28 January 1993) that 'the Union will not accept the involvement, in any aspect of the Burnsall dispute, by members of the Birmingham support group', threatening that further interference would result in the union's 'bringing to the attention of the wider trade union and Labour movement the activities of this group'. There then followed a period of exchange of letters, with the support group insisting that it had a legitimate role to play, and that its activities had been agreed with the union, and the union accusing the support group of rewriting history and concealing the true nature of its activities. By the time the strike was called off, one of the union officers described the support group intervention as 'a campaign to undermine the GMB leadership of the strike' and an 'additional burden which the union leadership has had to shoulder'. The London support group issued a statement accusing the GMB of intimidating and threatening the strikers to force them to end the strike. In reply, one of the black strikers issued a statement accusing the support group of intimidating the strikers into breaking the law.

Another problem which made the relationship between the union and the strikers difficult was the fact that many of the strikers had limited or no English-language skills, and the union could not provide a full-time officer who could speak the language of the Asian strikers. The union officers therefore relied heavily upon an Asian community activist to translate for them. However, because this activist was an active member of the IWA and the support group, the full-time officers felt, rightly or wrongly, that he was misleading the strikers as to the union's position. The IWA strongly denied this allegation; either way, the union officers conceded that the union had been seriously weakened by not having a sympathetic Punjabi speaker to speak on their behalf.

THE POST MORTEM

The ending of the strike generated much debate on what went wrong, and on the degree of blame to be attached to various parties in the struggle. The strike illustrates the fact that the issue of 'community support' for trade unions in disputes involving minority ethnic workers is more problematic than many have realised, not least because of the often very different ideologies and aims of many of these groups and unions. After the strike was called off the IWA(GB) stated:

> The calling off of the strike has vindicated the IWA(GB)'s view that it was never possible for this action to succeed within the law. The GMB line of conducting the action within the law has resulted in a failure to win either trade union recognition or to secure the reinstatement of their dismissed members. . . . The IWA calls upon all its members to campaign, inside and outside trade unions, to change the policy of those unions who are committed to conducting industrial disputes strictly within the law, even though the law is unjust and biased.
>
> (Press release by IWA(GB) on the calling off of the Burnsall strike)

For the IWA, the lesson of the strike was that unions must sometimes be prepared to campaign *outside* the law, in order to build a mass movement and secure fundamental rights. A similar statement by the London support group urged that in the context of anti-union legislation, strikes such as Burnsall's can only be successful through mobilising wider community support and developing new strategies. They accused the GMB officials of being 'less interested in winning the strike than in keeping it within their control', which led ultimately to the 'bitter betrayal' of the strikers.

One local white activist tried to put the union's actions in a more sympathetic context:

> Most of us on the left are all too familiar with cases of union bureaucrats selling out winnable struggles and treating the rank and file membership with contempt. We are also well aware of the British trade union movement's shameful record of indifference, neglect, and downright racism towards black workers. The knee-jerk reaction is to believe the worst when the GMB is accused of betraying the mainly Asian (and majority female) strikers at Burnsall. . . . The uncomfortable fact is, however, that in this instance the GMB conducted an honest, determined and surprisingly principled struggle. If the left's usual accusations of 'selling out' and 'betrayal' against bureaucrats are to carry any credibility, we have to give credit where it's due and avoid spreading lies and slander.
>
> (Denham 1993)

The GMB's actions in this case should not be seen as of the same order as those of the blinkered and racist union officials who abandoned and undermined black struggle at Imperial Typewriters and other earlier industrial struggles. Indeed, many of the sorts of initiatives which we have argued were lacking in the first case study in this chapter were in fact adopted by the union in this one. The strike began with a genuine and determined commitment by the union to the Burnsall strikers. As Denham argues, although it was a 'legal' strike, the union 'sailed close to the wind' in its attempts to obtain blacking of Burnsall. Although in theory the union could have refused strike pay because of the short duration of the strikers' membership, the union paid the strike pay immediately. (Normally, 53 weeks' membership was the qualifying period for any union benefit.)

The union devoted a lot of effort to raising the public profile of the strike, in the first six months of the strike issuing twelve press releases. Indeed, media pressure forced a previously unsympathetic Health and Safety Executive to write a critical report of the factory, imposing a four-part improvement notice, and demanding other alterations to current company practice. The union saw this as having an important effect on the morale of the strikers and the continuation of the strike. The strikers had been suffering real financial hardship, and were unable to get DHSS benefit because the Social Security Act forbids benefit to those involved in an industrial dispute. However, because of the now very public health and safety issue it was ruled that the workers' refusal to return to work was justified, so that the workers were able to receive unemployment benefit and income support. Thus, while the support groups felt the union had sold the strikers short, the union felt it had done all it was able to do, including initiating some rather innovatory tactics.

DISCUSSION

One of the problems of this dispute was that key players were often operating according to different and incompatible assumptions. Sometimes, at various stages in the strike, the allegiance of different individuals to these different positions was blurred, concealed or confused. To clarify these different sets of assumptions, we will first postulate three different historical positions held by union members regarding the preferred relationship between trade unions and migrant or minority ethnic workers. This will be followed by three different positions held by external black groups on their relationship with trade union struggle (see Table 8.2).

Table 8.2 The relationship between trade unions and minority ethnic workers

Union members and minority ethnic workers	Groups external to the union
1 Racist exclusion	1 Black separatist
2 Incorporation	2 Incorporation
3 Partial autonomy	3 Race and class

UNION MEMBERS AND MINORITY ETHNIC WORKERS

The first position is that of *racist exclusion*, as characterised by many trade unionists in the pre-war and early post-war periods, and by some members and officials in the disputes of the 1960s and early 1970s. The preference is first, to keep migrant workers out of the labour market; later, to keep them out of the union, and when in the union, to keep them excluded from the union benefits to which they were entitled.

The second position is one of *incorporation*, where union membership is extended to minority ethnic workers, but where the basis of inclusion goes no further than that consistent with a traditional trade union class analysis. Membership unity is seen as central; thus any special measures which distinguish between types of workers are to be discouraged. The natural preference is to be 'colour blind'. The 'hard' position within this was to extend no special measures at all to migrant workers, as was the position of many unions in the 1960s. A later, more flexible, position is to encourage the adoption of some measures which take account of the different circumstances of minority ethnic members, such as producing literature in different languages. The incorporation model forms the premise upon which most of the 'race' structures of individual unions are currently based.

The third position is one of *partial autonomy*, held by many black trade unionists and some white activists, who argue that union rules, structures and policies should change to allow for the experiences of exclusion and racism of the minority black membership, as these disadvantages are suffered over and above those suffered by the white membership. Furthermore, the fact that black members are generally in a minority within unions means that normal union structures operate to prevent their voice from being heard by the majority (Lee 1987). Thus many minority ethnic workers feel that the way to get their voices heard is by self-organisation within unions, in their own separate structures. (This chapter has not time to address the current 'self-organisation' debate – for an overview of this see Virdee and Grint 1994.)

The tactic of self-organisation tends to be regarded with suspicion by the white union hierarchy, who generally prefer what could be called the 'passive assimilation' strategy associated with the previous 'incorporation' position. The assumptions within this model are described by Virdee and Grint:

eventually, minorities will rise through the ranks of the union movement and provide role models for others to follow; in the meantime the unions themselves will become progressively more liberal, thereby setting up a virtuous circle to bind minorities properly into the labour movement, where their similar experience and interests as *workers* will transcend what differentiates them along ethnic lines. Whatever problems minorities suffer from can best be resolved through a strategy that asserts from the beginning that all are equal.

(Virdee and Grint 1994: 208)

A common argument used by those within the union who oppose self-organisation is one which draws upon a simplistic Marxist approach, namely that class-based interests as employees and workers take precedence over any other sectional interest such as race or ethnicity. (Virdee and Grint find this ironic as the British trade union movement has traditionally been hostile to Marxist approaches.) Only rarely has a union itself actively facilitated the development of self-organised groups, the best-known example being the white-collar union NALGO, the National and Local Government Officers' Association, before the UNISON merger.

The self-organisation debate is currently generating a lot of heat in some unions. However, it could be argued that, in itself, self-organisation doesn't necessarily raise fundamental contradictions within the unions, and may merely operate to serve the interests of a new and relatively middle-class black trade union bureaucracy. If self-organisation were to allow the large-scale involvement of minority ethnic workers in union structures, then many of the demands that minority ethnic workers make to address the issue of racism would push the trade unions beyond what they regard as the 'normal' economistic defensive position of protecting the sectional interests of their members, and move them towards a more overtly political position. However, at the moment it seems that such mass involvement in the 'race' structures has rarely occurred (Virdee forthcoming), and therefore it seems that some of the more fundamental tensions and contradictions within the union position are more likely to be exposed in relation to *external* groups at moments of struggle rather than *internally* through the tensions of self-organisation.

GROUPS EXTERNAL TO THE UNION

There are at least three identifiably different positions which in theory could be held by external black groups on their relationship with trade union struggle:

The *black separatist* position is the other side of the coin of the racist/exclusionist position historically held by some white trade unionists. This is the view that after years of evidence of white trade union racism to black members and workers, black people can only be properly represented by their own organisations, perhaps even including their own black trade unions. Any organisation where black workers are led by white leaders is bound to neglect black interests in favour of the white majority.

The second position is similar to the straightforward trade union class position put forward in the white unionists' *incorporation* model. This view is that black groups can help black members integrate into unions, and give some assistance to the unions in limited special measures, such as providing community links in recruitment campaigns, assisting with the translation and distribution of union material, etc. Black workers are not seen in any sense as having a special role as a 'vanguard' movement within unions – this would be a sort of inverted racism, carrying a danger of distancing black workers from their white class allies. At least one faction of the IWA could be seen to subscribe to this traditional class solidarity view (Josephides 1991: 22).

The third position is a more radical *race and class* perspective, stressing the potential of external groups for galvanising unions into more radical and political action. On this view, British unions are reformist and non-political organisations concerned only with the immediate remuneration of their members. Black workers can offer the labour movement the opportunity to break the reformist distinction between the political and the economic (Joshi and Carter 1984). Sivanandan writes:

> Trade unions, once an instrument of class struggle, have in the course of achieving legitimacy, come to act as a buffer between the classes – absorbing the impact of working class radicalism on behalf of capital in exchange for wage concessions on behalf of labour. . . . Black workers . . . have been forced by the racist ethos of British society (worker and capitalist alike) to address themselves more directly to the political dimensions of their economic exploitation. They

have . . . been compelled to recognise that a purely quanti-
tative approach to the improvement of their conditions can
by itself have no bearing on the quality of their lives. Their
economic struggle is at once a political struggle. And that puts
them in the vanguard of working class struggle.

(Sivanandan, Editorial, *Race Today*, August 1973)

This position is similar to that of the West Midlands-based IWA(GB),
involved in the Burnsall dispute. The IWA(GB) believes that because
many white workers have been corrupted into racism, while black
workers have at the same time become more politicised, through their
experiences of exploitation as well as through their earlier struggles
against imperialism, black workers will often find themselves taking
the initiative in workplace struggle.

In the same way that a class analysis is used by white trade
unionists when arguing against self-organisation for black workers,
so a class analysis can be drawn upon to defuse radical black
intervention in struggle. In the Burnsall dispute, one of the white
union leaders clearly identified the London Support Group as
'Black Separatists' and drew on a class argument to oppose them.

Unfortunately, what the London Support Group cannot
accept is that it is the strikers' membership of a British trade
union that gives them coherence. It is their organisation
along class lines that makes them so potentially powerful and
a pole of attraction for others and it is the championing of
their cause and the vigorous leadership given by the GMB
that has brought their struggle to national prominence. The
London Support Group view the Burnsall strike instead as a
struggle of black workers and their community against the
forces of state repression and its leadership by a white trade
union and its officers as an unfortunate minor inconvenience
best ignored as much as possible.

(GMB letter, 23 March 1993)

While the union officials used class arguments to criticise the
support groups, black members of the support groups used race
arguments to criticise the union officials. The union was seen to
have 'sold out' its black members; accusations of white union
leaders unsympathetic to black struggle, with implications of
racism, came to the surface, rooted in memories of the experience
of black trade unionists in the 1950s, 1960s and early 1970s. Both

these arguments were overstated. The external support groups were not predominantly peopled by 'black separatists'; the union officials concerned with the Burnsall dispute were not 'racist exclusionists' such those revealed in the disputes of 20 or 30 years ago. Indeed, one of the officials consciously saw the dispute as an attempt to put to rest the old image of unions seen only as working for the benefit of 'white, male, skilled workers over the age of 35':

> The union's record was a pretty unimpressive one. We consciously saw ourselves as doing something to rectify that imbalance of commitment from the union to the workers, given the commitment that ethnic minority workers in terms of their union membership had given to unions over many years.
>
> (Quoted in Büyüm 1993: 23)

The GMB trade unionists involved in the Burnsall dispute attempted to win recognition and improve the working conditions of their newly recruited members through action which remained within the law, and insisted on retaining control of the dispute to make sure that actions of their members did not transgress the law and jeopardise union funds. Inevitably this was seen by some as incorporation by white union bureaucracy to contain black struggle. Memories of this went back to Grunwick, where the mobilisation of official union support for the strikers was seen as a tactic of incorporation:

> Grunwick marked the end of an era of vibrant and creative black struggles which had threatened to bring a political dimension to industrial struggle. It was an end brought about by the invasion of official trade unionism, which had moved from a policy of opposition or apathy to a strategy of control through co-option.
>
> (Gordon 1985)

Nevertheless, those who were critical of the union's actions are still not to be labelled 'black separatist', a position which groups such as the IWA(GB) are strongly opposed to.

> We feel unity [between black and white] will develop in struggle. This does not in any sense deny the need for black workers to have their own caucuses in every factory and place of work. We do not advocate separate black unions;

that would be to play the capitalists' game of dividing the working class.

(Report of the General Secretary, IWA(GB), J. Joshi, 1970: 21–2, quoted in Josephides 1990: 119)

The perspective of 'black separatism' is rarely found amongst black union members. In general, the term is over-used by white trade unionists, and is often attributed to black activists when they begin to move beyond the normal limits of traditional trade union activity. A recent study of four trade unions found no evidence of this perspective being articulated by either rank and file black workers or their representatives within the 'race' structures of the union (Virdee forthcoming). The perspective is more likely to be held by activists *external* to trade unions. Activists in the London support group held varying positions on 'separatism': while some made pronouncements during the strike which were quite sympathetic to separate black organisation, others threatened to withdraw if the group became 'separatist'. However, for some individuals the failure of the Burnsall strike itself seemed to stimulate a 'separatist' perspective. After the strike, one of the members of the London support group became even more convinced of the importance of black support organisations, and was clearly giving serious thought to the issue of separate black union organisation:

I think the other thing that comes out is that black workers need their own structures as well. The need for . . . even a black trade union, if need be. . . . Structures need to be created where black workers can fight through. It's becoming so difficult to work and struggle within the mainstream unions. They have managed, during the Burnsall strike, to do quite a lot of damage. Despite everything it was getting a lot of propaganda, getting a lot of publicity, getting a lot of mainstream support at one level. But at the end of the day it didn't win. . . . It didn't manage to get the mass support that was needed on that picket line every other day. There was no mass pickets. So we as black people do need to construct a strategy in order to have counter structures. Maybe we haven't been doing the right structures. And I think that there are ideas floating around about black trade unions, or black workers' organisations. But more black support groups. And I think that's the biggest contribution the strikers have made.

(Quoted in Büyüm 1993: 52)

PROBLEMS OF 'COMMUNITY SUPPORT'

In the earlier-mentioned strikes of the 1960s and 1970s, community action played a significant role in support of the strikers. This led to a rather romanticised view among the left as to the power in struggle of a union allied to broader black community organisations. In the earlier case study of the Heathrow cleaners in this chapter we too have argued that the failure of the TGWU to work with community organisations weakened their hand. However, in the Burnsall case, community support is shown to be a more problematic issue. More specifically, there is a clear distinction to be made between those forms of community support which are lawful and those which are not.

In the early stages of the Burnsall dispute, the union did engage the broader local community in the action, and, with the support of local groups and key religious and commercial figures, succeeded for over two months in preventing the company from securing an alternative workforce. In this, the union had the support of the IWA(GB), which used its local influence to try to shame the scabs in their local communities:

> We've put their names up in local temples and distributed leaflets, naming them and the Indian villages they come from. Some might say it's direct humiliation. But we're saying, by crossing the picket line for a few bob, you are a disgrace to your community.
>
> (IWA spokesman, *Guardian*, 7 October 1992)

Nevertheless, in this case the community support did not produce the desired outcome. Despite the local popular support for the strikers the company was able to secure a replacement workforce, including many from the local Punjabi community. Some have argued that this reflects the fact that in recent years the IWA has lost some of its mobilising force in the Asian community, as the activities on which it mobilised in the 1960s and 1970s have less relevance for a new generation within minority ethnic communities. A further critique comes from those who see part of the problem to be the fact that the IWA is less attuned to *women's* struggles. In her study of Punjabi women workers in Birmingham, Guru (1987) was critical of the attitudes of some of the IWA men she interviewed, those who were in their late thirties and over, and who had spent much of their lives in rural areas of India: she felt they had 'patronising and paternalistic' attitudes to the participation of women in organised politics. On this argument, the influence of this particular community-based organisation was less than it might have been in relation to the groups of strikers and scab workers, who were both predominantly female.

This organisation of community support in union recruitment drives, or in attempts to prevent the recruitment of scab labour, does not in theory create problems for the union concerned. However, when community support becomes mass picketing and potentially unlawful secondary action, it becomes an issue of a different order, and may pose a direct threat to trade union assets. Although the other previously mentioned cases where industrial struggle involved community support were often quite innovative and radical by the standards of normal official and unofficial disputes at that time, they nevertheless complied with the laws of the day. These struggles, which seemed to confirm the left's best ideals about unity and solidarity between workers and the extension of economic struggle into new and exciting political areas, were therefore not as 'radical' as mythology would have it. One major difference in the context of similar struggles today is the undermining of workers' collective power through structural unemployment and the increasingly repressive employment legislation. In particular the legislation has made once-normal collective action much more likely to be defined as unlawful activity.

CONCLUSION

One of the case studies described in this chapter is located in the service sector, the other in manufacturing. They both represent typical workplaces for minority ethnic groups; at the same time they are in their different ways both quite characteristic of the contemporary service and manufacturing sectors. Heathrow typifies the profitable, dynamic and expanding part of the service sector whose glamorous superstructure rests upon the labour of thousands of sub-contracted, poorly paid and highly exploited workers. Although Burnsall's appears to be an old-fashioned traditional sweat shop, it represents an important component of the 'new workplace'. Through the growth of sub-contracting from core, assembly and manufacturing customers, factories such as Burnsall's are an increasingly central element in the new two-tier manufacturing world, in this case supplying major car

assemblers such as Jaguar and Rover. The introduction in manufacturing of Japanese-style management practices, JIT (Just-in-Time),
contracting out and so on has increased the numbers of small- to
medium-sized employers who are under intense pressure from their
customers, the major assemblers, and who become even more
opposed to trade unions than they would normally be. In the service
sector, competitive tendering and contracting out have the same
effect. The over-representation of women, minority ethnic workers
and migrants in these sectors provides extra opportunities for
employers to divide, segment and individualise their workforce.
Increasingly, this is the context in which trade unions must operate.

Many labour movement activists now argue that the trade union
movement has no hope of bringing unionisation to these workers
unless it works in co-operation with communities and links unionisation to broader issues such as workplace discrimination, sexual
and racial harassment at the workplace, health and safety, cultural,
linguistic and religious rights, harassment by the police and immigration authorities and so on.

> If the trade union movement wants to tackle the creation of
> low-paid, racially defined ghettos in employment, it has to
> shift its priorities. It must encourage community initiatives
> rather than fearing where they might lead. It must offer
> resources and be willing to stick with the local and com-
> munity groups when the inevitable industrial disputes arise.
> This means working jointly to build solidarity and, most
> importantly, confront anti-union legislation.
> (Campaign Against Racism and Fascism, March/April 1994: 5)

We argued in the first case study that if the union had worked
with the local community groups it would have had more success
in its recruitment drive. However, this success would then have led
naturally to the problems of the second case study. Here, officials
who were sympathetic to the idea of broader community links as
well as to some of the principles of 'self-organisation' still drew the
line at unlawful action to challenge anti-union laws, even though
it could be argued that such laws are having a more oppressive
effect on these new groups of workers than workers in the
relatively strong, already unionised, sectors.

The problem for unions here is that the highly visible failure of
campaigns such as Burnsall's could lead to a more general disillusion with unions on the part of minority ethnic workers and

make further union recruitment more difficult. As one of the GMB officials recognised: 'there is no doubt that we are going to find it more difficult to recruit Asian workers in the future, because of what happened in the Burnsall strike' (quoted in Büyüm 1993: 37).

One of the key differences between a radical and a reformist position is the readiness in the former to take action outside the law, when that law is seen as unjust and representing the narrow interests of the ruling elite. However, unions by their very nature are not easily radical organisations in this sense. Much has been argued as to the radical or conservative potential of unions in social transformation (see, e.g., Hyman 1971; Kelly 1988). Many have argued since the times of Lenin and Gramsci that trade unions are basically defensive organisations operating within the confines laid down by capitalist society, are essentially competitive, and are unlikely to be the instrument of a radical transformation of society (see Harman 1983). Although unions in Britain have shown their effectiveness in factory-level issues, 'they studiously avoid any coherent theory of their role in changing the economic base of society. The question is a political one, and the unions separate the industrial struggle from the political struggle. Politics is seen as something outside of the industrial process' (Rice 1977: 164). Thus in Britain 'union membership has never meant that members should have any fundamental commitment to a new society' (Rice 1977: 164).

Some commentators argue that the current period of crisis of the labour movement cannot be separated from the historical question of the division between 'politics' and 'economics'. The critiques of trade unions by Hobsbawm (1981) and Lane (1982) have been summarised as follows:

> the crisis affecting trade unions is the result of the inter-weaving of long-term structural change with economic crisis and high and sustained levels of unemployment. Together these have exposed union practices that rested upon 'economism' as inadequate and ill-suited to retaining membership, morale and influence in a recessionary period.
>
> (Eldridge *et al*. 1991: 81)

These commentators are critical of the failure of the movement to demonstrate an alternative vision upon which unionism can be based: 'one that extends beyond the plant and the pay packet and into issues regarding the social purposes of work and a wider quest for a society founded on equity' (Eldridge *et al*. 1991: 81). Eldridge,

Cressey and MacInnes write that even in periods of relative strength for unions, there has been constant conflict over the strategies, values and fundamental orientations that unions should adopt; 'this ambiguity is historically embedded and becomes particularly acute in periods of recession' (Eldridge *et al.* 1991: 79). The context of recession heightened the ambiguities, conflicts and tensions of the Burnsall dispute. It might be argued that in the future such tensions are going to be sharpened by the conjunction of a number of factors:

> In both the service and manufacturing sectors pressures have increased the proportional significance of marginalised, low-paid and heavily exploited workers, so that these 'poor work' sectors now form an important component of the 'new workplace'. Unions need to recruit and organise workers within these sectors to replace their falling membership and arrest the effect this sector has on dragging down wages elsewhere. For a number of reasons, women and minority ethnic workers are disproportionately represented within these 'poor work' sectors.
>
> The problems of organising this sector mean that broader forms of action are likely to be necessary to achieve success. At the same time the increasingly restrictive legislation means that such action is far more vulnerable to being defined as unlawful. Black workers and their communities, due to the politicising nature of their life and work experiences, are far more ready to embrace a political and radical dimension to economic struggles and struggles of union recognition.

The combination of all these factors means that when unions embark upon similar campaigns they are more likely to find themselves addressing political questions broader than 'economism' and outside the remit of conventional trade union action. By this analysis the tensions which arose during the Burnsall dispute are understandable, and almost predictable. They cannot be reduced simply to individual personalities who are 'racist', 'separatist', or 'bureaucratic'. Given the combination of factors described above it is clear that in some other form and setting these issues will arise to face the labour movement again.

NOTES

1 In this chapter the term 'minority ethnic' is used to refer to people of Afro-Caribbean and Asian descent, and other 'visible' minorities. As many of the writers and activists referred to in this chapter also use the term 'black' to mean the same thing, we also employ this term in the chapter.

2 Twelve interviews were undertaken with cleaning workers and TGWU representatives. They comprised six interviews with cleaning workers, three interviews with local TGWU district officers and three interviews with regional TGWU officers. Four out of the six cleaning workers were Asian women; one was an Asian man and the other was a white man. Of the three local TGWU officers, one was an Asian man and two were white men. Of the three regional TGWU officers, one was a white man, one a white woman and the other an Afro-Caribbean man. The interviews were undertaken in 1991 and early 1992. (The interviews with the cleaning workers took place in their homes because of the employer's refusal to allow the TGWU to make contact with them on airport premises.) A full account of this research can be found in Virdee (forthcoming).

3 Of these 800 (80 per cent) were Asian, of whom the overwhelming majority were women. Of the remaining 200 cleaners, 150 (15 per cent) were white, and 50 (5 per cent) were African or Afro-Caribbean.

4 Much of the material referred to over the next few pages comes from unpublished documents generated by the GMB, the support groups, and activists during the course of the dispute.

REFERENCES

Ashton, D. N. and Maguire, M. (1991) 'Patterns and Experiences of Unemployment', in Brown, P. and Scase, R. (eds) (1991) *Poor Work: Disadvantage and the Division of Labour*, Milton Keynes: Open University Press.

BAA (1992) *Heathrow Airport: Facts and Figures*, London.

BAA (1994) *Annual Review 1994*, London.

Bentley, S. (1976) 'Industrial Conflict, Strikes and Black Workers: Problems of Research Methodology', *New Community* **1**, 2, Summer.

Brown, C. (1984) *Black and White Britain: The Third PSI Survey*, London: Heinemann.

Brown, P. and Scase, R. (eds) (1991) *Poor Work: Disadvantage and the Division of Labour*, Milton Keynes: Open University Press.

Büyüm, M. (1993) 'The Burnsall Strike: Account of a Struggle', MA dissertation, Department of Sociology, University of Warwick.

CARF/SR (1981) *Southall: The Birth of a Black Community*, London: IRR and Southall Rights.

Castles, S. (1990) *Labour Migration and the Trade Unions in Western Europe*, Occasional Paper No. 18, University of Wollongong: Centre for Multicultural Studies.

CRE (1992) *Part of the Union? Trade Union Participation by Ethnic Minority Workers*, London: Commission for Racial Equality.

Denham, J. (1993) 'Burnsall: The Aftermath', *Socialist Organiser*, 22 July.

Eldridge, J., Cressey, P. and MacInnes, J. (1991) *Industrial Sociology and Economic Crisis*, Hemel Hempstead: Harvester Wheatsheaf.

Fryer, P. (1984) *Staying Power: The History of Black People in Britain*, London: Pluto Press.

Gordon, P. (1985) 'If They Come in the Morning . . .', in B. Fine and R. Millar (eds), *Policing the Miners' Strike*, London: Lawrence and Wishart.

Guru, S. (1987) 'Struggle and Resistance: Punjabi Women in Birmingham', Ph.D. thesis, University of Keele.

Harman, C. (1983) *Gramsci versus Reformism*, Bookmarks.

Hobsbawm, E. (1981) *The Forward March of Labour Halted*, London: Verso.

Hyman, R. (1971) *Marxism and the Sociology of Trade Unions*, London: Pluto Press.

Jones, T. (1993) *Britain's Ethnic Minorities*, London: Policy Studies Institute.

Josephides, S. (1990) 'Principles, Strategies and Anti-racist Campaigns: The Case of the Indian Workers' Association', in H. Goulbourne (ed.), *Black Politics in Britain*, Aldershot: Avebury.

Josephides, S. (1991) 'Towards a History of the Indian Workers' Association', Research Paper in Ethnic Relations No. 18, University of Warwick.

Joshi, S. and Carter, B. (1984) 'The Role of Labour in the Creation of a Racist Britain', *Race and Class* **XXV**, 3.

Kelly, J (1988) *Trade Unions and Socialist Politics*, London: Verso.

Lane, T. (1982) 'The Unions: Caught on an Ebb Tide', *Marxism Today* **26**, 9.

Lee, G. (1987) 'Black Members and their Unions', in G. Lee and R. Loveridge (eds), *The Manufacture of Disadvantage*, Milton Keynes: Open University Press.

London Borough of Ealing (1988) *Minutes of the Economic Development Division*, London: London Borough of Ealing.

Martens, A. (1993) 'Migratory Movements: The Position, the Outlook. Charting a Theory and Practice for Trade Unions', Paper presented to the Conference on Trade Union Strategies to Combat Racism and Xenophobia, ETUC, Brussels.

Mason, D. (1994) 'Employment and the Labour Market', *New Community* **20**, 2, January.

Morris, L. (1991) 'Women's Poor Work', in P. Brown and R. Scase (eds), *Poor Work: Disadvantage and the Division of Labour*, Milton Keynes: Open University Press.

Penninx, R. and Roosblad, J. (1994) 'Trade Unions, Immigration and Immigrant and Ethnic Minority Workers in Western Europe 1960–1993', unpublished paper, Institute for Migration and Ethnic Studies, University of Amsterdam.

Phizacklea, A. and Miles, R. (1980) *Labour and Racism*, London: Routledge & Kegan Paul.

Radin, B. (1966) 'Coloured Workers and British Trade Unions', *Race* **VIII**, 2.

Rice, M. (1977) 'The State of the Unions', in R. N. Ottoway (ed.), *Humanising the Workplace*, London: Croom Helm.

Sivanandan, A. (1982) *A Different Hunger: Writings on Black Resistance*, London: Pluto Press.

Sivanandan, A. (1989) 'Racism 1992', *Race and Class*, January–March.

Smith, P. and Morton, G. (1993) 'Union Exclusion and the Decollectivization of Industrial Relations in Contemporary Britain', *British Journal of Industrial Relations* **31**, 1, March.

Snape, E. (1994) 'Reversing the Decline? The TGWU's Link-Up Campaign', *Industrial Relations Journal* **25**, 3, September.

TGWU (1989) *Forward T and G*, London: Transport and General Workers' Union.

TUC (1983a) *Race Relations at Work*, London: Trades Union Congress.

TUC (1983b) *TUC Workbook on Racism*, London: Trades Union Congress.

TUC (1991) *Involvement of Black Workers in Trade Unions*, London: Ruskin College/Northern College, Trades Union Congress.

Virdee, S. (forthcoming) *Black Workers' Participation and Representation in Trade Unions*, Monographs in Ethnic Relations, University of Warwick.

Virdee S. and Grint, K. (1994) 'Black Self Organisation in Trade Unions', *Sociological Review* **42**, 2, May.

Vranken, J. (1990) 'Industrial Rights', in Z. Layton-Henry (ed.), *The Political Rights of Migrant Workers in Western Europe*, London: Sage.

Workers Against Racism (1985) *The Roots of Racism*, London: Junius.

Wrench, J. (1987) 'Unequal Comrades: Trade Unions, Equal Opportunity and Racism', in R. Jenkins and J. Solomos (eds), *Racism and Equal Opportunity Policies in the 1980s*, Cambridge: Cambridge University Press.

Wrench, J. (1990) 'The 1990s and Black Employment: Britain and the European Community', *Trades Union Congress*, (booklet), June.

Wrench, J. (1993) 'Ethnic Minorities and Workplace Organisation in Britain: Trade Unions, Participation and Racism', conference paper, Bonn, December 1992, published as: 'Ethnische Minderheiten und Organisation am Arbeitsplatz in Grossbritannien: Gewerkschaften, Mitbestimmung und Rassismus', *Gesprachskreis Arbeit und Soziales* No. 22, Bonn: Friedrich Ebert Stiftung.

9

POWER, SURVEILLANCE
AND RESISTANCE

Inside the 'factory of the future'

Alan McKinlay and Phil Taylor

INTRODUCTION

Critical studies of the impact of HRM techniques have been hampered by a lack of longitudinal empirical research. With few exceptions, existing studies of worker reactions to HRM are snapshots, report *managerial* perceptions of changes in employee commitment, or are based on extremely limited qualitative research (Scott 1994). Our analysis is based on the experience of a greenfield microelectronics plant – Pyramid – in a booming global market. The Pyramid plant is owned by an American multinational – PhoneCo – which has deliberately encouraged a high degree of experimentation in work organisation and labour regulation. The cornerstone of the corporation's unitarist ideology is individual commitment to personal growth and collective pursuit of total quality. But we will argue that the liberal humanism of the corporate mission statement is derived from a reading of the demands of a business which straddles high technology and mass consumer electronics. For PhoneCo, innovatory personnel policies are an essential precondition of competitive advantage in a highly competitive, fragmented global market.

Three complementary methodologies were used to chart the development of the greenfield plant: extensive interviews with managers and shopfloor employees; participant observation; and four surveys of employee attitudes to work, supervision and teamworking over a three-year period. A series of face-to-face interviews were conducted with key corporate, divisional and operational managers at critical moments in the plant's development. Extensive interviews were also conducted with shopfloor employees. Participant observation involved both researchers going through the standard induction process for new employees and daily contact with two production teams. Finally, we administered four surveys which included, for instance, standard questions on commitment, pace of work and attitudes towards specific innovatory personnel practices. This combination of methodologies allowed us to construct an intimate record of the *process* of change rather than a series of static snap-shots of work experience.

The chapter is in four sections. The first considers the importance of Foucault's concept of power/knowledge and discipline for understanding HRM practices. The second section reviews the dynamics of discipline within a team-based organisation and culture. This is followed by an examination of peer review, a formal process designed to force workers to rate each other's work performance and adherence to PhoneCo's cultural norms. Finally, we examine the lessons management drew from their experience of employee resistance to the peer review process and how their disciplinary objectives were reaffirmed by a series of organisational innovations.

FOUCAULT AND THE FACTORY

> the major effect of the Panopticon: to induce in the inmate a sense of conscious and permanent visibility that assures the automatic functioning of power. So to arrange things that the surveillance is permanent in its effects, even if it is discontinuous in its action; that the perfection of power should tend to render its actual exercise unnecessary . . . in short, that the inmates should be caught up in a power situation of which they are themselves the bearers.
>
> (Foucault 1977: 201)

For Foucault, power and knowledge are necessarily related. Just as power creates, so it also presupposes, knowledge (Dandeker 1990: 23). Although concerned with the general transformation of society from the late eighteenth century, Foucault chose to trace the development of power/knowledge through histories of specific institutions: the prison, clinic and asylum. These were more than case studies, however: they were grand, overarching metaphors offered by a philosopher who eschewed totalising philosophies. Particular fields of knowledge emerged, defined, confirmed and transformed power exercised through specific institutions. Foucault viewed power and powerlessness as mutually constitutive rather than defined in terms of cause and effect. Equally, Foucault was careful to stress the historicity of disciplinary practices and their institutional forms.

The central motif of each of Foucault's studies is laying open the subjective factors of social life to calculation, manipulation, in a word, making them governable. The conventional depiction of the move from the physical torture to the psychological rehabilitation of prisoners as socially progressive is rejected by Foucault. Rather, he regards the increased attention to moral rehabilitation as the alternative to corporal punishment as symptomatic of a new set of disciplinary practices, and not as the humanisation of carceral practices. The parallels with the development of the factory system are striking. As Nikolas Rose aptly puts it, the twentieth century has witnessed the psychologisation of work, providing managers with 'a vocabulary and a technology for rendering the labour of the worker visible, calculable, and manageable' (Rose 1990: 95). In this sense, the 'soft' management techniques following in the tradition of Mayo's human relations are *potentially* more penetrating and more pernicious than those in the Taylorist lineage. The psychological pressure on workers to seek personal satisfaction through their assimilation of corporate goals of quality, flexibility and involvement implies a profound subjection of individual subjectivity. Even the individual's most private domain does not offer the opportunity for the most temporary of refuges before the psyche is exposed to interrogative pressure (Townley 1993: 221–38).

Perhaps Foucault's most striking image is that of the panopticon. He draws on Jeremy Bentham's unrealised plan for a prison in which individuals isolated in their cells would never know if they were being scrutinised from a central observatory. Crucially, the 'carceral gaze' is based on one-way looking which objectifies the individuals under scrutiny. 'Power', explained Foucault, 'is exercised by virtue of things being known and people being seen' (Foucault 1980: 154). The gaoler peering through the judas hole is simultaneously exercising power *and* consolidating a knowledge base of what constitutes normal or acceptable behaviour. In this way, power and knowledge are mutually reinforcing. For Bentham the panopticon was the optimal form of prison architecture which enclosed and individualised inmates, and efficiently combined surveillance and discipline. Parallels in the contemporary corporate world include the exercise of power/knowledge over managers through financial controls or, on the shopfloor, through employee attitude studies to fine-tune involvement strategies. In other words, the panoptic organisation has the capacity to identify any deviation from the norm and compel convergence or improvement on targets: resistance by prisoners or workers can confirm and, indeed, strengthen an emerging body of knowledge and set of disciplinary practices.

So seductive is Foucault's panopticon metaphor, however, that if simply transposed on to the labour process perspective it can seriously overestimate the scope and depth of management control. Equally, such a transposition risks obliterating the novelty of Foucault's thinking. Consider, for example, Sewell and Wilkinson's (1992) thesis that JIT–TQM enormously enhances central control over the labour process while minimising the role of front-line supervisors. While we accept that this may be the case, we part company with them when they contend that sophisticated management information systems coupled with horizontal surveillance of workers by workers *necessarily* squeezes out 'negative divergences from expected behaviour and management defined norms' (*ibid.*: 279). Sewell and Wilkinson are not alone in overstating the depth of control achieved by what Barker (1993: 408) calls 'concertive control': 'a form of control more powerful, less apparent, and more difficult to resist than . . . bureaucracy'. Similarly, Garrahan and Stewart's study of the Nissan 'enigma' concludes that so claustrophobic is the quality circle that it:

> represents a form of powerlessness for many workers. [Nissan's] success depends upon a tight nexus of subordination that can be read as control, exploitation and surveillance – the other side of quality, flexibility, and teamwork.
>
> (Garrahan and Stewart 1992: 59)

The image in these accounts is of a form of self-subordination so complete, so seamless that it stifles any dissent, however innocuous. These are factories in which 'lean' managements have dispersed the control function so effectively that the only expression of workers' collectivity is to intensify their levels of mutual subjugation. To paraphrase Foucault, in team-based work regimes every 'prisoner' becomes a 'warder' and every 'warder' a 'prisoner'. In so far as workers have a voice in these accounts, they offer an ethnography of the factory as a total institution in which surveillance is constant, immutable and inescapable. Our objectives are first, to present an alternative view in which workers actively engage with the teamworking ideology, seek to prise open spaces for individual dissent, and remain capable of collective opposition, however limited in scope and duration. And second, to consider how PhoneCo management have developed their knowledge of the dynamics of a team-based disciplinary regime.

EMPOWERMENT, DISCIPLINE AND SURVEILLANCE

power would be a fragile thing if its only function were to repress, if it worked only through the mode of censorship, exclusion, blockage and repression . . . exercising itself only in a negative way. . . . Far from preventing knowledge, power produces it.

(Foucault 1980: 59)

From its foundation in the inter-war period PhoneCo's strategy was to make and market rather than innovate, to exploit cost advantages by rapidly building market share. Corporate structure remained highly centralised with tight strategic and tactical control over overseas subsidiaries. Corporate planning was strictly top-down and exclusively driven by financial measures (Sciberras 1977: 117–21). PhoneCo played little part in the wave of corporate restructuring from 1960 to 1975 which witnessed the emergence of powerful regional divisions within, for example, Ford and IBM (Dassbach 1989).

In 1980, however, PhoneCo completely overhauled its strategy and structure, rejecting its administrative heritage in favour of rapid 'Japanisation'. This sharp change in corporate priorities stemmed from humiliating losses to Japanese competitors in its core domestic markets during the mid-1970s (Scherer 1992: 52–7). PhoneCo's strategy of low-cost, low-quality production was re-placed by mass customisation. The central concerns were to accelerate new product development and to exceed the new quality and efficiency standards set by its Japanese competitors (Caruso 1992: 3–4). Indeed, achieving 'total customer satisfaction' is the cornerstone of PhoneCo's post-1980 differentiation strategy, which displaced its former cost leadership policy (Belohlav 1993: 57–9). Structural changes were no less profound: the corporation progressively decentralised decision-making and loosened the control exercised from its American headquarters. There was, however, an inverse relationship between operational de-centralisation and the corporate centre's continued control of strategic agendas (Amin and Dietrich 1991: 64–5). Over the last 15 years, PhoneCo has been making a gradual transition from being a global corporation dominated by the American parent to an innovative transnational company based on polycentric decision-making (Bartlett and Ghoshal 1989). The transnational company seeks to gain competitive advantage through the efficiency gains of a world-wide production and sourcing system while retaining maximum responsiveness to international variations in demand. By monitoring different structural arrangements PhoneCo is gradually shifting core corporate functions, such as systems development, from hierarchy to network as the dominant organisational archi-tecture. In transnational networks, national affiliates become equal contributors to the development of global organisational com-petencies rather than subsidiary companies reliant on control by an American headquarters. The impact of corporate restructuring on organisational learning is closely scrutinised by PhoneCo head-quarters. Crucially, at all levels within PhoneCo, management information systems are interrogated to gauge the scope and frequency of interaction: the network rather than individual becomes the focus of corporate control.

For PhoneCo, the cellular phone market epitomised the con-flicting pressures of intense price competition within a fragmented marketplace. The harmonisation of cellular networks across Europe and their rapid introduction in developing economies such as China resulted in an explosive growth in demand for portable phones from the late 1980s. In the western economies, the shift from luxury to mass market was paralleled, moreover, by rapid product innovation and the continuing fragmentation of demand, by functionality and design. Equally, the market rapidly became fiercely price competitive with the entrance of global players in microelectronics, notably NEC and Sony. Over the last five years, prices have tumbled by between 20 and 25 per cent per year. If PhoneCo's decision to open a new plant to service non-American markets reflected buoyant global demand, then its choice of work organisation reflected intensifying cost and customisation press-ures. In contrast to its conventionally organised American sister plant, the new Pyramid plant was to test the viability of team-working rather than hierarchy, of commitment rather than control. The importance of the new plant's output for PhoneCo's global strategy and its novel organisation ensured that Pyramid's performance was closely monitored by corporate headquarters. Pyramid was attempting to go far beyond PhoneCo's existing employee involvement initiatives in its American plants (Lawler 1986).

PhoneCo was one of a number of leading American microelectronics multinationals which located in Scotland's 'silicon glen' in 1965–75. As a result of regional policies designed to counteract the collapse of Scotland's traditional industrial base and corporate moves towards mass customisation the gender division of labour was fundamentally altered. The traditional reliance on female labour in assembly work was reversed with a significant masculinisation of microelectronics employment during the 1980s (Goldstein 1992). American multinationals in the sector have consistently prohibited trade union organisation (Findlay 1993). PhoneCo's 'direct dealing' policy places an absolute priority on the psychological, as well as the legal, contract between the *individual* and the corporation, to the exclusion of trade unions. In its rigorous selection process to search for clusters of psychological types to form production teams, flat organisational structure, and application of HRM techniques, PhoneCo is atypical of electronics plants in Scotland. Innovation in process technologies or the social organisation of production is confined to American-owned electronics plants rather than characteristic of the sector as a whole (Findlay 1990: 213–16). Even within this group, new production concepts such as JIT and innovatory HRM practices were only gradually introduced through the 1980s (Webb and Dawson 1991: 194). The trigger for changes in patterns of labour regulation was market fragmentation and increased price competition. A central objective behind the introduction of JIT, Total Quality Management and problem-solving workgroups was to increase plant responsiveness and efficiency. But step gains in productivity did not necessarily result in work intensification. Indeed, by producing only to order and not for stock such firms freed time for workgroups to work on quality or process improvements (Dawson and Webb 1989: 233). This reorientation towards work organisation constituted a radical change in labour regulation. The autonomy and creativity of the worker is no longer an obstacle to the enterprise's success to be cowed – as in Taylorism – but 'a central economic resource' to be mobilised (Miller and Rose 1990: 26).

The assumption by workgroups of technical and co-ordinative roles normally confined to management fundamentally altered the nature of authority on the shopfloor. Managerial authority is thus derived from inter-personal skills and technical competence rather than office or hierarchy. But if the authority of the individual manager was opened up to scrutiny from below through employee involvement, then managerial power per se became more opaque. By dispersing the functions of management, efficiency, flexibility and quality were suffused as the rationality of the organisation as a whole rather than the prerogative of specific functionaries (Cressey *et al.* 1985: 53–4). The authority of the individual manager becomes more personalised and contingent as the factory's power structure becomes more anonymous and unquestioned. Organisationally, PhoneCo's Pyramid plant was to extend these trends towards dispersed control: the social processes of teamworking were to be monitored continuously, evaluated, and engineered.

Prospective managers for the new plant were warned to 'be patient, you and your team are learning a completely new method of management. The managers of the future will be measured on how well their team manages itself, not on how well you manage them' (PhoneCo Internal Memo, 1990). More important than any lessons drawn from the parent corporation or from previous managerial experience was a year-long period of experimentation in a small pilot plant – Stewartfield – employing approximately 100 workers, whilst the new facility was under construction. The pilot plant concentrated on a single product using well-established technology to minimise technical uncertainty. Production schedules were secondary to the process of social experimentation. Technological, product and marketing choices were selected so as to focus managerial and employee attention on the social dynamics of production. No external or corporate consultants were hired to provide blueprints. Rather, the implicit assumption was that Stewartfield would yield an organic organisational strategy deeply embedded in managerial and employee experience, and that this intense socialisation would form a bedrock of collective commitment for the new, much larger facility. Self-managing teams encompassed a range of productive and organisational functions. Each month every team member was required to assume one of a number of rotating co-ordinating roles: component supplies, liaison with other teams, holiday rotas. Teams were allocated a range of support staff – personnel, technical and facilitative. Such 'Staff Associates' had no authority within the teams: their roles were designed to be supportive rather than directive. The team was imagined as a private social space whose boundaries would only be breached at the behest of the team itself, and then only temporarily.

From the first, management anticipated that the Stewartfield workforce would play a pivotal role in the new Pyramid plant scheduled to employ 2,000 within two years of opening. The Stewart-field workers were to act as the bearers of the team-working culture, spearheading the diffusion of behavioural norms in the new plant. In practice, however, the employees socialised into the team culture of Stewartfield played an ambiguous role in extending the principles of teambuilding. Such workers found themselves juggling unfamiliar responsibilities for vetting potential new recruits, training new starts, and ensuring that the team-working culture was not diluted by the flood of new arrivals. The hiring and training roles, coupled with their knowledge of the principles of the teamworking culture, consolidated the informal authority exercised by Stewartfield veterans on the assembly lines. Pyramid expanded from a single production line to fourteen in under two years. Against a background of constantly expanding production targets and chronic material shortages, the teams were forced to improvise, shifting between work stations in an attempt to compensate for successive droughts and surges in components. In this context, the Stewartfield cohort found their first months inside Pyramid immensely stressful. 'In other jobs', one influential woman worker explained, 'you could switch off your mind and just work – not in here. And it doesn't stop when you clock off: your mind's still buzzing with this place hours after you've left' (Interview, line worker, October 1992).

From being the bearers of a managerially sanctioned team ideology, a significant minority of Stewartfield veterans increasingly conceived themselves as guardians of a set of norms which they had played an active role in creating. Paradoxically, the diffusion of the teamworking culture in Pyramid assumed a defensive quality in which workers resented any deviation from the practice of collective decision-making established in Stewartfield. Any team member or manager whose actions crossed the line separating facilitative from directive behaviour was openly criticised. The Stewartfield veterans articulated a vision of the 'factory of the future' in which teamworking always took precedence over production. For one exasperated manager this friction was based on experienced employees 'making the mistake of thinking

PhoneCo is a team-driven organisation. It's not: it's a *business*-driven organisation' (Interview, HR Development Manager, November 1993).

In Stewartfield managers were deeply impressed by the tight discipline maintained by the teams. Indeed, for management the success of self-policing absenteeism, time-keeping, and less tangible 'cultural' indices of teambuilding reaffirmed their belief that flexible volume production was best 'managed through culture, not structure' (Interview, HR Director, May 1992). That a visiting corporate executive was upbraided by a line worker for breaking an elementary safety rule or that an absent worker was confronted by his fellow team-members symbolised the potency of team-based control. In Pyramid, however, the lack of clear factory-wide rules quickly led to wide variations in disciplinary actions in different teams. The fast-changing composition of the teams highlighted differing propensities to take 'corrective actions' against individuals. 'Corrective action' was the generic term for any sanction imposed by a team to improve an individual's performance or as punishment for an infraction of quality, efficiency, or behavioural standards. The Pyramid teams varied widely in their interpretation of the broadly defined behavioural standards laid down by PhoneCo. The 'corrective action' imposed for absenteeism without alerting the team ranged from a mild rebuke at a team meeting to a suspension of overtime for three weeks.

Discipline was rapidly perceived as *ad hoc*, arbitrary, and distorted by personality clashes. A further complication was added by management's decision to hire temporary workers rather than relax their stringent recruitment procedure. The use of temporary workers was always regarded as a temporary expedient – 'a necessary evil' – rather than the creation of a permanent layer of 'peripheral' workers (Interview, Production Manager, May 1993). Temporary workers were excluded from the internal decision-making processes of the teams and restricted to the most de-skilled tasks on the line. Control of temporary workers rested with permanent members of PhoneCo teams. Experienced employees were gate-keepers in the company's recruitment process. After successfully negotiating psychometric and dexterity tests, prospective employees were interviewed by a representative of the team they would join. At this stage, the team delegate could veto the appointment of an applicant. In the case of temporary workers, the teams played an even more important role. Temporary workers could apply to become permanent employees. However, they still had to go through the full selection process, irrespective of their length of service on the line. More than this, to fail any stage of the recruitment process was to have one's contract immediately terminated, with no right to appeal. Temporary workers were, therefore, in an extremely vulnerable position. Divisions emerged over the treatment of temporary workers among the group of Stewartfield veterans. On the one hand stood a minority who enforced extraordinarily tight discipline on temporary workers and gained a reputation for rejecting all but a few applicants for permanent employment. On the other hand, the majority of experienced employees considered such draconian discipline a breach of the teamworking ethos by individuals determined to bring themselves to the attention of management. In these circumstances, the majority of permanent workers became increasingly protective towards temporary workers. For management, the net result was that fewer temporary workers applied for permanent status while the teams became indiscriminate in their support of transfer applications.

The result of this complex process was that the teams gradually withdrew from their disciplinary role. Even where easily remedied flaws in routine tasks caused frustrating disruptions to work flows and the teams maintained the façade of peer review, this did not mean that effective 'corrective actions' were imposed. One line worker explained that the lack of basic discipline was damaging efficiency and corrosive of personal relations within his team: 'You'd just be getting in to the swing of production and – bang! – you'd discover two or three wrong spools [of components had been loaded]. The team would meet and "Willie" would promise not to do it again. But next week it was the same story' (Interview, Line Worker, April 1994). In turn, this compelled shopfloor managers to intervene to enforce discipline. Inevitably, such interventions drew heavy criticism from the teams as yet another sign of the emergence of traditional managerialism. Within the first year of Pyramid's existence, both management and workforce were confronted with the disintegration of the original conception of a team-based organisation.

Team-based work organisation and an empowerment ideology do not eliminate the control imperative from the workplace. Nor do they necessarily smother worker dissent and resistance. Rather, even in this non-union environment, opposition was articulated *through* the empowerment ideology. Equally, the disciplinary purpose of team-based organisation can be deflected, moderated, or completely thwarted by a tacit campaign of non co-operation by the workforce. Even this mildest form of protest posed serious questions for a work regime whose whole rationale was not just to manufacture consent but to sustain the positive commitment of the workforce.

PEER REVIEW AND MUTUAL CONTROL

One confesses – or is forced to confess. When it is not spontaneous or dictated by some internal, the confession is wrung from a person by violence or threat; it is driven from its hiding place in the soul or extracted from the body.

(Foucault 1979: 59)

With testimony, testing and observation, confession has, argues Foucault, become 'one of the West's most highly valued techniques for producing truth' (Foucault 1979: 59). Confession, supplemented by personal confrontation, is the core of peer review, the technique used to reveal and measure individual psychological performance within work teams. 'Peer review is', argue Kenney and Florida (1993: 27–8),

> perhaps the most important element of social control in the Japanese transplants (in the US) because it does not involve a direct confrontation between management and labour. The work teams and peer review committees become the first line of discipline. Team members are expected to counsel workers who miss work or experience other problems, and if problems persist to transmit that information to management . . . teams provide the peer pressure required to keep most workers in line.

In Japanese transplants in the US auto industry, the formal peer review process stands to one side of work teams, and is composed of workers and managers. Peer review committees are formal mechanisms which complement the informal discipline of the teams. More than this, peer review committees are responsible for setting individual pay awards. In PhoneCo, however, peer review is conceptualised as an integral element of team functioning. Management's role was defined as setting the overall vision of team appraisal; as supportive rather than directive with minimal outside intervention. Peer review was to be the cornerstone of the plant's reward system, a method which would effectively displace management both from maintaining routine discipline and annual wage adjustments.

For PhoneCo management, the success of peer review was the key to gauging the embeddedness of the team culture. Peer review had a dual purpose: to provide managerial knowledge *and* to provide a forum for the teams to reflect individually and collectively on the teambuilding process. It is difficult to exaggerate the importance management attributed to understanding the dynamics of team development through constant monitoring of 'the subjective process at work through the Peer Review Process' (PhoneCo Corporate HR Manual, 1994). For management, transparency and universality legitimised peer review:

> assembly workers were simply being put into a 'goldfish bowl' analogous to control processes within PhoneCo's corporate structure.
>
> (Interview, Production Manager, May 1993)

> Visibility is a two-way thing. The engineers who vet my progress today know that I will scrutinise their projects tomorrow. So we all know that we will flip-flop between these roles inside the development network: nobody is permanently in charge of controlling other systems engineers.
>
> (Interview, Systems Engineer, December 1993)

Peer review was conceived as the critical arena of the disciplinary process within the production teams. This involved each team member rating every other member on ten dimensions of in- dividual behaviour and attitudes. These ranged from behaviour which indicated their assimilation of the teamworking culture to assessments of an individual's conscientiousness and readiness to pioneer innovations in work organisation. To 'show a positive attitude' is defined as:

> Talks about and emphasises positive aspects of team goals and performance; positive about team members and the factory; makes constructive suggestions; gives recognition and praise to other team members/teams; has a will to do spirit; willing to give constructive and honest feedback to others.
>
> (Internal Briefing Document, May 1993)

This definition captures a tension at the heart of the peer review process. To 'show a positive attitude' involves not just encouraging other individuals and the team as an entity; rather individuals were asked to assess each other's readiness to encourage *and* criticise. In other words, peer review was conceived as a microscopic disciplinary process which would lay bare individual and collective shortcomings in team development. Indeed, management made a direct link between the effectiveness of peer review as a disciplinary practice and corporate competitiveness.

> The rating placed on anyone's contribution is important. However, what is more important is the prior discussion of the views of the team, the agreement on the ratings, the recognition of effort and the carrying out of corrective actions. These are essential in order to improve performance and ensure we develop to be world class.
>
> (Internal Training Document, June 1993)

Peer review was viewed as neither individual, anonymous nor episodic, but as a collective, transparent and continuous process. Equally, peer review was to be insulated from the demands of production: meetings were not to be contaminated with discussion of output targets. The ideal was to hold monthly meetings at which the relative scores of all permanent team members would be displayed on graphs and subjected to extensive discussion. The monthly meeting was the formal and symbolic expression of the constant and collective nature of discipline within the workgroup. In itself, this open forum at which detailed comparisons of three individuals' performance was the sole topic was the first level of corrective action. Simply exposing weaknesses in individual performance to collective scrutiny was intended to increase the team member's motivation to comply with expected behaviour and norms. The monthly peer review meeting was not only the moment at which internal tensions were to be dispersed and the team ideology reinforced, but also when disciplinary issues were explicitly confronted by the team. This was the opportunity to exercise collective discipline over individuals with, for instance, poor time-keeping records or suspect attitudes towards co-operation.

Peer review was pioneered in microelectronics by Digital and Motorola (Katzenbach and Smith 1993: 187). Even in these corporations, peer review has been introduced in only a few locations and in a highly circumscribed fashion (Hodson and Hagan 1988: 121).

Beyond noting a general – and durable – dissatisfaction with peer review, particularly in terms of annual wage adjustment, no study has yet examined the dynamics of the process in detail (Buchanan and McCalman 1989: 151–3, 165). Successive surveys of the PhoneCo workforce revealed a deep and pervasive distrust of peer review. In our first survey two-thirds of the respondents affirmed that they understood peer review's objectives but at the same time they were critical of it in practice. Fewer than 20 per cent of respondents favoured assessing – or being assessed by – their co-workers. Indeed, the workforce's attitudes were the exact opposite of management's intention: it drained individual and team confidence, was an intimidating experience, created or sharpened tensions in the teams, and, most of all, workers intensely disliked reviewing their team-mates. Broadly speaking, the level of antipathy to peer review was greatest among those with an employment history outside microelectronics and those who had previous membership of a trade union. For all categories, the distrust of peer review hardened over time and the most profound opposition was displayed by the longest-serving employees.

As production pressures intensified, team meetings increasingly concentrated on issuing top-down instructions and exhortation to the virtual exclusion of team development. Physical constraints became more apparent as the workforce expanded. Team meetings grew ever more chaotic as around forty people struggled to hear, far less participate in, the proceedings. Even the formalities of peer review slowly collapsed under the strain. In those teams in which peer review continued it proved an incredibly divisive practice, often embittering personal relationships. Retaliatory scoring – marking down someone who had scored you low in the previous month – was not uncommon. Workers drawn from outside the microelectronics sector were particularly hostile to peer review and quickly learnt to subvert its surveillance objective. These workers developed the practice of tacitly trading monthly scores, negating the discriminatory intent of the system. This practice spread throughout the plant as established teams were broken up to form the basis of new lines: equalised scoring became the norm among all categories of employees. Ironically, the subversion of peer review was justified through an identification with Pyramid's team-based culture. That is, if teams were meeting their output and quality targets, then it was widely considered unfair for any individual team-member to receive a negative peer review. This shift in employee opinion was paralleled by a deterioration in the formal disciplinary processes of the teams. While informal pressures continued to be applied to any recalcitrant team-member, it was rare for individuals to be exposed to the full glare of peer review.

Both responses to peer review undermined its dual purpose of team development and discipline. On the one hand, tit-for-tat scoring was corrosive of team morale while, on the other, tacit trading nullified its disciplinary content. Managerial facilitators were acutely aware that the disciplinary content of peer review was being collectively exorcised by the workgroups but powerless to reverse the trend. One desperate facilitator was openly ridiculed when she suggested that team members should keep private notebooks recording their observations of their colleagues. We must stress the limits to worker opposition to peer review which remained individualised and was expressed *through* the company culture. Hostility to peer review co-existed with widespread endorsement of the principle of teamwork and the rotation of secondary jobs, co-ordinative roles normally performed by front-line management. The only exception to this pattern was from temporary workers who hankered after traditional supervision. This reflects the exclusion of temporary workers from team decision-making and the absence of any clear indicators of the performance required from them if they were successfully to make the transition to permanent PhoneCo employees.

The only moment of collective opposition resulted from Pyramid's first annual pay review. The virtual collapse of peer review had left management with no mechanism to rank workers' performance. Confronted with this vacuum in their knowledge, management were left with little option but to classify the workforce arbitrarily into five bands with each receiving a fixed percentage rise ranging from zero to 8 per cent. The most extreme reaction came on one line which halted work completely for a shift. Throughout the day, workers congregated in small groups and, when asked, told anxious plant managers that they were considering production issues. This silent strike was followed by what the workers involved called a three-week 'go-slow' (Interview, line worker, January 1994).

Everybody's unhappy at the moment because of the bands people have been given. They've marked this line lower than any of the other lines. We've been hammered. I've seen the figures: we almost made our targets last year. People are very pissed off. The other shift went on strike on the Thursday before Christmas. Not one board came off the line. . . . We're on a go-slow at the moment and so is the other shift. There's no way that we are going to hit our targets. We grafted hard last year and we got that slap in the face for all the work we put in. Why should we be motivated? The only shift on this line that isn't on a go-slow is the night shift because they all got A's and B's. We mostly got 'C's and 'D's.

(Interview, Line Worker, January 1994)

That there would be dissatisfaction at a grading exercise which identified only 10 per cent of workers as Band 'A' was entirely predictable. The extent of dissatisfaction, however, was staggering: more than two-thirds of the permanent workforce lodged a complaint about their grading. For the core workers who had been socialised into the PhoneCo culture in Stewartfield – 'the elect' – the grading awards simply confirmed the profound shift away from the original team culture (Geary 1992: 48). On the shopfloor the consensus was that the gradings were arbitrary and reflected the ill-informed judgements of inexperienced Line Leaders rather than the continuous and, above all, transparent appraisal promised through peer review.

The grading process was widely criticised as arbitrary, ill-informed and divisive: the death-knell of the team culture. 'It's about individuals', said one 'A'-graded assembly worker, 'and not the team': 'I think it's worse on Assembly. They are doing the same job more or less. Let's say they are hitting their targets and the quality is good, so they are working well as a team. Why should somebody get a "B" and somebody next to them get a "D"?' (Interview, Line Worker, February 1994).

For management, a prime virtue of the peer review process was its transparency. There would be no surprise gradings: workers would be constantly informed of their colleagues' opinion of their performance and conformance to PhoneCo culture. Line leaders usurped the team's disciplinary purpose and compromised the internal transparency of the team-based reward system. A 'B'-graded assembler satisfied with her award explained that her secondary jobs increased her visibility: 'Take me. I get a "B" because I do secondary jobs and the bosses can see me doing them. That takes me off the line. The girls who replace me got a "D" and an "E". That's not right at all' (Interview, line worker, January 1994).

The link between worker visibility and grading also systematically discriminated against 'back-end' workers who were quite literally invisible to management. Similarly, the vital training roles routinely assumed by Stewartfield veterans kept them on the line, and this was widely perceived as the main reason for their disappointing gradings.

THE LIMITS OF MANAGERIAL POWER/KNOWLEDGE

From the first, there were significant limits to managerial understanding of the processual, team-based control regime being developed in Pyramid. By relying on managers' allegiance to the principles grounded in their personal experience of the Stewartfield experimental plant, PhoneCo risked diluting this attachment when it numerically expanded this group. Indeed, a key member of the founding management team acknowledged that their new appointments, particularly in the technical areas, 'became operational assets but cultural liabilities' (Interview, HR Development Manager, October 1993). Increased production, in other words, was achieved at the expense of teamworking. Nor did a manager's use of the teamworking language necessarily signify personal identification with, or understanding of, its principles:

> It's all about rites of passage and membership. American electronics companies have a very strong sense of culture and corporateness. And there are badges you have to wear and buzz words you have to know the meaning of. . . . It doesn't mean knowledge or understanding, it simply means that you have to know the meaning. That allows you to be a member, to engage in conversation.
>
> (Interview, HR Development Manager, October 1993)

Even before the pay award fiasco, management were acutely aware that peer review had fallen into abeyance, but given the centrality of peer review there was no way that it could simply be scrapped. Rather, management redesigned peer review around a rating process which forced employees to discriminate between their fellow team- members. A major failing of the original system was that management had no knowledge of its collapse under the weight of production pressures or subversion by reciprocal scoring within teams. The depth of opposition to the pay award was a watershed moment, precipitating managerial strategy. Peer reviews became quarterly rather than monthly events, compulsory rather than voluntary, and team scoring was automated to permit management to monitor its implementation and minimise the opportunities for retrospective manipulation of scores. In essence, the new rating system was designed to prevent team-members tacitly trading scores. Each employee has a fixed quota of points to allocate between their team members. The individual's score is multiplied by a factor allocated by management to reflect overall team performance. The manager who designed the new rating system emphasised that the objective was to sharpen the disciplinary dimension of teamworking.

> The changes to the peer review process will force the teams to confront the discipline issue. We're trying to force the issue. People in the past have used the scoring scale as a way out, give everyone four. Now we're going to force distri-bution but not about the norm. We're not interested in normalising the scores. What we're interested in is forcing people to take responsibility. Each team member has only a limited number of points to distribute. In other words, if I give you a four then I have to give someone else a three.
>
> (Interview, HR Director, November 1993)

In contrast to the *ad hoc* nature of the initial peer review process, in the new system the roles of all participants are more tightly specified. Detailed documentation now codifies management's expectations of each person's role in the process and the scope of the actual review meeting. Each individual is to sit silent while the team explains how their behaviour is reflected in their respective scoring: all team members must contribute at this stage. As the instruction manual states, 'the person being reviewed remains silent during this part of the review until each person has taken their turn to give recognition and feedback'. The individual under scrutiny then explains their self-assessment and asks for 'clarification' from any of their scrutineers. The content of the exchanges is noted for future reference. This time the tension at the core of such highly charged exchanges is explicitly recognised: facilitators are warned that they have to tread a fine line between ensuring that the team is judgemental in its scrutiny of the individual and avoiding alienating the team from the process itself.

CONCLUSION

We began by suggesting that the power of HRM techniques to defuse employees' resistance and channel their individual and collective aspirations through corporate agendas had been greatly exaggerated. PhoneCo employees created a variety of methods to subvert the disciplinary intent of innovatory HRM practices. In terms of surveillance, the teams shifted from a tight self-policing *internal* regime to protecting the integrity of the team concept from *external* – managerial – intrusions. The teams' first line of defence against an emerging managerialism was the managerially sanctioned rhetoric of empowerment. When management intervened in team matters, their most potent defence was to make the disciplinary processes inoperable. Furthermore, we argued that there is a danger that insensitive application of Foucauldian concepts of surveillance and discipline risked overstating the reach of panoptic organisation. There is never simply a stark alternative between 'empowerment' and 'emasculation', nor is this categorisation conclusive and irreversible. Empowerment is both an ideological construct and part of the daily experience of the Pyramid workforce. Pyramid employees endorsed key elements of teamworking as an ideology and as practice while decisively rejecting its disciplinary objectives. The nature of teamworking itself becomes a contested issue through workers constantly probing the depth of management commitment to maintaining the integrity of devolved decision-making. If the disciplinary intent had been undermined slowly by the workgroups' refusal to enforce the peer review system, the ideology of the managerless organisation was punctured by the first annual pay evaluation. The visible, sovereign power of management was re-established at this critical juncture. The revamped peer review system was designed not just to sharpen its disciplinary edge but also in an attempt to restore the dispersed, anonymous power of a panoptic factory organisation.

Overstatements of the reach and depth of panoptic organisations are based on an unquestioned assumption that management practices are informed by a coherent body of knowledge, in this case, of teamworking and peer review. But, as Pyramid's managers admit, they are only now constructing mechanisms which will *begin* to provide them with continuous information about the internal dynamics of teamworking. Given the limited conceptual framework underpinning management's vision of 'the factory of the future', developing new forms of power/knowledge from this information flow will be a project requiring analytical skills drawn from outside Pyramid. At this point, corporate priorities regarding production and understanding of the dynamics of teamworking may well conflict. The past record suggests that production will be prioritised over building a comprehensive and continuous understanding of teamworking. There is, then, a constant tension between the imperatives of the market and those of factory managers charged with expanding output volume and extending knowledge of HRM simultaneously.

ACKNOWLEDGEMENTS

We gratefully acknowledge the financial support of the Leverhulme Trust. Our thanks to Paul Smith for his patience and persistence as an editor.

REFERENCES

Amin, A. and Dietrich, M. (1991) 'From Hierarchy to "Hierarchy" – The Dynamics of Contemporary Corporate Restructuring in Europe', in A. Amin and M. Dietrich (eds), *Towards a New Europe? Structural Change in the European Economy*, Aldershot: Edward Elgar.

Barker, J. R. (1993) 'Tightening the Iron Cage: Concertive Control in Self-Managing Teams', *Administrative Science Quarterly* **38**, 2: 408–37.

Bartlett, C. A. and Ghoshal, S. (1989) *Managing Across Borders: The Transnational Solution*, Cambridge, Mass: Harvard Business School Press.

Belohlav, J. (1993) 'Quality, Strategy, and Competitiveness', *California Management Review* **36**, 55–67.

Buchanan, D. and McCalman, J. (1989) *High Performance Work Systems: The Digital Experience*, London: Routledge.

Caruso, R. (1992) *Mentoring and the Business Environment: Asset or Liability?*, Aldershot: Dartmouth.

Cressey, P., Eldridge, J. and MacInness, J. (1985) *Just Managing: Authority and Democracy in Industry*, Milton Keynes: Open University Press.

Dandeker, C. (1990) *Surveillance, Power and Modernity: Bureaucracy and Discipline from 1700 to the Present Day*, Oxford: Polity Press.

Dassbach, C. (1989) *Global Enterprises and the World Economy, Ford, General Motors, and IBM: The Emergence of the Transnational Enterprise*, New York: Garland.

Dawson, P. and Webb, J. (1989) 'New Production Arrangements: The Totally Flexible Cage?', *Work, Employment and Society* **3**, 2: 221–38.

Findlay, P. (1990) 'What Management Strategy? Labour Utilisation and Regulation at Scotland's "Leading Edge"', unpublished D.Phil. thesis, Oxford University.

Findlay, P. (1993) 'Union Recognition and Non-unionism: Shifting Fortunes in the Electronics Industry in Scotland', *Industrial Relations Journal* **24**, 1: 28–43.

Foucault, M. (1977) *Discipline and Punish: The Birth of the Prison*, Harmondsworth: Allen Lane.

Foucault, M. (1979) *The History of Sexuality: Volume 1*, Harmondsworth: Allen Lane.

Foucault, B. (1980) *Power/Knowledge: Selected Interviews and Other Writings 1972–1977*, ed. C. Gordon, Brighton: Harvester.

Garrahan, P. and Stewart, P. (1992) *The Nissan Enigma: Flexibility at Work in a Local Economy*, London: Mansell.

Geary, J. F. (1992) 'Pay, Control and Commitment: Linking Appraisal and Reward', *Human Resource Management Journal* **2**, 4: 36–54.

Goldstein, N. (1992) 'Gender and the Restructuring of High-Tech Multinational Corporations: New Twists to an Old Story', *Cambridge Journal of Economics* **16**, 3: 269–84.

Hodson, R. and Hagan, J. (1988) 'Skills and Job Commitment in High Technology Industries in the US', *New Technology, Work and Employment* **3**, 2: 112–24.

Katzenbach, J. R. and Smith, D. K. (1993) *The Wisdom of Teams: Creating the High Performance Organization*, Cambridge, Mass.: Harvard Business School Press.

Kenney, M. and Florida, R. (1993) *Beyond Mass Production: The Japanese System and its Transfer to the US*, Oxford: Oxford University Press.

Lawler, E. (1986) *High Involvement Management: Participative Strategies for Improving Organizational Performance*, San Francisco: Jossey-Bass Publishers.

Miller, P. and Rose, N. (1990), 'Governing Economic Life', *Economy and Society* **19**, 1: 1–31.

Rose, N. (1990) *Governing the Soul: The Shaping of the Private Self*, London: Routledge.

Scherer, F. M. (1992) *International High-Technology Competition*, Cambridge, Mass.: Harvard University Press.

Sciberras, E. (1977) *Multinational Electronics Companies and National Economic Policies*, Greenwich, Conn.: JAI Press.

Scott, A. (1994) *Willing Slaves? British Workers Under Human Resource Management*, Cambridge: Cambridge University Press.

Sewell, B. and Wilkinson, B. (1992) '"Someone to Watch over Me": Surveillance, Discipline and the Just-In-Time Labour Process', *Sociology* **26**, 2: 271–89.

Townley, B. (1993) 'Performance Appraisal and the Emergence of Management', *Journal of Management Studies* **30**: 221–38.

Webb, J. and Dawson, P. (1991) 'Measure for Measure: Strategic Change in an Electronic Instruments Corporation', *Journal of Management Studies*, **28**, 2: 191–206.

10

INSIDE THE NON-UNION FIRM

Ian McLoughlin

INTRODUCTION

Collective industrial relations in Britain have been in steady decline since the early 1980s. Under one in four employees in the private sector are now union members, the majority of workplaces have no recognised unions present, and there has been a 'dramatic' decline in the proportion of establishments and employees covered by collective bargaining (Millward *et al*. 1992; Brown 1993; Bird and Corcoran 1994). Commentators on these trends have talked of the end of institutional industrial relations and argued that the 'traditional, distinctive "system" of British industrial relations' no longer characterises the economy as a whole (Millward *et al*. 1992: 350). However, compared to our knowledge of declining unionised settings, we know surprisingly little about industrial relations in the growing proportion of non-union workplaces. The aim of this chapter is to look inside the non-union firm and explore the implications for its organisation by trade unions.

What follows will focus on three questions. First, how are industrial relations in non-union settings managed and to what extent do new techniques of Human Resource Management predominate? Second, how do employees in non-union workplaces respond to the managerial regimes under which they work? Is it the case, for example, that these employees have a low propensity to join a union or do they in fact show a propensity to unionise which is frustrated by the absence of a union to join? Third, what are the implications of the findings of the study for trade unions as they seek to broaden their appeal to the non-union employee?

The vehicle for exploring these questions will be the findings from the first major in-depth study in Britain of industrial relations in non-union settings in the 'high technology' sector (see McLoughlin and Gourlay 1994).[1] The chapter is structured as follows. First, the relationship between HRM techniques and non-unionism is explored and a typology for analysing management styles in non-union settings outlined. Second, some of the results of the study concerning management approach and employee responses are presented and discussed. Finally, some of the implications for trade unions are outlined. The conclusion points to some grounds for optimism for trade unions in organising the non-union workplace. However, this is tempered by the very real and considerable difficulties that will have to be faced in attracting non-union employees to membership and in gaining recognition from non-union employers.

HRM AND MANAGEMENT STYLE IN NON-UNION SETTINGS

The decline of trade union organisation has drawn attention to strategies and styles for managing without unions. On the one hand, new and sophisticated techniques of HRM have been highlighted as both a potential challenge to trade union organisation (Storey 1992; Bacon and Storey, Chapter 2) and as a means of managing without unions (Guest 1987, 1989). On the other, large-scale survey evidence has pointed to a lack of sophistication of management style in non-union workplaces. Instead a 'Bleak House' picture of non-union industrial relations has been painted where, in contrast to unionised settings, 'employee voice' is said to be more circumscribed, irregular and informal; pay determination more individualised; and job security significantly weaker (Millward *et al.* 1992; Sisson 1993). What, then, is the analytical link between HRM and non-unionism and what other approaches to managing without unions can be conceptualised?

One distinctive feature of new HRM techniques, it has been claimed, is that they can be defined as a cluster of polices with a high degree of *strategic integration* (Guest 1987, 1989). That is, in contrast to traditional personnel management, HRM is a strategic activity which utilises a framework of highly integrated policy levers to deliver employee commitment beyond contractual obligation to core business values (Storey 1992). Through sophisticated employee resourcing, development, communication and reward policies, work and employment conditions are created which, through a 'substitution effect', effectively reduce employee demands for union services (Guest 1989). Moreover, HRM is founded upon an explicit and tight coupling between strategic intent at corporate level and line management attitudes and behaviour at the workplace.

High levels of strategic integration in management style do not, in themselves, necessarily present a terminal challenge to trade unions. Indeed, in so far as such an approach places an emphasis on the recognition of the value of employees as humans, it might arguably be seen to represent a step towards the very management sophistication that many reformers and observers of British industrial relations have called for since the report of the Donovan Commission in the late 1960s. However, a second key aspect of HRM appears to reject the pluralist and collectivist assumptions that underlie such an analysis. This aspect draws attention to the unitarist and 'individualist' view of the employment relationship that is embedded in HRM theory and its apparent practice, especially in the USA. As Guest has observed, the perspectives and values at the core of HRM apparently 'leave little scope for collective arrangements and assume little need for collective bargaining' and thereby pose 'considerable challenge to traditional industrial relations and more particularly to trade unionism' (Guest 1989: 43).

However, the extent to which HRM is necessarily 'unitarist' has been questioned. Storey, for example, argues that it is perfectly possible that trade unions could be accommodated within an HRM model if a collective relationship which is co-operative rather than adversarial is posited. Indeed, Storey's (1992: 243) extensive research in mainstream British organisations in the private and public sector appears to show that HRM initiatives have developed quite extensively in the context of established and well-organised trade union representation – an approach which he terms 'dualism'. Nevertheless, Storey's qualifications to this observation suggest that the relationship between HRM initiatives and trade unions is far from complementary. Although, in the firms he studied, the adoption of HRM did not involve an 'overt all-out assault' on trade unions, it was also the case that unions did, in most instances, become 'marginalised'.

Nonetheless, such arguments do highlight the need to develop a disaggregated understanding of HRM which takes account of its development in different contexts, sometimes alongside existing highly collectivised employment relations. More generally, and by the same token, it is also necessary to develop a conceptualisation of the management of the non-union employment relationship which allows for the possibility for the collective regulation of certain issues. In other words, non-unionism should not simply be equated either with the practice of 'HRM' or with high levels of individualisation of employer/employee relations to the exclusion of collective regulation.

Indeed, the degree to which individualism and collectivism are in reality mutually exclusive aspects of management style has been a matter of some argument (Marchington and Parker 1990; Purcell and Ahlstrand 1994; Bacon and Storey, Chapter 2). There is not space to explore this debate here (for a discussion see McLoughlin and Gourlay 1994); suffice it to say that the empirical observation that management can pursue both individualistic and collectivist approaches at the same time does not necessarily undermine the analytical usefulness of making such a distinction in the first place. The important point is to seek to locate management styles in terms of the *balance* or *mix* they seek between individualism and collectivism, rather than expect to find in practice the pursuit of one to the exclusion of the other (Storey and Sisson 1993). This is emphasised by Bacon and Storey (1993), who suggest that management may adopt individualist and collectivist approaches in relation to different aspects of the employment relationship depending on whether they are concerned with industrial relations (in its narrow sense), work organisation, or human resourcing (*ibid.*: 6).

By viewing the individualism/collectivism issue in this way it is possible to start to develop a more disaggregated understanding of HRM and its relationship to trade unions. For example, Keenoy (1990: 5) identifies two versions of HRM that suggest contrasting positions in this regard. First, 'traditional HRM', which has as its basic assumption that 'investment in people is good business if not the basis of good business'. Here the values of enterprise founders become institutionalised into a particular management style. According to Keenoy, 'traditional HRM' rests on the 'strategic and *philosophical* assumption that recognising and seeking to meet the needs of people leads to a competitive advantage [italics in the original]' (1990: 5). The assumption is that such investment in human resources will lead to a situation where demands on the part of employees for union services are reduced if not eliminated. If such demands arise, they are a function of managerial failings in meeting employee needs.

A second approach, 'strategic HRM', is viewed by Keenoy as the more novel variant. This begins with the question, 'what HRM strategy will maximise competitive advantage, optimise control, and minimise unit and labour replacement costs?' (1990: 5). 'Strategic HRM' assesses the relevance of union presence in terms of contingent factors such as product and labour market conditions. If an HRM approach without unions provides the best 'fit' with such contingencies, then this is likely to be the preferred approach. Alternatively, if an approach based on collective bargaining – or at least certain forms of bargaining arrangement – provide a better 'fit', then this should prevail (1990: 6). In this way, therefore, strategic HRM may involve a relatively high degree of collectivism *alongside* a more individualised approach – what Storey, as noted above, refers to as 'dualism'.

Rather than a rejection of collectivism *in toto*, therefore, it may be the type of collectivism which is both embodied in the independent representation of employee interests by trade unions *and* which results in *adversarial* employment relations that is called into question by HRM. Where trade union presence is based around more co-operative relationships – 'new style' single union arrangements might be an example here – then HRM and unions may be deemed by management, in certain circumstances, more complementary (see on this Guest, 1995). Moreover, as Legge (1989: 35–6) observes, there is in fact a more general tension in HRM between the management rhetoric of an individualised employment relationship and the use in practice of collective forms of work organisation or problem-solving (e.g. team working, quality circles). This 'new collectivism' (Bacon and Storey, Chapter 2) is designed to achieve individual employee commitment to collective organisational goals.

In non-union settings where the management approach lacks strategic integration similar kinds of arguments apply. For example, the 'Bleak House' image of non-union industrial relations noted above would be most likely where management approach lacked strategic integration and employees were viewed as a commodity rather than as a resource. One would also expect this approach to be characterised by the absence of extensive and formalised personnel policies and to be coupled to strong statements of the managerial prerogative and overt opposition to the trade union organisation of the workforce.

Such a management approach, of course, is often associated with non-union small enterprises. However, recent research in the small business sector indicates that the way employees are managed in such settings is rather more varied and complex (Goss 1991). This suggests we should be cautious in assuming that the management style in medium- to large-sized non-union enterprises, even if unsophisticated in comparison to new HRM techniques, can be simply characterised as an authoritarian assertion of the managerial prerogative. For example, the reliance of many employers in sectors such as high technology on key technical skills amongst the core workforce may mean that what Goss (1991) has termed 'benevolent autocracy' is a more likely management approach. This refers to a style type characteristic of situations where the employer's position of power is clearly established in relation to employees but, by virtue of their skills or competencies, workers are not entirely dependent upon the employer and can exert a degree of labour-market independence. As a result, management may seek to foster a close identification between the employee and the enterprise reflecting the need to retain highly skilled and valued human resources.

Finally, where management approach lacks strategic integration it is also possible that a more collective approach to the regulation of the employment relationship will exist. While one might expect this approach normally to be associated with the presence of trade unions and collective bargaining, there are circumstances when this might not be the case. For example, management might seek to manage *without* unions but still regulate the employment relationship through largely collective means. This may include, e.g., the provision of elected staff councils for the purposes of information disclosure, communication and consultation. Similarly, pay determination may take place on the basis of company, local labour market or industry rates set outside the establishment or enterprise by reference to collective agreements to which the establishment/enterprise itself is not party. Such 'shadow bargaining' has, for instance, been observed in non-union settings in the USA (see Kochan *et al.* 1986). Alternatively, in settings where firms have previously had a history of union recognition, trappings of a collective approach may still remain – not just in institutional form but also in the mind-sets of managers (Dunn 1993). Whatever the precise arrangements, this approach is one that seeks to follow agendas set elsewhere or simply to pursue short-term advantages. For this reason, non-union management style types of this variety can be regarded as *ad hoc*, reactive and opportunistic in character.

We can pull the threads of this discussion together by suggesting the following typology of management styles in non-union settings based on the two dimensions of *strategic integration* and *individualism/collectivism*. This yields four 'ideal-type' management styles (see Figure 10.1).[2] New HRM techniques would obviously be those which lie towards the 'high' end of the strategic integration dimension. Where the regulation of the employment relationship is highly individualised, this is likely to be associated with non-union status. This style type would therefore correspond to what was referred to above as 'traditional HRM'. Where overall business strategy involves a more contingent stance on the extent of individual and collective regulation, this would correspond more to what was termed above 'strategic HRM'.

In this case a mix of both union and non-union elements might be anticipated. Approaches which lack strategic integration and are highly individualised would be suggestive of an unsophisticated management style where individual employees are regarded as commodities rather than 'human resources'. This would be consistent with the 'Bleak House' picture of non-unionism, although as

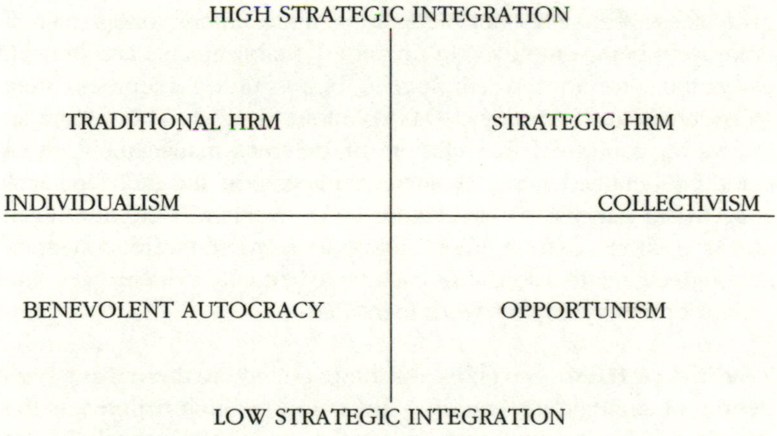

HIGH STRATEGIC INTEGRATION

TRADITIONAL HRM	STRATEGIC HRM
INDIVIDUALISM	COLLECTIVISM
BENEVOLENT AUTOCRACY	OPPORTUNISM

LOW STRATEGIC INTEGRATION

Figure 10.1 A typology of management styles

noted this may be highly qualified in certain circumstances by more benevolent management styles which recognise employer dependence on employees with a degree of labour market power. Finally, where significant elements of collective regulation of the employment relationship remain, this may point to the close organisational, geographical or historical proximity of non-unionism to unionised employment relations, and a reactive and opportunistic stance on the part of management.

NON-UNIONISM AND MANAGEMENT STYLE IN THE HIGH TECHNOLOGY SECTOR

The nature of non-union industrial relations in the high technology sector was explored using data from four main sources.[3] First, a postal questionnaire survey of 115 establishments with over 100 employees drawn from the 'high technology' sector in the South-East region, excluding Greater London. Second, a follow-up interview survey of personnel managers or persons responsible for personnel matters at thirty locations representative of and drawn mainly from the original postal survey sample. Third, detailed case studies of management policies and practices in three firms (a US-owned computer company and a UK-owned consumer electronics firm drawn from the main sample, and a US-owned engineering design contractor – see Table 10.1). Finally, surveys of four contrasting workforces were conducted in these three case study firms.

The postal survey revealed a high level of non-unionism, 80 per cent of establishments not recognising trade unions, under half of employees being employed in unionised establishments and only an estimated one in ten employees being union members (see McLoughlin and Gourlay 1994 for more details). The follow-up interviews confirmed that clusters of different management styles could be identified along the strategic integration and individualism/ collectivism dimensions (see Figure 10.1).[4] Neither 'HRM' nor 'Bleak House' notions of non-union industrial relations were dominant, although elements resonant of each were certainly evident.

Four broad style types were identified:

Traditional HRM (seven establishments), where there was a high degree of strategic integration – illustrated by such features as the presence of a personnel director for the enterprise as a whole, the existence of formal statements of employment philosophy and

Table 10.1 The case study firms

Company	Engineering design contractor	Consumer electronics company	Computer company
Ownership	US	UK	US
UK employees	2,500	400[*]	2,400
World employees	5,200	–	30,000
Date founded in UK	1,959	1984[†]	1,978

[*]One of our main UK divisions of the UK holding company. A further 3,000 were employed by the other divisions
[†]Formed as a result of a management buy-out in 1984. Previously the company had been part of a major UK consumer electronics group

early personnel management involvement in change programmes – and the regulation of the employment relationship was largely individualised. All these establishments, for example, were non-union and part of larger non-union firms.

Strategic HRM (four establishments), where there were high levels of strategic integration but a greater mix of collective with individual regulation. For example, all four establishments had recognised trade unions for significant elements of the workforce, although in all cases this had been under review in the light of changing business circumstances. In two instances this meant a move towards individualising aspects of the employment relationship, leading in one case to a partial de-recognition of trade unions.

Benevolent autocracy (nine establishments), in this and the following style type the level of strategic integration was relatively low. For example, personnel specialists were conspicuous by their absence or marginal status, personnel policies were fragmented and lacked formalisation, and line management tended to play the dominant role, although not in a manner defined by strategic considerations. In fact, most of the establishments in the study in this category faced highly competitive labour market conditions and the absence of unions was usually explained by management as simply a function of the fact that it was an issue that had never been raised by employees.

Opportunists (ten establishments), in these cases personnel policies and practices were again fragmented and sometimes lacked formalisation. However, unlike the 'benevolent autocrat' approach, the regulation of employment relations usually involved a higher level of collectivisation. In fact, in three cases unions were recognised, at least for one category of employee; in three more, unions had been de-recognised during the 1980s but a predominantly collective approach retained; and, in four others, unions had always been absent from the establishment, although in some instances present in the company of which the establishment was a part.

In their various ways the management styles in all these cases tended to be reactive and opportunistic responses to circumstances, e.g. by exploiting labour market weakness in the cases of de-recognition.

Management styles were explored in more depth through the three case studies of non-union firms. In fact, none of these three firms could be said to have a well-developed HRM approach of either a 'traditional' or 'strategic' type. Instead the cases turned out to provide examples of 'benevolent autocracy' (computer company and design engineering contractor) and 'opportunism' (consumer electronics company).

In the case of the design engineer and consumer electronics company, for example, personnel policies were relatively formalised but the personnel function operated in a purely administrative role. However, in the computer company, only rudimentary personnel policies were evident and personnel matters were dealt with by an administration manager in the finance function. In all three firms, it was line management who played the key role in shaping personnel practice but, in the absence of integrated and consistent personnel policies, the approach tended towards what Brewster and Larson refer to as a 'wild west' model, where 'every manager is free to develop his or her own style of relationship with employees' (1992: 414–15). The most extreme case was the computer company, where departmental heads had developed and followed their own remuneration and performance appraisal policies with no attempt to ensure consistency of approach. Notably, there was also considerable opposition amongst departmental heads to a proposal to recruit a personnel specialist. This, it was feared, would result in unacceptable constraints on line management discretion.[5] The management styles of both the computer company and the contract design engineer placed a great stress on the individual nature of the employment relationship and the mutual benefits of dealing with employees on a 'one-to-one' basis. In both companies, while the managerial prerogative was paramount, it was also clearly recognised that the nature of the product and labour market made them highly dependent on recruiting and retaining highly skilled and motivated staff whose services were much in demand by competitors. Thus, the management of employees exhibited many 'benevolent' trappings, manifested, for example, in a collegiate and informal working atmosphere, a stress on 'being a member of the team', and a relatively high degree of autonomy and trust.[6] In such a context, the issue of trade union organisation did not appear to be a salient one as far as management were concerned.

The consumer electronics company was rather different in so far as, unlike the other two firms, it had a previous history of union recognition. The company had been owned by a major UK electronics group but had been the subject of a management buy-out in 1984. At its peak, the firm had employed over 1,000 employees, the vast majority of whom, by the time of the buy-out, had been made redundant. At this point the owners of the new company decided to de-recognise the existing trade unions. This decision appeared to be an opportunistic one, made on the back of the belief that the unions had done little to save employees' jobs and that management could, in the wake of the buy-out, present themselves as more effective custodians of employee interests.

Significantly, however, most of the trappings of a collective approach to managing the employment relationship were retained. For example, in place of the trade unions management instituted a staff committee with elected representatives from both manual and office grades. Senior management interviewees claimed that derecognition had been a success and that the company had no 'in principle' opposition to trade unions. The workforce, it was asserted, now simply saw no need for trade union representation (a view not supported by our survey results). It is worth noting that no concerted attempt to reorganise the plant had been made. Indeed, management reported a half-hearted demand for recognition from the EETPU (now part of the AEEU), who asserted that they had 'sufficient members' at the plant to warrant recognition (this claim was not supported by our survey either).

However, numerous events did point towards an emergent collectivisation of this young and predominantly female workforce. For example, a number of grievances had emerged and, on management's own admission, the loyalty that employees once felt to the company for saving their jobs was being diluted as the company expanded. In one notable incident, a few months prior to the start of fieldwork, the first short stoppage of work by shop-floor employees since de-recognition had taken place in a protest over working conditions. Staff committee representatives noted that after this management had adopted a more conciliatory line. In particular, the committee had been more actively consulted over changes to a bonus scheme, as a result of which the representatives felt that they had exercised a not insignificant influence over the outcomes. At the same time, some managers appeared more ready to admit, albeit with reservations, that renewed demands for union representation could be a possibility in the long term.

EMPLOYEE PROPENSITY TO UNIONISE

The propensity of employees to unionise in the three case study firms was explored through the four workforce surveys. These ranged from technicians (engineering design contractor), manual assembly workers (consumer electronics), office staff (consumer electronics) and technicians and computer professionals (computer company).[7] The surveys revealed a low level of union membership in each of the three firms. Overall, out of a sample of 215 respondents, only 30 per cent had ever been union members, and only 5 per cent were currently union members (see Table 10.2).

Why did the employees in these three non-union settings not join unions? As indicated above, an explanation consistent with the 'HRM' thesis would be that their levels of satisfaction with the content of and rewards from their employment were such that they had no perceived need for union services. At the same time, the individualisation of their attitudes would be such that they might even have ideological objections to trade unions. However, as we have seen, none of the three case study firms were exponents of HRM-type policies and practices, so one would expect such 'union substitution' effects on employee propensity to join a union in these cases to be slight. An alternative explanation could be that

Table 10.2 Union membership and propensity to join a union

	Design company %	Consumer electronics Manual %	Computer company Non-manual %	%	ALL %
Current union member	0	4	3	2	5
Previously union member	25	25	41	29	30
No propensity to join a union	62	26	69	58	50
A propensity to join a union	35	68	31	38	46

non-membership of unions was a product of structural features of the work situation which resulted in a lack of a union to join (Gallie 1989; Hartley 1992). In other words, employees had a high propensity to join unions, but this was frustrated by an anti-union employer or, as likely perhaps in these cases, the absence of meaningful union recruitment activity.

In order to test these propositions a slightly modified version of Kochan's (1980) model of the 'critical determinants' of individual motivations to join a union was used to analyse propensity to unionise amongst the four workforces. Briefly, this model posits that if an individual experiences *dissatisfaction* with economic aspects of the job (i.e. bread-and-butter issues such as wages, benefits, working conditions or the process of pay determination itself), this can act as a 'trigger' to union-joining behaviour. This may be reinforced where the individual's desire for participation or influence on the job is frustrated, that is where there is a *negative view of the utility of management-provided 'voice mechanisms'* as a means of resolving grievances. In these circumstances, if the individual has *positive instrumental beliefs* about a union's ability to have an effect on pay and conditions over and above that which they might achieve as an individual, then a high propensity to join a union is likely. Conversely, where an individual's satisfaction is high, they have a *positive view of the utility of 'voice mechanisms'* and hold *negative instrumental beliefs* about unions, then the propensity to unionise is likely to be low. The assumptions made by the model are therefore broadly consistent with those which are deemed to underlie the 'union substitution' effect of HRM.

At first sight the findings of the workforce surveys appeared to support the Kochan model. For example, a high propensity to join a union was found in the manual workforce at the consumer electronics company. This was associated with low levels of job satisfaction, a low perceived utility of management voice mechanisms (including the staff committee), and a high instrumental support for union as opposed to individual pay determination. Similarly, a low propensity to join a union was evident amongst the employee samples from the engineering design contractor and the computer company. In both cases, as the Kochan model predicts, this was associated with high levels of job satisfaction, a high perceived utility of management voice mechanisms, and a negative instrumental view of union involvement in negotiating their pay.

However, in the case of the staff sample at the consumer electronics company, a low propensity to join a union was associated with a low (*not* high) level of job satisfaction – in other words, dissatisfaction with the job did not seem to 'trigger' union-joining behaviour. This might have been explained by the fact that this group *did* tend to see the management voice mechanism in a positive light: in other words, they felt job-related grievances could be resolved by complaining to management. This would be consistent with the Kochan model. However, like the manual workforce, they viewed the utility of the staff committee – the core of management's consultative and communication policy – negatively, suggesting that their job-related grievances were not perceived as being dealt with adequately. Finally, this group had a strong negative instrumental view of unions. Thus, the office workers in the consumer electronics firm appeared to view 'putting-up' with job dissatisfaction or even quitting as preferable to joining a union.

However, further light was thrown on our findings through a log-linear analysis which allowed us to assess the relative contribution of the three independent variables – job satisfaction, utility of voice and instrumental beliefs – on the dependent variable *propensity to join a union* (see McLoughlin and Gourlay 1994 for further details). In brief, the results of this analysis revealed that *instrumental beliefs* about unions had by far the strongest effect and that the influence of other variables, including organisational identification and commitment, on propensity to unionise was far weaker, if not negligible.

In sum, on the basis of these findings it appeared that, in the case of the consumer electronics manual workforce, the lack of union availability was the key reason for non-union membership. If a union was to become available, the majority of these employees would, on the basis of the survey, apparently join. In the case of the other three workforces, it appeared that union availability would make no difference to the majority who held negative instrumental views of unions. Nevertheless, it should be noted that at least 30 per cent of the design contractor technicians, consumer electronics non-manuals and computer company professionals exhibited a propensity to join a union, at least in the sense that their reasons for non-membership were not based on principled opposition. The key point, however, is that the low propensity to join a union amongst these workforces did not appear to be an attitudinal outcome of the practice of new HRM techniques. Of course, given our earlier observations regarding management style in the three case study firms, this should not come as any surprise.

IMPLICATIONS FOR TRADE UNIONS

The 'Bleak House' image of non-unionism could be taken to suggest that unions might have considerable grounds for optimism in recruiting in non-union firms in the mid-1990s and beyond. Compared to their unionised counterparts, for example, employees in non-union workplaces are more likely to be subject to arbitrary managerial authority, have low pay, less job security and, apart perhaps from quitting, no means to air their grievances. However, expanding their membership base beyond existing well-organised areas may be a more complex task than such a reading of the non-union sector would suggest. For example, Willman *et al.* (1993) have argued that unions operate in an employer as well as an employee market place. For employees, unions supply a range of collective (e.g. pay bargaining), semi-collective (e.g. grievance representation) and individual services (e.g. traditional 'friendly society' benefits and newer financial and legal services). For the employer, unions potentially offer a reliable 'voice' mechanism and assistance in the process of skill formation. A key objective for trade unions, therefore, is not only to package their services in a manner attractive to potential employee recruits, but also to convince employers to grant recognition, which will enable them to deliver the full range of union services to their members.

The findings from the study have some bearing on these issues. For example, unions with ambitions to expand their membership base into hitherto relatively weakly organised employee markets, such as found here in the high technology sector, might view the findings reported above with some optimism. First, it was found in the case of one of the surveyed workforces – the consumer electronics manuals, which comprised mainly young females – that a collective recognition of interests opposed to those of management was emerging, evidenced by a high propensity to join a union. Second, even in the other three workforces, whose technical and professional composition might have been expected to underpin a low propensity to unionise, it was found that at least three out of ten employees showed a propensity to join a union. Overall, taking all four workforces together, nearly half of the surveyed employees indicated a propensity to join a union. Third, the findings also suggested that HRM strategies were not dominant in 'high tech' non-union firms, contrary to what has often been claimed, and that low levels of union membership were not explained by a 'union substitution' effect.

Against this, however, must be put the view that whilst the absence of a union to join might have explained the low level of union membership in a significant proportion of cases, it was the case for the majority of employees that union availability was not a decisive consideration. That is, as far as the findings of the study were concerned, many employees appeared to enjoy sufficient advantage from their employment, not only from remuneration, but also the satisfaction that they gained from the content of their jobs, to make judgements that they 'did not need' a union appear genuine. In short, an available union to join would have apparently made no difference since these employees would see no instrumental advantage in membership, while a small proportion would harbour ideological objections to joining anyway.

In circumstances such as these, and even where employees did exhibit a propensity to unionise, it is arguable that for recruitment to be successful, union membership would have to be 'sold' to potential members as something more than a collective defence against the actual or potential experience of an unscrupulous employer, uncompetitive pay, poor working conditions or job loss.[8] In other words, far more emphasis would have to be placed on the 'marketing' of a wider range of individual services, such as financial, legal and support services – in other words, the 'AA of the workplace' role for trade unions which Tony Blair recently endorsed (Mason and Bain 1991; Basset and Cave 1993; Cave 1994; Blair 1994). However, the problem, as Kessler and Bayliss (1992: 270) observe, is that 'British trade unions are not used to recruiting members by the same methods as the Automobile Association.' Neither, it might be added, is there any consensus amongst the unions that they should do so.

To turn to the employer market, clearly, gaining new members in hitherto weakly organised sectors is but the first step for trade unions. They are also eventually faced with the task of winning recognition from employers. Again, the findings give some ground for optimism. As already noted, the evidence suggests that, even in a sector such as 'high tech', non-union employers do not appear to have found a universally applicable solution to the problem of managing without unions. This does not mean that non-union employers are about to invite union recognition as a potential source of resolving their industrial relations difficulties. However, it does suggest that many of the situations in which employers seek to sustain or move to non-union status may hold some hope for unions. This is because employers may seek to remain, or become, 'free' of unions for opportunistic and pragmatic reasons, possibly with a misguided perception of what managing a workforce without unions might entail as the firm matures and the workforce expands. For such employers – and the consumer electronics company discussed above could be regarded as indicative – managing without unions could conceivably turn out to be perceived as more trouble than managing with them.

Against this possibility, however, is the observation that a reluctance to see the worth of trade union presence may be particularly entrenched amongst some managements in high technology firms. In such cases demand for union services by employees might be seen as an indication of managerial 'failure' and/or as antithetical to managers' own ideological predispositions. Thus, at best, unions might well find themselves restricted in many instances to just 'marketing' individual membership services, which are not dependent upon employer recognition of the union, and without any realistic prospect of such recognition ever being forthcoming. This has a major inbuilt disadvantage for unions since the financial implications of such a recruitment strategy are profound as the *per capita* cost of the individual and semi-collective servicing of members is high relative to offering recognition-dependent collective services which also deliver a reliable flow of subscription income (Willman *et al*. 1993). The likely response would be a rise in individual subscriptions which might render union membership uncompetitive in the eyes of potential recruits – in relation to other sources of individual financial services or in relation to the 'no up-front cost' option of dealing on a one-to-one basis with the employer.

The findings of the employee surveys also point to an additional consideration for unions with ambitions to expand their membership base into relatively unorganised areas. An approach advocated by the TUC in the past has been to launch 'blanket' recruitment campaigns in geographically defined labour markets (TUC 1988, 1989, 1993). However, it could be suggested that this runs the risk of being rather 'hit and miss' unless the labour market intelligence upon which it is based is highly detailed and specific. It also assumes that non-union status is largely a function of structural factors constraining union availability (TUC 1993).

One consequence may be that a relatively large amount of resources, which might have been better utilised in a more focused campaign, are necessarily committed to organise employees, many of whom may have a low rather than high propensity to unionise. For example, assuming the three case study enterprises were located in a local labour market targeted for recruitment efforts, the manual employees at consumer electronics might have been highly receptive to the message of such an initiative, while the majority of the non-manuals and the employees at the design contractor and the computer company would have largely been hostile. A blanket recruitment campaign, however, would assume that the reasons for non-union membership in each case are structural ones constraining union availability. Of course, this begs the question of how unions are to identify non-union locations and work-forces where employees do have a high propensity to unionise. Nevertheless, it does indicate the dangers of seeking to explain non-unionism entirely in terms of structural factors without reference to variations in employee propensity to join unions irrespective of union availability.

All of this points to the likely difficulties for trade unions in both identifying and attracting new members in circumstances where a higher priority and far more resources are likely to be required to sustain successful recruitment campaigns than in the past. If the four workforces in this study are anything to go by, even given a potentially attractive and appropriately targeted package of membership services – and of course a more favourable economic climate and legal framework – unions will still need to research their membership 'markets' carefully in order to make sure that recruitment resources are not wasted on 'lost causes'.

CONCLUSION

The findings discussed in this chapter add to a more general picture which suggests that non-unionism in the high technology sector is not fully explained by the widespread use of new HRM techniques. While examples of 'traditional' and 'strategic' HRM were evident, other management styles of a non-HRM type were also common. Further, it was not the case, at least in the case study firms, that low employee demands for union services was a direct result of a 'union substitution' effect. Finally, although a rare occurrence, union de-recognition appeared to be driven by management opportunism rather than strategic thinking. However, while these conclusions do not endorse the image of the high technology sector as a 'no go' area for unions, neither do they give unqualified support for the more optimistic view that the impediments to union organisation are largely structural ones to do with union availability. The basis for arguing this lies not so much in the nature of management styles in non-union settings as in employees' instrumental attitudes towards union membership. If these findings are anything to go by, trade unions with organising ambitions in this area will find 'selling' the benefits of union membership to many of these non-union employees a major challenge, especially as employers will be particularly resistant in most cases to granting recognition.

NOTES

1 This study was funded by the National Advisory Board and the Economic and Social Research Council. I am grateful to the editors of this volume and participants in seminars in the Faculty of Social Sciences at Brunel University and the London School of Economics for their comments and views on earlier drafts of this chapter.

2 In the light of our earlier discussion, it should be emphasised that the polarities of the *individualism/collectivism* dimension are meant to be analytically, not necessarily empirically, distinct. The placing of the 'strategic HRM' approach in a collectivist segment is not meant to indicate that individualised approaches to particular issues in the employment relationship, or towards some segments of the workforce more generally, are necessarily absent in practice; rather that, on balance, a collectivist approach is the more prominent. It should also be remembered that, since a strategic HRM approach is likely to involve adjustments in policy and practice in response to perceived changes in contingent circumstances, then significant alterations in the mix between collective and individual regulation (e.g. through the introduction of more individualised pay determination or even de-recognition for all, or more likely, some categories of employee) may be particularly apparent, e.g. as manifested in the 'dualistic' approach identified by Storey.

3 The reasons for this particular sectoral and geographical focus were as follows. First, the sector and the region have both been associated in some, although not in all, previous studies with disproportionately low levels of union membership density, recognition and collective bargaining coverage (Beaumont and Harris 1988; Sproull and MacInnes 1989; Findlay 1993). Second, HRM techniques designed as an explicit alternative to managing with unions are frequently associated with firms (especially North American multi-nationals) operating in this sector, along with a more general resistance to union organisation (Basset 1986; Beaumont 1986; Morgan and Sayer 1988). Third, the sector at the time was one of employment growth and, in the South-East, had been targeted with little success as a focus for trade union recruitment efforts (McLoughlin 1984). The definition of 'high technology' used was based on the official definition given in Butchart (1987).

4 A total of 115 usable returns were received giving an effective response rate of 23 per cent for the postal survey. In total these establishments employed 30,553 employees and the firms of which they were a part, 150,438 employees. In order to classify the management approaches in the thirty follow-up interview survey establishments drawn from the initial sample, data were drawn from the original postal questionnaire and a short questionnaire on human resource policies and practices completed at or near the time of the follow-up interviews. This information was used to place management approaches on our strategic integration and individualism/collectivism dimension based on the presence or absence of particular policies or practices. The classification was subsequently corroborated and adjusted with reference to qualitative data derived from our semi-structured interviews at the establishment and through reference to company documents, such as mission statements, employee handbooks and the like, provided at the time of the follow-up interview. For further details see McLoughlin and Gourlay (1994).

5 Much of this antagonism was based on the perceived role of the human resources function in the US parent company. Indeed, the function and all its works were viewed with considerable suspicion

and cynicism by senior line management in the UK. This view, it was claimed, was shared by their counterparts in the USA, even at the highest level. The UK Managing Director – who did not share such views – recounted his experience on asking the Vice-President of the US parent what he thought of the role of the function. The Vice-President replied with some candour, 'Well, if you ask me they're all a bunch of fucking social workers!'

6 At the engineering design contractor, for example, an illustration of a 'benevolent' management style was provided by the case of one employee who had been told to cancel a family holiday in order to help meet a contract deadline. Subsequently he enjoyed a family vacation at Disneyland in the USA paid for by the company. More commonly, it was said that project managers frequently sent flowers to the spouses of members of their team as compensation for the regular absence of their partners!

7 The employee survey samples contrasted in a number of respects. At the engineering design contractor the sample was predominantly qualified to technician level, just over 40 per cent were aged over 40, and all were male. At the consumer electronics company surveys were conducted of the manual workforce and of office workers, including some technical personnel. Over half of the former had no formal educational qualifications and nearly 65 per cent were under 30 years of age and 80 per cent were female. The majority of the consumer electronics office sample had 'O' level or technician qualifications and were aged between 20 and 39, and slightly more were male than female. In the case of the computer company over 65 per cent of the sample were 'professionally' qualified to first degree or above (14 per cent had higher degrees), the vast majority were aged between 20 and 39, and nearly 90 per cent were male.

8 A possible counter to this view is provided by a recent survey of over 1,000 new members of twelve different trade unions (Whitston and Waddington 1994). The survey revealed that the principal reasons for joining a union remained traditional 'collective-solidaristic' rather than 'individualistic'. Moreover, professional and managerial employees – a key category in many high tech settings – were the most likely to cite 'belief in unions' as the reason for joining. However, it is not particularly surprising that those with strong ideological beliefs would be well represented amongst managers and professionals who had chosen to join unions in recent years. It is also noteworthy that it was also this group who most frequently cited financial services amongst the two principal reasons for joining. It is a moot point whether the latter motivation might be the more salient for those who remain non-union members than the former.

REFERENCES

Bacon, N. and Storey, J. (1993) 'Individualisation of the Employment Relationship and the Implications for Trade Unions', *Employee Relations* **15**, 1: 5–17.

Basset, P. (1986) *Strike Free: New Industrial Relations in Britain*, London: Macmillan.

Basset, P. and Cave, A. (1993) 'All for One: The Future of the Unions', *Fabian Society Pamphlet*, No. 559, London: Fabian Society.

Beaumont, P. B. (1986) 'Industrial Relations Policies in High Tech Firms', *New Technology, Work and Employment* 1, 2: 152–9.

Beaumont, P. B. and Harris, R. I. D. (1988) 'High Technology Industries and Non-union Establishments in Britain', *Relations Industrielles* 43, 4: 829–46.

Beaumont, P. B. and Harris, R. I. D. (1989) 'The North-South Divide in Britain: The Case of Trade Union Recognition', *Oxford Bulletin of Economics and Statistics* 51, 4: 413–28.

Blair, T. (1994) 'No Favours. Unions '94: Campaigning for the Future, Special Supplement', *New Statesman and Society*, 18 November: 33–4.

Bird, D. and Corcoran, L. (1994) 'Trade Union Membership and Density in 1994', *Employment Gazette*, June: 189–96.

Brewster, C. and Larson, H. (1992) 'Human Resource Management in Europe: Evidence from Ten Countries', *International Journal of Human Resource Management* 3, 3, December: 409–34.

Brown, W. (1993) 'The Contraction of Collective Bargaining in Britain', *British Journal of Industrial Relations* 3, 2: 189–200.

Butchart, R. L. (1987) 'A New Definition of the High Technology Industries', *Economic Trends* No. 400, February: 82–8.

Cave, A. (1994) *Managing Change in the Workplace: New Approaches to Employee Relations*, London: Coopers & Lybrand/Kogan Page.

Dunn, S. (1993) 'From Donovan to . . . Wherever', *British Journal of Industrial Relations* 31, 2: 169–87.

Findlay, P. (1993) 'Union Recognition and Non-unionism: Shifting Fortunes in the Electronics Industry in Scotland', *Industrial Relations Journal* 24, 1: 28–43.

Gallie, D. (1989) 'Trade Union Allegiance and Decline in British Urban Labour Markets', ESRC Social Change and Economic Life Initiative Working Paper 9, Oxford: Nuffield College.

Goss, D. (1991) *Small Business and Society*, London: Routledge.

Guest, D. (1987) 'Human Resource Management and Industrial Relations', *Journal of Management Studies* 24, 5: 503–21.

Guest, D. (1989) 'Human Resource Management: Its Implications for Industrial Relations and Trade Unions', in J. Storey (ed.), *New Perspectives on Human Resource Management*, London: Routledge.

Guest, D. (1995) 'Human Resource Management, Trade Unions and Industrial Relations', in J. Storey (ed.), *Human Resource Management: A Critical Text*, London: Routledge.

Hartley, J. F. (1992) 'Trade Union Membership and Joining', in J. F. Hartley and G. M. Stephenson (eds), *Employment Relations: The Psychology of Influence and the Control of Work*, Oxford: Blackwell.

Keenoy, T. (1990) 'HRM: A Case of the Wolf in Sheep's Clothing?', *Personnel Review*, 19, 2: 3–9.

Kessler, S. and Bayliss, F. (1992) *Contemporary British Industrial Relations*, London: Macmillan.

Kochan, T. A. (1980) *Collective Bargaining and Industrial Relations*, Homewood Ill.: Richard D. Irwin.

Kochan, T. A., Katz, H. C. and McKersie, R. B. (1986) *The Transformation of American Industrial Relations*, New York: Basic Books.

Legge, K. (1989) 'Human Resource Management: A Critical Analysis', in J. Storey (ed.), *New Perspectives on Human Resource Management*, London: Routledge.

McLoughlin, I. P. (1984) 'Engineering *Their* Future: Recent Changes in the Organisation of British Professional Engineers', *Industrial Relations Journal* **15**, 4: 64–73.

McLoughlin, I. P. and Gourlay, S. N. (1994) *Enterprise Without Unions: Industrial Relations in the Non-Union Firm*, Buckingham: Open University Press.

Marchington, M. and Parker, P. (1990) *Changing Patterns of Employee Relations*, London: Harvester Wheatsheaf.

Mason, B., and Bain, P. (1991) 'Trade Union Recruitment Strategies: Facing the 1990s', *Industrial Relations Journal* **22**, 1: 36–45.

Millward, N., Stevens, M., Smart, D. and Hawes, W. R. (1992) *Workplace Industrial Relations in Transition*, Aldershot: Dartmouth Press.

Morgan, K. and Sayer, A. (1988) *Microcircuits of Capital: 'Sunrise' Industries and Economic Development*, Cambridge: Polity Press.

Purcell, J. (1987) 'Mapping Management Styles in Employee Relations', *Journal of Management Studies* **23**, 2: 205–23.

Purcell, J. and Ahlstrand, B. (1994) *Human Resource Management in the Multi-divisional Company*, Oxford: Oxford University Press.

Purcell, J. and Sisson, K. (1983) 'Strategies and Practice in the Management of Industrial Relations', in G. S. Bain (ed.), *Industrial Relations in Britain*, Oxford: Blackwell.

Sisson, K. (1993) 'In Search of HRM', *British Journal of Industrial Relations* **31**, 2: 201–10.

Sproull, A. and MacInnes, J. (1989) 'Union Recognition, Single Union Agreements and Employment Change in Scottish Electronics', *Industrial Relations Journal* **20**, 1: 33–46.

Storey, J. (1992) *Developments in the Management of Human Resources*, Oxford: Blackwell.

Storey, J. and Sisson, K. (1993) *Managing Human Resources and Industrial Relations*, Buckingham: Open University Press.

TUC (1988) *Meeting the Challenge*, First Report of the Special Review Body, London: Trades Union Congress.

TUC (1989) *Organising for the 1990s*, Second Report of the Special Review Body, London: Trades Union Congress.

TUC (1993) Minutes of Evidence to the Employment Committee hearing on 'The Future of Trade Unions', London: HMSO.

Whitston, C. and Waddington, J. (1994) 'Why Join a Union?', *New Statesman and Society*, 18 November: 36–8.

Willman, P., Morris, T. and Aston, B. (1993) *Union Business: Trade Union Organisation and Financial Reform in the Thatcher Years*, Cambridge: Cambridge University Press.

INDEX

ACAS 56, 88, 90
adversarial trade unionism 8, 77, 79, 81, 305: *see also* militant unionism
advice provided by trade unions 56–9, 315, 317
AEEU 10, 66, 179, 211, 218–20, 225, 226
AEU 21, 61, 63, 67, 86, 96, 101
agreements: interpretation of as grievance 169, 170, 171, 172, 174
annualised hours 15, 51
appraisals 54, 112, 117, 123, 153, 156, 157, 161, 162–4, 223, 233
apprenticeships 1
arbitration agreements 11, 77, 86
Asda 14
Association of Professional Ambulance Personnel 85
Association of University and College Lecturers 93
Australia 4, 5

ballots for industrial action 20, 241
banks 60, 67, 89
'beauty contests' 10, 27
Belgium 2
Benefits Agency: management structure of 120–2; union organisation in 129–33, 134
BIFU 41, 64, 71, 92
boilermakers 12

bonuses 153, 156, 157, 161
brownfield sites 10, 65
BT 13, 88, 90
Burnsall dispute 258 *ff*
business cycles 6
business unionism 26

Cadbury 10, 24, 44, 60, 61–2, 66–7, 91
capitalism: ambivalent role of unions within 3; change as characteristic of 7; worker consent to working within system 212–13
car industry 22–3, 25, 26, 84, 272–3: *see also* Nissan; Rover
Cassidy, David 41
casual workers 14, 195
Catholic unions 2
CBI 42, 90
CEGB 50
change in the workplace: elements of 151; existing procedures and 151; generally 6 *ff*; piecemeal nature of 151, 154; trade unionists' view 155 *ff*; unionised workplaces, incidence at 24, 90–1, 151, 154, 178, 303
civil service: Benefits Agency case study 120–2; Benefits Agency unions 129–33; collective organisation in 110; conditions of work and employment 110;

324